Casual Country

HOME PLANS

HDA, Inc.
Saint Louis, Missouri

Contents

Casual Country Home Plans is published by HDA, Inc., 944 Anglum Road, St. Louis, MO 63042. All rights reserved. Reproduction in whole or part without written permission of the publisher is prohibited. Printed in the U.S.A. © 2007.

Artist drawings and photos shown in this publication may vary slightly from the actual working drawings. Some photos are shown in mirror reverse. Please refer to the floor plan for accurate layout. All plans appearing in this publication are protected under copyright law.

COVER HOME - The house shown on the front cover is Plan #597-040D-0016 and is featured on page 162. Photo courtesy of Greg Marquis.

Current Printing   5 4 3 2 1

This house shown on the cover is Plan #597-032D-0026 and is featured on page 343. Photo courtesy of Drummond Design.

This house shown on the cover is Plan #597-021D-0003 and is shown on page 366. Photo courtesy of Breland and Farmer.

This house shown on the cover is Plan #597-038D-0023 and is featured on page 113. Photo courtesy of The Garlinghouse Company.

At Home

Encompassing many different architectural design elements, the Country Home is more defined by its inviting appeal

*C*ountry Homes exude a warm, inviting feeling. Filled with emotion, these family friendly designs offer an atmosphere that envelops all who enter with comfort and relaxation. More than just an architectural style, Country Home Plans reflect a natural sense of affection.

The Country design can include many different architectural styles, including Farmhouse, Southern Country, Ranch, and Craftsman. All of these homes have distinct characteristics that define their specific style. Read on to determine which Country Home fits your personal style the most.

Plan #597-026D-0183, see page 209.

Farmhouse

As a nation that relies on farming, the indistinguishable Farmhouse is an American favorite. A contemporary version of Colonial homes, Farmhouses are simply framed and usually rectangular in shape. The primary feature that always stands out with this design is the covered wrap-around porch, which beckons people to sit back and relax, generation after generation. Most Farmhouse-style homes are two-stories with all the bedrooms on the second floor. A steep gable roof leads into a more shallow covering for the porch to create extra shade. These homes can very easily take on Victorian style elements by adding details on the porch overhangs and railings, or by adding a significant bay window on the side. With its old-fashioned country appeal, the Farmhouse continues to be a popular choice for any setting.

Plan #597-016D-0049, see page 17.

Ranch

The ever-popular Ranch home, inspired by Spanish-American homes in the Southwest, dates back to the 19th century. It wasn't until after World War II, however, that the popularity of this design exploded, expanding to every corner of the nation. With the advent of the Federal Housing Authority and the 30-year mortgage, many more people were choosing to become homeowners. And with the rising cost of labor and materials, the demand for affordable housing was at an all-time high, making the small size of a Ranch a great bargain. Many developers emerged, buying huge plots of land and mass-producing almost identical homes, bringing the cost down even further. Today any one-story home can be defined as a Ranch, however true Ranch homes are simple, low to the ground and one room in depth.

Plan #597-020D-0013, see page 415.

Southern Country

A welcoming front porch, second-floor dormers and symmetrical windows characterize the Southern Country home. Combining elements from several different American home styles, this design was seen throughout the South during the 18th and 19th centuries. On most homes, the roof flares out to cover the porch. As a grand space to enjoy the outdoors, the front porch is the focal point of this design. And symmetrical windows help to accentuate the exterior, while flooding the interior with natural light. Dormers, brought back from Colonial styles, also contribute to the vast amount of interior light, as well as increasing the living area. Even with its simplicity of design, the Southern Country home is an elegant fixture in America's landscape, seen today in all areas of the nation.

Plan #597-091D-0017, see page 163.

Arts & Crafts

Gaining popularity in the early 20th century was the Arts & Crafts home, also known as Craftsman. Upon seeing the rise of factories and mass production, architects were searching for a way to get back to nature. Using materials such as wood and stone, these homes blend in with any landscape. Simplicity and lack of ornamentation are characteristics of every Craftsman home. These homes also usually feature a wide, open porch anchored by foundation pillars for an enchanting outdoor living space. Architects moved the simplicity indoors as well, designing open floor plans with an abundance of windows to flood the interior with natural light. Today, as everything in the world continues to increase its pace, building an Arts & Crafts home is a way to slow down and enjoy Mother Nature.

Choosing a home plan is an exciting but difficult task. Many factors play a role in what home plan is best for you and your family. If a Country-style home is what you're looking for, you will definitely find it in this book. This beautiful collection includes over 400 plans that exude pure Country charisma.

In addition to overall style, many other factors need to be considered when choosing a home plan. Take time to evaluate your family's needs and you will have an easier time sorting through all of the designs offered in this book.

BUDGET: Many items take part in this budget, from ordering the blueprints to the last doorknob purchased. When you find your dream design, visit our website at **www.houseplansandmore.com** to get a cost-to-build estimate to ensure that the finished product will be within your price range.

FAMILY LIFESTYLE: Think about the stage of life you are at now, and what stages you will be going through in the future. Ask yourself questions to figure out how much room you will need now and if you will need room for expansion.

FLOOR PLAN LAYOUTS: When you find a plan you want to purchase, be sure to picture yourself actually living in it. Consider the flow from the entry to the living, sleeping and gathering areas. Think about furniture you have now or that you plan to buy to make sure everything and everyone will fit nicely.

EXTERIOR SPACES: Be sure to incorporate your home building site when choosing your plan. Picture any landscaping you may incorporate into the design. Use your imagination to plan ahead your dream home and its surroundings.

Have fun searching for your new home! With the stunning plans offered in this book, and thousands more on our website **www.houseplansandmore.com**, we are sure you will find your perfect home.

Casual Country
❖ Home Plans ❖

Inviting wrap-around porches. Stylish dormers. Abundant windows. Family-friendly floor plans. All of these features are offered within this stunning collection of best-selling Casual Country Home Plans. These plans, from the nation's leading designers and architects, showcase amazing craftsmanship that proves country homes are packed with style, beauty and function. From cozy cottages to exquisite Southern styles, there is something for everyone who is ready to build a home filled with warmth and charm. Turn the page, start the journey and discover the home of your dreams.

Special features

- 1,440 total square feet of living area
- Foyer adjoins massive-sized great room with sloping ceiling and tall masonry fireplace
- The kitchen connects to the spacious dining room and features a pass-through to the breakfast bar
- Master bedroom enjoys a private bath and two closets
- An oversized two-car side entry garage offers plenty of storage for bicycles, lawn equipment, etc.
- 3 bedrooms, 2 baths, 2-car side entry garage
- Basement foundation, drawings also include crawl space and slab foundations

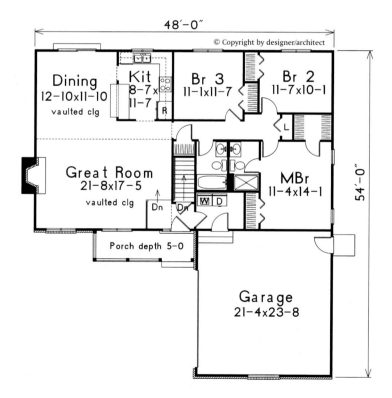

48'-0"

© Copyright by designer/architect

Dining
12-10x11-10
vaulted clg

Kit
8-7x
11-7

Br 3
11-1x11-7

Br 2
11-7x10-1

Great Room
21-8x17-5
vaulted clg

MBr
11-4x14-1

Dn   Dn   W D

54'-0"

Porch depth 5-0

Garage
21-4x23-8

Special features

- 2,074 total square feet of living area
- Unique sewing room is ideal for hobby enthusiasts and has counterspace for convenience
- Double walk-in closets are located in the luxurious master bath
- A built-in bookcase in the great room adds charm
- 3 bedrooms, 2 1/2 baths, 2-car side entry garage
- Slab foundation

Some vegetable plants and flowers are easier to start from seed. Marigolds, zinnias, squash and corn are good easy-to-start flowers and vegetables for the beginner gardener.

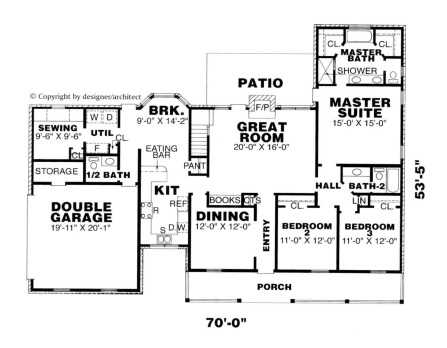

© Copyright by designer/architect

SEWING 9'-6" X 9'-6"

W D

UTIL CL.

F

STORAGE

CL.

1/2 BATH

BRK. 9'-0" X 14'-2"

EATING BAR

PANT

PATIO

F/P

GREAT ROOM 20'-0" X 16'-0"

MASTER BATH

SHOWER

CL. CL.

MASTER SUITE 15'-0" X 15'-0"

DOUBLE GARAGE 19'-11" X 20'-1"

KIT

REF

R

S D.W.

DINING 12'-0" X 12'-0"

BOOKS CTS

ENTRY

CL.

BEDROOM 2 11'-0" X 12'-0"

HALL BATH-2

LIN

CL.

BEDROOM 3 11'-0" X 12'-0"

53'-5"

PORCH

70'-0"

Special features

* 1,529 total square feet of living area
* A wrap-around porch adds country charm and offers a wonderful place to relax
* The kitchen, dining and breakfast rooms combine with a handy laundry area nearby that includes a walk-in pantry
* A covered breezeway connects the detached garage to the home
* 3 bedrooms, 2 baths, 2-car detached side entry garage
* Crawl space foundation

Spicy hues, from chili red to sari pink, blend well with organic shapes, well-worn books, and objects collected on travels. Coordinate these seasoned colors with your most cherished collections.

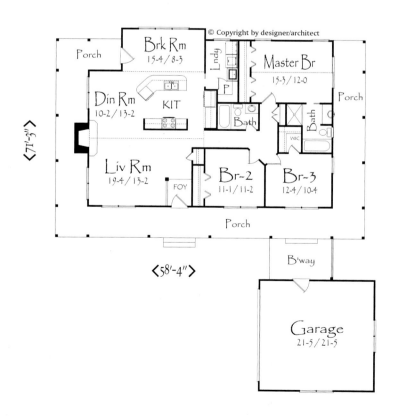

© Copyright by designer/architect

Special features

❖ 1,400 total square feet of living area
❖ Master bedroom is secluded for privacy
❖ The large utility room has additional cabinet space
❖ Covered porch provides an outdoor seating area
❖ Roof dormers add great curb appeal
❖ Living room and master bedroom feature vaulted ceilings
❖ Oversized two-car garage has storage space
❖ 3 bedrooms, 2 baths, 2-car garage
❖ Basement foundation, drawings also include crawl space foundation

One common mistake when decorating is homeowners tend to push all pieces of furniture up against the wall. It is much more inviting to separate areas within a space by creating little conversation areas.

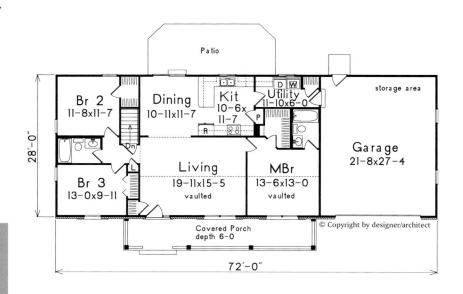

Patio

Br 2
11-8x11-7

Dining
10-11x11-7

Kit
10-6x
11-7

Utility
11-10x6-0

storage area

28'-0"

Br 3
13-0x9-11

Living
19-11x15-5
vaulted

MBr
13-6x13-0
vaulted

Garage
21-8x27-4

© Copyright by designer/architect

Covered Porch
depth 6-0

72'-0"

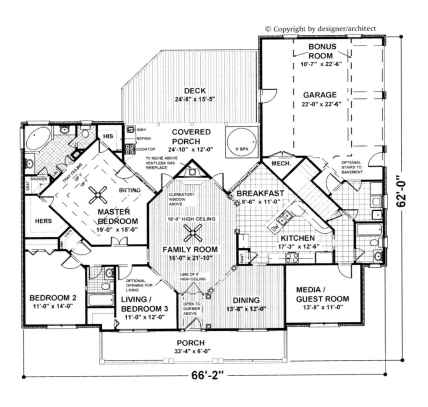

© Copyright by designer/architect

BONUS ROOM 10'-7" x 22'-6"

DECK 24'-8" x 15'-5"

GARAGE 22'-0" x 22'-6"

COVERED PORCH 24'-10" x 12'-0"

6' SPA

SINK
REFRIG.
COOKTOP

HIS

TV NICHE ABOVE VENTLESS GAS FIREPLACE

MECH.

OPTIONAL STAIRS TO BASEMENT

TRAY CEILING

SHOWER

SEAT

UP 1'
UP 1'

SITTING

CLERESTORY WINDOW ABOVE

BREAKFAST 8'-6" x 11'-0"

MASTER BEDROOM 19'-0" x 15'-0"

HERS

19'-9" HIGH CEILING

KITCHEN 17'-3" x 12'-6"

DW

PANT.

FAMILY ROOM 16'-0" x 21'-10"

LINE OF 9' HIGH CEILING

62'-0"

OPTIONAL OPENING FOR LIVING

BEDROOM 2 11'-0" x 14'-0"

LIVING / BEDROOM 3 11'-0" x 12'-0"

OPEN TO DORMER ABOVE

DINING 13'-8" x 12'-0"

MEDIA / GUEST ROOM 13'-8" x 11'-0"

PORCH 33'-4" x 6'-0"

66'-2"

Special features

- ❖ 1,992 total square feet of living area
- ❖ Interesting angled walls add drama to many of the living areas including the family room, master bedroom and breakfast area
- ❖ Covered porch includes a spa and an outdoor kitchen with sink, refrigerator and cooktop
- ❖ Enter the majestic master bath to find a dramatic corner oversized tub
- ❖ 4 bedrooms, 3 baths, 2-car side entry garage
- ❖ Basement, crawl space or slab foundation, please specify when ordering

Special features

- ❖ 1,360 total square feet of living area
- ❖ Kitchen/dining room features an island workspace and plenty of dining area
- ❖ Master bedroom has a large walk-in closet and private bath
- ❖ Laundry room is adjacent to the kitchen for easy access
- ❖ Convenient workshop in garage
- ❖ Large closets in secondary bedrooms maintain organization
- ❖ 3 bedrooms, 2 baths, 2-car side entry garage
- ❖ Basement foundation, drawings also include crawl space and slab foundations

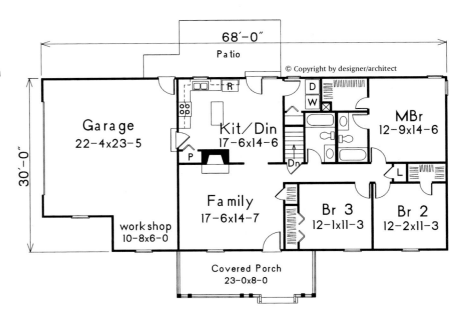

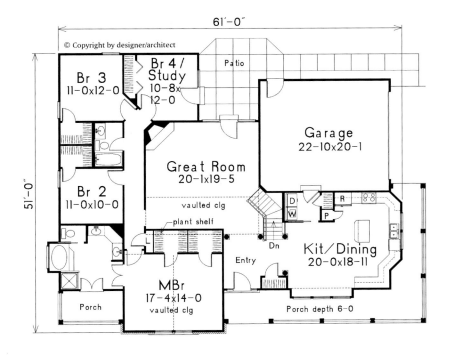

Special features

- ❖ 2,029 total square feet of living area
- ❖ Stonework, gables, roof dormer and double porches create a country flavor
- ❖ Kitchen enjoys extravagant cabinetry and counterspace in a bay, island snack bar, built-in pantry and cheery dining area with multiple tall windows
- ❖ Angled stair descends from large entry with wood columns and is open to a vaulted great room with corner fireplace
- ❖ Master bedroom boasts two walk-in closets, a private bath with double-door entry and a secluded porch
- ❖ 4 bedrooms, 2 baths, 2-car side entry garage
- ❖ Basement foundation, drawings also include crawl space and slab foundations

Special features

- ❖ 1,475 total square feet of living area
- ❖ Family room features a high ceiling and prominent corner fireplace
- ❖ Kitchen with island counter and garden window makes a convenient connection between the family and dining rooms
- ❖ Hallway leads to three bedrooms all with large walk-in closets
- ❖ Covered breezeway joins the main house and garage
- ❖ Full-width covered porch entry lends a country touch
- ❖ 3 bedrooms, 2 baths, 2-car detached side entry garage
- ❖ Slab foundation, drawings also include crawl space foundation

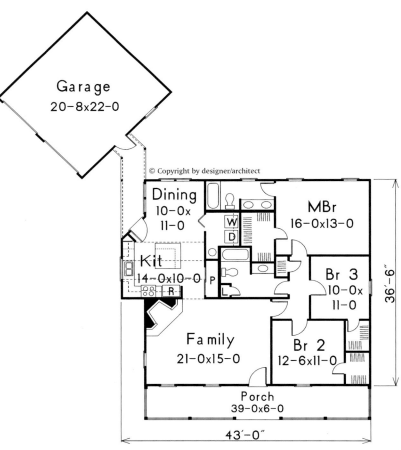

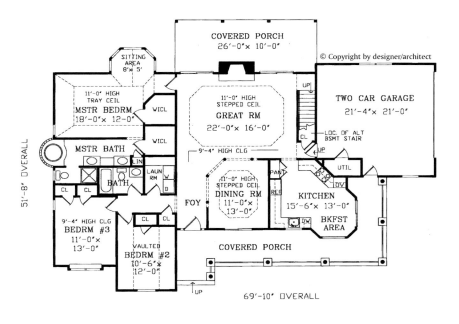

Special features

- ❖ 1,793 total square feet of living area
- ❖ A beautiful foyer leads into the great room that has a fireplace flanked by two sets of transomed doors both leading to a large covered porch
- ❖ Dramatic eat-in kitchen includes an abundance of cabinets
- ❖ Optional bonus room above the garage has an additional 779 square feet of living area
- ❖ 3 bedrooms, 2 baths, 2-car side entry garage
- ❖ Basement, crawl space or slab foundation, please specify when ordering

Special features

❖ 1,761 total square feet of living area
❖ Exterior window dressing, roof dormers and planter boxes provide visual warmth and charm
❖ Great room boasts a vaulted ceiling, fireplace and opens to a pass-through kitchen
❖ The vaulted master bedroom includes a luxury bath and walk-in closet
❖ Home features eight separate closets with an abundance of storage
❖ 4 bedrooms, 2 baths, 2-car side entry garage
❖ Basement foundation

Painting the cabinets in the kitchen with a high gloss paint bounces even more light around making the space seem bigger.

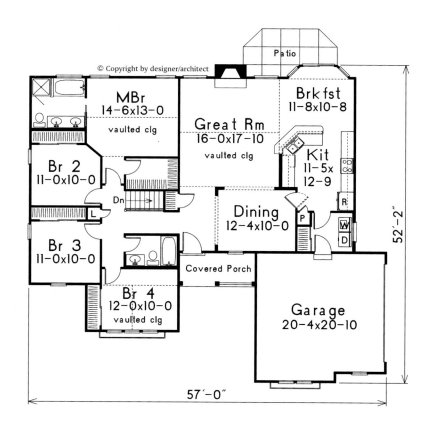

© Copyright by designer/architect

- MBr 14-6x13-0 vaulted clg
- Br 2 11-0x10-0
- Br 3 11-0x10-0
- Br 4 12-0x10-0 vaulted clg
- Dn
- Patio
- Great Rm 16-0x17-10 vaulted clg
- Brk fst 11-8x10-8
- Kit 11-5x 12-9
- Dining 12-4x10-0
- Covered Porch
- Garage 20-4x20-10
- 52'-2"
- 57'-0"

Special features

- 1,721 total square feet of living area
- Roof dormers add great curb appeal
- Vaulted dining and great rooms are immersed in light from the atrium window wall
- Breakfast room opens onto the covered porch
- 3 bedrooms, 2 baths, 3-car garage
- Walk-out basement foundation, drawings also include crawl space and slab foundations
- 1,604 square feet on the first floor and 117 square feet on the lower level atrium

83'-0"

42'-0"

Covered Porch

Brk
11-5x12-0

Atrium Below
Dn

© Copyright by designer/architect

Great Rm
16-0x16-10
vaulted

MBr
16-0x14-0
vaulted

Kit
11-5x12-0

Garage
29-4x21-4

Dining
11-0x11-6

vaulted

Br 3
11-1x13-3

Br 2
11-0x12-9

Porch
27-8x5-0

Special features

* 1,339 total square feet of living area
* Full-length covered porch enhances front facade
* Vaulted ceiling and stone fireplace add drama to the family room
* Walk-in closets in the bedrooms provide ample storage space
* Combined kitchen/dining area adjoins the family room for the perfect entertaining space
* 2" x 6" exterior walls available, please order plan #597-058D-0072
* 3 bedrooms, 2 1/2 baths
* Crawl space foundation

One of the most popular trends in home decorating currently is creating intimacy in a space. Look for ways to create small intimate seating areas by fireplaces, in a nook, alcove or a small room. Decorate in warm tones to make it a family comfort zone no one will ever want to leave.

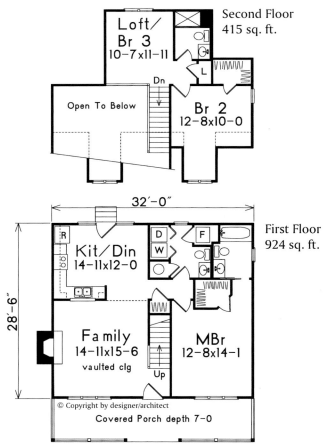

Loft/Br 3
10-7x11-11

Second Floor
415 sq. ft.

Open To Below

Dn

Br 2
12-8x10-0

32'-0"

First Floor
924 sq. ft.

Kit/Din
14-11x12-0

28'-6"

Family
14-11x15-6
vaulted clg

MBr
12-8x14-1

Up

© Copyright by designer/architect

Covered Porch depth 7-0

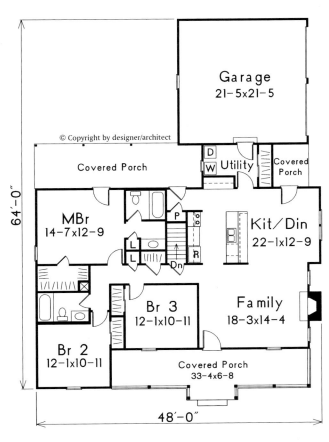

Garage
21-5x21-5

© Copyright by designer/architect

Covered Porch

D
W Utility

Covered Porch

MBr
14-7x12-9

P

L
L

Dn

R

Kit/Din
22-1x12-9

Br 3
12-1x10-11

Family
18-3x14-4

Br 2
12-1x10-11

Covered Porch
33-4x6-8

64'-0"

48'-0"

Special features

- ❖ 1,501 total square feet of living area
- ❖ Spacious kitchen with dining area is open to the outdoors
- ❖ Convenient utility room is adjacent to the garage
- ❖ Master bedroom features a private bath, dressing area and access to the large covered porch
- ❖ Large family room creates openness
- ❖ 3 bedrooms, 2 baths, 2-car side entry garage
- ❖ Basement foundation, drawings also include crawl space and slab foundations

Although planting dates are printed on most seed packets, they're easy to miss at planting time. Rewrite the date on each package in large letters, with a thick marker, and you won't miss any sowing seasons.

BLUE RIDGE LIBRARY

Special features

* 1,567 total square feet of living area
* Energy efficient home with 2" x 6" exterior walls
* Living room flows into the dining room shaped by an angled pass-through into the kitchen
* Cheerful, windowed dining area
* Master bedroom is separated from other bedrooms for privacy
* Future area available on the second floor has an additional 338 square feet of living area
* 3 bedrooms, 2 baths, 2-car side entry garage
* Partial basement/crawl space foundation, drawings also include slab foundation

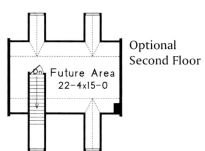

Optional Second Floor

Future Area 22-4x15-0

Dn

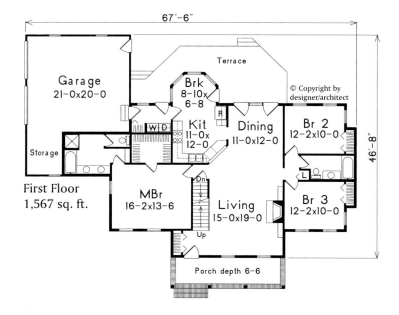

67'-6"

Garage 21-0x20-0

Terrace

Brk 8-10x 6-8

© Copyright by designer/architect

Kit 11-0x 12-0

Dining 11-0x12-0

Br 2 12-2x10-0

Storage

46'-8"

MBr 16-2x13-6

Dn

Living 15-0x19-0

Br 3 12-2x10-0

Up

First Floor 1,567 sq. ft.

Porch depth 6-6

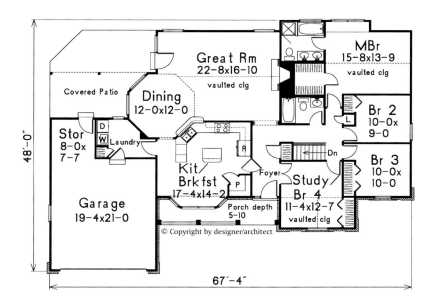

Special features

- ❖ 1,791 total square feet of living area
- ❖ Vaulted great room and octagon-shaped dining area enjoy a spectacular view of the covered patio
- ❖ Kitchen features a pass-through to the dining area, center island, large walk-in pantry and breakfast room with large bay window
- ❖ The master bedroom enjoys a vaulted ceiling and a sitting area
- ❖ The garage includes extra storage space
- ❖ 4 bedrooms, 2 baths, 2-car garage with storage
- ❖ Basement foundation, drawings also include crawl space and slab foundations

Special features

- ❖ 1,611 total square feet of living area
- ❖ Sliding doors lead to a delightful screened porch creating a wonderful summer retreat
- ❖ Master bedroom has a lavishly appointed dressing room and large walk-in closet
- ❖ The kitchen offers an abundance of cabinets and counterspace with convenient access to the laundry room and garage
- ❖ 3 bedrooms, 2 baths, 2-car side entry garage
- ❖ Basement foundation

Not wild about draperies? Then shutters may be your window treatment of choice. Uncluttered and classically stylish, shutters offer a range of choices in color, depth and style. They also look fabulous in any type of home, from purely traditional to country.

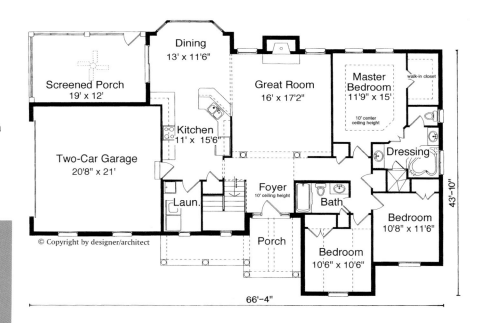

Special features

- 1,708 total square feet of living area
- Massive family room is enhanced with several windows, a fireplace and access to the porch
- Deluxe master bath is accented by a step-up corner tub flanked by double vanities
- Closets throughout maintain organized living
- Bedrooms are isolated from living areas
- 3 bedrooms, 2 baths, 2-car garage
- Basement foundation, drawings also include crawl space foundation

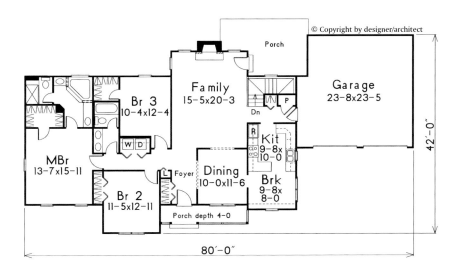

© Copyright by designer/architect

Porch

Family
15-5x20-3

Garage
23-8x23-5

Br 3
10-4x12-4

Dn

P

R

Kit
9-8x
10-0

MBr
13-7x15-11

W D

Foyer

Dining
10-0x11-6

Brk
9-8x
8-0

Br 2
11-5x12-11

Porch depth 4-0

42'-0"

80'-0"

A gable is the triangular top end of a wall where it meets the sloping part of a roof. Or, any roof that has two slopes that meet at the top to form an upside down "V".

Special features

- 2,097 total square feet of living area
- Angled kitchen, family room and eating area add interest to this home
- Family room includes a TV niche making this a cozy place to relax
- Sumptuous master bedroom includes a sitting area, double walk-in closet and a full bath with double vanities
- Bonus room above garage has an additional 452 square feet of living space
- 3 bedrooms, 3 baths, 3-car side entry garage
- Basement, crawl space or slab foundation, please specify when ordering

© Copyright by designer/architect

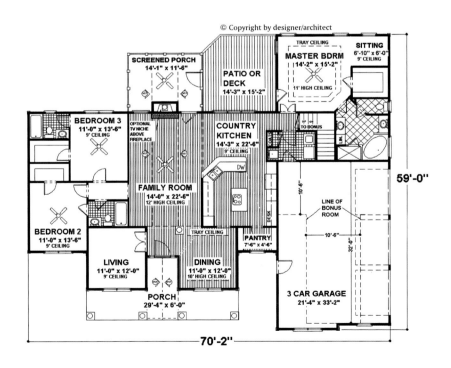

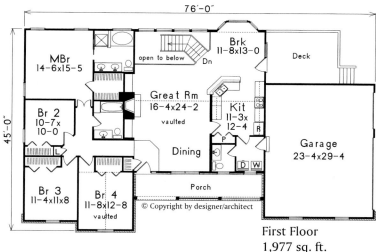

First Floor
1,977 sq. ft.

76'-0"

MBr
14-6x15-5

open to below   Dn

Brk
11-8x13-0

Deck

Great Rm
16-4x24-2
vaulted

Kit
11-3x
12-4

Br 2
10-7x
10-0

Dining

Garage
23-4x29-4

Br 3
11-4x11x8

Br 4
11-8x12-8
vaulted

Porch

© Copyright by designer/architect

45'-0"

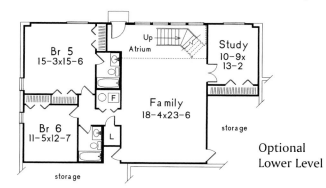

Optional
Lower Level

Br 5
15-3x15-6

Up
Atrium

Study
10-9x
13-2

Family
18-4x23-6

storage

Br 6
11-5x12-7

storage

Special features

❖ 1,977 total square feet of living area
❖ Classic traditional exterior is always in style
❖ Spacious great room boasts a vaulted ceiling, dining area, atrium with elegant staircase and feature windows
❖ Atrium opens to 1,416 square feet of optional living area below which consists of a family room, two bedrooms, two baths and a study
❖ 4 bedrooms, 2 1/2 baths, 3-car side entry garage
❖ Walk-out basement foundation

To freshen the air in your home, put a few drops of lemon juice in your vacuum bag when you change it. The fresh smell will spread throughout the house when you vacuum.

Special features

- 2,874 total square feet of living area
- Large family room with sloped ceiling and wood beams adjoins the kitchen and breakfast area with windows on two walls
- Large foyer opens to the family room with a massive stone fireplace and open stairs to the basement
- Private master bedroom includes a raised tub under the bay window, dramatic dressing area and a huge walk-in closet
- 4 bedrooms, 2 1/2 baths, 2-car side entry garage
- Basement foundation

To make the most of a shared bathroom, consider these guidelines. For adequate elbowroom, the minimum clearance between two sinks in the bath should be 30 inches, centerline to centerline. Using pocket doors rather than hinged doors in the entrance way can save space.

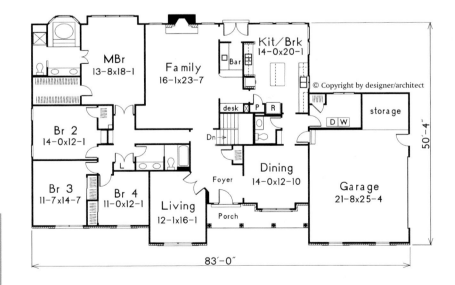

Second Floor
1,233 sq. ft.

Special features

❖ 2,300 total square feet of living area
❖ Cozy fireplace in the master suite
❖ 9' ceilings on the first floor
❖ Energy efficient home with 2" x 6" exterior walls
❖ 3 bedrooms, 2 1/2 baths, 2-car side entry garage
❖ Basement foundation

© Copyright by designer/architect

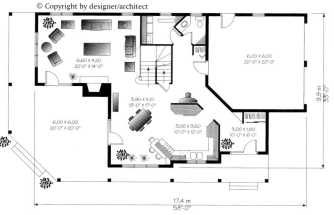

First Floor
1,067 sq. ft.

Positioning the sink beneath a window gives a cheery outlook to anyone on washing-up duty.

Special features

- 3,379 total square feet of living area
- A popular outdoor kitchen is incorporated into the covered rear porch perfect for year-round outdoor enjoyment with family and friends
- Enter double doors off the great room to find a media/hobby room with plenty of storage space
- Double walk-in closets in the master bedroom and bath help keep the homeowners organized
- The bonus room above the garage has an additional 334 square feet of living area
- 3 bedrooms, 2 1/2 baths, 2-car side entry garage
- Slab or crawl space foundation, please specify when ordering

Optional
Second Floor

Unfinished Bonus Room
14-0 x 23-10
(Clear)
8-0 Clg. Ht.

ATTIC ACCESS

SLOPED CLG.

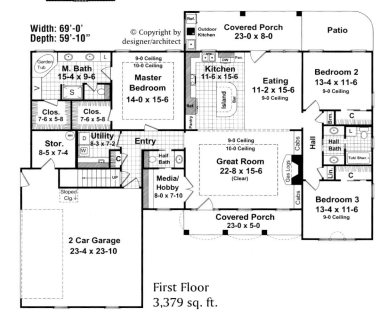

Width: 69'-0'
Depth: 59'-10"

© Copyright by designer/architect

Ref.
Outdoor Kitchen

Covered Porch
23-0 x 8-0

Patio

Garden Tub

M. Bath
15-4 x 9-6

9-0 Ceiling
10-0 Ceiling

Master Bedroom
14-0 x 15-6

Kitchen
11-6 x 15-6

DW
Pan.

Island
Bar

Eating
11-2 x 15-6
9-0 Ceiling

Bedroom 2
13-4 x 11-6
9-0 Ceiling

Clos.
7-6 x 5-8

Clos.
7-6 x 5-8

Ref.

Pantry

Brm.
C

Stor.
8-5 x 7-4

Utility
8-3 x 7-2

Entry

Half Bath

9-0 Ceiling
10-0 Ceiling

Great Room
22-8 x 15-6
(Clear)

Cabs
Hall

Hall Bath

L

Tub/ Shwr.

Gas Logs

Cabs

Lin.

Media/ Hobby
8-0 x 7-10

Bedroom 3
13-4 x 11-6
9-0 Ceiling

Sloped Clg.

UP

Cabs

C

2 Car Garage
23-4 x 23-10

Covered Porch
23-0 x 5-0

First Floor
3,379 sq. ft.

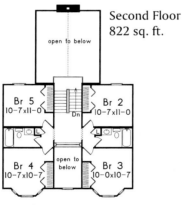

Second Floor
822 sq. ft.

open to below

Br 5
10-7x11-0

Dn

Br 2
10-7x11-0

Br 4
10-7x10-7

open to below

Br 3
10-0x10-7

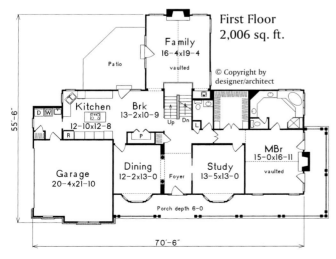

First Floor
2,006 sq. ft.

Family
16-4x19-4
vaulted

Patio

© Copyright by designer/architect

Kitchen
12-10x12-8

Brk
13-2x10-9

Up Dn

MBr
15-0x16-11
vaulted

Garage
20-4x21-10

Dining
12-2x13-0

Foyer

Study
13-5x13-0
vaulted

55'-6"

Porch depth 6-0

70'-6"

Special features

- ❖ 2,828 total square feet of living area
- ❖ Popular wrap-around porch gives home country charm
- ❖ Secluded, oversized family room with vaulted ceiling and wet bar features many windows
- ❖ Any chef would be delighted to cook in this smartly designed kitchen with island and corner windows
- ❖ Spectacular master bedroom and bath
- ❖ 5 bedrooms, 3 1/2 baths, 2-car side entry garage
- ❖ Basement foundation, drawings also include crawl space and slab foundations

To keep rodents out of your house, tidy up your garage. Store pet food and birdseed in hard plastic containers. Remove shoes, blankets and other cozy home sites. A mouse can squeeze through holes as small as a dime, so plug gaps around pipes with coarse steel wool and then caulk over it.

Special features

- ❖ 1,191 total square feet of living area
- ❖ Energy efficient home with 2" x 6" exterior walls
- ❖ Master bedroom is located near living areas for maximum convenience
- ❖ Living room has a cathedral ceiling and stone fireplace
- ❖ 3 bedrooms, 2 baths, 2-car side entry garage
- ❖ Slab foundation, drawings also include crawl space foundation

Use the "W" technique when painting walls. Start in a corner of the wall and roll on a 3' x 3' W pattern, then fill it in without lifting the roller. Always paint one wall at a time and paint trim last.

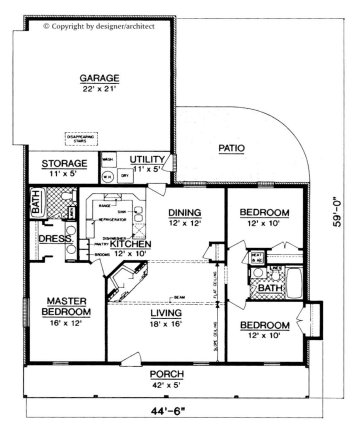

© Copyright by designer/architect

GARAGE
22' x 21'

DISAPPEARING STAIRS

PATIO

STORAGE
11' x 5'

WASH
W.H.   DRY

UTILITY
11' x 5'

BATH

RANGE
SINK
REFRIGERATOR
DISHWASHER
PANTRY   KITCHEN
12' x 10'
BROOMS

DRESS

DINING
12' x 12'

BEDROOM
12' x 10'

HEAT & AC

LINEN

BATH

MASTER BEDROOM
16' x 12'

BEAM

LIVING
18' x 16'

SLOPE CEILING   FLAT CEILING

BEDROOM
12' x 10'

PORCH
42' x 5'

44'-6"

59'-0"

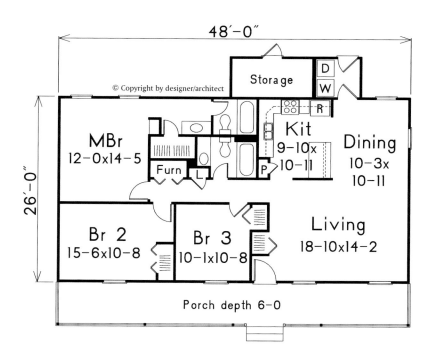

© Copyright by designer/architect

48'-0"

26'-0"

Storage

D
W

MBr
12-0x14-5

Kit
9-10x
10-11

Dining
10-3x
10-11

Furn   L

R

P

Br 2
15-6x10-8

Br 3
10-1x10-8

Living
18-10x14-2

Porch depth 6-0

Special features

❖ 1,285 total square feet of living area
❖ Accommodating home with ranch-style porch
❖ Large storage area on back of home
❖ Master bedroom includes dressing area, private bath and built-in bookcase
❖ Kitchen features pantry, breakfast bar and complete view to the dining room
❖ 2" x 6" exterior walls available, please order plan #597-001D-0119
❖ 3 bedrooms, 2 baths
❖ Crawl space foundation, drawings also include basement and slab foundations

Check local retail stores for discount kitchen appliances. Major appliances will drop drastically in price as the specific model becomes out of date.

Special features

- ❖ 2,357 total square feet of living area
- ❖ 9' ceilings on the first floor
- ❖ Secluded master bedroom includes a private bath with double walk-in closets and vanity
- ❖ Balcony overlooks living room with large fireplace
- ❖ The future game room on the second floor has an additional 303 square feet of living area
- ❖ 4 bedrooms, 3 1/2 baths, 2-car side entry garage
- ❖ Slab foundation, drawings also include crawl space foundation

In the winter, opening drapes and curtains on sunny days takes advantage of the sun's heating power. Then, close all drapes, blinds or shades at night in the winter to make use of their insulating properties.

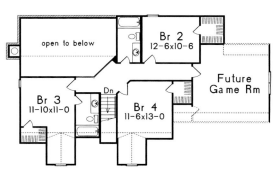

Second Floor
865 sq. ft.

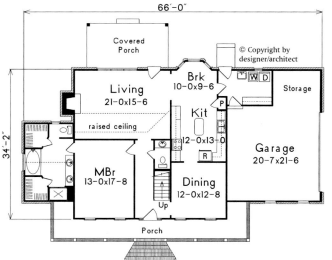

First Floor
1,492 sq. ft.

© Copyright by designer/architect

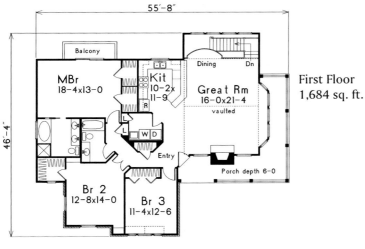

First Floor
1,684 sq. ft.

55'-8"

46'-4"

Balcony

MBr
18-4x13-0

Kit
10-2x
11-9

Great Rm
16-0x21-4
vaulted

Dining   Dn

Entry

Porch depth 6-0

Br 2
12-8x14-0

Br 3
11-4x12-6

© Copyright by designer/architect

Optional
Lower Level

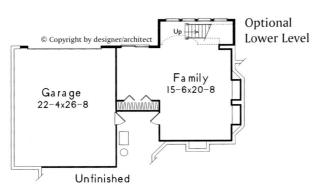

Up

Garage
22-4x26-8

Family
15-6x20-8

Unfinished

Special features

❖ 1,684 total square feet of living area
❖ Delightful wrap-around porch is anchored by a full masonry fireplace
❖ The vaulted great room includes a large bay window, fireplace, dining balcony and atrium window wall
❖ Double walk-in closets, large luxury bath and sliding doors to an exterior balcony are a few fantastic features of the master bedroom
❖ Atrium opens to 611 square feet of optional living area on the lower level
❖ 3 bedrooms, 2 baths, 2-car drive under garage
❖ Walk-out basement foundation

Special features

- 1,408 total square feet of living area
- Energy efficient home with 2" x 6" exterior walls
- A bright country kitchen boasts an abundance of counterspace and cupboards
- The front entry is sheltered by a broad veranda
- A spa tub is brightened by a box-bay window in the master bath
- 3 bedrooms, 2 baths, 2-car side entry garage
- Basement or crawl space foundation, please specify when ordering

If wall or floor space is limited in a bedroom, think vertical. Maximize your storage area by using tall chests of drawers or armoires instead of horizontal dressers.

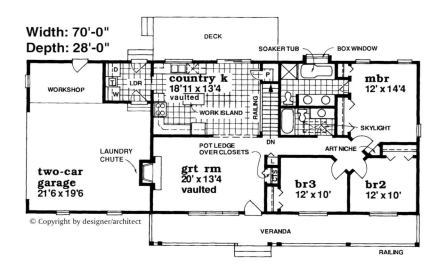

Width: 70'-0"
Depth: 28'-0"

DECK

SOAKER TUB   BOX WINDOW

WORKSHOP

D
LDR
T
W

country k
18'11 x 13'4
vaulted

WORK ISLAND

RAILING

P

mbr
12' x 14'4

SKYLIGHT

LAUNDRY
CHUTE

POT LEDGE
OVER CLOSETS

DN

ART NICHE

two-car
garage
21'6 x 19'6

grt rm
20' x 13'4
vaulted

L
CTS

br3
12' x 10'

br2
12' x 10'

© Copyright by designer/architect

VERANDA

RAILING

Special features

- 2,669 total square feet of living area
- Nice-sized corner pantry in kitchen
- Guest bedroom, located off the great room, has a full bath and would make an excellent office
- Master bath has double walk-in closets, whirlpool tub and a large shower
- 4 bedrooms, 3 1/2 baths, 2-car side entry garage
- Basement, crawl space or slab foundation, please specify when ordering

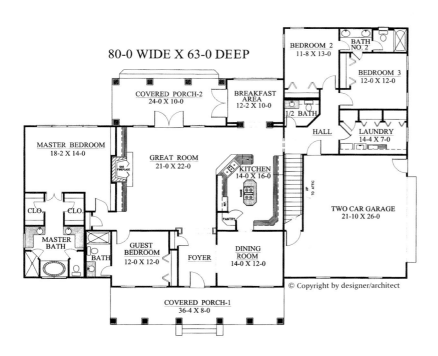

80-0 WIDE X 63-0 DEEP

BEDROOM 2
11-8 X 13-0

BATH NO. 2

BEDROOM 3
12-0 X 12-0

COVERED PORCH-2
24-0 X 10-0

BREAKFAST AREA
12-2 X 10-0

1/2 BATH

HALL

LAUNDRY
14-4 X 7-0

MASTER BEDROOM
18-2 X 14-0

GREAT ROOM
21-0 X 22-0

GAS FIREPLACE

KITCHEN
14-0 X 16-0

UP TO ATTIC

RANGE

REF

CLO. CLO.

PANTRY

TWO CAR GARAGE
21-10 X 26-0

MASTER BATH

BATH

GUEST BEDROOM
12-0 X 12-0

FOYER

DINING ROOM
14-0 X 12-0

© Copyright by designer/architect

COVERED PORCH-1
36-4 X 8-0

Watering your lawn can be a tricky task as watering too much can be as harmful as too little. Too much water drains nutrients out of the soil and drives it down beyond the root system. Apply only enough water to soak the soil slightly below the roots. On average roots are 6 to 8 inches deep.

Special features

- ❖ 1,253 total square feet of living area
- ❖ Sloped ceiling and fireplace in family room add drama
- ❖ U-shaped kitchen is efficiently designed
- ❖ Large walk-in closets are found in all the bedrooms
- ❖ 3 bedrooms, 2 baths, 2-car garage
- ❖ Crawl space or slab foundation, please specify when ordering

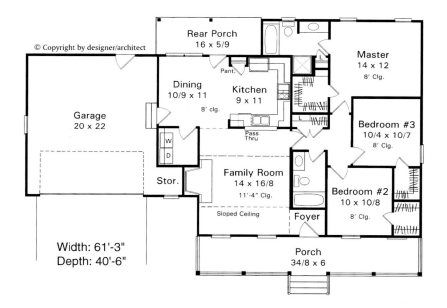

© Copyright by designer/architect

Rear Porch
16 x 5/9

Master
14 x 12
8' Clg.

Dining
10/9 x 11
8' clg.

Kitchen
9 x 11

Pant.

Bedroom #3
10/4 x 10/7
8' Clg.

Garage
20 x 22

W
D

Stor.

Pass
Thru

Family Room
14 x 16/8
11'-4" Clg.

Bedroom #2
10 x 10/8
8' Clg.

Sloped Ceiling

Foyer

Width: 61'-3"
Depth: 40'-6"

Porch
34/8 x 6

The clothesline was a backyard necessity before the advent of the clothes dryer, and even today people continue to prefer the fresh smell that only sun drying provides. To turn the poles into a landscape asset, plant climbing annuals at the base.

Special features

- 1,937 total square feet of living area
- Energy efficient home with 2" x 6" exterior walls
- Upscale great room offers a sloped ceiling, fireplace with extended hearth and built-in shelves for an entertainment center
- Gourmet kitchen includes a cooktop island counter and a quaint morning room
- Master suite features a sloped ceiling, cozy sitting room, walk-in closet and a private bath with whirlpool tub
- 3 bedrooms, 2 baths, 2-car side entry garage
- Crawl space foundation

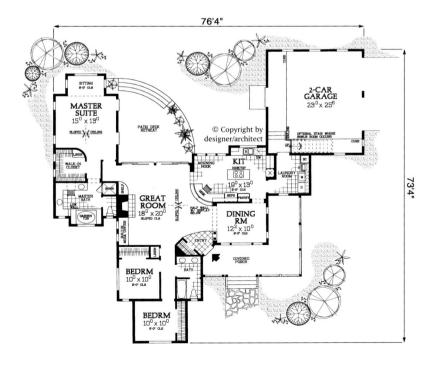

Plan #597-027D-0007

Special features

- ❖ 2,444 total square feet of living area
- ❖ Laundry room with workspace, pantry and coat closet is adjacent to the kitchen
- ❖ Two bedrooms, a study, full bath and plenty of closets are located on the second floor
- ❖ Large walk-in closet and private bath make this master bedroom one you're sure to enjoy
- ❖ Kitchen enjoys a cooktop island and easy access to the living area
- ❖ 3 bedrooms, 2 1/2 baths, 2-car side entry garage
- ❖ Basement foundation

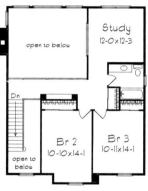

Second Floor
772 sq. ft.

First Floor
1,672 sq. ft.

© Copyright by designer/architect

Second Floor
951 sq. ft.

Special features

- ❖ 2,729 total square feet of living area
- ❖ Energy efficient home with 2" x 6" exterior walls
- ❖ Formal dining room has lovely views into the beautiful two-story great room
- ❖ Second floor loft area makes a perfect home office or children's computer area
- ❖ Bonus room on the second floor has an additional 300 square feet of living area
- ❖ 3 bedrooms, 2 1/2 baths, 2-car garage
- ❖ Basement foundation

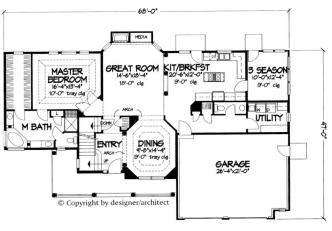

First Floor
1,778 sq. ft.

© Copyright by designer/architect

The tray ceiling gets its name from its resemblance to an inverted tray. Tray ceilings can be a terrific option when trying to hide recessed lighting in bedrooms.

Special features

- ❖ 1,140 total square feet of living area
- ❖ Open and spacious living and dining areas for family gatherings
- ❖ Well-organized kitchen has an abundance of cabinetry and a built-in pantry
- ❖ Roomy master bath features a double-bowl vanity
- ❖ 3 bedrooms, 2 baths, 2-car drive under garage
- ❖ Basement foundation

In 1949, Arthur Levitt and his two sons began a project that literally changed the look of the country forever. Under their control, a swath of empty field on Long Island became the country's first subdivision which was called Levittown.

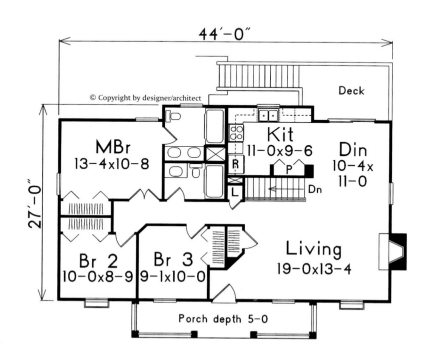

44'-0"

27'-0"

© Copyright by designer/architect

Deck

MBr
13-4x10-8

Kit
11-0x9-6

Din
10-4x
11-0

R

P

L

Dn

Br 2
10-0x8-9

Br 3
9-1x10-0

Living
19-0x13-4

Porch depth 5-0

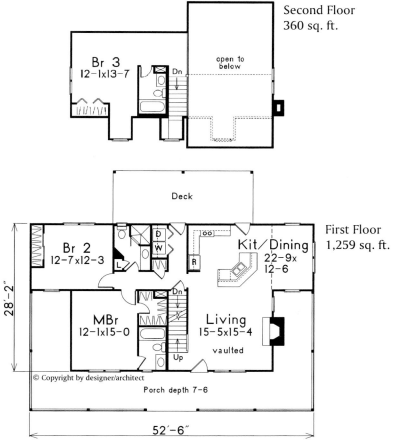

Second Floor
360 sq. ft.

Br 3
12-1x13-7

open to below

Dn

First Floor
1,259 sq. ft.

Deck

Br 2
12-7x12-3

Kit/Dining
22-9x
12-6

28'-2"

MBr
12-1x15-0

Living
15-5x15-4

vaulted

Dn

Up

© Copyright by designer/architect

Porch depth 7-6

52'-6"

Special features

❖ 1,619 total square feet of living area
❖ Private second floor bedroom and bath
❖ Kitchen features a snack bar and adjacent dining area
❖ Master bedroom has a private bath
❖ Centrally located washer and dryer
❖ 3 bedrooms, 3 baths
❖ Basement foundation, drawings also include crawl space and slab foundations

Phones, switch plates and doorknobs get dirty on a regular basis. To clean them quickly, just put a little rubbing alcohol on a soft cloth and wipe. It cleans and disinfects all of those areas in no time.

Special features

- ❖ 1,428 total square feet of living area
- ❖ Large vaulted family room opens to the dining area and kitchen with breakfast bar
- ❖ First floor master bedroom offers a large bath, walk-in closet and nearby laundry facilities
- ❖ A spacious loft/bedroom #3 overlooking the family room and an additional bedroom and bath complement the second floor
- ❖ 2" x 6" exterior walls available, please order plan #597-058D-0080
- ❖ 3 bedrooms, 2 baths
- ❖ Basement foundation

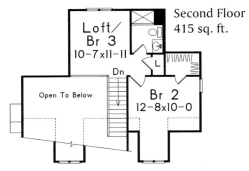

Second Floor
415 sq. ft.

Loft/ Br 3
10-7x11-11

Br 2
12-8x10-0

Open To Below

Dn

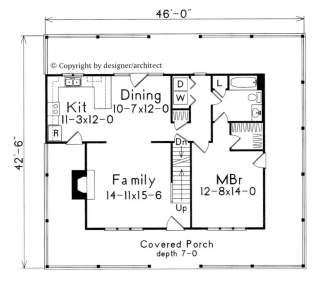

First Floor
1,013 sq. ft.

46'-0"

42'-6"

© Copyright by designer/architect

Kit
11-3x12-0

Dining
10-7x12-0

Family
14-11x15-6

MBr
12-8x14-0

Dn

Up

Covered Porch
depth 7-0

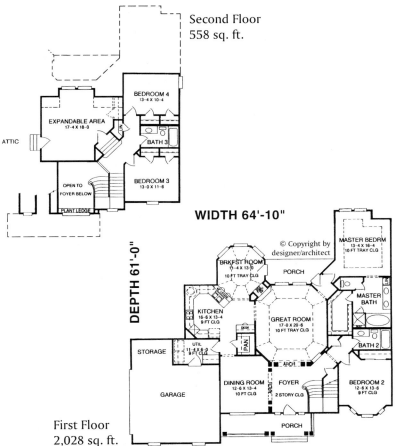

Second Floor
558 sq. ft.

BEDROOM 4
13-4 X 10-4

EXPANDABLE AREA
17-4 X 18-0

ATTIC

BATH 3

LIN

BEDROOM 3
13-0 X 11-6

OPEN TO
FOYER BELOW

PLANT LEDGE

WIDTH 64'-10"

DEPTH 61'-0"

© Copyright by
designer/architect

MASTER BEDRM
13-4 X 16-4
10 FT TRAY CLG

BRKFST ROOM
11-4 X 13-0
10 FT TRAY CLG

PORCH

KITCHEN
16-6 X 13-4
9 FT CLG

MASTER
BATH

GREAT ROOM
17-0 X 20-6
10 FT TRAY CLG

UTIL
11-4 X 6-0
9 FT CLG

STORAGE

DESK

PAN

BATH 2

GARAGE

ARCH

DINING ROOM
12-6 X 13-4
10 FT CLG

FOYER
2 STORY CLG

ARCH

BEDROOM 2
12-6 X 13-6
9 FT CLG

PORCH

First Floor
2,028 sq. ft.

Special features

❖ 2,586 total square feet of living area
❖ Great room has an impressive tray ceiling and see-through fireplace into the bayed breakfast room
❖ Master bedroom has a walk-in closet and private bath
❖ Decorative columns and arches adorn the foyer and entry into the formal dining room
❖ Expandable area on the second floor has an additional 272 square feet of living area
❖ 4 bedrooms, 3 baths, 2-car side entry garage
❖ Basement foundation, drawings also include crawl space and slab foundations

Special features

- ❖ 1,600 total square feet of living area
- ❖ Energy efficient home with 2" x 6" exterior walls
- ❖ Impressive sunken living room features a massive stone fireplace and 16' vaulted ceiling
- ❖ The dining room is conveniently located next to the kitchen and divided for privacy
- ❖ Special amenities include a sewing room, glass shelves in the kitchen, a grand master bath and a large utility area
- ❖ Sunken master bedroom features a distinctive sitting room
- ❖ 3 bedrooms, 2 baths, 2-car side entry garage
- ❖ Slab foundation, drawings also include crawl space and basement foundations

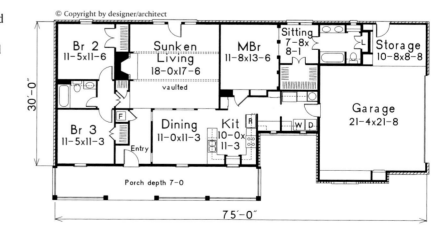

© Copyright by designer/architect

Br 2 11-5x11-6

Sunken Living 18-0x17-6 vaulted

MBr 11-8x13-6

Sitting 7-8x 8-1

Storage 10-8x8-8

30'-0"

Br 3 11-5x11-3

Entry

Dining 11-0x11-3

Kit 10-0x 11-3

W D

Garage 21-4x21-8

Porch depth 7-0

75'-0"

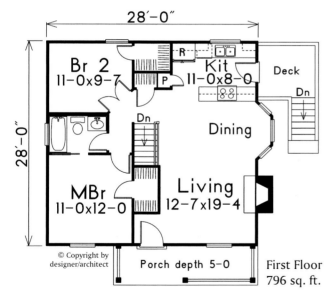

28'-0"

28'-0"

Br 2
11-0x9-7

Kit
11-0x8-0

R

P

Deck

Dn

Dn

Dining

MBr
11-0x12-0

Living
12-7x19-4

© Copyright by
designer/architect

Porch depth 5-0

First Floor
796 sq. ft.

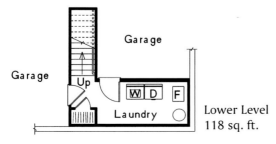

Garage

Garage

Up

W D F

Laundry

Lower Level
118 sq. ft.

Special features

- ❖ 914 total square feet of living area
- ❖ Large porch for leisure evenings
- ❖ Dining area with bay window, open stair and pass-through kitchen create openness
- ❖ Basement includes generous garage space, storage area, finished laundry and mechanical room
- ❖ 2 bedrooms, 1 bath, 2-car drive under garage
- ❖ Basement foundation

If your washer and dryer are located in a place where you can't hear the end of the cycle buzzer, set an alarm elsewhere in the house (like the timer on your microwave) to alert you of a finished load.

Special features

- 1,785 total square feet of living area
- 9' ceilings throughout the home
- Luxurious master bath includes a whirlpool tub and separate shower
- Cozy breakfast area is convenient to the kitchen
- 3 bedrooms, 3 baths, 2-car detached garage
- Basement, crawl space or slab foundation, please specify when ordering

Dormers have been featured in American architecture since the late 1600's. Although they come in a variety of shapes and sizes, all dormers are windows with their own roof, which is set vertically into the roof of the house. Being able to recognize different types of dormers will give you a clue to a home's architectural style.

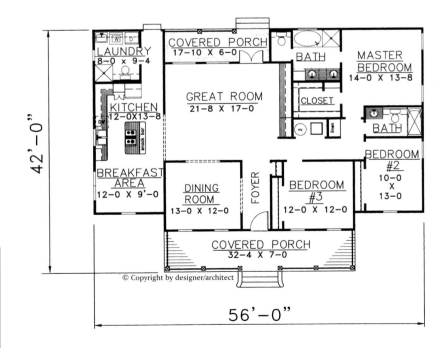

© Copyright by designer/architect

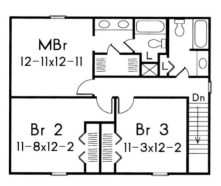

Second Floor
832 sq. ft.

MBr
12-11x12-11

Br 2
11-8x12-2

Br 3
11-3x12-2

Dn

Special features

- ❖ 1,664 total square feet of living area
- ❖ L-shaped country kitchen includes pantry and cozy breakfast area
- ❖ Bedrooms are located on the second floor for privacy
- ❖ Master bedroom includes a walk-in closet, dressing area and bath
- ❖ 2" x 6" exterior walls available, please order plan #597-001D-0121
- ❖ 3 bedrooms, 2 1/2 baths, 2-car garage
- ❖ Crawl space foundation, drawings also include basement and slab foundations

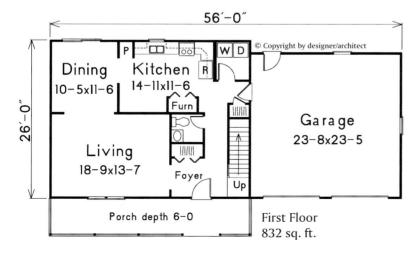

56'-0"

26'-0"

P

Dining
10-5x11-6

Kitchen
14-11x11-6

R

W D

© Copyright by designer/architect

Furn

Living
18-9x13-7

Garage
23-8x23-5

Foyer

Up

Porch depth 6-0

First Floor
832 sq. ft.

Cleaning scuff marks off a vinyl floor can be a real chore. But, using an art gum eraser (the tan one you used in school) or a pink pearl eraser makes the job simple and easy.

Special features

❖ 1,597 total square feet of living area
❖ Spacious family room includes a fireplace and coat closet
❖ Open kitchen and dining room provide a breakfast bar and access to the outdoors
❖ Convenient laundry area is located near the kitchen
❖ Secluded master bedroom enjoys a walk-in closet and private bath
❖ 4 bedrooms, 2 1/2 baths, 2-car detached garage
❖ Basement foundation

Second Floor
615 sq. ft.

Br 4
12-0x12-4

Br 3
14-0x10-0

Br 2
14-0x10-10

One of the top trends in home design currently is the use of "flexible" floor plans. Traditionally designed styles with separate living and dining rooms are being replaced by large family areas or great rooms which offer more flexibility for family living.

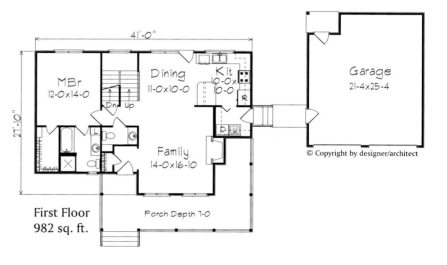

41'-0"

27'-10"

MBr
12-0x14-0

Dining
11-0x10-0

Kit
10-0x10-0

Garage
21-4x25-4

Family
14-0x16-10

© Copyright by designer/architect

First Floor
982 sq. ft.

Porch Depth 7-0

Plan #597-020D-0009

Optional Second Floor

OPEN TO LIVING ROOM BELOW

UNFINISHED ATTIC
15'0" x 30'0"

Special features

- ❖ 2,123 total square feet of living area
- ❖ Energy efficient home with 2" x 6" exterior walls
- ❖ Living room has a wood burning fireplace, built-in bookshelves and a wet bar
- ❖ Skylights make the sunporch bright and comfortable
- ❖ Unfinished attic has an additional 450 square feet of living area
- ❖ 3 bedrooms, 2 1/2 baths, 2-car side entry garage
- ❖ Crawl space foundation, drawings also include slab and basement foundations

Quoins are the dressed stones at the corner of buildings. They are typically rusticated meaning they are cut in large blocks separated by deep joints and are used to give a bold, exaggerated look to the corners of a structure.

First Floor Plan

58'-0"

71'-0"

GARAGE 22' x 21'

MASTER BATH

WIC

WIC

STORAGE 11' x 7'

SUNPORCH 20' x 11'
SKYLT. SKYLT.

MASTER BEDROOM 20' x 14'

ENTRY 2

UTIL 8' x 8'

HALL 2

KITCHEN 14' x 11'

BOOKS

LIVING 21' x 15'

HALL 1

BEDROOM 2 12' x 12'

© Copyright by designer/architect

BAR

PDR. RM.

WIC DRESS 2

WIC

EATING 13' x 12'

DINING 12' x 12'

ENTRY 1

BEDROOM 3 12' x 12'

DRESS 1

BATH 3

PORCH 30' x 8'

First Floor 2,123 sq. ft.

Special features

❖ 3,149 total square feet of living area

❖ 10' ceilings on the first floor and 9' ceilings on the second floor

❖ All bedrooms include walk-in closets

❖ Formal living and dining rooms flank the two-story foyer

❖ 4 bedrooms, 3 1/2 baths, 2-car detached garage

❖ Slab foundation, drawings also include crawl space foundation

The word porch is used freely to mean any sort of covered area that attaches to a home. Other variations include breezeway, veranda, portico or even a sleeping porch. Each different term typically is popularized depending on the region of the country you reside.

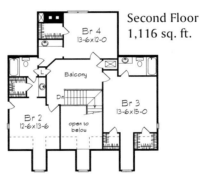

Second Floor
1,116 sq. ft.

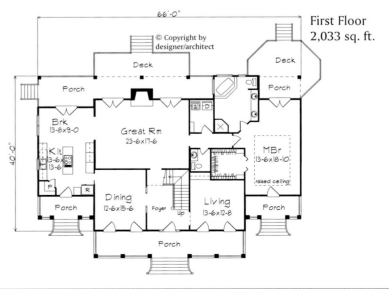

First Floor
2,033 sq. ft.

Bedroom
12' x 10'6"

Bath

Bath

Bonus Room
17'5" x 10'7"

Hall

Bedroom
13'7" x 11'6"

Master Bedroom
14'10" x 14'10"

Second Floor
830 sq. ft.

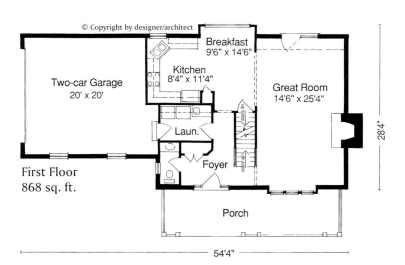

© Copyright by designer/architect

Breakfast
9'6" x 14'6"

Kitchen
8'4" x 11'4"

Two-car Garage
20' x 20'

Great Room
14'6" x 25'4"

Laun.

Foyer

28'4"

First Floor
868 sq. ft.

Porch

54'4"

Special features

❖ 1,698 total square feet of living area

❖ The massive great room runs the entire depth of the home offering a view of the front porch and easy access to the backyard

❖ The adjacent breakfast area offers a relaxed atmosphere and enjoys the close proximity of the U-shaped kitchen

❖ All bedrooms are located on the second floor, including the master suite that features a deluxe bath and walk-in closet

❖ The optional bonus room over the garage has an additional 269 square feet of living area

❖ 3 bedrooms, 2 1/2 baths, 2-car side entry garage

❖ Basement or crawl space foundation, please specify when ordering

Special features

- 2,069 total square feet of living area
- 9' ceilings throughout this home
- Kitchen has many amenities including a snack bar
- Large front and rear porches offer outdoor living spaces
- 3 bedrooms, 2 1/2 baths, 2-car garage
- Slab or crawl space foundation, please specify when ordering

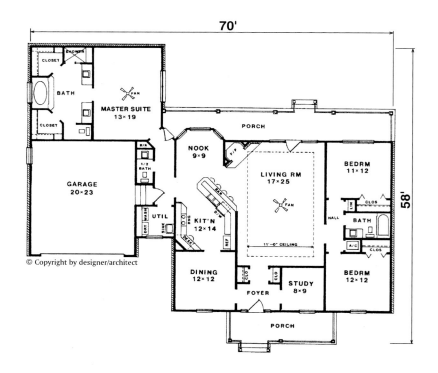

© Copyright by designer/architect

For centuries beeswax candles were used to light the homes of European nobility. Beeswax, considered to be a precious material during these times, was typically only cultivated by the noblemen themselves on their own land in fear that the wax would be stolen or sold.

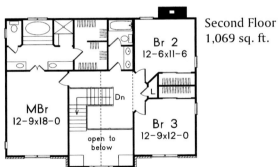

Second Floor
1,069 sq. ft.

Br 2
12-6x11-6

MBr
12-9x18-0

Br 3
12-9x12-0

open to below

Dn

L

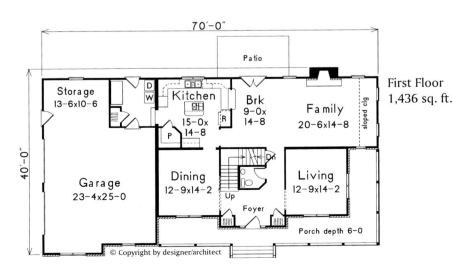

70'-0"

Patio

Storage
13-6x10-6

Kitchen
15-0x14-8

Brk
9-0x14-8

Family
20-6x14-8

sloped clg

D
W

P

R

40'-0"

Garage
23-4x25-0

Dining
12-9x14-2

Living
12-9x14-2

Up

Dn

Foyer

Porch depth 6-0

© Copyright by designer/architect

First Floor
1,436 sq. ft.

Special features

- 2,505 total square feet of living area
- The garage features extra storage area and ample workspace
- Laundry room is accessible from the garage and the outdoors
- Deluxe raised tub and an immense walk-in closet grace the master bath
- 3 bedrooms, 2 1/2 baths, 2-car side entry garage
- Basement foundation, drawings also include crawl space foundation

If you are planning a new kitchen, don't miss the chance to build in space - creating touches such as a drawer - front that pulls out to reveal a useful extra work surface. Some ranges even incorporate drawers into the base area below the cabinets.

Special features

- ❖ 1,787 total square feet of living area
- ❖ Large great room with fireplace and vaulted ceiling features three large skylights and windows galore
- ❖ Cooking is sure to be a pleasure in this L-shaped well-appointed kitchen which includes a bayed breakfast area with access to the rear deck
- ❖ Every bedroom offers a spacious walk-in closet with a convenient laundry room just steps away
- ❖ 415 square feet of optional living area available on the lower level
- ❖ 3 bedrooms, 2 baths, 2-car drive under garage
- ❖ Walk-out basement foundation

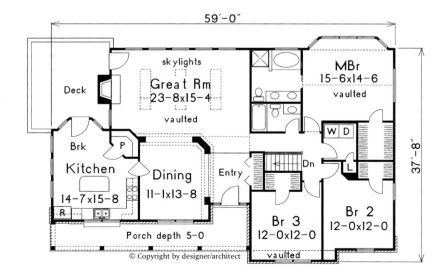

© Copyright by designer/architect

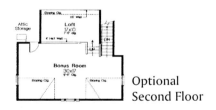

Optional
Second Floor

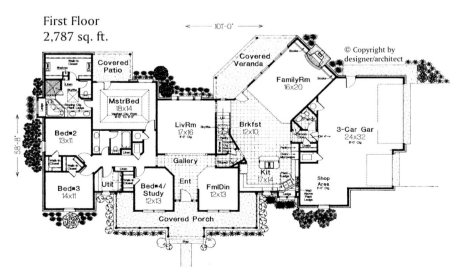

First Floor
2,787 sq. ft.

© Copyright by
designer/architect

Special features

- 2,787 total square feet of living area
- 9' ceilings on the first and second floors
- The enormous shop area in the garage is ideal for hobbies or extra storage
- An interesting gallery is the focal point of the entry
- Optional second floor has an additional 636 square feet of living area
- 4 bedrooms, 2 1/2 baths, 3-car side entry garage
- Crawl space, basement or slab foundation, please specify when ordering

White and creamy off-white are always safe bets when painting a home office or study. Any shade of a warm yellow tone helps stimulate creativity and brings clarity of thought to the person who inhabits the space.

Special features

- ❖ 3,269 total square feet of living area
- ❖ Stately stonework, cedar shakes and clipped gables combine to create a captivating facade
- ❖ A large country porch has access to the garage
- ❖ The grand-sized family room, open to the sunny breakfast room, features a fireplace, lots of windows and convenient adjacent powder room
- ❖ A sensationally designed kitchen includes all the amenities
- ❖ 4 bedrooms, 3 1/2 baths, 2-car garage
- ❖ Basement foundation

Decorating with mirrors illuminates your home. Hang them strategically to capture the light of glowing candles, sconces and chandeliers.

First Floor
1,675 sq. ft.

Second Floor
1,594 sq. ft.

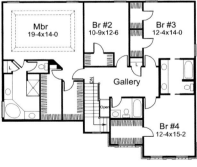

© Copyright by designer/architect

**Second Floor
576 sq. ft.**

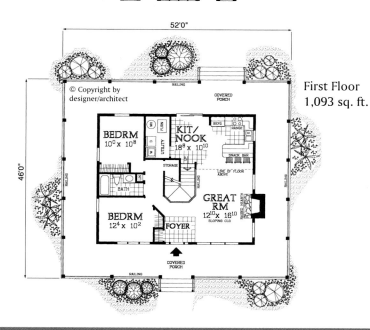

52'0"

46'0"

© Copyright by
designer/architect

**First Floor
1,093 sq. ft.**

Special features

❖ 1,669 total square feet of living area
❖ Energy efficient home with 2" x 6" exterior walls
❖ Windows add exciting visual elements to the exterior as well as plenty of natural light to the interior
❖ Two-story great room has a raised hearth
❖ Second floor loft/study would easily make a terrific home office
❖ 3 bedrooms, 2 baths
❖ Crawl space foundation

In the 18th century, small seats were made to fit into deep window recesses. Now, a window seat is more likely to be a built-in bench sometimes with a lift-up lid for storage, with a seat cushion and pillows for a functional yet relaxing space.

Special features

- ❖ 2,599 total square feet of living area
- ❖ Office/home school room could easily be converted to a fifth bedroom
- ❖ Recreation room on the second floor would make a great casual living area or children's play room
- ❖ Large shop/storage has an oversized work bench for hobbies or projects
- ❖ Bonus room on the second floor has an additional 385 square feet of living area
- ❖ 4 bedrooms, 2 1/2 baths, 2-car garage with shop/storage
- ❖ Basement, crawl space or slab foundation, please specify when ordering

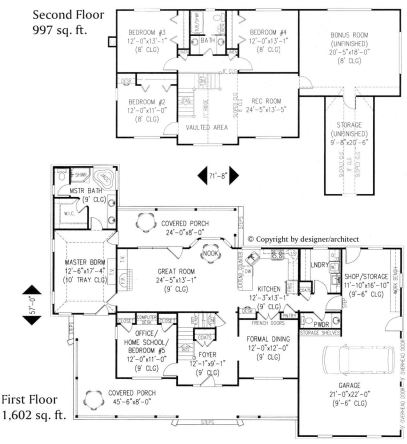

Second Floor
997 sq. ft.

First Floor
1,602 sq. ft.

© Copyright by designer/architect

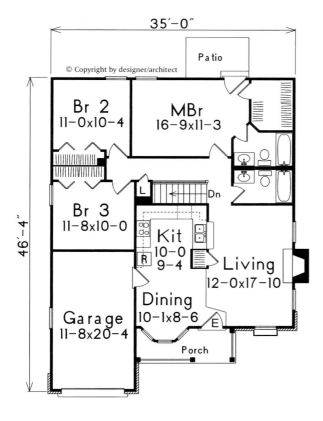

Special features

- ❖ 1,169 total square feet of living area
- ❖ Front facade features a distinctive country appeal
- ❖ Living room enjoys a wood-burning fireplace and pass-through to kitchen
- ❖ A stylish U-shaped kitchen offers an abundance of cabinet and counterspace with view to living room
- ❖ A large walk-in closet, access to rear patio and private bath are many features of the master bedroom
- ❖ 3 bedrooms, 2 baths, 1-car garage
- ❖ Basement foundation

To help bring the outdoors in to your home use natural materials. Stone, wood and all different kinds of tile are great for contributing to an outdoor feel. Granite, iron or bamboo are other elements that help add color and texture creating contrast to an interior.

Special features

- 2,184 total square feet of living area
- Delightful family room has access to the screened porch for enjoyable outdoor living
- Secluded master suite is complete with a sitting area and luxurious bath
- Formal living room has a double-door entry easily converting it to a study or home office
- Two secondary bedrooms each have their own full bath
- Bonus room above garage has an additional 379 square feet of living space
- 3 bedrooms, 3 baths, 2-car side entry garage
- Basement, crawl space or slab foundation, please specify when ordering

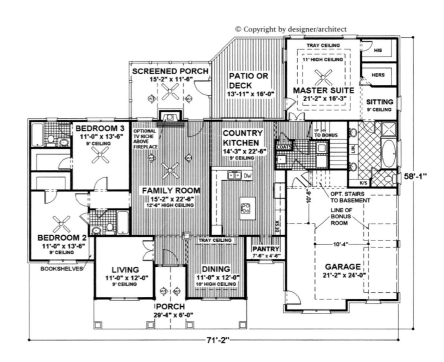

© Copyright by designer/architect

Second Floor
600 sq. ft.

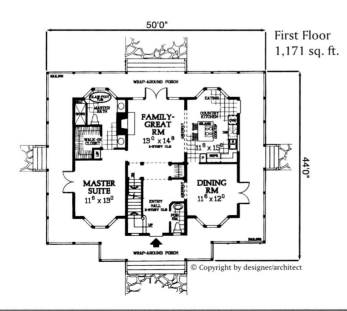

First Floor
1,171 sq. ft.

© Copyright by designer/architect

Special features

- ❖ 1,771 total square feet of living area
- ❖ Energy efficient home with 2" x 6" exterior walls
- ❖ Efficient country kitchen shares space with a bayed eating area
- ❖ Two-story family/great room is warmed by a fireplace in winter and open to outdoor country comfort in the summer with double French doors
- ❖ First floor master suite offers a bay window and access to the porch through French doors
- ❖ 3 bedrooms, 2 1/2 baths, optional 2-car detached garage
- ❖ Basement foundation

Special features

- ❖ 2,331 total square feet of living area
- ❖ Kitchen overlooks living area with fireplace and lots of windows
- ❖ Conveniently located first floor master bedroom
- ❖ Second floor features computer area with future gameroom space
- ❖ The future gameroom on the second floor has an additional 264 square feet of living area
- ❖ 3 bedrooms, 2 1/2 baths, 2-car side entry garage
- ❖ Slab foundation

Shingles made of asphalt or fiberglass are best repaired on warm days, when they are pliable. Stiff, cold shingles are easily damaged and are difficult to work with. Plan your work for a nice, sunny day in the fall or you'll have to wait for late spring.

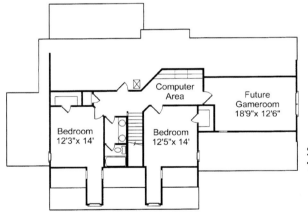

Second Floor
774 sq. ft.

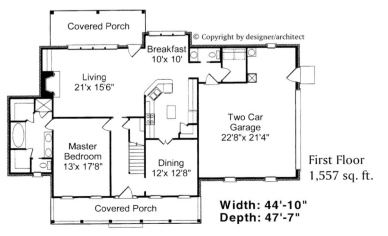

First Floor
1,557 sq. ft.

Width: 44'-10"
Depth: 47'-7"

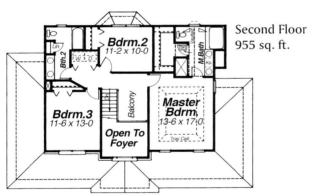

Second Floor 955 sq. ft.

Bdrm.2 11-2 x 10-0
Bth.2
Lin.
W.D.
M.Bath
Bdrm.3 11-6 x 13-0
Balcony
Master Bdrm. 13-6 x 17-0
Open To Foyer
Tray Cell.

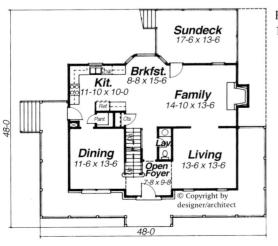

First Floor 1,038 sq. ft.

Sundeck 17-6 x 13-6
Brkfst. 8-8 x 15-6
Kit. 11-10 x 10-0
Ref
Pant.
Cts
Family 14-10 x 13-6
Dining 11-6 x 13-6
Lav
Living 13-6 x 13-6
Open Foyer 7-8 x 9-8
48-0
48-0

© Copyright by designer/architect

Special features

❖ 1,993 total square feet of living area
❖ All bedrooms on the second floor for privacy
❖ Cheerful bayed breakfast room connects the kitchen to the living area
❖ A two-story foyer greets guests upon entering the front door
❖ 3 bedrooms, 2 1/2 baths, 2-car drive under garage
❖ Walk-out basement foundation

Before dipping a brush in paint, dip it into water (for water based paints) or paint thinner (for oil-based paints) and spin out the excess. This wets the bristles in the ferrule (the metal base) and prevents paint from building up in there, which makes cleanup easier and extends the brush's life.

Special features

- ❖ 1,541 total square feet of living area
- ❖ Energy efficient home with 2" x 6" exterior walls
- ❖ Dining area offers access to a screened porch for outdoor dining and entertaining
- ❖ Country kitchen features a center island and a breakfast bay for casual meals
- ❖ Great room is warmed by a woodstove
- ❖ 3 bedrooms, 2 baths, 2-car garage
- ❖ Basement or crawl space foundation, please specify when ordering

The owner's manuals for your major appliances are filled with valuable information for everyday operation and maintenance. If you can't locate a manual, contact the manufacturer and ask the customer service department to send you one.

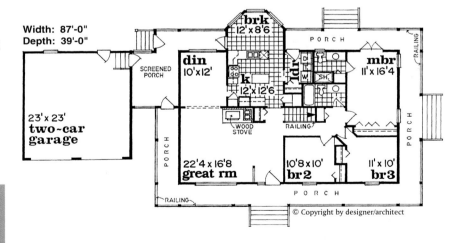

Width: 87'-0"
Depth: 39'-0"

© Copyright by designer/architect

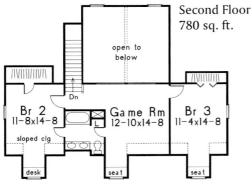

**Second Floor
780 sq. ft.**

open to below

Dn

Br 2
11-8x14-8

sloped clg

Game Rm
12-10x14-8

Br 3
11-4x14-8

desk

seat

seat

Special features

- ❖ 2,449 total square feet of living area
- ❖ Striking living area features fireplace flanked with windows, cathedral ceiling and balcony
- ❖ First floor master bedroom has twin walk-in closets and large linen storage
- ❖ Dormers add space for desks or seats
- ❖ 3 bedrooms, 2 1/2 baths, 2-car detached garage
- ❖ Slab foundation, drawings also include crawl space foundation

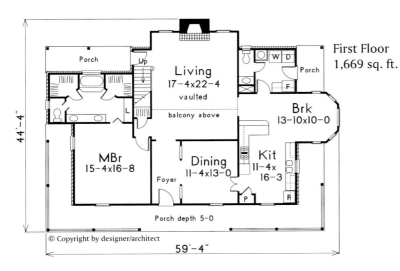

Porch

Up

Living
17-4x22-4
vaulted

W D

Porch

F

balcony above

Brk
13-10x10-0

**First Floor
1,669 sq. ft.**

44'-4"

MBr
15-4x16-8

Foyer

Dining
11-4x13-0

P

Kit
11-4x
16-3

R

Porch depth 5-0

© Copyright by designer/architect

59'-4"

Wood flooring is no longer used solely in living and family rooms. Increasingly it is being used in high-traffic areas such as hallways and kitchens. Be sure to pick the right wood as some types are less likely to hold up. Avoid softwoods such as pine and spruce. Instead, look for oak, maple, or ash.

Special Features

- ❖ 2,126 total square feet of living area
- ❖ Elegant bay windows in the master bedroom welcome the sun
- ❖ Double vanities in the master bath are separated by a large whirlpool tub
- ❖ Secondary bedrooms each include a walk-in closet
- ❖ Nook has access to the outdoors onto the rear porch
- ❖ 3 bedrooms, 2 baths, 2-car side entry garage
- ❖ Slab foundation

An engineered roof truss system is two to three times stronger than conventional stick framing and will ensure that a house and its roof remain married throughout the most horrific storms.

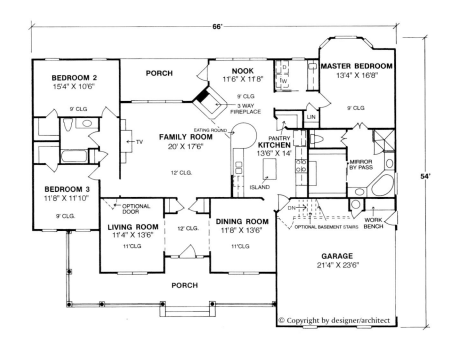

Special features

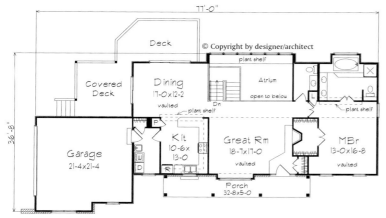

© Copyright by designer/architect

First Floor
1,297 sq. ft.

Lower Level
1,234 sq. ft.

- ❖ 2,531 total square feet of living area
- ❖ Charming porch with dormers leads into the vaulted great room with atrium
- ❖ Well-designed kitchen and breakfast bar adjoin an extra-large laundry/mud room
- ❖ Double sinks, tub with window above and plant shelf complete the vaulted master bath
- ❖ 4 bedrooms, 2 1/2 baths, 2-car side entry garage
- ❖ Walk-out basement foundation

Special features

- 1,833 total square feet of living area
- Large master bedroom includes a spacious bath with garden tub, separate shower and large walk-in closet
- The spacious dining area is brightened by large windows and patio access
- Detached two-car garage with walkway leading to house adds charm to this country home
- 3 bedrooms, 2 1/2 baths, 2-car detached side entry garage
- Crawl space foundation, drawings also include slab foundation

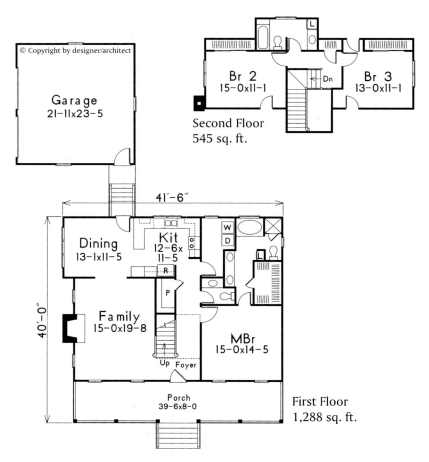

© Copyright by designer/architect

Garage
21-11x23-5

Br 2
15-0x11-1

Br 3
13-0x11-1

Second Floor
545 sq. ft.

41'-6"

40'-0"

Dining
13-1x11-5

Kit
12-6x
11-5

W D

Family
15-0x19-8

MBr
15-0x14-5

Up Foyer

Porch
39-6x8-0

First Floor
1,288 sq. ft.

Second Floor
580 sq. ft.

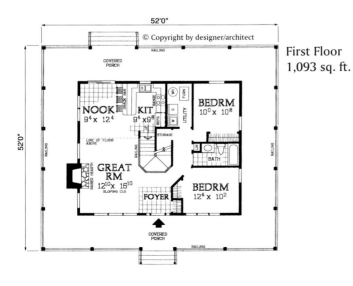

First Floor
1,093 sq. ft.

Special features

- ❖ 1,673 total square feet of living area
- ❖ Energy efficient home with 2" x 6" exterior walls
- ❖ Great room flows into the breakfast nook with outdoor access and beyond to an efficient kitchen
- ❖ Master bedroom on the second floor has access to a loft/study, private balcony and bath
- ❖ Covered porch surrounds the entire home for outdoor living area
- ❖ 3 bedrooms, 2 baths
- ❖ Crawl space foundation

Change your HVAC filter monthly. A clogged filter can cause the unit to overheat and can lead to premature damage to the air conditioning system.

Special features

- 2,674 total square feet of living area
- First floor master bedroom has a convenient location
- Kitchen and breakfast area have an island and access to the covered front porch
- Second floor bedrooms have dormer window seats for added charm
- Optional future rooms on the second floor have an additional 520 square feet of living area
- 4 bedrooms, 3 baths, 3-car side entry garage
- Basement or slab foundation, please specify when ordering

Second Floor
600 sq. ft.

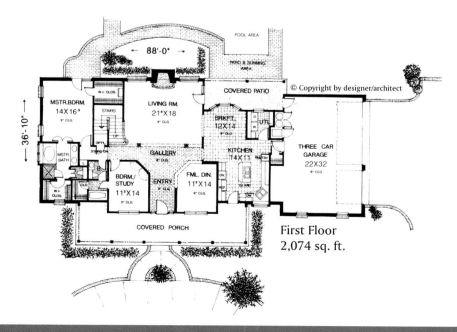

© Copyright by designer/architect

First Floor
2,074 sq. ft.

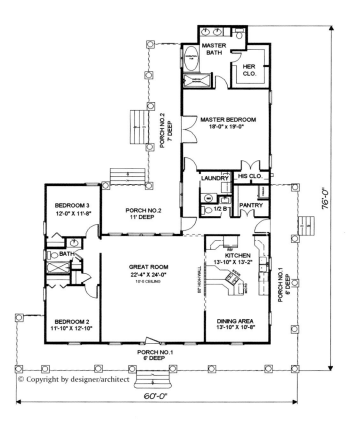

© Copyright by designer/architect

Special features

❖ 2,123 total square feet of living area
❖ L-shaped porch extends the entire length of this home creating lots of extra space for outdoor living
❖ Master bedroom is secluded for privacy and has two closets, double vanity in bath and a double-door entry onto covered porch
❖ The kitchen is designed for efficiency
❖ 3 bedrooms, 2 1/2 baths
❖ Crawl space or slab foundation, please specify when ordering

Furnishing a covered porch or patio by mixing indoor and outdoor furniture and accessories is a terrific way to combine the interior and the exterior. Plus, it allows the decorating scheme to flow seamlessly from the indoor spaces into the more seasonal space without the places looking disconnected.

Special features

- ❖ 2,547 total square feet of living area
- ❖ Grand-sized great room features a 12' volume ceiling, fireplace with built-in wrap-around shelving and patio doors with sidelights and transom windows
- ❖ The walk-in pantry, computer desk, large breakfast island for seven and bayed breakfast area are the many features of this outstanding kitchen
- ❖ The master bedroom suite enjoys a luxurious bath, large walk-in closets and patio access
- ❖ 4 bedrooms, 2 1/2 baths, 3-car side entry garage
- ❖ Basement foundation

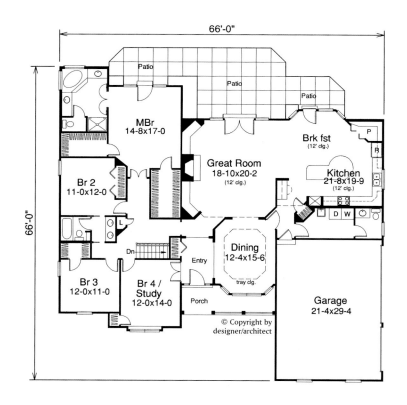

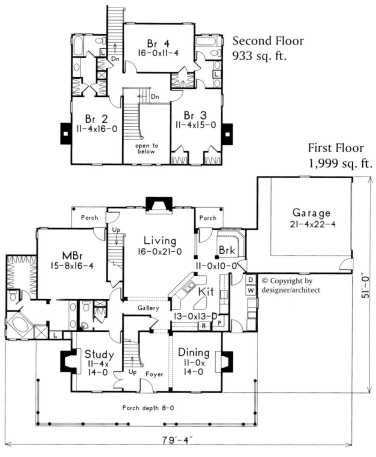

Second Floor
933 sq. ft.

Br 4
16-0x11-4

Br 2
11-4x16-0

Br 3
11-4x15-0

open to below

First Floor
1,999 sq. ft.

Garage
21-4x22-4

Porch

Porch

Up

Living
16-0x21-0

Brk
11-0x10-0

MBr
15-8x16-4

Kit
13-0x13-0

Gallery

© Copyright by designer/architect

D W R P L

51'-0"

Study
11-4x 14-0

Up Foyer

Dining
11-0x 14-0

Porch depth 8-0

79'-4"

Special features

- ❖ 2,932 total square feet of living area
- ❖ 9' ceilings throughout home
- ❖ Rear stairs provide convenient access to the second floor from living area
- ❖ Spacious kitchen has pass-through to the family room, a convenient island and pantry
- ❖ Cozy built-in table in breakfast area
- ❖ Secluded master bedroom has a luxurious bath and patio access
- ❖ 4 bedrooms, 3 1/2 baths, 2-car side entry garage
- ❖ Slab foundation

Don't place all of your furniture against the walls. This accentuates the straight lines of a room and can create a boxy feel. Try arranging it at 45-degree angles to the walls along with a rug for a fresh look.

Special features

- 2,698 total square feet of living area
- Great room feels spacious with a vaulted ceiling and windows overlooking the covered porch
- Master bath has a glass shower and whirlpool tub
- Laundry area includes counterspace and a sink
- 5 bedrooms, 3 baths, 2-car side entry garage
- Crawl space or slab foundation, please specify when ordering

Second Floor
885 sq. ft.

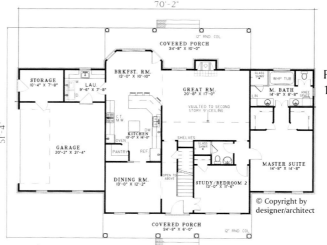

First Floor
1,813 sq. ft.

© Copyright by designer/architect

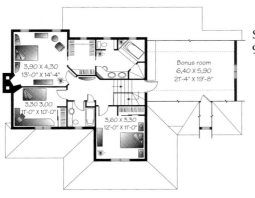

Second Floor
943 sq. ft.

Special features

- ❖ 2,089 total square feet of living area
- ❖ First floor garden solarium
- ❖ 9' ceilings on the first floor
- ❖ Energy efficient home with 2" x 6" exterior walls
- ❖ Bonus room on the second floor has an additional 313 square feet of living area
- ❖ 3 bedrooms, 2 1/2 baths, 2-car side entry garage
- ❖ Basement foundation

First Floor
1,146 sq. ft.

© Copyright by designer/architect

Special features

- ❖ 1,325 total square feet of living area
- ❖ Sloped ceiling and a fireplace in the living area create a cozy feeling
- ❖ Formal dining and breakfast areas have an efficiently designed kitchen between them
- ❖ Master bedroom has a walk-in closet and luxurious private bath
- ❖ 3 bedrooms, 2 baths, 2-car drive under garage
- ❖ Basement or crawl space foundation, please specify when ordering

Distressed cabinetry or flooring has become a popular trend in recent years. Artificially antiquing the wood by adding deliberate marks of wear and tear creates the feeling of timeless appeal and a custom look as well.

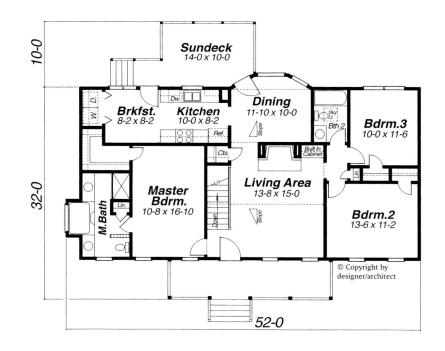

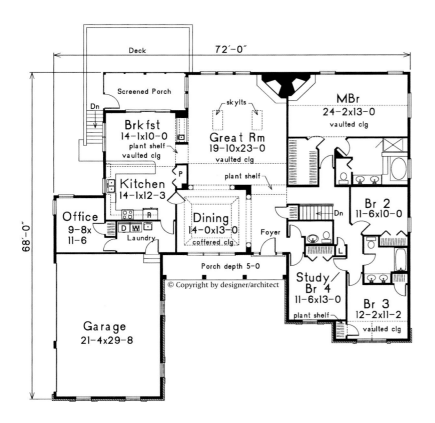

Special features

- ❖ 2,758 total square feet of living area
- ❖ Energy efficient home with 2" x 6" exterior walls
- ❖ Vaulted great room excels with fireplace, wet bar, plant shelves and skylights
- ❖ Fabulous master bedroom enjoys a fireplace, large bath, walk-in closet and vaulted ceiling
- ❖ Trendsetting kitchen and breakfast area adjoins the spacious screened porch
- ❖ Convenient office near kitchen is perfect for a computer room, hobby enthusiast or fifth bedroom
- ❖ 4 bedrooms, 2 1/2 baths, 3-car side entry garage
- ❖ Basement foundation

Special features

❖ 1,609 total square feet of living area
❖ Kitchen captures full use of space with pantry, ample cabinets and workspace
❖ Master bedroom is well secluded with a walk-in closet and private bath
❖ Large utility room includes a sink and extra storage
❖ Attractive bay window in the dining area provides light
❖ 3 bedrooms, 2 1/2 baths, 2-car garage
❖ Slab foundation

Café curtains are short curtains hung from a rod suspended halfway across a window. This sort of curtaining is sometimes hung in a double tier and is a useful treatment for windows that open inward or face directly onto a street since the tier system allows privacy with a minimal loss of light.

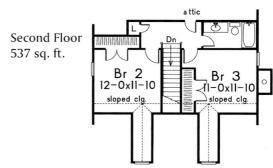

Second Floor
537 sq. ft.

attic
Br 2
12-0x11-10
sloped clg.
Br 3
11-0x11-10
sloped clg.
Dn

First Floor
1,072 sq. ft.

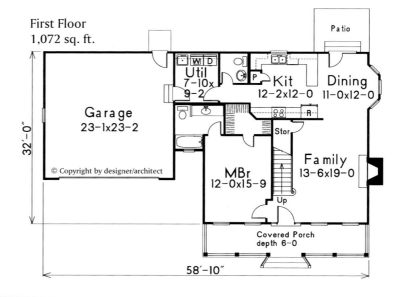

Patio

Garage
23-1x23-2

Util
7-10x
9-2

Kit
12-2x12-0

Dining
11-0x12-0

Stor

MBr
12-0x15-9

Family
13-6x19-0

Up

© Copyright by designer/architect

Covered Porch
depth 6-0

32'-0"

58'-10"

Special features

- ❖ 1,594 total square feet of living area
- ❖ Corner fireplace in the great room creates a cozy feel
- ❖ Spacious kitchen combines with the dining room creating a terrific gathering place
- ❖ A handy family and guest entrance is a casual and convenient way to enter the home
- ❖ 3 bedrooms, 2 baths, 2-car garage
- ❖ Slab or crawl space foundation, please specify when ordering

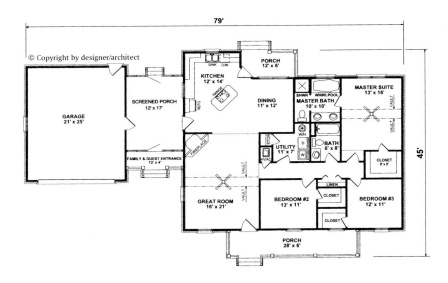

© Copyright by designer/architect

Deadhead in the gardening world means to remove flower heads from plants after they have bloomed. This prolongs the flowering season and it's the perfect practice if you have window boxes where you want lots of colorful flowers.

Special features

❖ 2,327 total square feet of living area

❖ Bayed nook nestled between the great room and kitchen provides ample area for dining

❖ Vaulted second floor recreation room is an ideal place for casual family living

❖ Room off the entry has the ability to become an office, guest bedroom or an area for home schooling if needed

❖ 3 bedrooms, 2 1/2 baths, 2-car side entry garage with shop/storage

❖ Basement, crawl space or slab foundation, please specify when ordering

So much of the Southern culture, a porch placed in the front of the home creates many benefits such as a shady overhang, as well as an indoor/outdoor setting meant for relaxation for many months of the year.

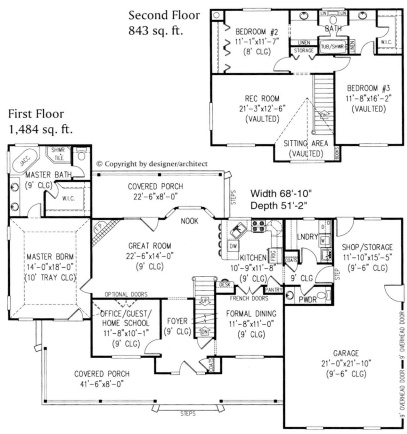

Second Floor
843 sq. ft.

First Floor
1,484 sq. ft.

Width 68'-10"
Depth 51'-2"

© Copyright by designer/architect

Special features

- ❖ 1,792 total square feet of living area
- ❖ Energy efficient home with 2" x 6" exterior walls
- ❖ Master bedroom has a private bath and large walk-in closet
- ❖ A central stone fireplace and windows on two walls are focal points in the living room
- ❖ Decorative beams and sloped ceilings add interest to the kitchen, living and dining rooms
- ❖ 3 bedrooms, 2 baths, 2-car drive under garage
- ❖ Basement foundation

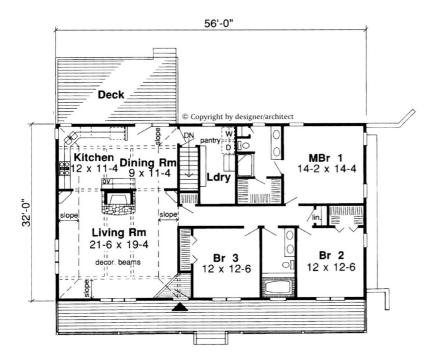

56'-0"

32'-0"

Deck

© Copyright by designer/architect

Kitchen
12 x 11-4

Dining Rm
9 x 11-4

Ldry

pantry

W
D

slope

DN

MBr 1
14-2 x 14-4

lin.

Living Rm
21-6 x 19-4

decor. beams

slope

Br 3
12 x 12-6

Br 2
12 x 12-6

Special features

- 1,600 total square feet of living area
- Energy efficient home with 2" x 6" exterior walls
- First floor master bedroom is accessible from two points of entry
- Master bath dressing area includes separate vanities and a mirrored makeup counter
- Second floor bedrooms have generous storage space and share a full bath
- 3 bedrooms, 2 baths, 2-car side entry garage
- Crawl space foundation, drawings also include slab foundation

Before a major cleaning session, take stock of your cleaning supplies. Don't wait until you're about to clean the oven to find out you don't have any oven cleaner left. Have everything you need on hand and ready to go for a smooth time.

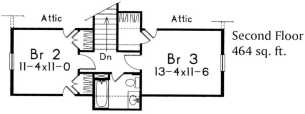

Attic

Br 2
11-4x11-0

Dn

Attic

Br 3
13-4x11-6

Second Floor
464 sq. ft.

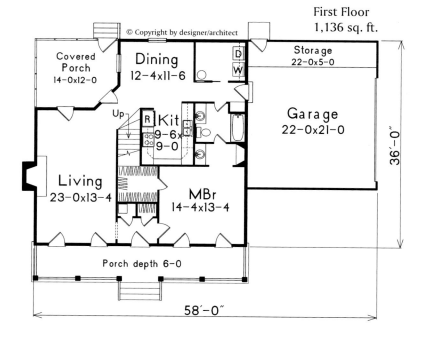

First Floor
1,136 sq. ft.

© Copyright by designer/architect

Covered Porch
14-0x12-0

Dining
12-4x11-6

Storage
22-0x5-0

Up

R Kit
9-6x
9-0

Garage
22-0x21-0

Living
23-0x13-4

MBr
14-4x13-4

36'-0"

Porch depth 6-0

58'-0"

Special features

* 1,406 total square feet of living area
* Master bedroom has a sloped ceiling
* Kitchen and dining area merge becoming a gathering place
* Enter the family room from the charming covered front porch to find a fireplace and lots of windows
* 3 bedrooms, 2 baths, 2-car detached garage
* Slab or crawl space foundation, please specify when ordering

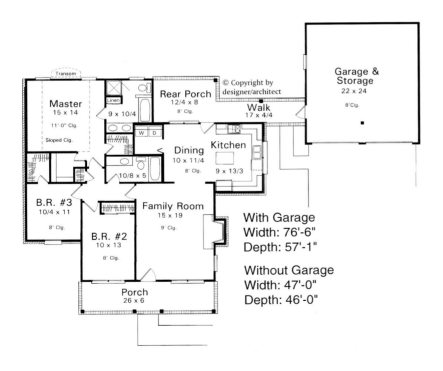

Master 15 x 14
11'-0" Clg.
Sloped Clg.

Linen

Transom

9 x 10/4

Rear Porch 12/4 x 8
8' Clg.

© Copyright by designer/architect

Walk 17 x 4/4

Garage & Storage 22 x 24
8' Clg.

W D

Dining 10 x 11/4
8' Clg.

Kitchen 9 x 13/3

10/8 x 5

B.R. #3 10/4 x 11
8' Clg.

Family Room 15 x 19
9' Clg.

B.R. #2 10 x 13
8' Clg.

Porch 26 x 6

With Garage
Width: 76'-6"
Depth: 57'-1"

Without Garage
Width: 47'-0"
Depth: 46'-0"

If you rub some waxed paper on your countertops and appliances after you clean, it will give them a nice, shiny finish and help repel dust and dirt.

Special features

- 929 total square feet of living area
- Spacious living room with dining area has access to an 8' x 12' deck through glass sliding doors
- Splendid U-shaped kitchen features a breakfast bar, oval window above sink and impressive cabinet storage
- Master bedroom enjoys a walk-in closet and large elliptical feature window
- Laundry, storage closet and mechanical space are located off the first floor garage
- 2 bedrooms, 1 bath, 3-car side entry garage
- Slab foundation

Barstools at a counter or center island in the kitchen are a convenient place for breakfast and other quick meals or school projects and homework that may need supervision or assistance from a parent.

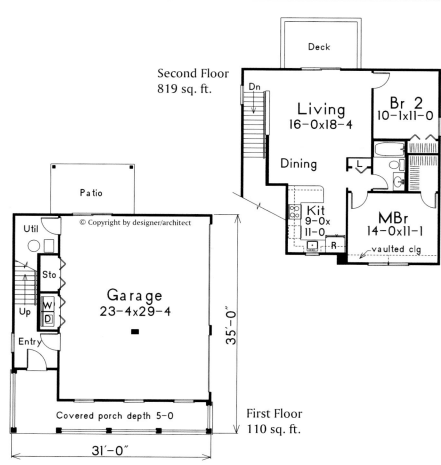

Second Floor
819 sq. ft.

Deck

Dn

Living
16-0x18-4

Br 2
10-1x11-0

Dining

Kit
9-0x
11-0

MBr
14-0x11-1

vaulted clg

© Copyright by designer/architect

Patio

Util

Sto

W
D

Up

Entry

Garage
23-4x29-4

35'-0"

Covered porch depth 5-0

First Floor
110 sq. ft.

31'-0"

Special features

- ❖ 1,344 total square feet of living area
- ❖ Family/dining room has sliding glass doors to the outdoors
- ❖ Master bedroom features a private bath
- ❖ Hall bath includes a double-bowl vanity for added convenience
- ❖ U-shaped kitchen features a large pantry and laundry area
- ❖ 2" x 6" exterior walls available, please order plan #597-001D-0108
- ❖ 3 bedrooms, 2 baths, 2-car garage
- ❖ Crawl space foundation, drawings also include basement and slab foundations

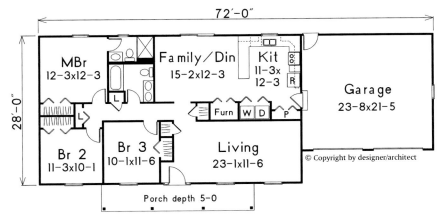

72'-0"

28'-0"

MBr
12-3x12-3

Family/Din
15-2x12-3

Kit
11-3x
12-3

Garage
23-8x21-5

Br 2
11-3x10-1

Br 3
10-1x11-6

Living
23-1x11-6

Furn   W D   P

Porch depth 5-0

© Copyright by designer/architect

Planning the layout of a living room is as important as choosing the color scheme. To make the task a little easier, draw a floor plan to scale on graph paper and cut out separate pieces for the furniture. Place these on the plan and move them around until you have an arrangement that suits your needs.

Special features

- 2,090 total square feet of living area
- The centrally located kitchen serves the dining and breakfast rooms with ease
- The expansive great room provides a cozy atmosphere with a warm fireplace
- Laundry area is located on the second floor convenient to the bedrooms
- 4 bedrooms, 2 1/2 baths, 2-car garage
- Basement foundation

Before storing your mower for the season, make it ready for next season. Lubricate linkages, change the oils, check for corrosion, and replace worn drive belts. Scrape matted grass from the underside of the mower deck, then place the tractor on blocks so its wheels hang free. Also, don't leave any gas in the tank or lines.

Second Floor
1,163 sq. ft.

First Floor
927 sq. ft.

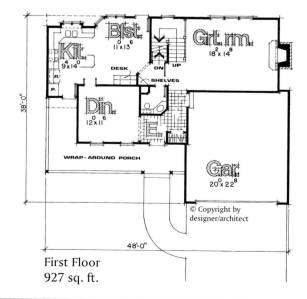

Second Floor
646 sq. ft.

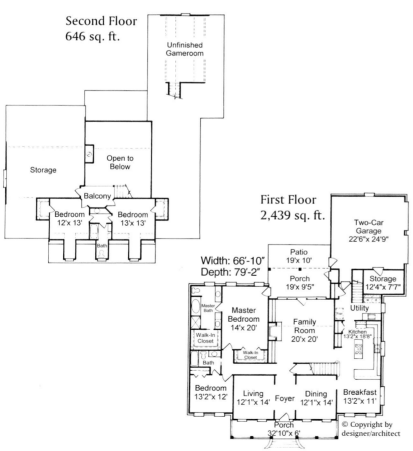

First Floor
2,439 sq. ft.

Width: 66'-10"
Depth: 79'-2"

© Copyright by
designer/architect

Special features

❖ 3,085 total square feet of living area
❖ The wonderful family room features a two-story ceiling, full wall of windows and a raised hearth fireplace flanked by built-in bookshelves
❖ The family chef is sure to enjoy the kitchen with a cooktop island and snack bar that opens to the breakfast area
❖ The unfinished gameroom has an additional 180 square feet of living area
❖ 4 bedrooms, 3 baths, 2-car side entry garage
❖ Slab, crawl space or basement foundation, please specify when ordering

Special features

❖ 1,998 total square feet of living area

❖ Large family room features a fireplace and access to the kitchen and dining area

❖ Skylights add daylight to the second floor baths

❖ Utility room is conveniently located near the garage and kitchen

❖ Kitchen/breakfast area includes a pantry, island workspace and easy access to the patio

❖ 3 bedrooms, 2 1/2 baths, 2-car side entry garage

❖ Basement foundation, drawings also include crawl space and slab foundations

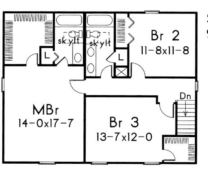

Second Floor
938 sq. ft.

Br 2
11-8x11-8

MBr
14-0x17-7

Br 3
13-7x12-0

First Floor
1,060 sq. ft.

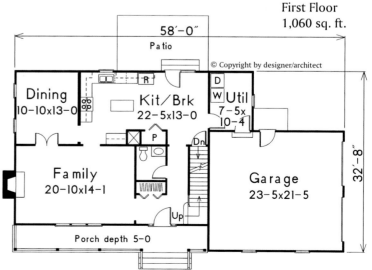

58'-0"

Patio

© Copyright by designer/architect

Dining
10-10x13-0

Kit/Brk
22-5x13-0

Util
7-5x
10-4

32'-8"

Family
20-10x14-1

Garage
23-5x21-5

Porch depth 5-0

© Copyright by designer/architect

Width 59'-0"
Depth 61'-0"

Special features

- ❖ 1,698 total square feet of living area
- ❖ Vaulted master bedroom has a private bath and a walk-in closet
- ❖ Decorative columns flank the entrance to the dining room
- ❖ Open great room is perfect for gathering family together
- ❖ 3 bedrooms, 2 1/2 baths, 2-car side entry garage with storage
- ❖ Basement, crawl space or slab foundation, please specify when ordering

Counters withstand an enormous amount of punishment, so choose your material wisely. Plastic tops run from moderately priced laminate to costly solid acrylic that looks like marble or granite. Hard-surface counters include tile, granite, organic glass, stainless steel and natural and synthetic marble.

Special features

❖ 2,198 total square feet of living area

❖ Great room features a warm fireplace flanked by bookshelves for storage

❖ Double French doors connect the formal dining room to the kitchen

❖ An oversized laundry room has extra counterspace

❖ The second floor bonus room has an additional 385 square feet of living area

❖ 4 bedrooms, 2 1/2 baths, 2-car side entry garage with shop/storage

❖ Basement, crawl space or slab foundation, please specify when ordering

Swapping out standard incandescent bulbs for ENERGY STAR® qualified compact flourescents in your five most frequently used fixtures could trim as much as $60 off your yearly energy bill.

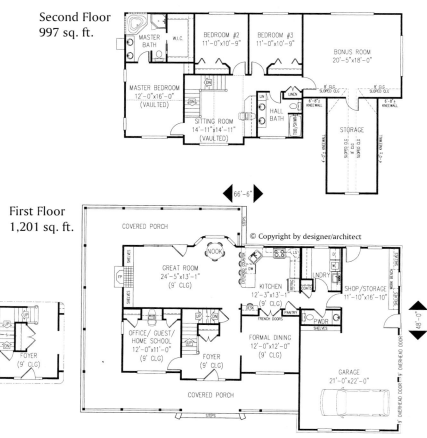

Second Floor
997 sq. ft.

First Floor
1,201 sq. ft.

© Copyright by designer/architect

Special features

- 1,550 total square feet of living area
- Wrap-around front porch is an ideal gathering place
- Handy snack bar is positioned so the kitchen flows into the family room
- Master bedroom has many amenities
- 3 bedrooms, 2 baths, 2-car detached side entry garage
- Slab or crawl space foundation, please specify when ordering

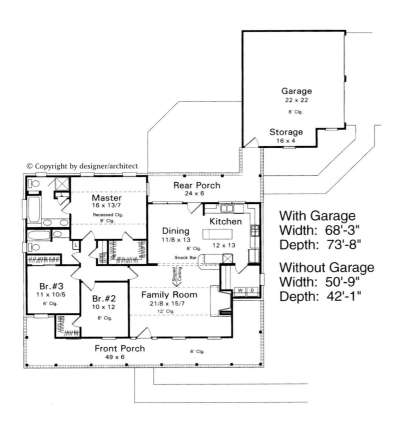

Garage
22 x 22
8' Clg.

Storage
16 x 4

© Copyright by designer/architect

Rear Porch
24 x 6

Master
16 x 13/7
Recessed Clg.
9' Clg.

Kitchen
12 x 13

Dining
11/8 x 13
8' Clg.

Snack Bar

Br.#3
11 x 10/5
8' Clg.

Br. #2
10 x 12
8' Clg.

Family Room
21/8 x 15/7
12' Clg.

W D

Front Porch
49 x 6   8' Clg.

With Garage
Width: 68'-3"
Depth: 73'-8"

Without Garage
Width: 50'-9"
Depth: 42'-1"

Cooking with your kids can be a scary thought for many parents. Here are a few tips to have a positive experience:
- Keep a sturdy stool nearby so kids can be a part of the action and aren't reaching for utensils over their heads.
- Organize a "kid's tools" drawer within their reach.

Special features

- 864 total square feet of living area
- Large laundry area accesses the outdoors as well as the kitchen
- Front covered porch provides an ideal outdoor living area
- Snack bar in kitchen creates a quick and easy dining area
- 2 bedrooms, 1 bath
- Crawl space or slab foundation, please specify when ordering

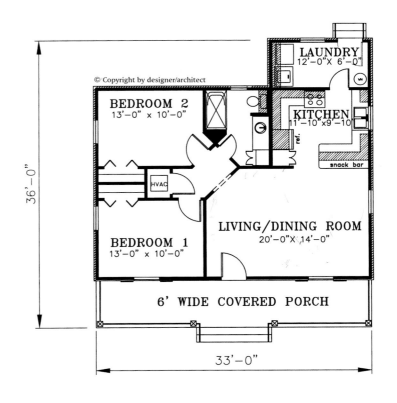

© Copyright by designer/architect

LAUNDRY
12'-0" X 6'-0"

BEDROOM 2
13'-0" x 10'-0"

KITCHEN
11'-10" x 9'-10"

ref.

snack bar

HVAC

36'-0"

BEDROOM 1
13'-0" x 10'-0"

LIVING/DINING ROOM
20'-0" X 14'-0"

6' WIDE COVERED PORCH

33'-0"

When making a bed, the top sheet or flat sheet always goes the "wrong" side up. This way when you fold back the top of the sheet the decorative or printed side will be seen.

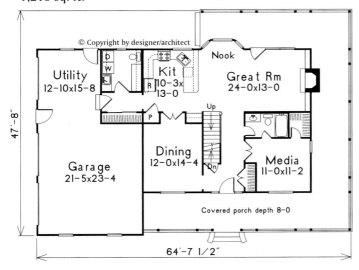

Second Floor
1,050 sq. ft.

Br 3
12-0x13-0

Br 2
12-0x13-0

MBr
14-0x17-3
coffered clg
sitting area

library

First Floor
1,216 sq. ft.

© Copyright by designer/architect

Utility
12-10x15-8

Kit
10-3x
13-0

Nook

Great Rm
24-0x13-0

Up

Garage
21-5x23-4

Dining
12-0x14-4

Dn

Media
11-0x11-2

47-8"

64'-7 1/2"

Covered porch depth 8-0

Special features

❖ 2,266 total square feet of living area
❖ Great room includes a fireplace flanked by built-in bookshelves and dining nook with bay window
❖ Unique media room includes a double-door entrance, walk-in closet and access to a full bath
❖ Master bedroom has a lovely sitting area and private bath with a walk-in closet, step-up tub and double vanity
❖ 3 bedrooms, 3 1/2 baths, 2-car side entry garage
❖ Basement foundation, drawings also include crawl space foundation

Small details make big impressions when entertaining. Take cues from the season. Some fun ideas for a place card include a ripe pear or another fruit of the season, a pine cone or even fall leaves. Attach a paper name tag to the stem or on the plate and you'll have a memorable reminder of the gathering.

163

Special features

- ❖ 1,772 total square feet of living area
- ❖ Extended porches in front and rear provide a charming touch
- ❖ Large bay windows lend distinction to the dining room and bedroom #3
- ❖ Efficient U-shaped kitchen
- ❖ Master bedroom includes two walk-in closets
- ❖ Full corner fireplace in family room
- ❖ 3 bedrooms, 2 baths, 2-car detached garage
- ❖ Slab foundation, drawings also include crawl space foundation

Flowers of one type in a vase will last longer than a bouquet of mixed varieties. Also, a single bloom will survive longer than many blossoms of the same type.

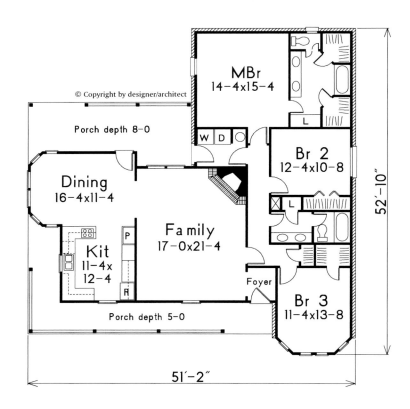

© Copyright by designer/architect

Porch depth 8-0

MBr
14-4x15-4

W D

Dining
16-4x11-4

Br 2
12-4x10-8

L

Family
17-0x21-4

Kit
11-4x
12-4

P

R

Foyer

Br 3
11-4x13-8

Porch depth 5-0

51'-2"

52'-10"

STORAGE

Second Floor
579 sq. ft.

BEDROOM 3
15X12

DN

OPEN TO BELOW

BEDROOM 2
15X12

Special features

- ❖ 1,643 total square feet of living area
- ❖ First floor master bedroom has a private bath, walk-in closet and easy access to the laundry closet
- ❖ Comfortable family room features a vaulted ceiling and a cozy fireplace
- ❖ Two bedrooms on the second floor share a bath
- ❖ 3 bedrooms, 2 1/2 baths, 2-car drive under garage
- ❖ Basement or crawl space foundation, please specify when ordering

DECK

DINING
12x12

KITCHEN
10x12

SKYLIGHT

First Floor
1,064 sq. ft.

34

D
W

DN

VAULT

UP

VAULT

MASTER BEDRM
15X13

FAMILY ROOM
18X15

© Copyright by designer/architect

38

The size of the American yard continues to shrink; currently it is only 9,000 square feet.

Special features

- 2,182 total square feet of living area
- Meandering porch creates an inviting look
- Generous great room has double-hung windows and sliding doors
- Highly functional kitchen features island/breakfast bar, menu desk and convenient pantry
- Each secondary bedroom includes generous closet space and a private bath
- 3 bedrooms, 3 1/2 baths, 2-car side entry garage
- Basement foundation, drawings also include crawl space and slab foundations

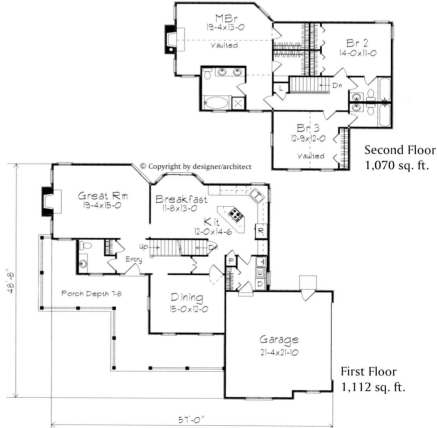

MBr
19-4x13-0
Vaulted

Br 2
14-0x11-0

Br 3
12-9x12-0
Vaulted

Second Floor
1,070 sq. ft.

© Copyright by designer/architect

Great Rm
19-4x15-0

Breakfast
11-8x13-0

Kit
12-0x14-6

Up

Entry

Porch Depth 7-8

Dining
15-0x12-0

Garage
21-4x21-10

48'-8"

57'-0"

First Floor
1,112 sq. ft.

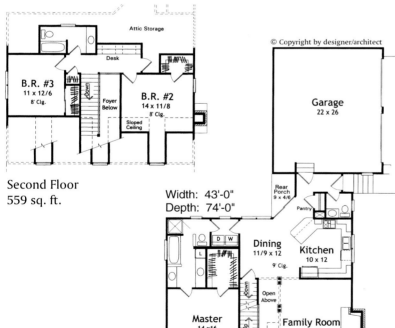

Second Floor
559 sq. ft.

Attic Storage

Desk

B.R. #3
11 x 12/6
8' Clg.

Foyer
Below

B.R. #2
14 x 11/8
8' Clg.

Sloped
Ceiling

© Copyright by designer/architect

Width: 43'-0"
Depth: 74'-0"

Garage
22 x 26

Rear
Porch
9 x 4/6

Pantry

Dining
11/9 x 12
9' Clg.

Kitchen
10 x 12

Open
Above

Master
14 x16
9' Clg

Family Room
14 x 18
9' Clg

Foyer
7/8 x 5/6

Porch
37 x 8

First Floor
1,256 sq. ft.

Special features

❖ 1,815 total square feet of living area
❖ Second floor has a built-in desk in the hall that is ideal as a computer work station or mini office area
❖ Two doors into the laundry area make it handy from the master bedroom and the rest of the home
❖ Inviting covered porch
❖ The kitchen provides an abundance of counterspace and cabinetry
❖ 3 bedrooms, 2 1/2 baths, 2-car side entry garage
❖ Basement foundation

When packing breakable items, use towels and washcloths to wrap them in instead of newspaper. You won't have to wash them when you unpack, and you don't need an extra box to pack those towels.

Special Features

- 2,252 total square feet of living area
- Large covered porch creates an enchanting country style
- Two rear covered porches and a screened porch offer an abundance of outdoor living area
- The family can enjoy an easy flow of activities with a wide open kitchen, nook and living room
- 4 bedrooms, 3 baths, 3-car side entry garage
- Slab foundation

Second Floor
516 sq. ft.

OPT. GAMEROOM
16' X 25'-8
8' CLG.

OPEN TO BELOW

JULIET BALCONY

ATTIC   LIN   DN

BEDROOM 2
12' X 12'8"
8' CLG.

BEDROOM 3
12' X 12'8"
8' CLG.

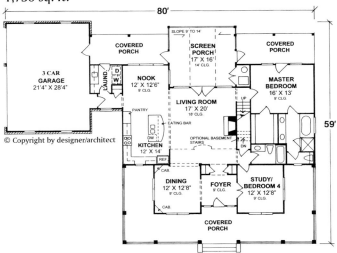

First Floor
1,736 sq. ft.

80'

59'

3 CAR GARAGE
21'4" X 28'4"

COVERED PORCH

SLOPE 9' TO 14'

SCREEN PORCH
17' X 16'
14' CLG.

COVERED PORCH

LAUND   D/W

NOOK
12' X 12'6"
9' CLG.

MASTER BEDROOM
16' X 13'
9' CLG.

PANTRY

LIVING ROOM
17' X 20'
18' CLG.

UP

EATING BAR

DW

OPTIONAL BASEMENT STAIRS

DN

KITCHEN
12' X 14'

REF   CAB.

DINING
12' X 12'8"
9' CLG.

FOYER
9' CLG.

STUDY/ BEDROOM 4
12' X 12'8"
9' CLG.

CAB.

COVERED PORCH

© Copyright by designer/architect

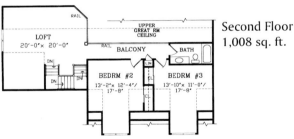

Second Floor
1,008 sq. ft.

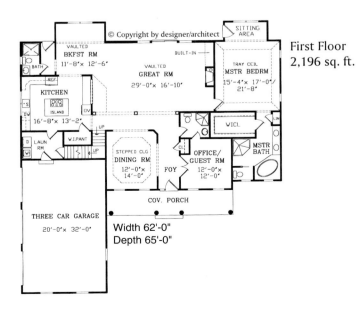

First Floor
2,196 sq. ft.

Width 62'-0"
Depth 65'-0"

Special features

❖ 3,204 total square feet of living area
❖ The master bedroom highlights a sunny sitting area, tray ceiling, huge walk-in closet and a corner spa tub in the bath
❖ Decorative columns introduce the expansive great room which features a fireplace, built-in shelves and a serving counter shared with the kitchen
❖ A handy office just off the entry doubles as a guest room and has private access to a full bath
❖ A full bath near the rear door from the kitchen is convenient
❖ 4 bedrooms, 4 baths, 3-car side entry garage
❖ Basement or crawl space foundation, please specify when ordering

Special features

- 1,800 total square feet of living area
- Energy efficient home with 2" x 6" exterior walls
- Covered front and rear porches add outdoor living area
- 12' ceilings in the kitchen, breakfast area, dining and living rooms
- Private master bedroom features an expansive bath
- Side entry garage has two storage areas
- Pillared styling with brick and stucco exterior finish
- 3 bedrooms, 2 baths, 2-car side entry garage
- Crawl space foundation, drawings also include slab foundation

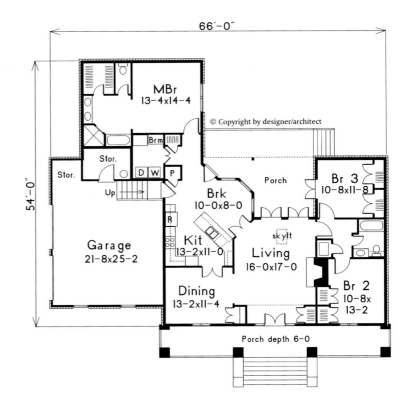

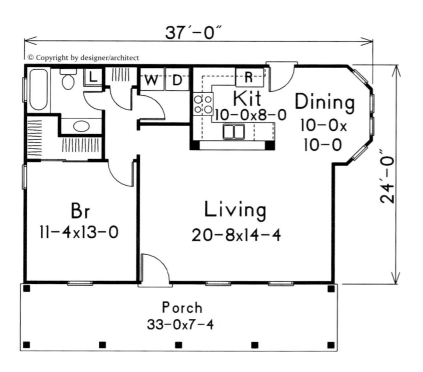

Special features

- ❖ 829 total square feet of living area
- ❖ U-shaped kitchen opens into living area by a 42" high counter
- ❖ Oversized bay window and French door accent dining room
- ❖ Gathering space is created by the large living room
- ❖ Convenient utility room and linen closet
- ❖ 1 bedroom, 1 bath
- ❖ Slab foundation

Ideally, your central air-conditioning compressor should be located on a shady side of your house. Studies show that shading a compressor can shave 1% to 2% off cooling costs. It's important to keep fences, shrubs, and anything else that might block airflow at least 24 inches away.

Special features

- 1,367 total square feet of living area
- Energy efficient home with 2" x 6" exterior walls
- Neat front porch shelters the entrance
- Dining room has a full wall of windows and convenient storage area
- Breakfast area leads to the rear terrace through sliding doors
- The large living room features a high ceiling, skylight and fireplace
- 3 bedrooms, 2 baths, 2-car garage
- Basement foundation, drawings also include slab foundation

Ceiling fans can save energy in both the summer and the winter. In the summer, fan blades should revolve in a counterclockwise direction. In winter months, set your fan at its slowest speed and reverse it in order to push warm air down.

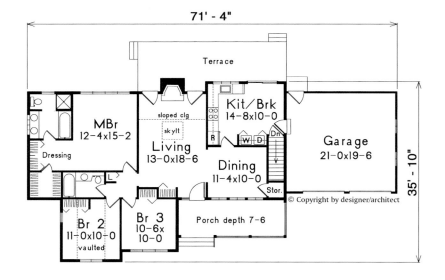

71' - 4"

Terrace

MBr 12-4x15-2

Dressing

sloped clg

skylt

Living 13-0x18-6

Kit/Brk 14-8x10-0

R

W D

Dn

Garage 21-0x19-6

35' - 10"

Dining 11-4x10-0

Stor.

© Copyright by designer/architect

Br 2 11-0x10-0 vaulted

Br 3 10-6x 10-0

Porch depth 7-6

Special features

❖ 1,783 total square feet of living area
❖ The front to rear flow of the great room, with built-ins on one side is a furnishing delight
❖ Bedrooms are all quietly zoned on one side of the home
❖ The master bedroom is separated for privacy
❖ Every bedroom features a walk-in closet
❖ 3 bedrooms, 2 baths, 2-car side entry garage
❖ Basement, crawl space or slab foundation, please specify when ordering

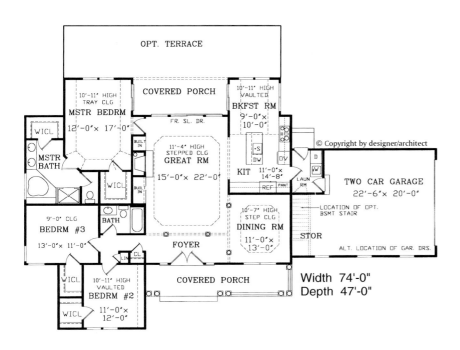

OPT. TERRACE

COVERED PORCH

10'-11" HIGH TRAY CLG
MSTR BEDRM
12'-0" x 17'-0"

WICL

MSTR BATH

WICL

9'-0" CLG
BEDRM #3
13'-0" x 11'-0"

BATH

FR. SL. DR.

11'-4" HIGH STEPPED CLG
GREAT RM
15'-0" x 22'-0"

BUILT IN

BUILT IN

FOYER

10'-11" HIGH VAULTED
BKFST RM
9'-0" x 10'-0"

KIT 11'-0" x 14'-8"

S
DW

REF

PANT

LAUN RM

D

W

© Copyright by designer/architect

TWO CAR GARAGE
22'-6" x 20'-0"

LOCATION OF OPT. BSMT STAIR

10'-7" HIGH STEP CLG
DINING RM
11'-0" x 13'-0"

STOR

ALT. LOCATION OF GAR. DRS.

CL

LIN

WICL

10'-11" HIGH VAULTED
BEDRM #2
11'-0" x 12'-0"

WICL

COVERED PORCH

Width 74'-0"
Depth 47'-0"

Special features

- 2,514 total square feet of living area
- An expansive porch welcomes you into the foyer, spacious dining area with bay and a gallery-sized hall with plant shelf above
- A highly functional U-shaped kitchen is open to a bayed breakfast room, study and family room with a 46' vista
- The family will enjoy time spent in the vaulted rear sunroom with fireplace
- 1,509 square feet of optional living area on the lower level with recreation room, bedroom #4 with bath and an office with storage closet
- 3 bedrooms, 2 baths, 3-car side entry garage with workshop/storage area
- Walk-out basement foundation

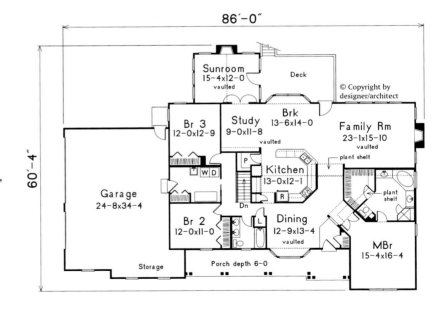

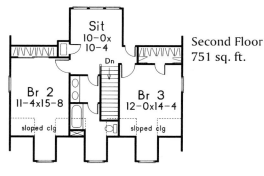

Sit
10-0x
10-4

Dn

Second Floor
751 sq. ft.

Br 2
11-4x15-8

Br 3
12-0x14-4

sloped clg

sloped clg

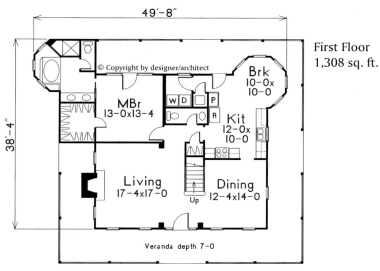

49'-8"

© Copyright by designer/architect

Brk
10-0x
10-0

First Floor
1,308 sq. ft.

MBr
13-0x13-4

W D   P

R

Kit
12-0x
10-0

38'-4"

Living
17-4x17-0

Dining
12-4x14-0

Up

Veranda depth 7-0

Special features

- ❖ 2,059 total square feet of living area
- ❖ Octagon-shaped breakfast room offers plenty of windows and creates a view to the veranda
- ❖ First floor master bedroom has a large walk-in closet and deluxe bath
- ❖ 9' ceilings throughout the home
- ❖ Secondary bedrooms and bath feature dormers and are adjacent to the cozy sitting area
- ❖ 3 bedrooms, 2 1/2 baths, 2-car detached garage
- ❖ Slab foundation, drawings also include basement and crawl space foundations

To add functional work space to a compact kitchen, think about purchasing a small rolling cart that can be moved around easily to free up space. Plus, when entertaining it can be moved out of sight.

Special features

- ❖ 1,655 total square feet of living area
- ❖ Master bedroom features a 9' ceiling, walk-in closet and bath with dressing area
- ❖ Oversized family room includes a 10' ceiling and masonry see-through fireplace
- ❖ Island kitchen has convenient access to the laundry room
- ❖ Handy covered walkway from the garage leads to the kitchen and dining area
- ❖ 3 bedrooms, 2 baths, 2-car garage
- ❖ Crawl space foundation

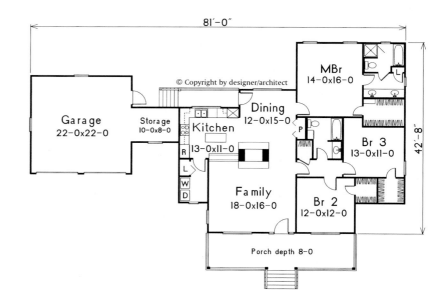

Outside your closet, install a hook or pull-out rod for hanging dry cleaning before putting away or to plan outfits for the next work day. This is a simple yet effective organizing move.

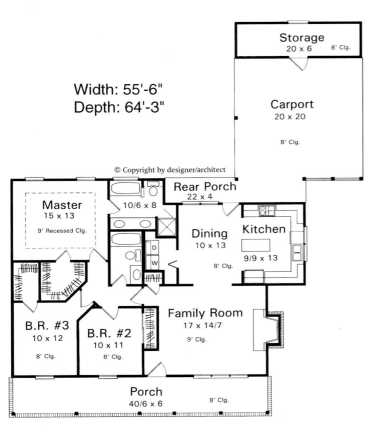

Width: 55'-6"
Depth: 64'-3"

Storage
20 x 6   8' Clg.

Carport
20 x 20

8' Clg.

© Copyright by designer/architect

Rear Porch
22 x 4

Master
15 x 13
9' Recessed Clg.

10/6 x 8

Dining
10 x 13
8' Clg.

Kitchen
9/9 x 13

B.R. #3
10 x 12
8' Clg.

B.R. #2
10 x 11
8' Clg.

Family Room
17 x 14/7
9' Clg.

Porch
40/6 x 6   8' Clg.

Special features

- ❖ 1,333 total square feet of living area
- ❖ Country charm with a covered front porch
- ❖ Dining area looks into the family room with fireplace
- ❖ Master suite has a walk-in closet and private bath
- ❖ 3 bedrooms, 2 baths, 2-car carport
- ❖ Slab or crawl space foundation, please specify when ordering

Prepare your bedroom for cold weather with freshly laundered winter linens and blankets. Save yourself a step next spring and wash summer linens before you store them. If you use lavender sachets in the closet or between the linens while stored, moths will be less attracted to the space.

Special features

- ❖ 1,389 total square feet of living area
- ❖ Energy efficient home with 2" x 6" exterior walls
- ❖ Formal living room has a warming fireplace and delightful bay window
- ❖ U-shaped kitchen shares a snack bar with the bayed family room
- ❖ Lovely master bedroom has its own private bath
- ❖ 3 bedrooms, 2 baths, 2-car garage
- ❖ Slab foundation

One of the hottest trends in kitchen products is filtered water on tap. For one-tenth of the cost of bottled water, you can have clean, fresh tasting water on tap. Some current models remove more than 99.9% of microbial cysts and dramatically reduces lead and chlorine, but retains beneficial fluoride.

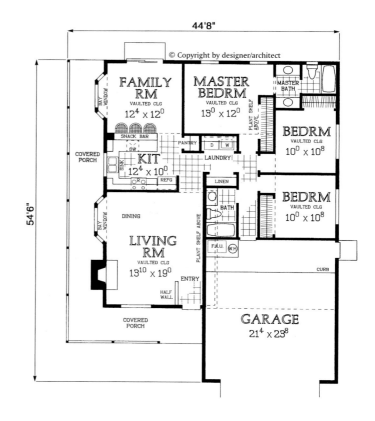

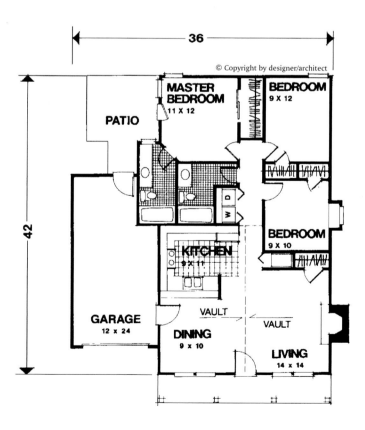

© Copyright by designer/architect

36

42

MASTER BEDROOM 11 X 12

BEDROOM 9 X 12

PATIO

BEDROOM 9 X 10

KITCHEN 9 X 11

GARAGE 12 x 24

VAULT

VAULT

DINING 9 X 10

LIVING 14 x 14

Special features

- ❖ 1,050 total square feet of living area
- ❖ Master bedroom has its own private bath and access to the outdoors onto a private patio
- ❖ Vaulted ceilings in the living and dining areas create a feeling of spaciousness
- ❖ The laundry closet is convenient to all bedrooms
- ❖ Efficient U-shaped kitchen
- ❖ 3 bedrooms, 2 baths, 1-car garage
- ❖ Basement or slab foundation, please specify when ordering

Plant deciduous trees (the type that lose their leaves in winter) on the south side of your house. They will provide summer shade without blocking winter sun. Plant evergreens on the north to shield your home from cold winter winds.

Special features

- ❖ 1,595 total square feet of living area
- ❖ Large great room features a tray ceiling and French doors to a screened porch
- ❖ Dining room and bedroom #2 have bay windows
- ❖ Master bedroom has a tray ceiling and a bay window
- ❖ 3 bedrooms, 2 baths, 2-car side entry garage
- ❖ Basement, crawl space, slab or walk-out basement foundation, please specify when ordering

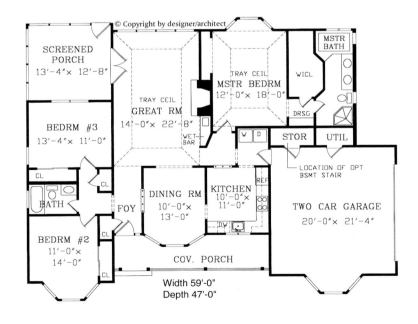

© Copyright by designer/architect

SCREENED PORCH 13'-4" x 12'-8"

MSTR BATH

TRAY CEIL GREAT RM 14'-0" x 22'-8"

TRAY CEIL MSTR BEDRM 12'-0" x 18'-0"

WICL

BEDRM #3 13'-4" x 11'-0"

DRSG

WET-BAR

W D

STOR

UTIL

CL

CL

BATH

FOY

DINING RM 10'-0" x 13'-0"

KITCHEN 10'-0" x 11'-0"

REF

LOCATION OF OPT BSMT STAIR

TWO CAR GARAGE 20'-0" x 21'-4"

BEDRM #2 11'-0" x 14'-0"

DW

CL

COV. PORCH

Width 59'-0"
Depth 47'-0"

Second Floor
970 sq. ft.

Br 2
12-0 x 12-5

LINEN

Master Br
12-0 x 15-4

FULL HT. WALLS

OPEN TO
FOYER
BELOW

RAILING

LINEN

DESK

Br 3
12-0 x 11-4

BUILT-IN
BOOK SHELVES

WINDOW
SEAT

First Floor
1,113 sq. ft.

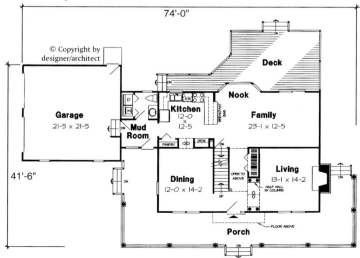

74'-0"

© Copyright by
designer/architect

Deck

DN

Garage
21-5 x 21-5

Kitchen
12-0
x
12-5

Nook

Family
23-1 x 12-5

BREAKFAST BAR

Mud
Room

PANTRY

DESK

DN

41'-6"

Dining
12-0 x 14-2

OPEN TO
ABOVE

UP

HALF WALL
W/ COLUMNS

Living
13-1 x 14-2

DN

FLOOR ABOVE

Porch

Special features

- ❖ 2,083 total square feet of living area
- ❖ Breakfast nook is a sunny bay window
- ❖ Half wall with columns creates a lovely entry into the living room
- ❖ Second floor landing has a cozy window seat surrounded on both sides by built-in bookshelves
- ❖ 3 bedrooms, 2 1/2 baths, 2-car side entry garage
- ❖ Basement or crawl space foundation, please specify when ordering

Special features

- ❖ 2,529 total square feet of living area
- ❖ Decorative columns enhance the exterior while a dramatic gallery is breathtaking upon entry
- ❖ The kitchen and breakfast nook are located between the family and living rooms for easy access
- ❖ The luxurious master bedroom includes a sitting area, private bath and access to the covered patio
- ❖ 4 bedrooms, 3 baths, 3-car side entry garage
- ❖ Slab foundation

The origin of dormer windows goes back centuries to French architect Francois Mansart (1598-1666). Mansart inserted a sequence of windows into the sloping roofs to make the attics inhabitable. This is reflected in the name dormer which comes from the French word dormir which means "to sleep."

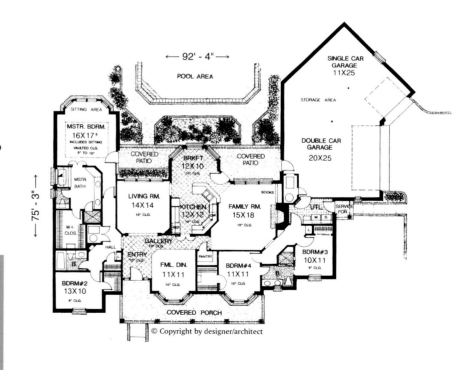

© Copyright by designer/architect

Second Floor
1,146 sq. ft.

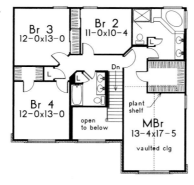

Br 3
12-0x13-0

Br 2
11-0x10-4

Dn

Br 4
12-0x13-0

open to below

plant shelf

MBr
13-4x17-5

vaulted clg

First Floor
1,375 sq. ft.

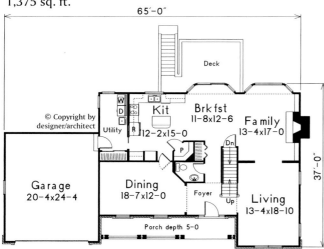

65'-0"

Deck

© Copyright by
designer/architect

W D

Kit
12-2x15-0

Brk fst
11-8x12-6

Family
13-4x17-0

Utility

R

Dn

37'-0"

Dining
18-7x12-0

Foyer

Up

Living
13-4x18-10

Garage
20-4x24-4

Porch depth 5-0

Special features

- ❖ 2,521 total square feet of living area
- ❖ Large living and dining rooms are a plus for formal entertaining or large family gatherings
- ❖ Informal kitchen, breakfast and family rooms feature a 37' vista and double bay windows
- ❖ Generously sized master bedroom and three secondary bedrooms grace the second floor
- ❖ 4 bedrooms, 2 1/2 baths, 2-car garage
- ❖ Basement foundation

To get your windows to really shine, mix a solution of half vinegar and half water and pour into a spray bottle. This should remove grit and grime from windows with little effort. To minimize lint, wipe windows clean with newspaper, coffee filters or a cloth diaper.

Special features

- 1,295 total square feet of living area
- Energy efficient home with 2" x 6" exterior walls
- Wrap-around porch is a lovely place for dining
- A fireplace gives a stunning focal point to the great room that is heightened with a sloped ceiling
- The master suite is full of luxurious touches such as a walk-in closet and a lush private bath
- 2 bedrooms, 2 baths, 2-car garage
- Basement foundation

Changing the spindles on a covered porch or patio can easily change the style of the facade. Using a smooth, more rounded spindle creates a Victorian feel while the use of a square, more angular spindle can reflect either a Craftsman, Rustic, Modern or Classic style influence to a design.

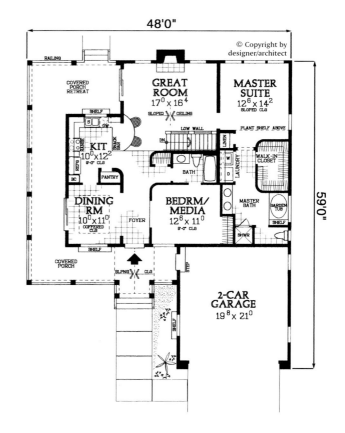

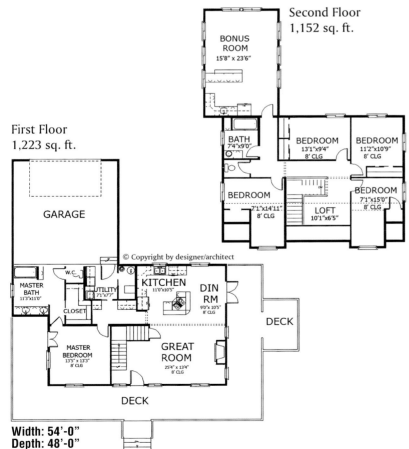

Second Floor
1,152 sq. ft.

BONUS
ROOM
15'8" x 23'6"

BATH
7'4"x9'0"

BEDROOM
13'1"x9'4"
8' CLG

BEDROOM
11'2"x10'9"
8' CLG

BEDROOM
7'1"x15'0"
8' CLG

BEDROOM
7'1"x14'11"
8' CLG

LOFT
10'1"x6'5"

First Floor
1,223 sq. ft.

GARAGE

© Copyright by designer/architect

MASTER
BATH
11'3"x11'0"

W.C.

UTILITY
7'1"x7'7"

KITCHEN
11'0"x10'5"

DIN
RM
9'0"x 10'5"
8' CLG

CLOSET

DECK

MASTER
BEDROOM
13'5" x 13'3"
8' CLG

GREAT
ROOM
25'4" x 13'4"
8' CLG

DECK

Width: 54'-0"
Depth: 48'-0"

Special features

- ❖ 2,375 total square feet of living area
- ❖ Beamed ceilings, French doors to the wrap-around porch and a stone fireplace add coziness to the open floor plan
- ❖ The large island kitchen with an eating bar is a cook's dream offering plenty of storage and a large window over the sink for viewing the backyard
- ❖ The bonus room with its own kitchen is located over the garage at the rear of the house and has an additional 408 square feet of living area
- ❖ 5 bedrooms, 2 baths, 2-car rear entry garage
- ❖ Crawl space foundation

Special features

- ❖ 1,945 total square feet of living area
- ❖ Great room has a stepped ceiling and a fireplace
- ❖ Bayed dining area enjoys a stepped ceiling and French door leading to a covered porch
- ❖ Master bedroom has a tray ceiling, bay window and large walk-in closet
- ❖ 3 bedrooms, 2 1/2 baths, 2-car side entry garage
- ❖ Basement, crawl space or slab foundation, please specify when ordering

Rotating and flipping your mattress avoids sagging and helps extend the life of the mattress.

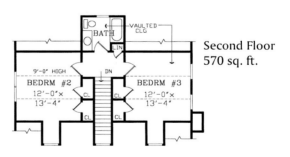

Second Floor
570 sq. ft.

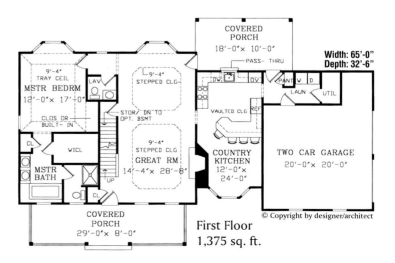

First Floor
1,375 sq. ft.

Width: 65'-0"
Depth: 32'-6"

© Copyright by designer/architect

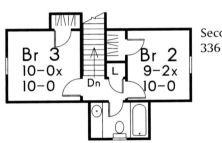

Second Floor
336 sq. ft.

Br 3
10-0x
10-0

Dn

L

Br 2
9-2x
10-0

Special features

- 954 total square feet of living area
- Kitchen has a cozy bayed eating area
- Master bedroom has a walk-in closet and private bath
- Large great room has access to the back porch
- Convenient coat closet is near the front entry
- 3 bedrooms, 2 baths
- Basement foundation

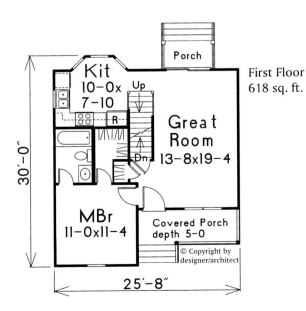

First Floor
618 sq. ft.

Porch

Kit
10-0x
7-10

Up

R

Great Room
13-8x19-4

Dn

MBr
11-0x11-4

Covered Porch
depth 5-0

© Copyright by
designer/architect

30'-0"

25'-8"

Maintaining a central air conditioner is easy if you follow the steps below. First, clear for airflow by hosing out leaves and pruning shrubs. Second, check the drain to be sure that it's carrying off excess moisture. Last, change filters several times per season; never run a system without a filter.

Special features

- ❖ 2,261 total square feet of living area
- ❖ Efficiently designed kitchen features a work island and snack bar
- ❖ Master bath has a double vanity, whirlpool tub and two walk-in closets
- ❖ Spacious laundry room includes workspace and a fold-down ironing board
- ❖ Optional second floor has an additional 367 square feet of living area
- ❖ 4 bedrooms, 2 1/2 baths, 2-car side entry garage
- ❖ Slab or crawl space foundation, please specify when ordering

Optional
Second Floor

First Floor
2,261 sq. ft.

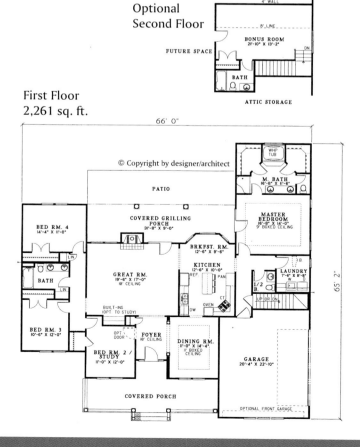

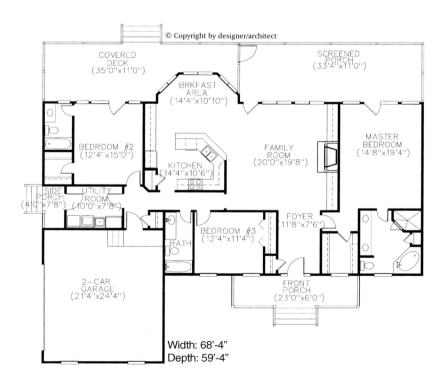

© Copyright by designer/architect

COVERED DECK (35'0"x11'0")

SCREENED PORCH (33'4"x11'0")

BRKFAST AREA (14'4"x10'10")

BEDROOM #2 (12'4"x15'0")

KITCHEN (14'4"x10'6")

FAMILY ROOM (20'0"x19'8")

MASTER BEDROOM (14'8"x19'4")

SIDE PORCH (4'0"x7'8")

UTILITY ROOM (10'0"x7'8")

BATH

BEDROOM #3 (12'4"x11'4")

FOYER (11'8"x7'6")

2-CAR GARAGE (21'4"x24'4")

FRONT PORCH (23'0"x6'0")

Width: 68'-4"
Depth: 59'-4"

Special features

- ❖ 2,038 total square feet of living area
- ❖ The spacious family room features a fireplace flanked by built-in shelves and access to the screened porch
- ❖ Bedroom #2 is an exciting room with a private bath, walk-in closet and access to the covered deck
- ❖ The kitchen offers an abundance of counterspace including a wrap-around counter with room for seating
- ❖ 3 bedrooms, 3 baths, 2-car side entry garage
- ❖ Pier foundation

If you clean brushes as soon as you're done painting, the job will be a lot easier. Use warm, soapy water for water-based paints; for other coatings, use the solvent specified on the can. Spin out excess cleaner, comb the bristles to straighten, and then lay the brush flat on a cloth to dry.

Special features

- ❖ 2,409 total square feet of living area
- ❖ Double two-story bay windows adorn the wrap-around porch
- ❖ A grand-scale foyer features a 40' view through morning room
- ❖ An eating area, fireplace, palladian windows, vaulted ceiling and balcony overlook are among the many amenities of the spacious morning room
- ❖ Two large second floor bedrooms and an enormous third bedroom enjoy two walk-in closets, a bay window and access to hall bath
- ❖ 4 bedrooms, 2 1/2 baths, 2-car side entry garage with storage
- ❖ Basement foundation

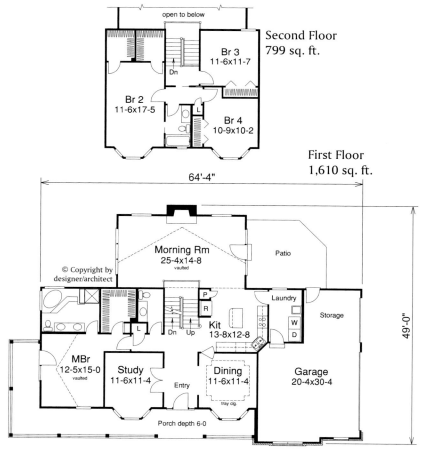

Second Floor 799 sq. ft.

Br 3 11-6x11-7

Br 2 11-6x17-5

Br 4 10-9x10-2

First Floor 1,610 sq. ft.

64'-4"

49'-0"

© Copyright by designer/architect

Morning Rm 25-4x14-8 vaulted

Patio

Laundry

Storage

Kit 13-8x12-8

MBr 12-5x15-0 vaulted

Study 11-6x11-4

Dining 11-6x11-4 tray clg.

Garage 20-4x30-4

Entry

Porch depth 6-0

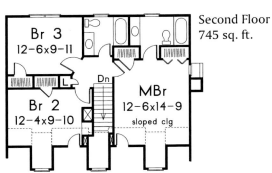

Second Floor
745 sq. ft.

Br 3
12-6x9-11

MBr
12-6x14-9
sloped clg

Br 2
12-4x9-10

Dn

L

Special features

❖ 1,582 total square feet of living area
❖ Conservative layout gives privacy to living and dining areas
❖ Large fireplace and windows enhance the living area
❖ Rear door in garage is convenient to the garden and kitchen
❖ Full front porch adds charm
❖ Dormers add light to the foyer and bedrooms
❖ 3 bedrooms, 2 1/2 baths, 1-car garage
❖ Slab foundation, drawings also include crawl space foundation

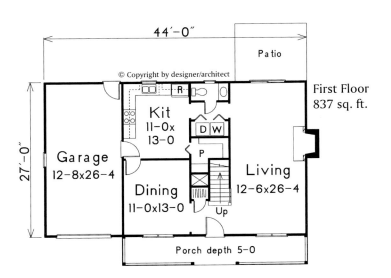

44'-0"

Patio

© Copyright by designer/architect

First Floor
837 sq. ft.

Kit
11-0x
13-0

D W

Garage
12-8x26-4

27'-0"

P

Living
12-6x26-4

Dining
11-0x13-0

Up

Porch depth 5-0

Plan on spending 1% of the purchase price of your home on home maintenance each year.

Special features

- 2,470 total square feet of living area
- All bedrooms are located on the second floor for privacy
- The U-shaped kitchen with island opens into the breakfast and family rooms
- The vaulted master bedroom features two walk-in closets and a private bath
- 4 bedrooms, 2 1/2 baths, 2-car garage
- Basement, walk-out basement, crawl space or slab foundation, please specify when ordering

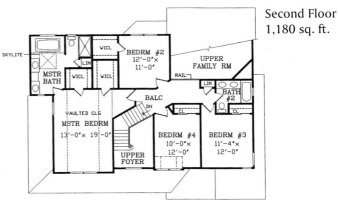

Second Floor
1,180 sq. ft.

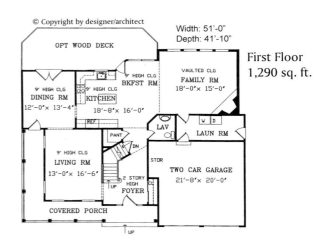

Width: 51'-0"
Depth: 41'-10"

First Floor
1,290 sq. ft.

© Copyright by designer/architect

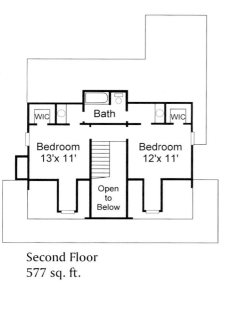

Second Floor
577 sq. ft.

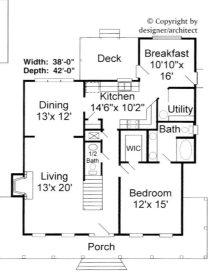

© Copyright by
designer/architect

Width: 38'-0"
Depth: 42'-0"

Deck

Breakfast
10'10"x
16'

Dining
13'x 12'

Kitchen
14'6"x 10'2"

Utility

Bath

1/2
Bath

WIC

Living
13'x 20'

Bedroom
12'x 15'

First Floor
1,242 sq. ft.

Porch

Special features

- ❖ 1,819 total square feet of living area
- ❖ Unique bath layout on the second floor allows for both bedrooms to have their own private sink area while connecting to the main bath
- ❖ Window wall in dining area floods area with sunlight
- ❖ Walk-in closets in every bedroom
- ❖ 3 bedrooms, 2 1/2 baths
- ❖ Crawl space or slab foundation, please specify when ordering

Studies show a home near or on a park can increase the property value as much as 20%.

Special features

- ❖ 2,107 total square feet of living area
- ❖ Kitchen has pantry and adjacent dining area
- ❖ Master bedroom has a bath and a large walk-in closet
- ❖ Second floor bedrooms have attic storage
- ❖ Bonus room above the garage has an additional 324 square feet of living area
- ❖ 3 bedrooms, 2 1/2 baths, 2-car garage
- ❖ Walk-out basement, basement, crawl space or slab foundation, please specify when ordering

Brick is one of the most durable siding materials: it doesn't need to be painted, doesn't rot, doesn't fade, and weathers handsomely.

Second Floor
983 sq. ft.

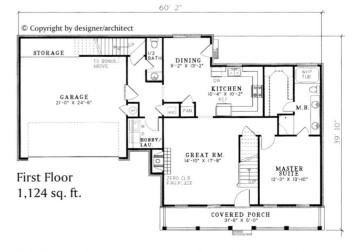

First Floor
1,124 sq. ft.

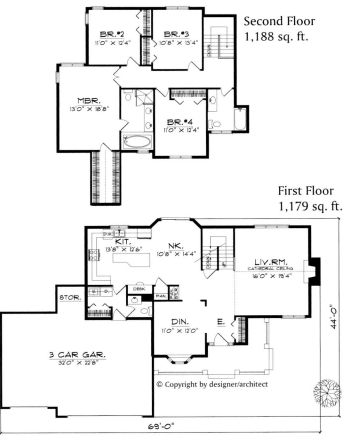

Second Floor
1,188 sq. ft.

BR.#2
11'0" x 12'4"

BR.#3
10'8" x 13'4"

MBR.
13'0" x 18'8"

BR.#4
11'0" x 12'4"

First Floor
1,179 sq. ft.

KIT.
13'8" x 12'6"

NK.
10'8" x 14'4"

LIV.RM.
CATHEDRAL CEILING
16'0" x 19'4"

STOR.

DESK

PAN.

DIN.
11'0" x 12'0"

E.

3 CAR GAR.
32'0" x 22'8"

© Copyright by designer/architect

44'-0"

69'-0"

Special features

- ❖ 2,367 total square feet of living area
- ❖ Energy efficient home with 2" x 6" exterior walls
- ❖ The spacious kitchen offers an abundance of counterspace including an extra-large center island
- ❖ A butler's pantry is located outside the formal dining room to assist with entertaining
- ❖ The airy living room features a cathedral ceiling and grand fireplace
- ❖ All bedrooms are located on the second floor for privacy
- ❖ 4 bedrooms, 2 1/2 baths, 3-car garage
- ❖ Basement foundation

Special features

❖ 1,841 total square feet of living area

❖ Sunny bayed breakfast room is cheerful for meals

❖ The master suite remains separate from the other bedrooms for privacy

❖ Second floor bonus rooms have a total of 295 square feet of additional living area

❖ 3 bedrooms, 2 1/2 baths, 2-car side entry garage

❖ Basement foundation

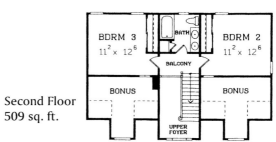

Second Floor
509 sq. ft.

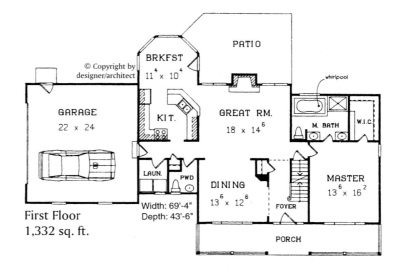

First Floor
1,332 sq. ft.

To avoid scuffing wood, vinyl or linoleum floors when rearranging furniture pieces, slide a folded towel under each side of the piece of furniture you wish to move. Not only does this avoid scratches and scrapes, but it tends to make moving the piece a lot easier.

Optional
Second Floor

Balc.

Bonus Rm.
21⁴ • 16⁴

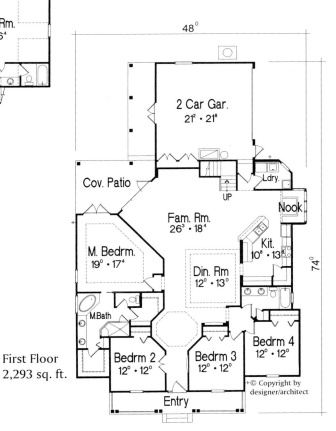

First Floor
2,293 sq. ft.

48⁰

2 Car Gar.
21² • 21⁸

Cov. Patio

Ldry.

UP

Nook

Fam. Rm.
26³ • 18⁴

Kit.
10⁸ • 13⁸

M. Bedrm.
19⁰ • 17⁴

Din. Rm.
12⁰ • 13⁰

74⁰

M.Bath

Bedrm 2
12⁰ • 12⁰

Bedrm 3
12⁰ • 12⁰

Bedrm 4
12⁰ • 12⁰

© Copyright by
designer/architect

Entry

Special features

- ❖ 2,293 total square feet of living area
- ❖ Formal dining area flows into large family room making great use of space
- ❖ Cozy nook off kitchen makes an ideal breakfast area
- ❖ Covered patio attaches to master bedroom and family room
- ❖ Optional second floor has an additional 509 square feet of living area
- ❖ 4 bedrooms, 2 baths, 2-car side entry garage
- ❖ Slab foundation

Avoid using fabric or paper light shades in a kitchen as they are likely to harbor grease and cooking odors. Glass and metal fittings are more practical.

Special features

❖ 1,256 total square feet of living area
❖ Energy efficient home with 2" x 6" exterior walls
❖ An open floor plan combined with vaulted ceilings offers spacious living
❖ The functional kitchen is complete with a pantry eating bar
❖ The master bedroom offers privacy and features a large walk-in closet and a private bath
❖ 3 bedrooms, 2 baths, 2-car garage
❖ Crawl space or slab foundation, please specify when ordering

Pliers are some of the most common and useful tools around the house. Variety is necessary – a good toolbox should have a number of types, including the standard and needle-nose pliers.

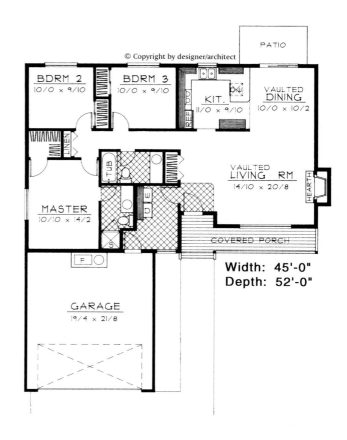

© Copyright by designer/architect

Width: 45'-0"
Depth: 52'-0"

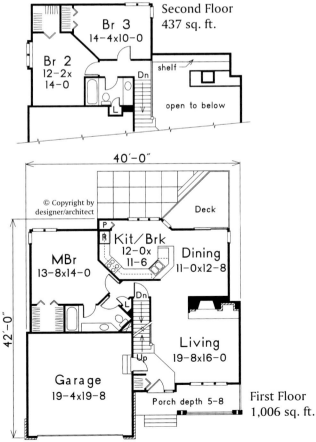

Second Floor 437 sq. ft.

Br 3 14-4x10-0

Br 2 12-2x 14-0

shelf

Dn

open to below

L

40'-0"

© Copyright by designer/architect

Deck

Kit/Brk 12-0x 11-6

Dining 11-0x12-8

MBr 13-8x14-0

42'-0"

Dn

L

Up

Living 19-8x16-0

Garage 19-4x19-8

Porch depth 5-8

First Floor 1,006 sq. ft.

Special features

- ❖ 1,443 total square feet of living area
- ❖ Raised foyer and cathedral ceiling in living room
- ❖ Impressive tall-wall fireplace between living and dining rooms
- ❖ Open U-shaped kitchen features a cheerful breakfast bay
- ❖ Angular side deck accentuates patio and garden
- ❖ First floor master bedroom has a walk-in closet and a corner window
- ❖ 3 bedrooms, 2 baths, 2-car garage
- ❖ Basement foundation

The common nail is used for general construction work and a wide variety of other purposes. When driving common nails with a hammer try to snap your wrist rather than hitting the nail with arm power.

Special features

❖ 2,871 total square feet of living area
❖ Energy efficient home with 2" x 6" exterior walls
❖ A grand two-story foyer greets guests upon entering the home
❖ A handy butler's pantry connects the kitchen and the formal dining room
❖ Luxurious master bedroom has a gorgeous bath with spa tub and double vanities
❖ Bonus room above the garage is included in the square footage
❖ 4 bedrooms, 2 1/2 baths, 2-car garage
❖ Crawl space foundation

Second Floor
1,552 sq. ft.

First Floor
1,319 sq. ft.

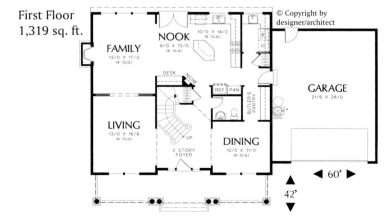

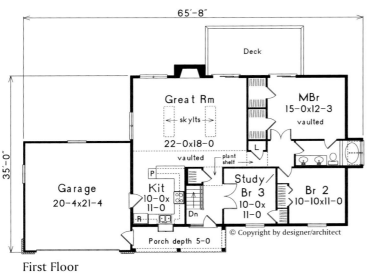

65′-8″

Deck

Great Rm
skylts
22-0x18-0
vaulted

plant shelf

MBr
15-0x12-3
vaulted

L

35′-0″

Garage
20-4x21-4

P

Kit
10-0x
11-0

R

Dn

Study/
Br 3
10-0x
11-0

Br 2
10-10x11-0

Porch depth 5-0

© Copyright by designer/architect

**First Floor
1,278 sq. ft.**

Family
21-6x14-4

Br 4
12-9x14-4

Up

Storage

**Optional
Lower Level**

Special features

- ❖ 1,278 total square feet of living area
- ❖ Excellent U-shaped kitchen with garden window opens to an enormous great room with vaulted ceiling, fireplace and two skylights
- ❖ Vaulted master bedroom offers a double-door entry, access to a deck and bath and two walk-in closets
- ❖ The bath has a double-bowl vanity and dramatic step-up garden tub with a lean-to greenhouse window
- ❖ 805 square feet of optional living area on the lower level with family room, bedroom #4 and bath
- ❖ 3 bedrooms, 1 bath, 2-car garage
- ❖ Walk-out basement foundation

Special features

- 2,928 total square feet of living area
- Triple windows brighten a pleasant office with views of the screen porch
- An enormous sitting room extends the master bedroom making it spacious and open
- The bayed breakfast room is a sunny place to start the day
- 3 bedrooms, 2 1/2 baths
- Slab foundation

Second Floor
577 sq. ft.

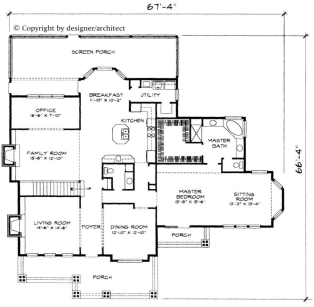

First Floor
2,351 sq. ft.

Termites are the most destructive wood-destroying pest in the nation. At least 1% of housing in the United States each year requires treatment. Most termite species swarm in late summer or fall. It is best to hire a professional pest control company to carry out a routine regimen and keep the pests under control.

Second Floor 863 sq. ft.

Special features

- ❖ 2,363 total square feet of living area
- ❖ Energy efficient home with 2" x 6" exterior walls
- ❖ Covered porches provide outdoor seating areas
- ❖ Corner fireplace becomes focal point of family room
- ❖ Kitchen features island cooktop and adjoining nook
- ❖ 3 bedrooms, 2 1/2 baths, 2-car garage
- ❖ Partial basement/crawl space foundation

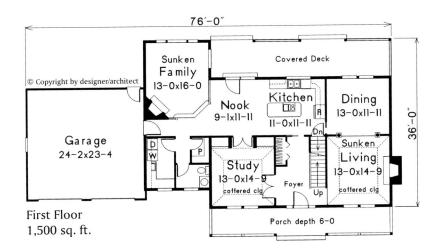

First Floor 1,500 sq. ft.

© Copyright by designer/architect

To maximize efficiency, wash only full loads of clothes when possible and always clean the dryer's lint filter after every load.

Special features

- 2,525 total square feet of living area
- The living room has a 10' ceiling and a large fireplace
- The parlor is a perfect place for entertaining guests
- The bayed breakfast room is flooded with light and opens to the optional deck
- 3 bedrooms, 2 1/2 baths, 2-car garage
- Basement, crawl space or slab foundation, please specify when ordering

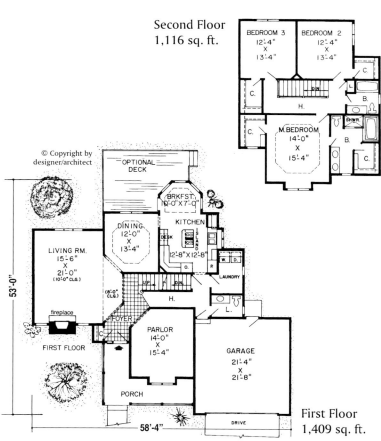

Second Floor
1,116 sq. ft.

First Floor
1,409 sq. ft.

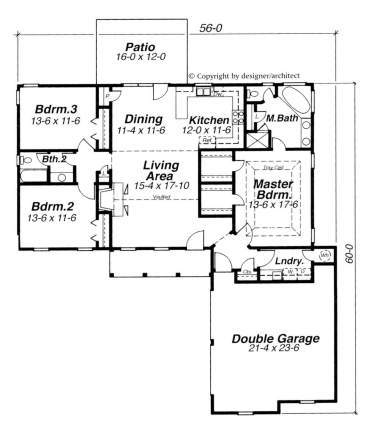

56-0

Patio
16-0 x 12-0

© Copyright by designer/architect

Bdrm.3
13-6 x 11-6

Dining
11-4 x 11-6

Kitchen
12-0 x 11-6

M.Bath

Bth.2

Living Area
15-4 x 17-10
Vaulted

Tray Ceil.

Master Bdrm.
13-6 x 17-6

Bdrm.2
13-6 x 11-6

60-0

Lndry.

Double Garage
21-4 x 23-6

Special features

- ❖ 1,675 total square feet of living area
- ❖ Country accents give this home curb appeal
- ❖ Spacious laundry room is located off the master bedroom
- ❖ Cathedral ceiling in the living area adds exceptional drama
- ❖ Alternate floor plan design includes handicap accessibility that is 100% ADA compliant
- ❖ 3 bedrooms, 2 baths, 2-car side entry garage
- ❖ Crawl space or slab foundation, please specify when ordering

Block sunlight from reaching weeds to stop growth in your vegetable garden. The best choice is to use landscaping fabric. Cover the entire area before planting, anchoring with brick or wire clips. Then cover the area with mulch. Cut small holes in the fabric to plant your seeds.

Special features

❖ 2,150 total square feet of living area
❖ Multiple gables and a charming covered porch add dramatic curb appeal to the facade
❖ A bay-shaped whirlpool tub area in the master bath is a stunning feature
❖ The home office off the entry is secluded from other parts of the home
❖ 3 bedrooms, 2 1/2 baths, 2-car side entry garage
❖ Basement foundation

Get rid of pests while beautifying your yard. Avoid using insecticides by planting marigolds, basil, mint, chives, onions and chrysanthemums near or in your garden. Secretions from these and many other plants act as a natural insect repellent.

Second Floor
1,014 sq. ft.

BR. #3
11/9X11/5

M. BR.
15/5X15/9
COFFERED CLG.

BR. #2
11/1X11/9

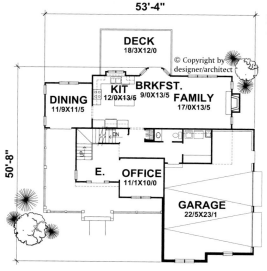

First Floor
1,136 sq. ft.

53'-4"

DECK
18/3X12/0

© Copyright by designer/architect

KIT
12/0X13/5

BRKFST.
9/0X13/5

FAMILY
17/0X13/5

DINING
11/9X11/5

50'-8"

E.

OFFICE
11/1X10/0

GARAGE
22/5X23/1

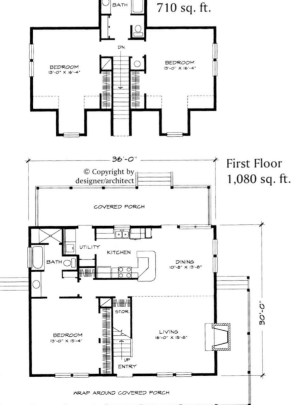

Second Floor
710 sq. ft.

BATH

BEDROOM
13'-0" X 16'-4"

DN

BEDROOM
13'-0" X 16'-4"

First Floor
1,080 sq. ft.

36'-0"

© Copyright by
designer/architect

COVERED PORCH

UTILITY

KITCHEN

BATH

DINING
10'-8" X 13'-8"

30'-0"

STOR

BEDROOM
13'-0" X 15'-4"

LIVING
16'-0" X 13'-8"

UP
ENTRY

WRAP AROUND COVERED PORCH

Special features

❖ 1,790 total square feet of living area
❖ A snack bar counter in the kitchen joins the spacious living and dining rooms to this family-friendly space
❖ The dining room enjoys corner windows and access to the expansive rear porch, perfect for extending meals to the outdoors
❖ The first floor bedroom with private bath access and full closet wall is the ideal master suite
❖ 3 bedrooms, 2 baths
❖ Slab foundation

Come fall, get your lawn ready for winter. Look for compacted soil in heavily used areas and loosen it with a core aerator. Reseed bare spots and top them with a thin layer of soil. Fix small drainage problems by filling low spots with fresh soil. A few precautions will ensure a healthy lawn come springtime.

Special features

- ❖ 1,799 total square feet of living area
- ❖ The vaulted ceiling in the great room creates a dynamic living space
- ❖ The garage offers an extra storage area with room to create a shop, bonus room or separate porch
- ❖ The bonus room with half bath has the potential to be a great guest room or play room and provides an additional 394 square feet of living area
- ❖ 3 bedrooms, 2 1/2 baths, 2-car garage
- ❖ Crawl space or slab foundation, please specify when ordering

Optional
Second Floor

Bonus Room 14-8 x 19-6

Sloped Clg.   Sloped Clg.

Future Half Bath

First Floor
1,799 sq. ft.

© Copyright by designer/architect

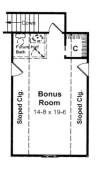

Bedroom 2 12-2 x 11-10, 9-0 Ceiling

Covered or Screened-in Porch 16-2 x 8-0

Gas Logs

Bath

Hall

Great Room 16-0 x 26-0

VAULT

Bedroom 3 12-0 x 11-4, 9-0 Ceiling

VAULT

Dining 12-0 x 17-4, 9-0 Ceiling

Raised Bar

Kitchen 13-4 x 12-8

DW

Island

Pan.

Jet Tub

Seat

Shr.

M. Bath

Master Bedroom 14-4 x 17-6, 9-0 Ceiling

Stairs Option

Utility 7-10 x 5-10

Half Bath

Hall

C 6-0 x 8-4

C 6-0 x 5-2

Optional Office, Shop, Bonus, Porch, or Storage 11-4 x 12-6

Opt. Door

Opt. Wall

Storage 11-4 x 5-0

Optional Side Entrance Garage

Two or Three-Car Garage 24-0 x 24-0

Covered Porch 41-6 x 6-0

Width: 78'-0"
Depth: 46'-0"

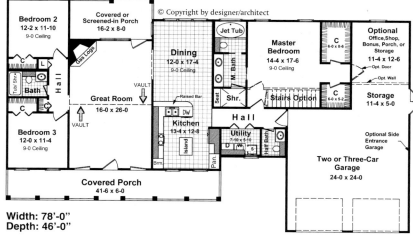

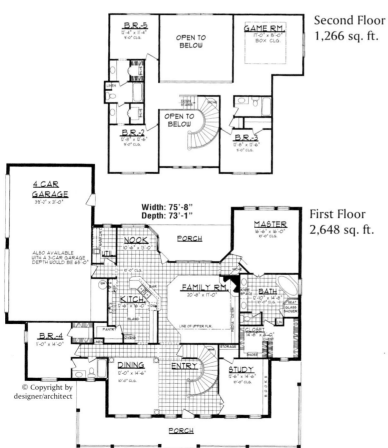

Second Floor
1,266 sq. ft.

Width: 75'-8"
Depth: 73'-1"

First Floor
2,648 sq. ft.

© Copyright by
designer/architect

Special features

❖ 3,914 total square feet of living area
❖ This beautiful two-story brick and stone country home is country living at its finest
❖ An elegant formal dining room and spacious study are on either side of the entry
❖ Bedroom #4 includes a walk-in closet and private bath access creating an ideal guest suite
❖ Three bedrooms, two baths and a large game room are located on the second floor making this a perfect family home
❖ 5 bedrooms, 4 baths, 4-car side entry garage
❖ Slab or crawl space foundation, please specify when ordering

Special features

- 1,711 total square feet of living area
- U-shaped kitchen joins the breakfast and family rooms for an open living atmosphere
- Master bedroom has a secluded covered porch and private bath
- Balcony overlooks the family room that features a fireplace and accesses the deck
- 3 bedrooms, 2 1/2 baths, 2-car garage
- Basement foundation

If you live in an area where there are large trees and desirable views, pruning trees can help remove branches that block your view. It is smart to prune out unwanted growth periodically. Plus, trees and shrubs stay healthier if you remove branches that are diseased, pest-ridden, or dead.

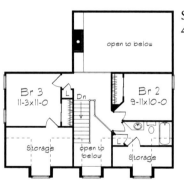

Second Floor
483 sq. ft.

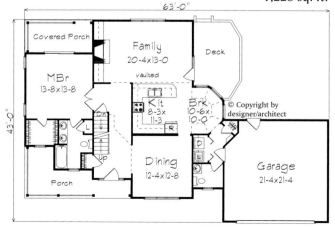

First Floor
1,228 sq. ft.

Second Floor
686 sq. ft.

First Floor
864 sq. ft.

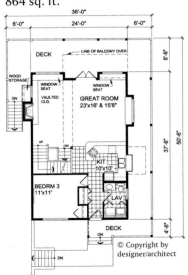

© Copyright by designer/architect

Lower Level
864 sq. ft.

Special features

- 2,414 total square feet of living area
- Energy efficient home with 2" x 6" exterior walls
- The partially covered rear wrap-around deck encourages family activity whatever the season
- The second floor bedrooms with 10' and 12' ceilings bring a soothing feeling to this vaulted space
- The lower level contains two additional bedrooms, a shared bath and a multi-purpose game room with patio access
- 5 bedrooms, 2 1/2 baths
- Walk-out basement foundation

Special features

- ❖ 2,448 total square feet of living area
- ❖ Energy efficient home with 2" x 6" exterior walls
- ❖ Enormous island in kitchen has enough space for food preparation as well as dining
- ❖ Cozy living area off kitchen has the feel of a hearth room with fireplace
- ❖ Bonus room has an additional 450 square feet of living area
- ❖ 3 bedrooms, 2 1/2 baths, 2-car side entry garage
- ❖ Basement foundation

The single most important fire preventive measure is to equip your home with working smoke detectors. Place one on the entry level and outside each sleeping area. Remember to test them every month and replace the batteries annually.

Second Floor
1,000 sq. ft.

First Floor
1,448 sq. ft.

© Copyright by designer/architect

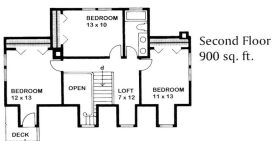

Second Floor
900 sq. ft.

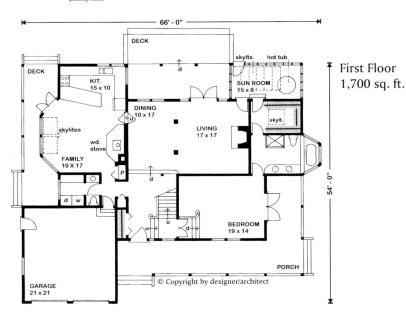

First Floor
1,700 sq. ft.

© Copyright by designer/architect

Special features

❖ 2,600 total square feet of living area
❖ Energy efficient home with 2" x 6" exterior walls
❖ All first floor rooms feature French doors for easy access to the great outdoors
❖ The large family room is brightened by the bay window and skylights and is warmed by a woodstove
❖ A unique stairway landing creates a sunken master suite with a luxurious bath and walk-in closet
❖ The private sun room has space for a hot tub creating a relaxing atmosphere
❖ 4 bedrooms, 2 1/2 baths, 2-car garage
❖ Crawl space foundation

Special features

* 1,772 total square feet of living area
* Bedroom #2 boasts a walk-in closet and built-in desk
* The centrally located kitchen serves the formal dining room and charming breakfast nook with ease
* A 10' ceiling adds spaciousness to the expansive living room
* The garage includes a large shop area which has convenient access from the rear yard
* 3 bedrooms, 2 baths, 2-car garage
* Slab or crawl space foundation, please specify when ordering

Universal design means creating spaces that meet the needs of all people, young and old, able and disabled. If universal design is something you are interested in, check with your local housing agencies and they will assist you with guidelines for design that promotes harmonious and stress-free living.

© Copyright by designer/architect

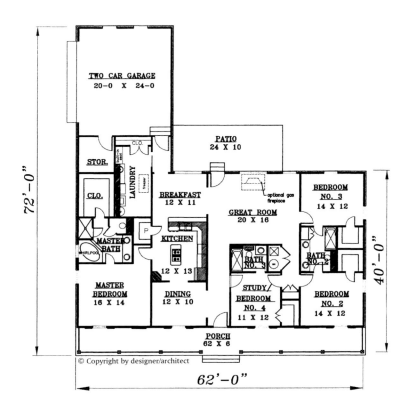

Special features

* 2,188 total square feet of living area
* The centrally located kitchen serves the dining room and breakfast area with ease and includes a walk-in pantry and cooktop island
* The study/bedroom #4 enjoys a walk-in closet and private bath making it an ideal guest suite
* The large laundry area includes a closet, built-in seat and has room for a freezer
* The garage includes an additional storage area
* 4 bedrooms, 3 baths, 2-car side entry garage
* Slab or crawl space foundation, please specify when ordering

Special features

- ❖ 1,978 total square feet of living area
- ❖ Den/guest room is private from other first floor living areas
- ❖ Extra storage in garage
- ❖ Second floor sitting area is open for all bedrooms to enjoy
- ❖ 4 bedrooms, 2 1/2 baths, 2-car garage
- ❖ Basement, crawl space or slab foundation, please specify when ordering

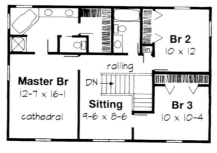

Second Floor
944 sq. ft.

Br 2
10 x 12

Master Br
12-7 x 16-1
cathedral

railing

DN

Sitting
9-6 x 8-6

Br 3
10 x 10-4

lin

First Floor
1,034 sq. ft.

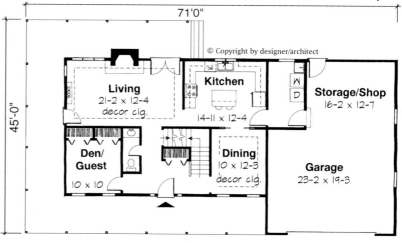

71'0"

45'-0"

© Copyright by designer/architect

Living
21-2 x 12-4
decor clg.

Kitchen
14-11 x 12-4

Storage/Shop
16-2 x 12-7

Den/Guest
10 x 10

Dining
10 x 12-3
decor clg.

Garage
23-2 x 19-3

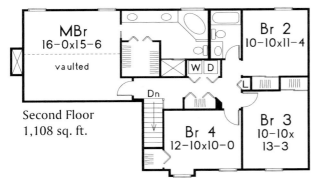

MBr
16-0x15-6
vaulted

Br 2
10-10x11-4

W **D**

Dn

Second Floor
1,108 sq. ft.

Br 4
12-10x10-0

Br 3
10-10x
13-3

Special features

- ❖ 2,135 total square feet of living area
- ❖ Family room features extra space, an impressive fireplace and full wall of windows that joins the breakfast room creating a spacious entertainment area
- ❖ Washer and dryer are conveniently located on the second floor near the bedrooms
- ❖ The kitchen features an island counter and pantry
- ❖ 4 bedrooms, 2 1/2 baths, 2-car garage
- ❖ Basement foundation

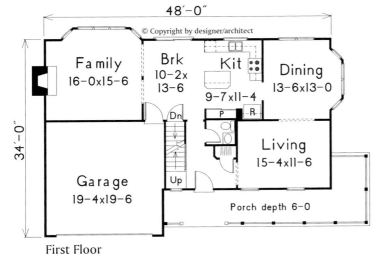

48'-0"

© Copyright by designer/architect

Family
16-0x15-6

Brk
10-2x
13-6

Kit
9-7x11-4

Dining
13-6x13-0

34'-0"

Dn

P R

Garage
19-4x19-6

Living
15-4x11-6

Up

Porch depth 6-0

First Floor
1,027 sq. ft.

Special features

- ❖ 4,058 total square feet of living area
- ❖ TV room on the second floor is secluded so not to disturb the bedrooms
- ❖ Screened porch is a relaxing escape
- ❖ Keeping room directly off kitchen has a cozy fireplace warming these casual living areas
- ❖ 4 bedrooms, 3 full baths, 2 half baths, 3-car side entry garage
- ❖ Slab foundation

When adding screens for your screened porch, consider pet-resistant screening which is seven times stronger than regular insect screening. It is composed of a vinyl-coated polyester that's installed like conventional screening products. It resists pet damage and offers terrific outward visibility.

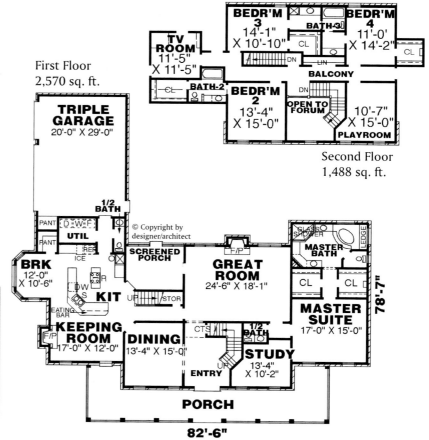

First Floor
2,570 sq. ft.

Second Floor
1,488 sq. ft.

© Copyright by designer/architect

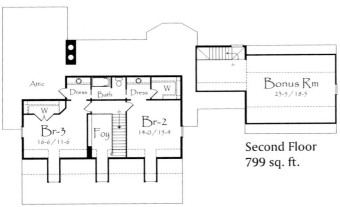

Attic

Dress Bath Dress W

W

Br-3
16-6 / 11-6

Foy

Br-2
14-0 / 15-4

Bonus Rm
23-5 / 18-5

Second Floor
799 sq. ft.

Special features

- ❖ 2,896 total square feet of living area
- ❖ A guest bedroom is located directly off the foyer to ensure privacy
- ❖ The bowed breakfast room is an exciting place to start the day
- ❖ A roomy laundry area makes the household chore a breeze
- ❖ Handy space above the garage can be finished for an additional 550 square feet of living space, complete with a private entrance
- ❖ 4 bedrooms, 3 baths, 2-car garage
- ❖ Walk-out basement foundation

Master Br
16-1 / 15-0

W

Bath

Great Rm
20-11 / 19-7

Brk
12-5 / 13-5

Kit

Lndy

Garage
23-5 / 23-5

© Copyright by designer/architect

Guest Br
11-1 / 11-8

Ba

Foy

DIN RM
14-0 / 12-4

Porch

⟨ 45'-4" ⟩

⟨ 85'-5" ⟩

First Floor
2,097 sq. ft.

Your lawn will tell you when it needs water. Two signs are when the grass changes from green to gray-green and also when footprints remain when you walk across the lawn.

Special features

- ❖ 1,770 total square feet of living area
- ❖ Energy efficient home with 2" x 6" exterior walls
- ❖ 12' ceilings enhance the living and dining rooms, kitchen, breakfast nook and foyer
- ❖ The secluded master bedroom enjoys a private bath with a walk-in closet and double-bowl vanity
- ❖ The kitchen opens to the living and dining rooms for an easy flow of family activities
- ❖ 3 bedrooms, 2 baths, 2-car side entry garage
- ❖ Slab foundation, drawings also include crawl space foundation

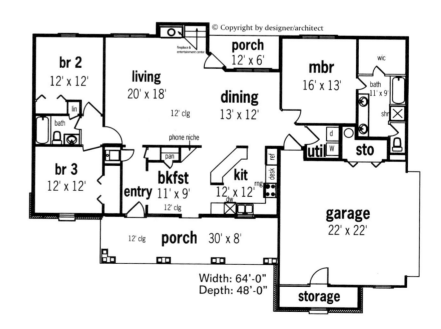

© Copyright by designer/architect

Width: 64'-0"
Depth: 48'-0"

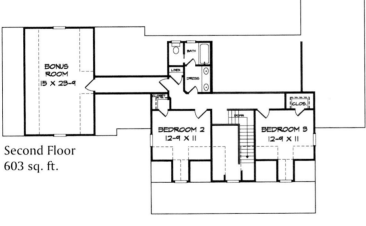

Second Floor
603 sq. ft.

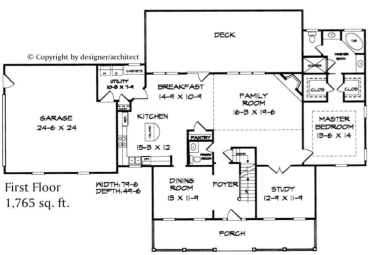

© Copyright by designer/architect

First Floor
1,765 sq. ft.

WIDTH: 79-6
DEPTH: 49-6

Special features

- 2,368 total square feet of living area
- Spacious family areas offer an easy flow of activities
- The breakfast area has access to the rear deck, expanding the dining to the outdoors
- Two secondary bedrooms on the second floor enjoy walk-in closets and window seats
- The bonus room has an additional 447 square feet of living area
- 3 bedrooms, 2 1/2 baths, 2-car side entry garage
- Basement foundation

Keeping your hedges and shrubs pruned around your home keeps areas from being hidden and making theft more easily attainable. Overgrown plants offer intruders a place to hide while they attempt to break in.

Special features

- 1,668 total square feet of living area
- Simple, but attractively styled ranch home is perfect for a narrow lot
- Front entry porch flows into the foyer which connects to the living room
- Garage entrance to home leads to the kitchen through the mud room/laundry area
- U-shaped kitchen opens to the dining area and family room
- Three bedrooms are situated at the rear of the home with two full baths
- Master bedroom has a walk-in closet
- 3 bedrooms, 2 baths, 2-car garage
- Partial basement/crawl space foundation, drawings also include crawl space and slab foundations

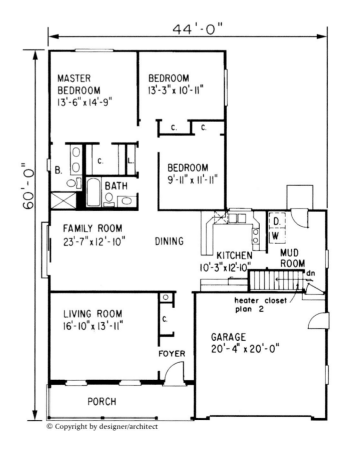

© Copyright by designer/architect

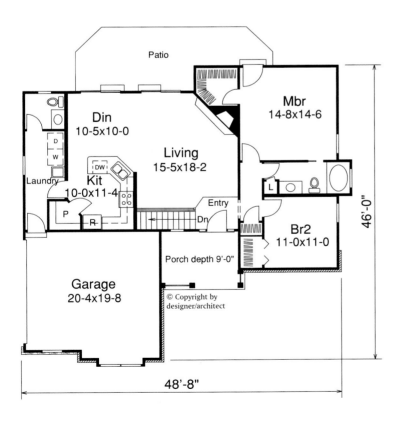

Patio

Din
10-5x10-0

Mbr
14-8x14-6

Living
15-5x18-2

Laundry

Kit
10-0x11-4

Entry
Dn

Br2
11-0x11-0

46'-0"

Porch depth 9'-0"

Garage
20-4x19-8

© Copyright by
designer/architect

48'-8"

Special features

❖ 1,248 total square feet of living area
❖ Harmonious design of stonework and gables create the perfect country retreat
❖ Large country porch is ideal for relaxing on evenings
❖ Great room and dining area enjoy a vaulted ceiling, corner fireplace and views of rear patio through two sets of sliding doors
❖ Large walk-in pantry, U-shaped cabinetry and pass-through snack bar are a few features of the smartly designed kitchen
❖ 2 bedrooms, 1 1/2 baths, 2-car side entry garage
❖ Basement foundation, drawings also include slab foundation

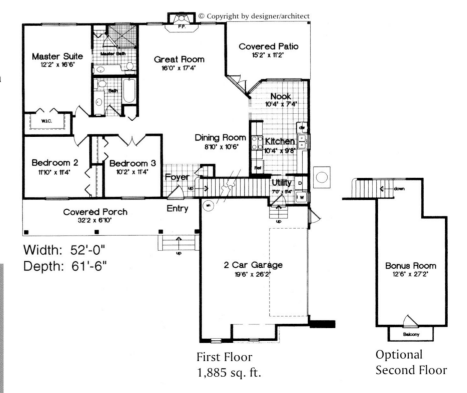

Special features

- ❖ 1,885 total square feet of living area
- ❖ Enormous covered patio
- ❖ Dining and great rooms combine to create one large and versatile living area
- ❖ Utility room is directly off the kitchen for convenience
- ❖ Bonus room above garage has an additional 327 square feet of living space
- ❖ 3 bedrooms, 2 baths, 2-car side entry garage
- ❖ Basement foundation

When hanging wallpaper, place pieces of tape over outlets and switches to minimize exposure to paste or water. But, keep in mind, tape won't protect you if the electricity is still on.

© Copyright by designer/architect

Master Suite 12'2" x 16'6"

Great Room 16'0" x 17'4"

Covered Patio 15'2" x 11'2"

Nook 10'4" x 7'4"

Dining Room 8'10" x 10'6"

Kitchen 10'4" x 9'8"

Bedroom 2 11'10" x 11'4"

Bedroom 3 10'2" x 11'4"

Foyer

Utility 7'0" x 5'4"

Covered Porch 32'2" x 6'10"

Entry

Width: 52'-0"
Depth: 61'-6"

2 Car Garage 19'6" x 26'2"

Bonus Room 12'6" x 27'2"

Balcony

First Floor 1,885 sq. ft.

Optional Second Floor

Special features

- ❖ 801 total square feet of living area
- ❖ A wrap-around porch, roof dormer and fancy stonework all contribute to a delightful and charming exterior
- ❖ The living room enjoys a separate entry, a stone fireplace, vaulted ceiling and lots of windows
- ❖ The well-equipped kitchen has a snack bar and dining area with bay which offers access to the rear patio
- ❖ An oversized two-car garage features a large vaulted room ideal for a shop, studio, hobby room or office with built-in cabinets and access to the porch
- ❖ 2 bedrooms, 1 bath, 2-car side entry garage
- ❖ Slab foundation

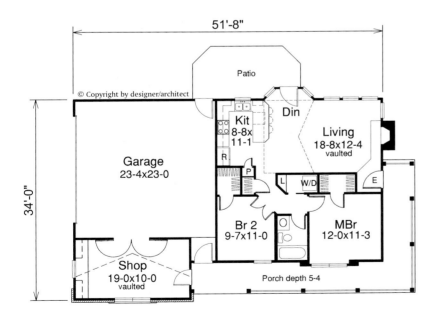

© Copyright by designer/architect

51'-8"

34'-0"

Patio

Garage
23-4x23-0

Kit
8-8x
11-1

Din

Living
18-8x12-4
vaulted

Shop
19-0x10-0
vaulted

Br 2
9-7x11-0

MBr
12-0x11-3

Porch depth 5-4

Special features

- 2,200 total square feet of living area
- The kitchen enjoys an abundance of counterspace along with an extra-large island
- False beams top the kitchen and dining area providing a cozy atmosphere
- Secondary bedrooms are located on the second floor along with a loft area with built-in bookshelves
- 3 bedrooms, 2 1/2 baths
- Slab foundation

Second Floor
746 sq. ft.

© Copyright by designer/architect

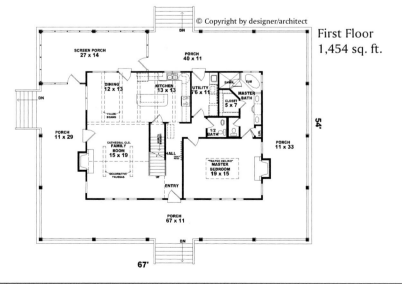

First Floor
1,454 sq. ft.

Oak is the most common type of flooring in the United States. Red oak has salmon tones while white oak is more ashen. Oak accepts just about every finish, installs easily and withstands heavy foot traffic. Oak floor boards can blacken if exposed to moisture, so do not install it in kitchens or bathrooms.

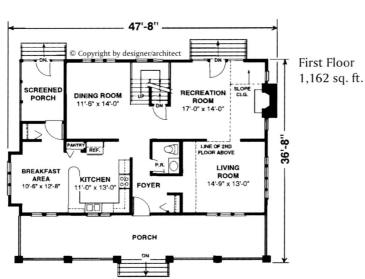

Second Floor
847 sq. ft.

First Floor
1,162 sq. ft.

Special features

❖ 2,009 total square feet of living area
❖ Spacious master bedroom has a dramatic sloped ceiling and private bath with a double-bowl vanity and walk-in closet
❖ Bedroom #3 has an extra storage area behind the closet
❖ Versatile screened porch is ideal for entertaining year-round
❖ Sunny breakfast area is located near the kitchen and screened porch for convenience
❖ 3 bedrooms, 2 1/2 baths
❖ Basement foundation

When shopping for furniture always look beneath the surface. Lift the cushions or turn the piece over to see how well it's constructed. Look for loose screws, padding that's not sewn correctly, insufficient support, and springs that are obvious or unprotected.

Special features

- ❖ 2,144 total square feet of living area
- ❖ The covered porch opens up to an exquisite foyer with arched opening to the study, living and dining rooms
- ❖ Efficient kitchen enjoys a large work island with seating and opens to the friendly nook and spacious living room
- ❖ All bedrooms enjoy walk-in closets for easy organization
- ❖ 4 bedrooms, 2 baths, 2-car side entry garage
- ❖ Slab foundation

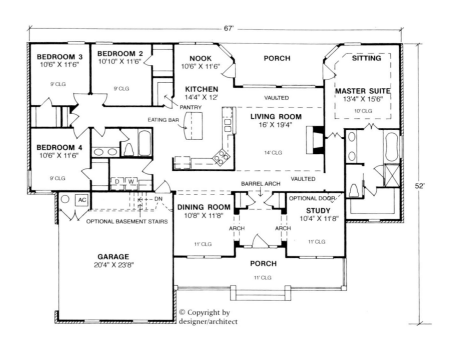

Art and photography should always be hung last after other decorating decisions have been made. The height of the sofa, the width of the armoire, even the curtain drape will affect the ultimate look of a hanging display.

Special features

* 1,860 total square feet of living area
* The spacious foyer opens to the combination living and dining rooms creating an attractive formal area for greeting guests
* The breakfast area is surrounded by windows, offering a spectacular view of the backyard
* The great room ceiling slopes to 12' high and offers a comfortable gathering space for family and friends
* 3 bedrooms, 2 baths, 2-car side entry garage
* Basement foundation

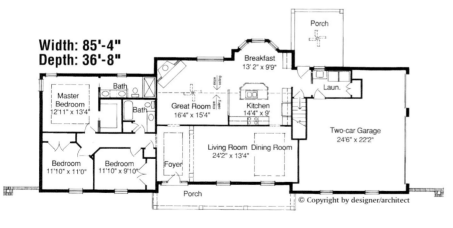

Width: 85'-4"
Depth: 36'-8"

Porch

Breakfast
13'2" x 9'9"

Laun.

Master Bedroom
12'11" x 13'4"

Bath

Bath

Great Room
16'4" x 15'4"

Kitchen
14'4" x 9'

Two-car Garage
24'6" x 22'2"

Bedroom
11'10" x 11'0"

Bedroom
11'10" x 9'10"

Foyer

Living Room
24'2" x 13'4"

Dining Room

Porch

© Copyright by designer/architect

Special features

- 3,013 total square feet of living area
- Oversized rooms throughout
- Kitchen features an island sink, large pantry and opens into the breakfast room with a sunroom feel
- Large family room with fireplace accesses the rear deck and front porch
- Master bedroom includes a large walk-in closet and private deluxe bath
- 4 bedrooms, 3 1/2 baths, 2-car side entry garage
- Basement foundation

Second Floor
1,554 sq. ft.

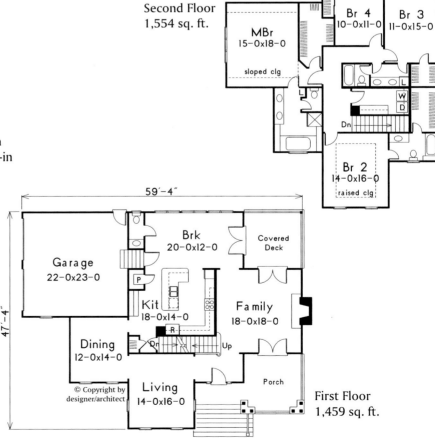

First Floor
1,459 sq. ft.

Second Floor
1,419 sq. ft.

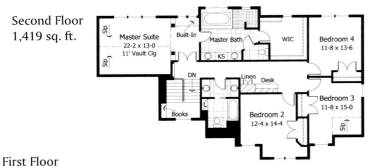

First Floor
1,563 sq. ft.

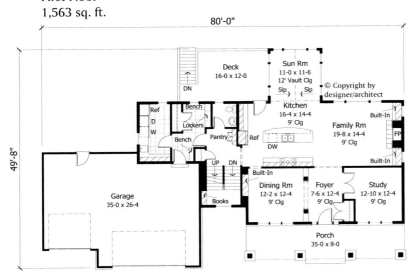

Special features

* 2,982 total square feet of living area
* French doors lead into a private study perfect for a home office
* An extra-large kitchen island offers space for quick meals or buffet dinners and opens to the enchanting sun room
* A double-door entry leads into the elegant master suite which features a vaulted ceiling and plush bath with walk-in closet
* 4 bedrooms, 2 1/2 baths, 3-car garage
* Walk-out basement foundation

Special features

- 1,480 total square feet of living area
- Enormous double-hung windows brighten every room
- Kitchen, living and dining rooms comprise the open space for easy flow of family activities
- A hearth fireplace keeps the home cozy, while the cooking island and breakfast bar screen the kitchen from the living/dining area
- The first floor bedroom boasts a walk-in closet, compartmented bath and laundry alcove
- 3 bedrooms, 2 baths
- Crawl space or basement foundation, please specify when ordering

Second Floor
570 sq. ft.

BEDROOM
13 x 12

H

attic

L

OPEN

BEDROOM
11 x 15

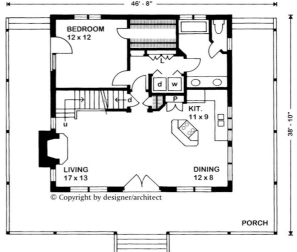

First Floor
910 sq. ft.

46' - 8"

38' - 10"

BEDROOM
12 x 12

L

d w

P

KIT.
11 x 9

u

LIVING
17 x 13

DINING
12 x 8

PORCH

© Copyright by designer/architect

Special features

- ❖ 1,902 total square feet of living area
- ❖ Great room with fireplace is easily viewable from the kitchen and breakfast area
- ❖ Luxury master bedroom has a bay window and two walk-in closets
- ❖ Formal living and dining rooms create a wonderful entertaining space
- ❖ 3 bedrooms, 2 baths, 2-car side entry garage
- ❖ Basement, crawl space or slab foundation, please specify when ordering

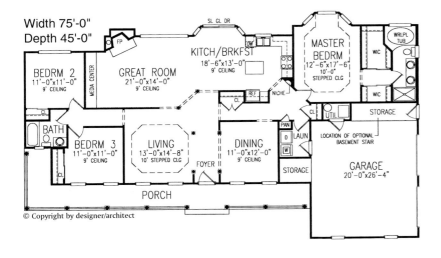

Width 75'-0"
Depth 45'-0"

© Copyright by designer/architect

To preserve and protect exterior doors and trim without hiding the wood's beauty, do what boaters do: use marine varnish. Also known as spar varnish, the high oil content of this finish coating makes it more flexible than other clear finishes.

Special features

- 2,582 total square feet of living area
- Energy efficient home with 2" x 6" exterior walls
- Both the family and living rooms are warmed by hearths
- The master bedroom on the second floor has a bayed sitting room and a private bath with whirlpool tub
- Old-fashioned window seat in the second floor landing is a charming touch
- 4 bedrooms, 3 baths, 2-car side entry garage
- Basement or crawl space foundation, please specify when ordering

Although many homeowners use a sponge when washing dishes, washcloths are easier to launder. Just remember if you use a sponge to sanitize it periodically in a hot water and bleach mixture to prevent germs from collecting inside.

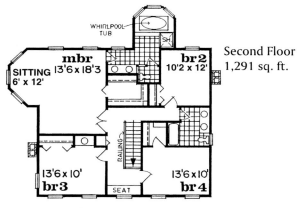

Second Floor
1,291 sq. ft.

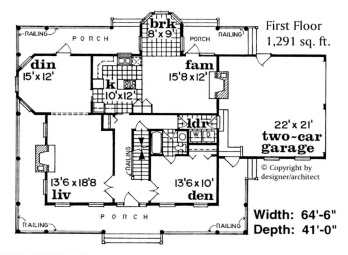

First Floor
1,291 sq. ft.

© Copyright by designer/architect

Width: 64'-6"
Depth: 41'-0"

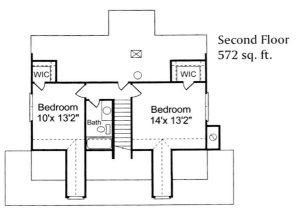

Second Floor
572 sq. ft.

WIC

Bedroom
10'x 13'2"

Bath

Bedroom
14'x 13'2"

WIC

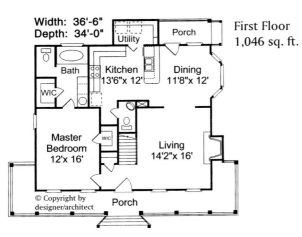

Width: 36'-6"
Depth: 34'-0"

Utility

Porch

First Floor
1,046 sq. ft.

Bath

Kitchen
13'6"x 12'

Dining
11'8"x 12'

WIC

Master
Bedroom
12'x 16'

WIC

Living
14'2"x 16'

© Copyright by
designer/architect

Porch

Special features

❖ 1,618 total square feet of living area
❖ Secondary bedrooms with walk-in closets are located on the second floor and share a bath
❖ Utility room is tucked away in the kitchen for convenience but is out of sight
❖ Dining area is brightened by a large bay window
❖ 3 bedrooms, 2 1/2 baths
❖ Slab or crawl space foundation, please specify when ordering

Special features

- ❖ 1,830 total square feet of living area
- ❖ Inviting covered verandas in the front and rear of the home
- ❖ Great room has a fireplace and cathedral ceiling
- ❖ Handy service porch allows easy access
- ❖ Master bedroom has a vaulted ceiling and private bath
- ❖ 3 bedrooms, 2 baths, 3-car side entry garage
- ❖ Basement, crawl space or slab foundation, please specify when ordering

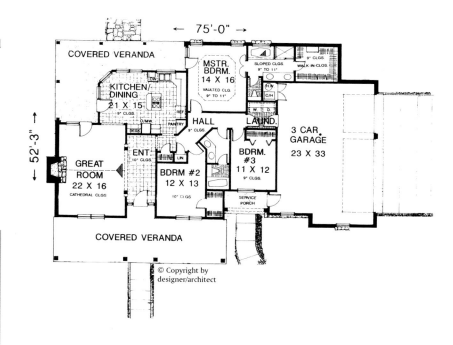

Adding wainscoting to an existing room creates an old-fashioned look especially when added to a kitchen or bedroom. This design idea works well when an update is needed to an older home but you don't want the renovation looking "too new" that it doesn't integrate with the rest of the home.

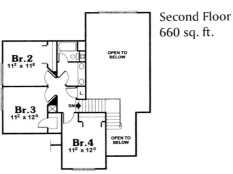

Second Floor
660 sq. ft.

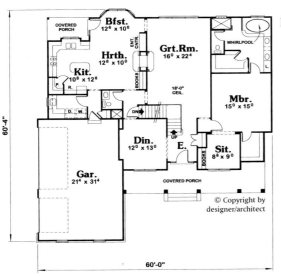

First Floor
1,955 sq. ft.

Special features

- ❖ 2,615 total square feet of living area
- ❖ Two-story great room is elegant with a see-through fireplace into the cozy hearth room
- ❖ Master bedroom has sitting area with built-in bookshelves
- ❖ Covered porch off breakfast area is a perfect place to spend quiet mornings
- ❖ 4 bedrooms, 2 1/2 baths, 3-car side entry garage
- ❖ Basement foundation

Clutter can really detract from an open floor plan. When planning your area, make a list of all of the items that will need to be stored. Often times when rooms are designed there is not enough storage. Designing a room with these needs in mind will not compromise the beauty of the space.

Special features

❖ 2,889 total square feet of living area
❖ Energy efficient home with 2" x 6" exterior walls
❖ Cathedral ceiling in family room is impressive
❖ 9' ceilings throughout the first floor
❖ Private home office is located away from traffic flow
❖ 4 bedrooms, 3 1/2 baths, 2-car side entry garage
❖ Basement foundation

Covering your gutters with either wire or plastic mesh drastically cuts down on drain clogging debris and also keeps your gutters from overflowing or damaging the exterior of your home.

Second Floor
962 sq. ft.

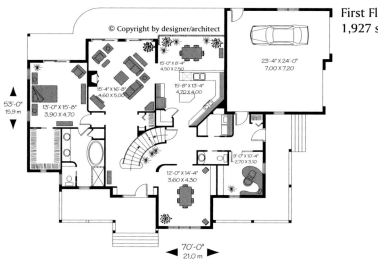

© Copyright by designer/architect

First Floor
1,927 sq. ft.

Special features

- ❖ 2,157 total square feet of living area
- ❖ The efficiently designed kitchen serves the bayed breakfast area and formal dining room with ease
- ❖ French doors lead onto the rear porch and connecting deck for an abundance of outdoor living space
- ❖ The massive garage features space for a golf cart and a work area that accesses the service yard
- ❖ The second floor guest room has an additional 464 square feet of living area
- ❖ 3 bedrooms, 2 baths, 2-car side entry garage
- ❖ Slab or pier foundation, please specify when ordering

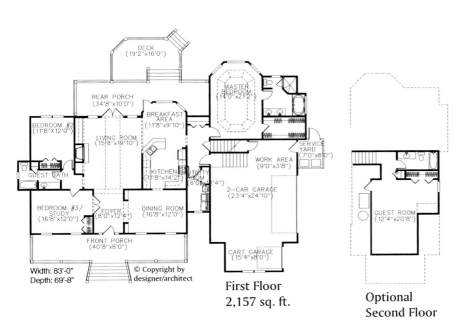

Width: 83'-0"
Depth: 69'-8"

© Copyright by designer/architect

First Floor
2,157 sq. ft.

Optional
Second Floor

Special features

- ❖ 2,428 total square feet of living area
- ❖ The formal dining room defined by elegant columns will grab your eye as you enter this inviting home
- ❖ The corner fireplace adds to the warm ambiance of the living room
- ❖ Two secondary bedrooms enjoy the unique space created by the charming dormers
- ❖ 4 bedrooms, 2 1/2 baths
- ❖ Basement foundation

Second Floor
895 sq. ft.

Bedroom
13'7"x 11'9"

Open to
Below

Bedroom
11'11"x 11'4"

Bedroom
15'x 11'11"

© Copyright by designer/architect

Utility

Porch
24'x 8'

Width: 45'-10"
Depth: 48'-5"

First Floor
1,533 sq. ft.

Breakfast
9'2"x 9'11"

Living
18'8"x 15'

Kitchen
11'6"x 12'

Dining
12'8"x 11'6"

Foyer
8'8"x 6'6"

Master
Bedroom
14'10"x 13'

Porch
35'10"x 5'

Lights with motion detectors are convenient and an efficient source for outdoor security lighting. Well positioned motion detectors make it virtually impossible for anyone to sneak up on your home.

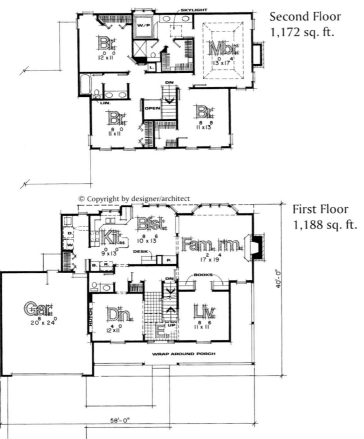

Second Floor
1,172 sq. ft.

© Copyright by designer/architect

First Floor
1,188 sq. ft.

Special features

❖ 2,360 total square feet of living area
❖ The formal dining room boasts a unique hutch
❖ The formal living room connects with the bayed family room which includes bookshelves and a grand fireplace
❖ The kitchen opens into the bayed breakfast area and includes a built-in desk and island
❖ 4 bedrooms, 2 1/2 baths, 2-car garage
❖ Basement foundation

Keeping a paint can from getting too messy can be the hardest part of the job. Here's a tip - slide a rubber band over the open can so it stretches top to bottom across the open can. Then, when you pull the brush out of the paint wipe the bottom against the rubber band each time to avoid unnecessary drips.

Special features

- ❖ 3,059 total square feet of living area
- ❖ Covered porches surround the exterior of this home
- ❖ Laundry area includes hobby area connected to the garage
- ❖ Bedroom #2 has a bayed sitting area making it also ideal as a study
- ❖ 4 bedrooms, 4 baths, 2-car side entry garage
- ❖ Basement foundation

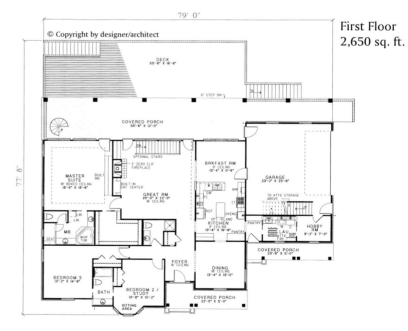

© Copyright by designer/architect

First Floor 2,650 sq. ft.

Lower Level 409 sq. ft.

Special features

- ❖ 1,716 total square feet of living area
- ❖ Great room boasts a fireplace and access to the kitchen/breakfast area through a large arched opening
- ❖ Master bedroom includes a huge walk-in closet and French doors that lead onto an L-shaped porch
- ❖ Bedrooms #2 and #3 share a bath and linen closet
- ❖ 3 bedrooms, 2 baths, 2-car detached garage
- ❖ Crawl space or slab foundation, please specify when ordering

7' DEEP PORCH

MASTER BEDROOM 16'8 X 16'0

© Copyright by designer/architect

STOR   **STOR**

DETACHED GARAGE 24'0 X 20'0

BD RM 3 12'0 X 11'8

11' DEEP PORCH

CLOSET 6'0 X 10'0

L

REF.   OVEN   P

SNACK BAR   COOKTOP

GREAT ROOM 19'6 X 22'0

KITCHEN/ BREAKFAST 12'8 X 21'10

BD RM 2 11'10 X 11'0

6' DEEP PORCH

44'-0" WIDE X 65'-0" DEEP - WITHOUT GARAGE

Cold weather shouldn't be an issue anymore with exterior painting. Most conventional paints need to be applied during temperatures 55 degrees or warmer. But cold weather paints are designed to resist moisture, frost and blisters in as low as 35 degrees.

Special features

- 2,837 total square feet of living area
- Office/sitting room directly off the master bedroom is perfect for a home office or quiet place to relax
- Living room/guest room offers a cozy fireplace adding a memorable touch
- A covered porch wraps around the sunny bayed breakfast room
- 3 bedrooms, 3 baths, 2-car side entry garage
- Basement, crawl space or slab foundation, please specify when ordering

Second Floor
685 sq. ft.

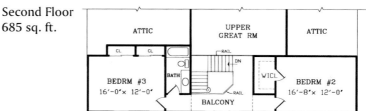

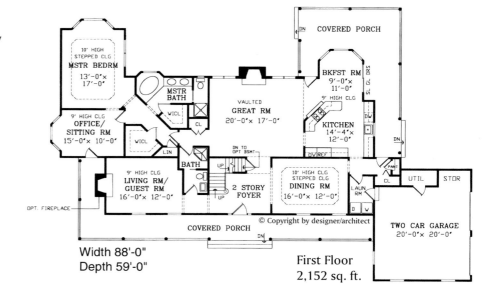

Width 88'-0"
Depth 59'-0"

First Floor
2,152 sq. ft.

© Copyright by designer/architect

Second Floor
1,158 sq. ft.

BR.3
10'6"x11'8"

BR.2
10'4"x11'8"

MBR.
TRAY CEILING
15'x19'0"

DOWN

OPEN TO FOYER

BR.4
CATHEDRAL CEILING
13'x13'6"

First Floor
1,333 sq. ft.

© Copyright by designer/architect

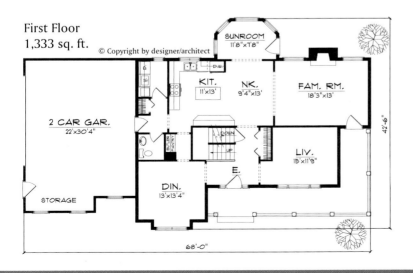

SUNROOM
11'8"x7'8"

2 CAR GAR.
22'x30'4"

KIT.
11'x13'

NK.
9'4"x13'

FAM. RM.
18'3"x13'

BUTLER PANTRY

DOWN

UP

LIV.
15'x11'9"

STORAGE

DIN.
13'x13'4"

E.

42'-6"

68'-0"

Special features

- ❖ 2,491 total square feet of living area
- ❖ Energy efficient home with 2" x 6" exterior walls
- ❖ Entry is flanked by formal living and dining rooms
- ❖ Hallway between dining room and kitchen includes a butler's pantry to ease serving a party
- ❖ The kitchen, breakfast nook and family room combine for an expansive gathering space
- ❖ All bedrooms are located on the second floor for privacy
- ❖ 4 bedrooms, 2 1/2 baths, 2-car side entry garage
- ❖ Basement foundation

Special features

- 1,936 total square feet of living area
- Covered porch creates an inviting entrance
- Kitchen, breakfast and great rooms combine for an open area and include access to the rear sundeck
- Second floor includes an abundance of storage area
- Bonus room on the second floor has an additional 528 square feet of living area
- 3 bedrooms, 2 1/2 baths, 2-car side entry garage
- Walk-out basement foundation

For a stylish flower arrangement, pick flowers from your garden in the early morning or late evening. Place them in water immediately, or the stems will form an air-lock that prevents them from drinking.

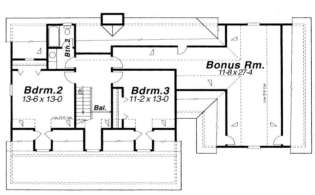

Second Floor
624 sq. ft.

Bonus Rm.
11-8 x 27-4

Bdrm.2
13-6 x 13-0

Bdrm.3
11-2 x 13-0

Bth.2

Bal.

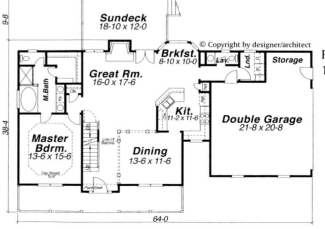

© Copyright by designer/architect

First Floor
1,312 sq. ft.

Sundeck
18-10 x 12-0

Brkfst.
8-10 x 10-0

Lav.

Lnd.

Storage

Great Rm.
16-0 x 17-6

M.Bath

Kit.
11-2 x 11-6

Double Garage
21-8 x 20-8

Master
Bdrm.
13-6 x 15-6

Dining
13-6 x 11-6

9-8

38-4

64-0

Special features

❖ 1,334 total square feet of living area

❖ This welcoming design is ideal for a vacation, starter or empty-nester home

❖ Relax on cozy front and rear porches that are large enough for rocking chairs

❖ The spacious first floor master suite features a walk-in closet, sitting area and private bath

❖ The second floor features two bedrooms that share a full bath

❖ 3 bedrooms, 2 1/2 baths

❖ Crawl space foundation

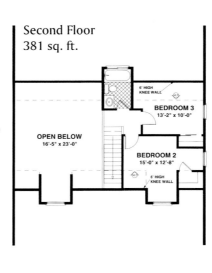

First Floor
953 sq. ft.

Second Floor
381 sq. ft.

PORCH
35'-8" x 7'-7"

COUNTRY KITCHEN
20'-0" x 11'-3"

PANTRY

D
W

STORAGE OR STAIRS TO BASEMENT

COATS

FAMILY ROOM
16'-5" x 14'-2"

MASTER SUITE
15'-0" x 14'-10"

SITTING

CLOSET
5'-3" x 6'-11"

PORCH
35'-8" x 7'-7"

42'-4"

36'-0"

Copyright © 2006 Atlanta Plan Source, Inc.

© Copyright by designer/architect

6' HIGH KNEE WALL

BEDROOM 3
13'-2" x 10'-0"

OPEN BELOW
16'-5" x 23'-0"

BEDROOM 2
15'-0" x 12'-8"

6' HIGH KNEE WALL

Small packages of screws are much more expensive than boxes of 100. The traditional, plain wood screw is easily replaced by new, innovative designs with sharper, wider threads that resemble drywall screws.

Special features

- 2,326 total square feet of living area
- Energy efficient home with 2" x 6" exterior walls
- A grand fireplace warms the adjoining family room, kitchen and nook
- The vaulted master bedroom features a private bath and double doors leading to the rear deck
- The bonus room above the garage has an additional 358 square feet of living area
- 3 bedrooms, 2 1/2 baths, 2-car side entry garage
- Basement foundation

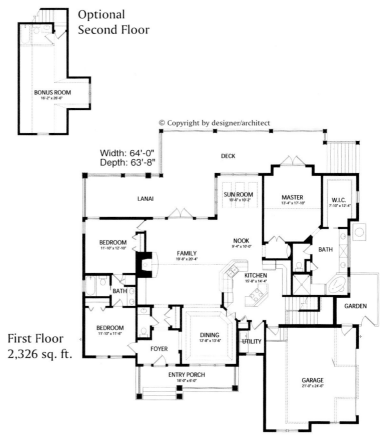

Optional Second Floor

BONUS ROOM
16'-2" x 26'-6"

© Copyright by designer/architect

Width: 64'-0"
Depth: 63'-8"

DECK

LANAI

SUN ROOM
10'-6" x 10'-2"

MASTER
13'-4" x 17'-10"

W.I.C.
7'-10" x 12'-4"

BEDROOM
11'-10" x 12'-10"

FAMILY
19'-8" x 20'-4"

NOOK
9'-4" x 10'-0"

BATH

BATH

KITCHEN
15'-8" x 14'-4"

GARDEN

First Floor
2,326 sq. ft.

BEDROOM
11'-10" x 11'-6"

FOYER

DINING
12'-8" x 13'-6"

UTILITY

GARAGE
21'-0" x 24'-6"

ENTRY PORCH
18'-0" x 6'-0"

Special features

- 480 total square feet of living area
- Inviting wrap-around porch and rear covered patio are perfect for summer evenings
- Living room features a fireplace, separate entry foyer with coat closet and sliding doors to a rear patio
- The compact but complete kitchen includes a dining area with bay window and window at sink for patio views
- 1 bedroom, 1 bath, 1-car garage
- Slab foundation

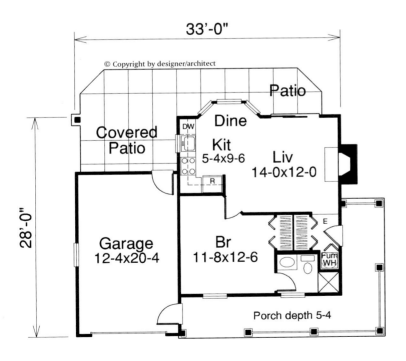

33'-0"

© Copyright by designer/architect

Patio

Covered Patio

Dine

DW

Kit 5-4x9-6

Liv 14-0x12-0

R

28'-0"

Garage 12-4x20-4

Br 11-8x12-6

E

Furn WH

Porch depth 5-4

Applying caulk can be messy but, for best results start by practicing on a scrap of paper so you get used to how quick the caulk comes out of the tube. Smoothing the caulk is best done with a damp finger or rag.

Special features

- 1,688 total square feet of living area
- The great room dazzles with a grand fireplace, built-in shelves and access to the rear porch
- The master bedroom enjoys two walk-in closets and a private bath with a double-bowl vanity
- Roomy laundry area makes the household chore a breeze
- 3 bedrooms, 2 baths, 2-car side entry garage
- Basement, crawl space or slab foundation, please specify when ordering

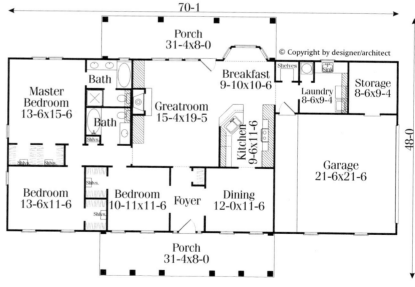

70-1

Porch
31-4x8-0

© Copyright by designer/architect

Breakfast
9-10x10-6

Shelves

Laundry
8-6x9-4

Sink

Storage
8-6x9-4

Bath

Master
Bedroom
13-6x15-6

Bath

Greatroom
15-4x19-5

Kitchen
9-6x11-6

48-0

Garage
21-6x21-6

Bedroom
13-6x11-6

Bedroom
10-11x11-6

Foyer

Dining
12-0x11-6

Porch
31-4x8-0

Special features

- ❖ 864 total square feet of living area
- ❖ L-shaped kitchen with convenient pantry is adjacent to the dining area
- ❖ Easy access to laundry area, linen closet and storage closet
- ❖ Both bedrooms include ample closet space
- ❖ 2 bedrooms, 1 bath
- ❖ Crawl space foundation, drawings also include basement and slab foundations

36'-0"

24'-0"

Br 1
13-2x10-1

Kit
10-2x6-8

D W Furn

Dining
9-5x
10-4

Br 2
11-8x13-0

Living
13-5x13-0

© Copyright by designer/architect

Porch depth 4-0

Never stack terra-cotta flower pots vertically. Changes in temperature and humidity will make them swell causing them to stick together making them easy to crack when trying to pull apart.

Special Features

- ❖ 1,463 total square feet of living area
- ❖ The covered porch welcomes guests and leads into the open family room with a fireplace and handy built-ins
- ❖ To the rear, a U-shaped kitchen with walk-in pantry connects with the bayed dining room which enjoys access to the outdoors
- ❖ The bedrooms have extra peace and quiet on the second floor and enjoy having the laundry closet close at hand
- ❖ The unfinished storage area has an additional 258 square feet that can be finished as needed
- ❖ 3 bedrooms, 2 1/2 baths, 2-car garage
- ❖ Basement foundation

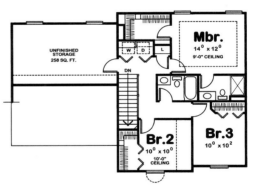

Second Floor
747 sq. ft.

© Copyright by designer/architect

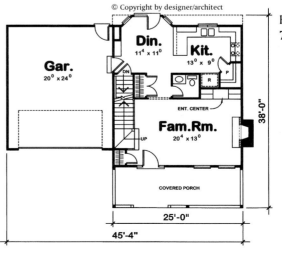

First Floor
716 sq. ft.

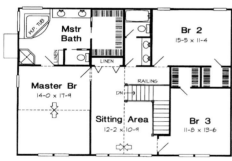

Second Floor
1,269 sq. ft.

Special features

❖ 2,647 total square feet of living area
❖ Master bath includes luxury with a corner whirlpool tub
❖ Vaulted second floor sitting area is a great place to relax
❖ The breakfast room has pocket doors that separate it from the family room
❖ 4 bedrooms, 3 baths, 2-car side entry garage
❖ Basement or crawl space foundation, please specify when ordering

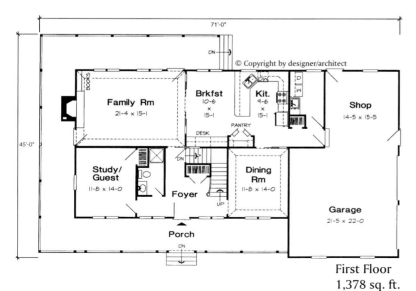

© Copyright by designer/architect

First Floor
1,378 sq. ft.

Special features

- 1,522 total square feet of living area
- The family room accessing a rear terrace through sliding glass doors flows into the large country kitchen
- The second floor master suite features a tray ceiling and private bath with a double vanity
- A wrap-around porch and a central gable with a half-circle window give this stylish country home a warm appeal
- 3 bedrooms, 2 1/2 baths, 2-car garage
- Slab, crawl space or basement foundation, please specify when ordering

Fill empty spaces in your refrigerator and freezer with water jugs. You'll save energy and money because it takes more energy to run an empty refrigerator and freezer than a full one.

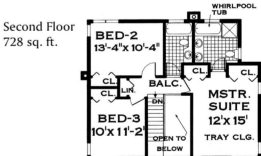

Second Floor
728 sq. ft.

WHIRLPOOL TUB

BED-2
13'-4" x 10'-4"

CL.

CL.

CL.

BALC.

MSTR. SUITE
12' x 15'

CL.

LIN.

DN

BED-3
10' x 11'-2'

OPEN TO BELOW

TRAY CLG.

SHELF

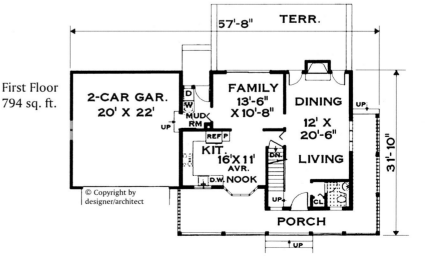

First Floor
794 sq. ft.

57'-8"

TERR.

2-CAR GAR.
20' X 22'

FAMILY
13'-6" X 10'-8"

DINING
12' X 20'-6"

UP

MUD RM

UP

31'-10"

REF P

KIT.
16' X 11'
AVR.

DN

LIVING

D.W.

NOOK

UP

CL.

© Copyright by designer/architect

PORCH

UP

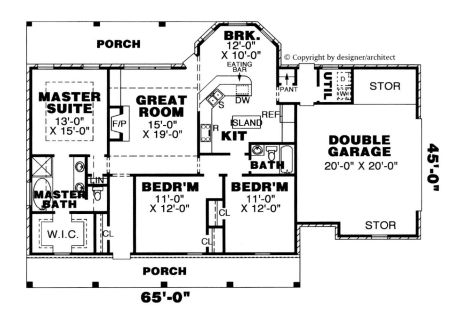

Special features

- ❖ 1,612 total square feet of living area
- ❖ Covered porch in rear of home creates an outdoor living area
- ❖ Master suite is separated from other bedrooms for privacy
- ❖ Eating bar in kitchen extends into breakfast area for additional seating
- ❖ 3 bedrooms, 2 baths, 2-car side entry garage
- ❖ Slab foundation

Clean off the countertops by storing mail, keys, and to-do lists in an organized built-in desk. This feature helps keep the kitchen the place for cooking and dining exclusively.

Special features

- 2,250 total square feet of living area
- The kitchen easily serves the casual bayed breakfast room or the formal dining room
- The master bedroom enjoys a luxurious bath, two walk-in closets, porch access and a nearby office/nursery
- A large laundry room complete with a sink and counterspace adds simplicity to the household chore
- The unfinished bonus room has an additional 310 square feet of living area
- 4 bedrooms, 3 baths, 2-car side entry garage
- Slab or crawl space foundation, please specify when ordering

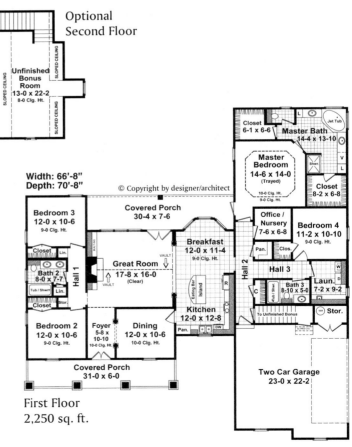

Optional Second Floor

Unfinished Bonus Room 13-0 x 22-2
8-0 Clg. Ht.

Attic Access

SLOPED CEILING

Width: 66'-8"
Depth: 70'-8"

© Copyright by designer/architect

Closet 6-1 x 6-6

Master Bath 14-4 x 13-10

Jet Tub

Master Bedroom 14-6 x 14-0 (Trayed)
10-0 Clg. Ht.
9-0 Clg. Ht.

Closet 8-2 x 6-8

Office / Nursery 7-6 x 6-8

Bedroom 4 11-2 x 10-10
9-0 Clg. Ht.

Bedroom 3 12-0 x 10-6
9-0 Clg. Ht.

Covered Porch 30-4 x 7-6

Breakfast 12-0 x 11-4
9-0 Clg. Ht.

Hall 2

Hall 3

Bath 3 8-10 x 5-0

Laun. 7-2 x 9-2

Closet

Lin.

Hall 1

Great Room 17-8 x 16-0 (Clear)
VAULT

Island
Eating Bar

To Unfinished Bonus

Stor.

Bath 2 8-0 x 7-7

Lin.

Kitchen 12-0 x 12-8

Closet

Stor.

Bedroom 2 12-0 x 10-6
9-0 Clg. Ht.

Foyer 5-8 x 10-10
10-0 Clg. Ht.

Dining 12-0 x 10-6
10-0 Clg. Ht.

Pan.

Covered Porch 31-0 x 6-0

Two Car Garage 23-0 x 22-2

First Floor
2,250 sq. ft.

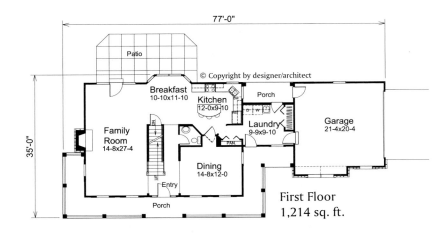

Mbr
14-10x15-8

Br #4
11-8x10-6

HALL

Br #2
12-6x10-0

Br #3
12-6x11-0

Open

Second Floor
1,154 sq. ft.

77'-0"

Patio

© Copyright by designer/architect

Breakfast
10-10x11-10

Kitchen
12-0x9-10

Porch

35'-0"

Family
Room
14-8x27-4

Laundry
9-9x9-10

Garage
21-4x20-4

PAN

Dining
14-8x12-0

Entry

Porch

First Floor
1,214 sq. ft.

Special features

❖ 2,368 total square feet of living area

❖ This country exterior with its wrap-around porch, impressive stonework and roof dormers is a delight to the eye

❖ A two-story foyer leads to an enormous family room with fireplace and access to the rear patio

❖ The family-sized laundry room with access to a rear covered porch is adjacent to the kitchen

❖ On the second floor, the master bedroom is generous in size and features a vaulted ceiling, two walk-in closets and an elegant private bath

❖ 4 bedrooms, 3 1/2 baths, 2-car side entry garage

❖ Basement foundation, drawings also include slab and crawl space foundations

Special features

- ❖ 1,479 total square feet of living area
- ❖ Enormous double-hung windows brighten every room
- ❖ Kitchen, living and dining rooms comprise the open space for easy flow of family activities
- ❖ A hearth fireplace keeps the home cozy, while the cooking island and breakfast bar screen the kitchen from the living/dining area
- ❖ The first floor bedroom boasts a walk-in closet, compartmented bath and laundry alcove
- ❖ 3 bedrooms, 2 baths
- ❖ Slab foundation

Second Floor
568 sq. ft.

First Floor
911 sq. ft.

© Copyright by designer/architect

Second Floor
986 sq. ft.

BONUS ROOM
11'9" x 32'1"

BEDROOM 4
14'9" x 13'0"

OPEN BELOW

MECHANICAL/ STORAGE
7'5" x 8'6"

BEDROOM 3
14'9" x 13'0"

OPEN BELOW

BEDROOM 2
14'9" x 15'5"

© Copyright by designer/architect

DECK
40'0" x 11'7"

SCREENED PORCH
11'10" x 11'7"

BREAKFAST
10'11" x 10'0"

First Floor
1,986 sq. ft.

GARAGE
21'4" x 32'1"

MASTER BDRM
14'9" x 18'5"

FAMILY
19'0" x 17'0"

KITCHEN
13'10" x 13'2"

49'-2" 36'-4"

LIVING
14'9" x 11'11"

ENTRY
11'7" x 14'5"

DINING
14'9" x 11'11"

55'-8"

22'-0"

Special features

- ❖ 2,972 total square feet of living area
- ❖ Extra storage available off the second floor bedroom
- ❖ Angled staircase in entry adds interest
- ❖ Charming screened porch is accessible from the breakfast room
- ❖ Bonus room above the garage has an additional 396 square feet of living area
- ❖ 4 bedrooms, 3 1/2 baths, 3-car side entry garage
- ❖ Walk-out basement, crawl space or slab foundation, please specify when ordering

When organizing, keep everything related to the task at hand within reach. Store detergent, softener, bleach and stain removers according to how regularly you use them.

Special features

- 2,665 total square feet of living area
- 9' ceilings on the first floor
- Spacious kitchen features many cabinets, a center island cooktop and bayed breakfast area adjacent to the laundry room
- Second floor bedrooms boast walk-in closets, dressing areas and share a bath
- Twin patio doors and fireplace grace living room
- 4 bedrooms, 3 baths, 2-car rear entry garage
- Slab foundation, drawings also include crawl space foundation

Put your recipes or project ideas into a photo album. It's easy to organize them because the pages can be moved as you add more ideas under a certain topic. Plus, if you splatter something, you can wipe off the plastic pages.

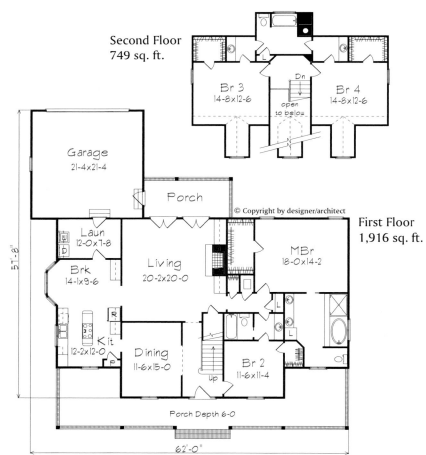

Second Floor
749 sq. ft.

© Copyright by designer/architect

First Floor
1,916 sq. ft.

Special features

- 1,568 total square feet of living area
- Multiple entrances from three porches help to bring the outdoors in
- The lodge-like great room features a vaulted ceiling, stone fireplace, step-up entrance foyer and opens to a huge screened porch
- The kitchen has an island and peninsula, a convenient laundry room and adjoins a spacious dining area which leads to a screened porch and rear patio
- The master bedroom has two walk-in closets, a luxury bath and access to the screened porch and patio
- 2 bedrooms, 2 baths, 3-car side entry garage
- Crawl space foundation

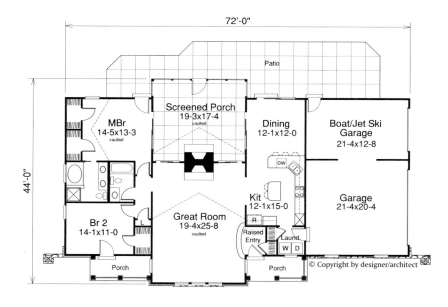

© Copyright by designer/architect

Special features

- ❖ 2,376 total square feet of living area
- ❖ The second floor bedroom with a private bath featuring a curved wall is the ideal master suite
- ❖ The garage enters the home to find an expansive utility area that houses a pantry, sink and space for a washer and dryer
- ❖ The bonus room on the second floor has an additional 420 square feet of living area
- ❖ 4 bedrooms, 2 1/2 baths, 2-car side entry garage
- ❖ Basement foundation

© Copyright by designer/architect

12'-0" X 15'-6"
3,60 X 4,65

10'-4" X 15'-6"
3,10 X 4,65

15'-2" X 16'-0"
4,55 X 4,80

10'-10" X 10'-10"
3,25 X 3,25

68'-6"
20,55 m

45'-0"
13,5 m

20'-4" X 33'-4"
6,10 X 10,00

First Floor
1,239 sq. ft.

11'-2" X 11'-0"
3,35 X 3,30

10'-10" X 11'-0"
3,25 X 3,30

13'-4" X 14'-8"
4,00 X 4,40

10'-10" X 11'-2"
3,25 X 3,36

14'-0" X 30'-0"
4,20 X 9,00

Second Floor
1,137 sq. ft.

Special features

- 1,197 total square feet of living area
- U-shaped kitchen includes ample workspace, breakfast bar, laundry area and direct access to the outdoors
- Large living room has a convenient coat closet
- Bedroom #1 features a large walk-in closet
- 2" x 6" exterior walls available, please order plan #597-001D-0102
- 3 bedrooms, 1 bath
- Crawl space foundation, drawings also include basement and slab foundations

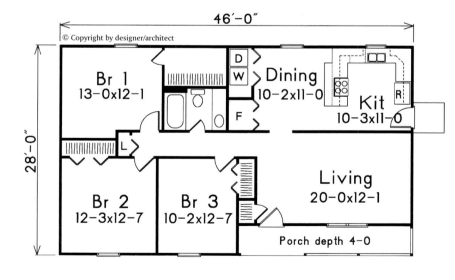

© Copyright by designer/architect

46'-0"

28'-0"

Br 1
13-0x12-1

D
W
F

Dining
10-2x11-0

Kit
10-3x11-0

R

L

Br 2
12-3x12-7

Br 3
10-2x12-7

Living
20-0x12-1

Porch depth 4-0

You can extend the flowering season by planting in both the warm and the cool microclimates of your yard. Patches of melting snow create a simple map for you to follow.

Special features

- ❖ 1,960 total square feet of living area
- ❖ Energy efficient home with 2" x 6" exterior walls
- ❖ The family room enjoys a bay window overlooking the backyard and an inviting fireplace
- ❖ The master bedroom features a beautiful vaulted ceiling and two walk-in closets
- ❖ A half wall visually separates the kitchen and family room
- ❖ 4 bedrooms, 2 1/2 baths, 2-car garage
- ❖ Basement, slab or crawl space foundation, please specify when ordering

Second Floor
1,005 sq. ft.

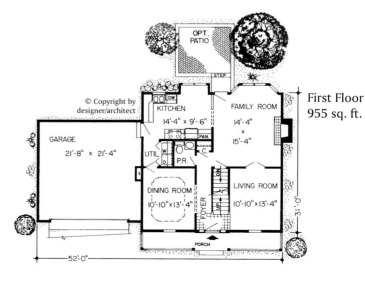

First Floor
955 sq. ft.

© Copyright by designer/architect

Special features

- 2,356 total square feet of living area
- Transoms above front windows create a custom feel to this design
- Spacious master bath has double vanities, toilet closet, and an oversized whirlpool tub
- Covered rear porch off the sunny breakfast area is ideal for grilling or relaxing
- 4 bedrooms, 2 1/2 baths, 2-car side entry garage
- Slab foundation

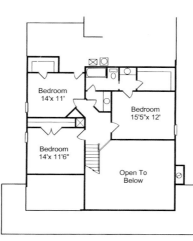

Width: 38'-11"
Depth: 68'-5"

Two Car Garage 22'x 23'6"

Porch

Breakfast

Master Bedroom 15'x 15'4"

Dining 13'6"x 12'

Living 18'x 17'6"

Porch

© Copyright by designer/architect

First Floor
1,516 sq. ft.

Bedroom 14'x 11'

Bedroom 15'5"x 12'

Bedroom 14'x 11'6"

Open To Below

Second Floor
840 sq. ft.

When you choose perennials, consider which have the best flowers, but don't ignore the leaves. In your garden, beautiful blooms will catch your eye first – interesting leaves, though, will keep your attention once the flowers have faded.

Special features

* 864 total square feet of living area
* Charming front porch welcomes guests and provides a wonderful place to relax
* The expansive living/dining room shares a snack bar with the kitchen
* The kitchen provides an abundance of storage with a nice pantry and cabinets
* Two generously sized bedrooms share a full bath and are separated from the main living areas for privacy
* 2 bedrooms, 1 bath
* Slab or crawl space foundation, please specify when ordering

Make sure that any fabrics you use for upholstery and curtains are flame retardant. All new sofas have to meet strict fire regulations but second-hand ones may have been made before they came into force.

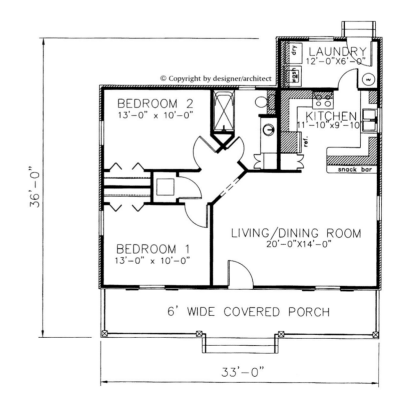

Special features

❖ 2,158 total square feet of living area
❖ Private master suite has a walk-in closet and bath
❖ Sloped ceiling in family room adds drama
❖ Secondary bedrooms include 9' ceilings and walk-in closets
❖ Covered porch adds a charming touch
❖ 4 bedrooms, 3 baths, 2-car side entry garage
❖ Crawl space or slab foundation, please specify when ordering

Width: 65'-1"
Depth: 69'-0"

More than one eighth of annual house fires are caused by space-heating equipment. Electric or liquid fuel heaters must be at least 3 feet away from any object, including walls.

Special features

- 1,700 total square feet of living area
- Energy efficient home with 2" x 6" exterior walls
- Cozy living area has plenty of space for entertaining
- Snack bar in kitchen provides extra dining area
- 3 bedrooms, 1 1/2 baths
- Basement foundation

Second Floor
840 sq. ft.

11'-8" X 11'-0"
3,50 X 3,30

13'-0" X 14'-0"
3,90 X 4,20

11'-0" X 11'-0"
3,30 X 3,30

First Floor
860 sq. ft.

11'-0" X 10'-0"
3,30 X 3,00

9'-0" X 14'-4"
2,70 X 4,30

28'-0"
8,4 m

14'-0" X 14'-0"
4,20 X 4,20

11'-0" X 12'-0"
3,30 X 3,60

© Copyright by designer/architect

30'-0"
9,0 m

If you use well water, be aware of agricultural activity in your area, which affects the quality of your water. After your first year on the property, test as you feel necessary.

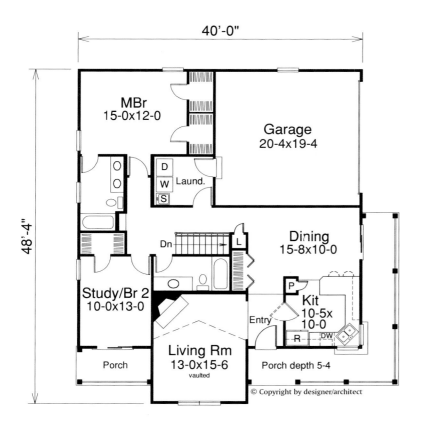

40'-0"

48'-4"

MBr
15-0x12-0

Garage
20-4x19-4

D
W Laund.
S

Dn

Dining
15-8x10-0

Study/Br 2
10-0x13-0

Kit
10-5x
10-0

Entry

P

R DW

Living Rm
13-0x15-6
vaulted

Porch

Porch depth 5-4

© Copyright by designer/architect

Special features

- ❖ 1,316 total square feet of living area
- ❖ Porches are accessible from entry, dining room and bedroom #2
- ❖ The living room enjoys a vaulted ceiling, corner fireplace and twin windows with an arched transom above
- ❖ A kitchen is provided with corner windows, an outdoor plant shelf, a snack bar, a built-in pantry and opens to a large dining room
- ❖ Bedrooms are very roomy, feature walk-in closets and have easy access to oversized baths
- ❖ 2 bedrooms, 2 baths, 2-car side entry garage
- ❖ Basement foundation, drawings also include crawl space and slab foundations

Special features

- ❖ 1,377 total square feet of living area
- ❖ Master bedroom has double-door access onto the screened porch
- ❖ Cozy dining area is adjacent to the kitchen for convenience
- ❖ Great room includes a fireplace
- ❖ Optional second floor has an additional 349 square feet of living area
- ❖ 3 bedrooms, 1 bath
- ❖ Crawl space or slab foundation, please specify when ordering

If you're considering a water feature for your yard, make safety a top priority. A water feature that doesn't contain standing water, such as a fountain without a pool, is safest. If you want a large pond or pool, the safest idea would be to encircle it with a fence if you have small children.

First Floor
1,377 sq. ft.

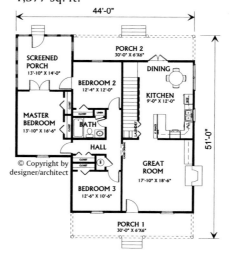

Optional
Second Floor

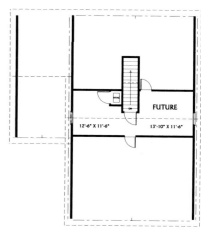

Special features

- 2,772 total square feet of living area
- 10' ceilings on the first floor and 9' ceilings on the second floor create a spacious atmosphere
- Large bay windows accent the study and master bath
- Breakfast room features a dramatic curved wall with direct view and access onto porch
- 4 bedrooms, 3 1/2 baths, 2-car side entry garage
- Slab foundation

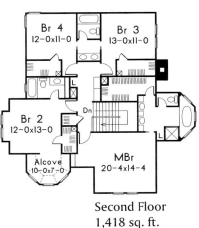

First Floor
1,354 sq. ft.

Second Floor
1,418 sq. ft.

Emphasize favorite accessories or pictures by giving them their own special lighting. Spotlights fitted into the top of display boxes or niches, or wall lamps that shine directly down onto prints or paintings, will increase their decorative value and impact.

Special features

❖ 3,033 total square feet of living area

❖ Sunroom warmed by fireplace and brightened by lots of windows

❖ Bedroom #4 and bath #2 on the second floor both lead to the balcony through French doors

❖ 4 bedrooms, 3 1/2 baths, 2-car side entry garage

❖ Basement, crawl space, walk-out basement or slab foundation, please specify when ordering

A compact kitchen can be efficient, but not when it lacks storage. One way to stretch the space without comprising design is to extend the cabinets to the ceiling. Although a harder reach, it is the perfect solution for items you rarely need.

Second Floor
1,115 sq. ft.

© Copyright by designer/architect

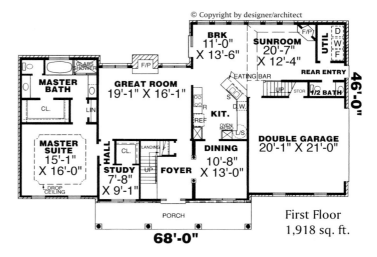

First Floor
1,918 sq. ft.

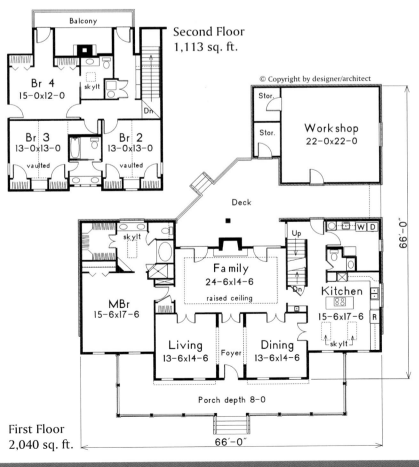

Second Floor
1,113 sq. ft.

© Copyright by designer/architect

Balcony

Br 4
15-0x12-0

skylt

Dn

Br 3
13-0x13-0

Br 2
13-0x13-0

vaulted   vaulted

Stor.

Stor.

Workshop
22-0x22-0

Deck

skylt

W D

Up

Family
24-6x14-6
raised ceiling

Kitchen
15-6x17-6

Dn

R

MBr
15-6x17-6

66'-0"

Living
13-6x14-6

Foyer

Dining
13-6x14-6

skylt

Porch depth 8-0

First Floor
2,040 sq. ft.

66'-0"

Special features

❖ 3,153 total square feet of living area
❖ Energy efficient home with 2" x 6" exterior walls
❖ Master bedroom has full amenities
❖ Covered breezeway and front and rear porches add a quality outdoor living area
❖ Full-sized workshop and storage with garage below is a unique combination
❖ 4 bedrooms, 2 full baths, 2 half baths, 2-car drive under garage
❖ Basement foundation, drawings also include crawl space and slab foundations

Preserve memories in a shadow box rather than a photo album for a more interesting three-dimensional approach to family mementos.

Special features

❖ 1,925 total square feet of living area
❖ Energy efficient home with 2" x 6" exterior walls
❖ Balcony off eating area adds character
❖ Master bedroom has a dressing room, bath, walk-in closet and access to the utility room
❖ 3 bedrooms, 2 baths, 2-car side entry garage
❖ Crawl space foundation, drawings also include slab foundation

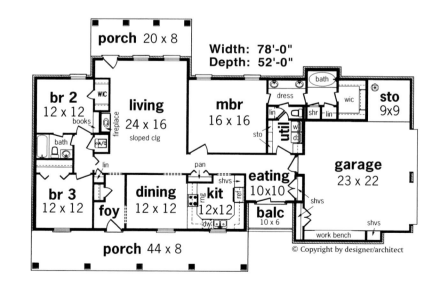

porch 20 x 8

Width: 78'-0"
Depth: 52'-0"

br 2
12 x 12

living
24 x 16
sloped clg

mbr
16 x 16

dress
bath
wic
sto
9x9

br 3
12 x 12

foy

dining
12 x 12

kit
12x12

eating
10x10

garage
23 x 22

balc
10 x 6

porch 44 x 8

work bench

© Copyright by designer/architect

To distress wooden furniture, first paint it a light color. When dry, rub a candle on areas where natural wear might occur, such as panel edges. Paint with a deeper color. When dry, rub the waxed areas with steel wool to expose patches of the base coat.

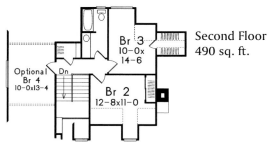

Second Floor
490 sq. ft.

Br 3
10-0x14-6

Optional
Br 4
10-0x13-4

Dn

Br 2
12-8x11-0

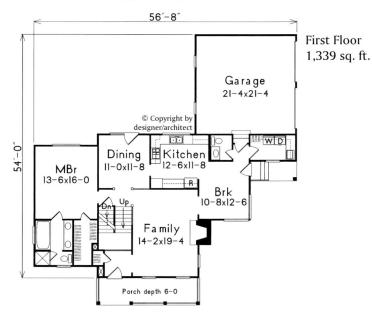

56'-8"

54'-0"

First Floor
1,339 sq. ft.

Garage
21-4x21-4

© Copyright by
designer/architect

Dining
11-0x11-8

Kitchen
12-6x11-8

W D

MBr
13-6x16-0

Brk
10-8x12-6

Dn Up

Family
14-2x19-4

R

Porch depth 6-0

Special features

- ❖ 1,829 total square feet of living area
- ❖ Entry foyer with coat closet opens to a large family room with fireplace
- ❖ Two second floor bedrooms share a full bath
- ❖ Optional bedroom #4 on the second floor has an additional 145 square feet of living area
- ❖ Cozy porch provides a convenient side entrance into the home
- ❖ 3 bedrooms, 2 1/2 baths, 2-car side entry garage
- ❖ Partial basement/crawl space foundation

Floor-to-ceiling mirrors definitely increase the sense of volume in a room. So, this style can be perfect when trying to make a room appear larger than its true size.

Special features

- ❖ 2,307 total square feet of living area
- ❖ A decorative arched window adds a dramatic touch to the front exterior as well as the interior of the living room
- ❖ A compact rear covered porch creates a functional place to grill or enter the home with groceries or packages
- ❖ Snuggle up to the fireplace in the cozy and casual family room
- ❖ 3 bedrooms, 2 1/2 baths, 2-car side entry garage
- ❖ Basement foundation

Second Floor
1,021 sq. ft.

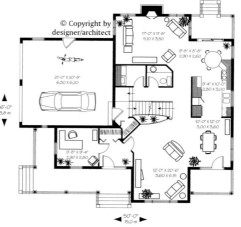

First Floor
1,286 sq. ft.

© Copyright by
designer/architect

Second Floor
707 sq. ft.

Br. 2
12⁰ x 12⁰

Br. 4
12⁰ x 11⁰

Br. 3
12⁰ x 11⁰

OPEN
TO
BELOW

PLANT SHELF

First Floor
1,570 sq. ft.

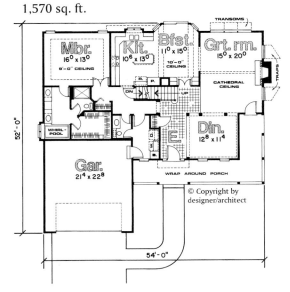

Mbr.
16⁰ x 13⁰

Kit.
10⁶ x 13⁰

Bfst.
11⁰ x 15⁰

Grt. rm.
15⁰ x 20⁰

Din.
12⁸ x 11⁴

Gar.
21⁴ x 22⁸

WRAP AROUND PORCH

© Copyright by
designer/architect

52' - 0"

54' - 0"

Special Features

- ❖ 2,277 total square feet of living area
- ❖ The two-story entry is impressive with a view to the formal dining room defined by decorative columns
- ❖ An efficient kitchen includes a pantry and work island with a nearby bayed breakfast area for easy meals
- ❖ Transom windows, a grand fireplace and cathedral ceiling create a stunning atmosphere in the great room
- ❖ 4 bedrooms, 2 1/2 baths, 2-car garage
- ❖ Basement foundation

Special features

- ❖ 1,595 total square feet of living area
- ❖ The front secondary bedroom could easily convert to a library or home office especially with its convenient double-door entry
- ❖ An expansive deck is enjoyed by the open great room and bayed dining area
- ❖ A walk-in closet organizes the master bedroom
- ❖ 3 bedrooms, 2 baths, 2-car garage
- ❖ Walk-out basement foundation

Using hairspray to clean a countertop, wall or wallpaper works fabulously. Lightly spray the hairspray onto the surface to treat and let it sit for a few seconds. Then, just wipe away. Repeat if necessary.

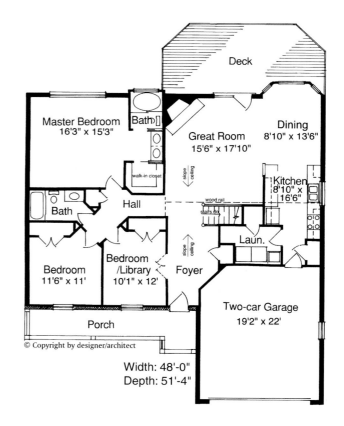

Width: 48'-0"
Depth: 51'-4"

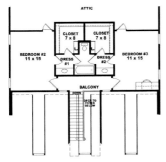

Second Floor
645 sq. ft.

First Floor
2,114 sq. ft.

© Copyright by
designer/architect

Special features

- ❖ 2,759 total square feet of living area
- ❖ Unique "friend's porch and entry" offers a casual place for relaxing as well as entering this home
- ❖ The combined kitchen, family and breakfast area is sure to be the main gathering space for the entire family
- ❖ The great room and formal dining room share a see-through fireplace creating a warm ambiance throughout
- ❖ 3 bedrooms, 3 1/2 baths, 2-car side entry garage
- ❖ Slab foundation

Adding a skylight is one of the quickest ways to make any room brighter, creating an open and airy feeling. Skylights produce a top-lit architectural drama that windows often can't match. Plus, dollar-for-dollar, they'll usually bring in more light than windows.

Special features

- 1,805 total square feet of living area
- Energy efficient home with 2" x 6" exterior walls
- Master bedroom forms its own wing
- Second floor bedrooms share a hall bath
- Large great room with fireplace blends into the formal dining room
- 3 bedrooms, 2 1/2 baths, 2-car side entry garage
- Basement foundation, drawings also include slab foundation

On open decks, water drains through gaps in the deck boards, but flooring on a covered porch fits tightly and therefore needs a pitch of at least ¼ inch per foot to shed water. Rot-resistant woods, stainless-steel fasteners, and protective coats of paint all help ensure that a porch will be able to withstand the elements.

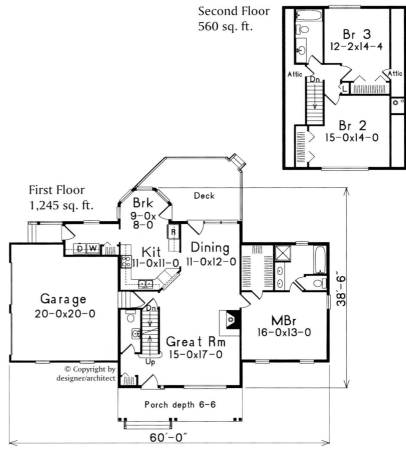

Second Floor
560 sq. ft.

Br 3
12-2x14-4

Attic

Attic

Dn

Br 2
15-0x14-0

First Floor
1,245 sq. ft.

Deck

Brk
9-0x 8-0

Kit
11-0x11-0

Dining
11-0x12-0

Garage
20-0x20-0

Dn

Great Rm
15-0x17-0

Up

MBr
16-0x13-0

38'-6"

© Copyright by designer/architect

Porch depth 6-6

60'-0"

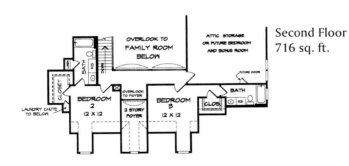

Second Floor
716 sq. ft.

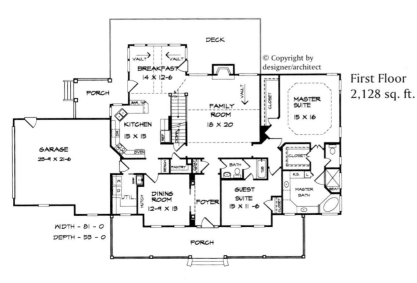

© Copyright by
designer/architect

First Floor
2,128 sq. ft.

WIDTH - 81 - 0
DEPTH - 53 - 0

Special features

- ❖ 2,844 total square feet of living area
- ❖ The U-shaped kitchen keeps everything within reach and easily serves the relaxing breakfast area or formal dining room
- ❖ The garage enters the home near the laundry workroom and the kitchen for easy unloading
- ❖ The master suite on the first floor and two bedrooms on the second floor enjoy private baths and walk-in closets
- ❖ 4 bedrooms, 4 baths, 2-car side entry garage
- ❖ Walk-out basement foundation

Big lawns are the American dream but are extremely labor-intensive. You can reduce yard maintenance by removing a portion of the lawn and replacing it with functional, yet relatively low-maintenance surfaces, such as wood decking, a brick patio or gravel paths.

Special features

- 2,092 total square feet of living area
- Dining room can used as an office or den
- Living room can be converted to a guest room
- Expansion loft is ideal for a playroom or a fourth bedroom and includes an additional 300 square feet of living area
- 3 bedrooms, 2 1/2 baths, 2-car garage
- Basement, crawl space or slab foundation, please specify when ordering

Hanging light and fan fixtures can be a nuisance when painting a ceiling. A simple solution to save the fixture from paint splatter without taking it down is to slip a large plastic trash bag over the light and seal it closed with a twist tie.

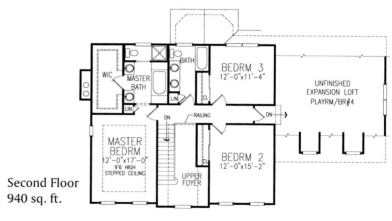

Second Floor
940 sq. ft.

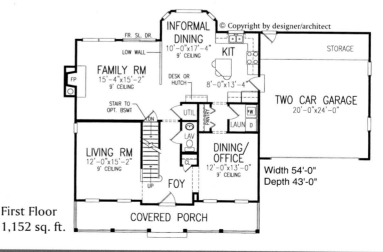

First Floor
1,152 sq. ft.

Width 54'-0"
Depth 43'-0"

© Copyright by designer/architect

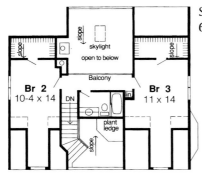

Second Floor
638 sq. ft.

Br 2
10-4 x 14

Br 3
11 x 14

skylight
open to below

Balcony

DN

plant
ledge

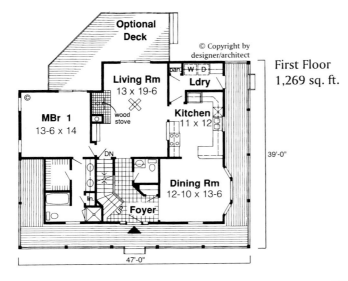

Optional Deck

© Copyright by designer/architect

Living Rm
13 x 19-6

Ldry

Kitchen
11 x 12

wood stove

MBr 1
13-6 x 14

DN

Dining Rm
12-10 x 13-6

Foyer

First Floor
1,269 sq. ft.

39'-0"

47'-0"

Special features

- ❖ 1,907 total square feet of living area
- ❖ Energy efficient home with 2" x 6" exterior walls
- ❖ Two-story living room is a surprise with skylight and balcony above
- ❖ Master bedroom is positioned on the first floor for convenience
- ❖ All bedrooms have walk-in closets
- ❖ 3 bedrooms, 2 1/2 baths
- ❖ Basement, crawl space or slab foundation, please specify when ordering

Special features

❖ 2,556 total square feet of living area

❖ A wrap-around porch that surrounds the entire exterior offers grand outdoor living space

❖ A bay window over the kitchen sink offers a wonderful place for growing plants, and windows on either side provide more light and added views of the porch

❖ The first floor master suite has its own set of French doors for outdoor access

❖ The bonus room over the garage has a separate entrance and offers an additional 482 square feet of living area

❖ 3 bedrooms, 2 1/2 baths, 2-car side entry garage

❖ Crawl space foundation

Second Floor
1,108 sq. ft.

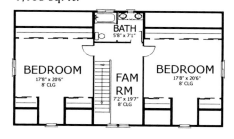

First Floor
1,448 sq. ft.

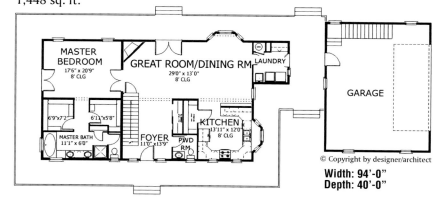

© Copyright by designer/architect

Width: 94'-0"
Depth: 40'-0"

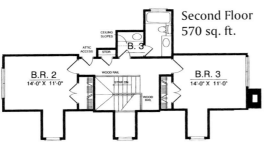

Second Floor
570 sq. ft.

CEILING SLOPES

ATTIC ACCESS

STOR.

B. 3

B.R. 2
14'-0" X 11'-0"

WOOD RAIL

STAIR DN.

B.R. 3
14'-0" X 11'-0"

WOOD RAIL

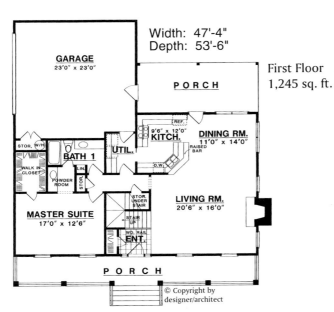

Width: 47'-4"
Depth: 53'-6"

First Floor
1,245 sq. ft.

GARAGE
23'0" x 23'0"

PORCH

REF.

KITCH.
9'6" x 12'0"

DINING RM.
11'0" x 14'0"
RAISED BAR

UTIL.

STOR. (W/H)

BATH 1

D.W.

WALK IN CLOSET

LIN.

POWDER ROOM

STOR.

MASTER SUITE
17'0" x 12'6"

STOR. UNDER STAIR

STAIR UP

LIVING RM.
20'6" x 16'0"

WD. RAIL   ENT.

PORCH

© Copyright by designer/architect

Special features

❖ 1,815 total square feet of living area
❖ Well-designed kitchen opens to the dining room and features a raised breakfast bar
❖ First floor master suite has a walk-in closet
❖ Front and back porches unite this home with the outdoors
❖ 3 bedrooms, 2 baths, 2-car side entry garage
❖ Basement, crawl space or slab foundation, please specify when ordering

To get extra life from any outdoor paint job, coat the bare wood with water repellent preservative before priming or painting it. Use only a repellent that is clearly labeled as paintable; some contain substances that will prevent paint from bonding properly.

Special features

- ❖ 2,685 total square feet of living area
- ❖ 9' ceilings throughout the first floor
- ❖ Vaulted master bedroom, isolated for privacy, boasts a magnificent bath with garden tub, separate shower and two closets
- ❖ The laundry area is located near the bedrooms for the ultimate in convenience
- ❖ Screened porch and morning room are both located off the well-planned kitchen
- ❖ 4 bedrooms, 2 1/2 baths, 3-car garage
- ❖ Basement foundation

Second Floor
1,325 sq. ft.

First Floor
1,360 sq. ft.

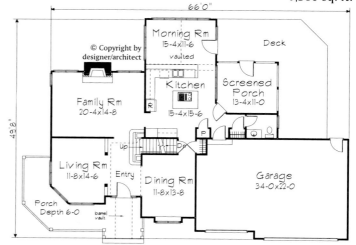

Second Floor 651 sq. ft.

BEDROOM 2
13'-0" x 11'-6"

BEDROOM 3
13'-0" x 11'-6"

OPEN BELOW

LOFT
13'-8" x 11'-0"

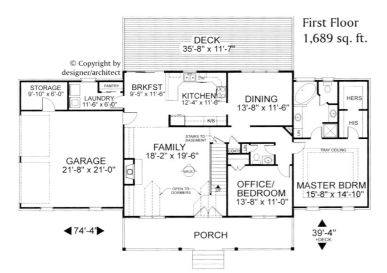

First Floor 1,689 sq. ft.

DECK
35'-8" x 11'-7"

© Copyright by designer/architect

STORAGE
9'-10" x 6'-0"

PANTRY

LAUNDRY
11'-6" x 6'-0"

BRKFST
9'-5" x 11'-6"

KITCHEN
12'-4" x 11'-6"

DINING
13'-8" x 11'-6"

HERS

HIS

STAIRS TO BASEMENT

GARAGE
21'-8" x 21'-0"

FAMILY
18'-2" x 19'-6"

VAULT

COATS

OPEN TO DORMERS

OFFICE/
BEDROOM
13'-8" x 11'-0"

TRAY CEILING

MASTER BDRM
15'-8" x 14'-10"

◀ 74'-4' ▶

39'-4"
+DECK

PORCH

Special features

❖ 2,340 total square feet of living area

❖ Large family room has a vaulted ceiling, bookcases and an entertainment center which surrounds a brick fireplace

❖ Highly functional kitchen is easily accessible from many parts of this home

❖ The second floor consists of two secondary bedrooms each having direct access to the bath

❖ The loft can serve as a recreation area or fifth bedroom

❖ 3 bedrooms, 2 1/2 baths, 2-car side entry garage

❖ Walk-out basement foundation

Special features

- ❖ 2,356 total square feet of living area
- ❖ Arched windows add elegance to the facade and shed an abundance of light into the dining and living rooms
- ❖ The kitchen includes a snack bar counter that opens to the relaxing breakfast area
- ❖ The secondary bedrooms share a Jack and Jill bath
- ❖ 4 bedrooms, 2 1/2 baths, 2-car side entry garage
- ❖ Slab foundation

Stucco has been used since the days of Renaissance Italy and was thought to give a building the appearance of being important. It was also used for weather and fire protection.

First Floor
1,516 sq. ft.

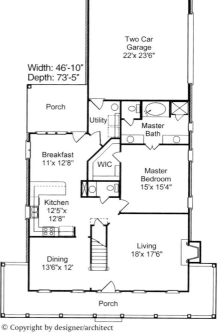

Second Floor
840 sq. ft.

© Copyright by designer/architect

Second Floor
1,063 sq. ft.

WINDOW SEAT

OPEN TO GRT.RM.

BR. #2
14'0" X 12'8"

BR. #3
14'0" X 12'0"

WINDOW SEAT

GUEST BR.
CATHEDRAL CEILING
12'0" X 14'8"

OPEN TO E.

PLANT LEDGE

UNHEATED STORAGE

OPTIONAL EXPANDED STORAGE

PORCH

KIT.
8'0" X 16'8"

NK.
10'4" X 13'0"

GRT.RM.
CATHEDRAL CEILING
19'8" X 26'0"

DIN.
12'0" X 15'0"

E.

MBR.
CATHEDRAL CEILING
14'0" X 18'8"

3 CAR GAR.
22'4" X 32'0"

PORCH

© Copyright by designer/architect

First Floor
2,109 sq. ft.

66'-0"

63'-0"

Special features

❖ 3,172 total square feet of living area
❖ Energy efficient home with 2" x 6" exterior walls
❖ The master bedroom is a luxurious retreat with two walk-in closets and a deluxe bath including a whirlpool tub in a bay window
❖ The kitchen features a cooktop island with eating bar and opens to the nook with access onto the rear porch
❖ Bedrooms #2 and #3 each feature a cozy window seat and share a Jack and Jill bath
❖ 4 bedrooms, 3 1/2 baths, 3-car side entry garage
❖ Basement foundation

Special features

- 1,578 total square feet of living area
- Wrap-around porch welcomes guests and enters the home at the living room and dining area
- The efficiently designed kitchen keeps everything close at hand
- The dining area and master bedroom enjoy sliding doors to the screened porch
- 3 bedrooms, 2 1/2 baths
- Pier foundation

Use newspapers to clean the windows of your house. It's a lot cheaper than paper towels, and the ink is a polishing agent that won't streak.

Second Floor
498 sq. ft.

BEDROOM #2
(11'4"x10'0")

BEDROOM #3
(11'8"x10'0")

© Copyright by designer/architect

SCREENED PORCH
(10'0"x10'0")

MASTER BEDROOM
(16'4"x12'0")

DINING AREA
(10'0"x14'8")

KITCHEN
(12'8"x9'0")

LAUNDRY

LIVING ROOM
(18'0"x13'8")

FRONT WRAP AROUND PORCH

Width: 36'-0"
Depth: 43'-8"

First Floor
1,080 sq. ft.

Second Floor
899 sq. ft.

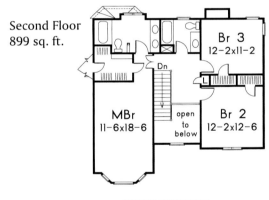

First Floor
1,023 sq. ft.

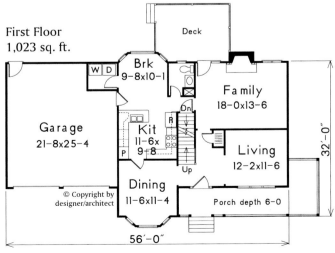

© Copyright by
designer/architect

Special features

- ❖ 1,922 total square feet of living area
- ❖ Varied front elevation features numerous accents
- ❖ Master bedroom suite is well-secluded with a double-door entry and private bath
- ❖ Formal living and dining rooms located off the entry
- ❖ 3 bedrooms, 2 1/2 baths, 2-car garage
- ❖ Basement foundation

To avoid cluttering countertops, store small appliances such as blenders and mixers or spices and cooking items out of sight keeping the countertops clean. It will make your kitchen seem a lot more spacious.

Special features

- ❖ 2,071 total square feet of living area
- ❖ Vaulted family room features a cozy fireplace
- ❖ Sunny breakfast room is brightened by triple windows
- ❖ Second floor includes two bedrooms, a bath and an unfinished area that offers an additional 149 square feet of living area
- ❖ 3 bedrooms, 2 1/2 baths, 2-car side entry garage
- ❖ Slab or crawl space foundation, please specify when ordering

Reconfigure a porch, sunroom or large living area for semi-outdoor living by installing ceiling fans, screens and natural stone floors that will weather. Outfit garden-style furnishings with weather-resistant cushions and pillows.

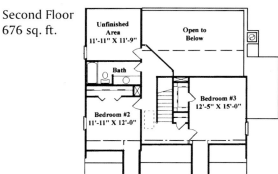

Second Floor
676 sq. ft.

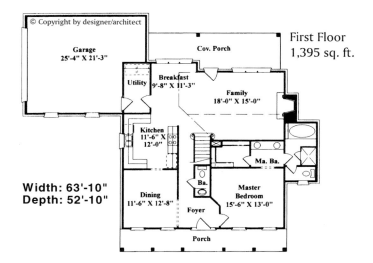

First Floor
1,395 sq. ft.

Width: 63'-10"
Depth: 52'-10"

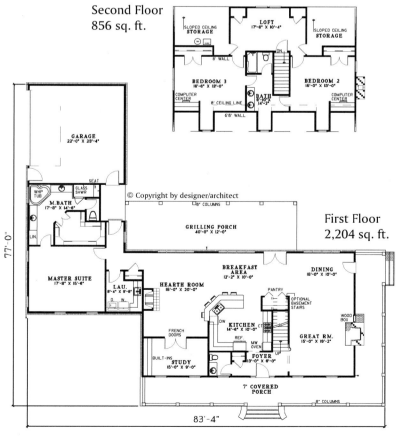

Second Floor
856 sq. ft.

© Copyright by designer/architect

First Floor
2,204 sq. ft.

Special features

- ❖ 3,060 total square feet of living area
- ❖ French doors in the hearth room lead into a private study with built-in shelves
- ❖ Kitchen includes a large wrap-around style eating counter capable of serving five
- ❖ Breakfast area has access onto a large covered grilling porch
- ❖ 3 bedrooms, 2 1/2 baths, 2-car side entry garage
- ❖ Crawl space or slab foundation, please specify when ordering

When designing the kitchen, locate the preparation area between the refrigerator and the sink. Place any ingredients, mixing equipment or bowls here for best usage.

Special features

- 1,124 total square feet of living area
- Energy efficient home with 2" x 6" exterior walls
- Wrap-around porch creates an outdoor living area
- Large dining area easily accommodates extra guests
- Sunken family room becomes a cozy retreat
- 2 bedrooms, 1 bath, 1-car garage
- Basement foundation

Engineered wood siding is a lot easier and less costly to install than real wood siding. It's lighter in weight and includes advancements making it easier to install. Engineered wood can be bought pre-primed, ready to paint or pre-finished in a number of options which reduces field and labor costs.

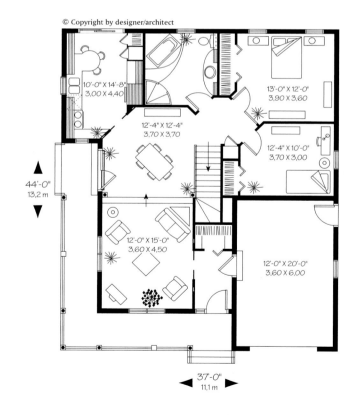

© Copyright by designer/architect

10'-0" X 14'-8"
3,00 X 4,40

12'-4" X 12'-4"
3,70 X 3,70

13'-0" X 12'-0"
3,90 X 3,60

12'-4" X 10'-0"
3,70 X 3,00

12'-0" X 15'-0"
3,60 X 4,50

12'-0" X 20'-0"
3,60 X 6,00

44'-0"
13,2 m

37'-0"
11,1 m

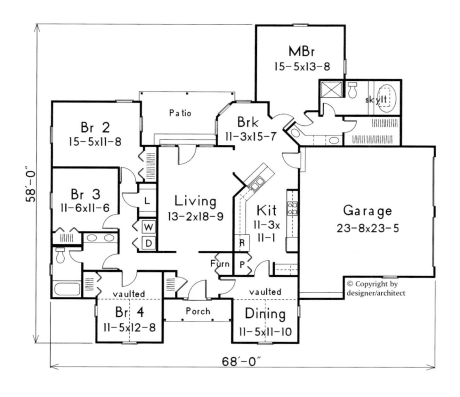

Special features

- 2,080 total square feet of living area
- Combined design elements create a unique facade
- Foyer leads into a large living room with a direct view of the patio
- Master bedroom includes spacious bath with garden tub, separate shower, walk-in closet and dressing area
- 2" x 6" exterior walls available, please order plan #597-001D-0126
- 4 bedrooms, 2 baths, 2-car side entry garage
- Crawl space foundation, drawings also include basement and slab foundations

The cheapest roofing materials are asphalt and fiberglass shingles. They are relatively easy to install. The heavier the shingle the better. Manufacturers guarantee their products, some types for 15 years and some for 25 years.

Special features

❖ 2,508 total square feet of living area

❖ Energy efficient home with 2" x 6" exterior walls

❖ Two-story foyer and family room add to the spaciousness of this home

❖ The kitchen opens to the bayed nook and expansive family room

❖ The master bedroom features private access onto the rear deck and a deluxe bath with a whirlpool tub and walk-in closet

❖ The bonus room above the garage has an additional 384 square feet of living area

❖ 3 bedrooms, 2 1/2 baths, 2-car side entry garage

❖ Basement or walk-out basement foundation, please specify when ordering

Second Floor
709 sq. ft.

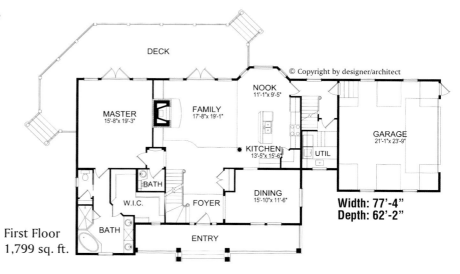

First Floor
1,799 sq. ft.

© Copyright by designer/architect

Width: 77'-4"
Depth: 62'-2"

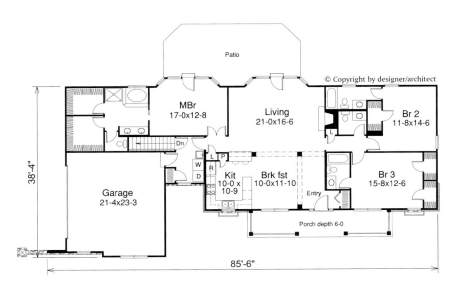

Special features

- ❖ 1,991 total square feet of living area
- ❖ A large porch with roof dormers and flanking stonework creates a distinctive country appeal
- ❖ The highly functional U-shaped kitchen is open to the dining and living rooms defined by a colonnade
- ❖ Large bay windows are enjoyed by both the living room and master bedroom
- ❖ Every bedroom features spacious walk-in closets and their own private bath
- ❖ 3 bedrooms, 3 1/2 baths, 2-car side entry garage
- ❖ Basement foundation

When painting interior walls, you'll eliminate a lot of backbreaking labor by mounting your roller on an extension pole. You won't have to bend over to load the roller, and you won't have to spend as much time on a ladder. And by standing away from the wall as you work, it is easier to see any missed areas.

Special features

❖ 1,554 total square feet of living area

❖ Bay-shaped kitchen has enough space for dining as well as a convenient closet for the washer and dryer

❖ A half wall divides the dining and living rooms creating privacy while maintaining a feeling of openness

❖ A cheerful sun room graces the front entry

❖ 3 bedrooms, 2 1/2 baths, 2-car garage

❖ Basement, crawl space or slab foundation, please specify when ordering

Choose a family-friendly paint type such as a satin or semigloss finish. A flat finish is not as family-friendly because it doesn't wipe clean as easily. Stick to high gloss for door frames where little hands touch frequently.

Second Floor
748 sq. ft.

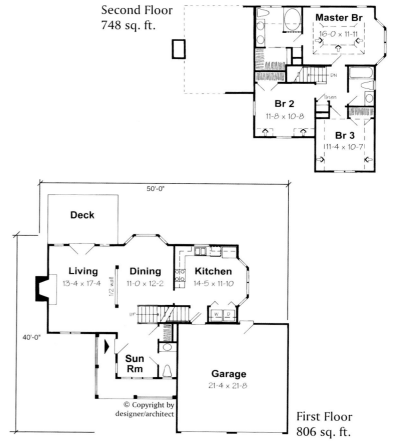

First Floor
806 sq. ft.

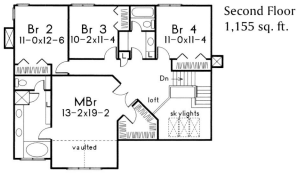

Second Floor
1,155 sq. ft.

Br 2
11-0x12-6

Br 3
10-2x11-4

Br 4
11-0x11-4

MBr
13-2x19-2

loft

Dn

skylights

vaulted

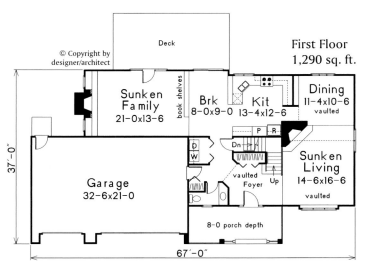

Deck

© Copyright by
designer/architect

Sunken
Family
21-0x13-6

book shelves

Brk
8-0x9-0

Kit
13-4x12-6

Dining
11-4x10-6
vaulted

P R

Dn

Up

Sunken
Living
14-6x16-6

vaulted

vaulted
Foyer

Garage
32-6x21-0

37'-0"

8-0 porch depth

67'-0"

First Floor
1,290 sq. ft.

Special features

- ❖ 2,445 total square feet of living area
- ❖ Sunken living room has a corner fireplace, vaulted ceiling and is adjacent to the dining room for entertaining large groups
- ❖ Large vaulted open foyer with triple skylights provides an especially bright entry
- ❖ Loft area overlooks foyer and features a decorative display area
- ❖ Bedrooms are located on the second floor for privacy and convenience, with a vaulted ceiling in the master bedroom
- ❖ 4 bedrooms, 2 1/2 baths, 3-car garage
- ❖ Basement foundation

Special features

- 1,894 total square feet of living area
- Decorative columns define the formal dining room from the foyer
- A charming breakfast nook is an enchanting place to start the day
- The bedrooms are situated next to each other and away from the main living areas to ensure privacy
- 3 bedrooms, 2 1/2 baths, 2-car side entry garage
- Crawl space, basement or slab foundation, please specify when ordering

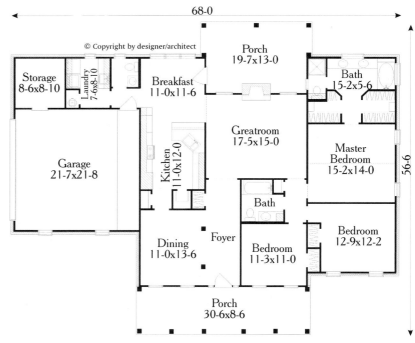

© Copyright by designer/architect

68-0

56-6

Porch
19-7x13-0

Storage
8-6x8-10

Laundry
7-6x8-10

Breakfast
11-0x11-6

Bath
15-2x5-6

Garage
21-7x21-8

Kitchen
11-0x12-0

Greatroom
17-5x15-0

Master Bedroom
15-2x14-0

Bath

Dining
11-0x13-6

Foyer

Bedroom
11-3x11-0

Bedroom
12-9x12-2

Porch
30-6x8-6

Dress Up
Your Outdoor Setting

One trademark of a Country home is a sprawling porch with grand outdoor living spaces. With an abundance of outdoor fabrics available today, you can create a wonderful retreat and maintain your Country style.

Imagine sitting in your favorite comfy chair with a good book, or while you chat with your friends. Prop your feet up on an ottoman. If there's a slight chill in the air, cover up with a throw. Relax.

Now imagine that you're outside. Does your vision change? If so, it doesn't have to anymore.

Gone are the days of outfitting your outdoor setting with only vinyl cushions and plastic chairs. Using beautiful, plush fabrics is one of the easiest ways to bring comfort and style to your outdoor setting, and will blur the line between your indoors and outdoors. And now, there's no need to worry about the gorgeous fabrics being ruined with the effects of Mother Nature.

Many companies today offer inspiring fabrics to add texture and comfort to your outdoor setting that are designed to weather any storm, and any amount of the sun's harsh rays. Created with revolutionary technology, these fabrics offer UV protection to resist fading, and anti-bacterial and anti-microbial characteristics to prevent the growth of mildew and fungi. And along with being stain-resistant, these new fabrics are much more durable than their cotton and canvas predecessors.

Sunbrella® Fabrics, well known for its quality and durability with awnings, boats and convertibles, has now become a leader in the outdoor furniture industry.

"Sunbrella delivers a complete package of color, design, durability, fade resistance and ease of cleaning," explains Harry Gobble, director of marketing for Glen Raven Custom Fabrics, the maker of Sunbrella Fabrics.

And with a 3-year warranty, you can rest easy the next time Mother Nature decides to mistreat your furniture.

At Left, Perennials Fabrics offer sophisticated style with an abundance of different fabric colors and textures. Visit www.perennialsfabrics.com for more information.

At Right, Sunbrella Fabrics can be found in a wide array of Country designs perfect to decorate any home. Visit www.sunbrella.com for more information.

Perennials™ Outdoor Fabrics and Weatherwize® are two additional companies that also utilize methods to create high-performance outdoor fabrics and back their promise with a 3-year warranty as well. With vivid, trendy hues, and lavish textures, it is easy to showcase your own personal style as you decorate your backyard retreat.

"Using fabrics that are 100% solution dyed acrylic and soil-, mildew-, and UV-resistant, there is never a need to sacrifice style for durability," says Nicole Gill-Ottinger of NGO Public Relations, a firm that represents Perennials Fabrics.

Another company adding style and comfort to outdoor living spaces is Laurie Bell. Founder Laurie Jenkins provides "high-tech, fashion-forward outdoor accessories that weather the storms of wear and tear as well as the demands of today's fashionistas."

At www.lauriebell.com you can find exciting patterns for pillows of all sizes, throws, and even ottomans. All covered with fabric that utilizes "a new chemistry that allows for almost complete saturation of the fabric" to prevent fading.

Another amazing characteristic of all these fabrics is that they are easy to clean. If any spills happen, just blot with mild soap and warm water.

With the exceptional array of outdoor fabrics available today, you and your family will be able to decorate your outdoor spaces with the same sophistication and style as any other room.

Second Floor
761 sq. ft.

Width: 82'-8"
Depth: 44'-4"

First Floor
1,891 sq. ft.

© Copyright by designer/architect

Special features

❖ 2,652 total square feet of living area
❖ Energy efficient home with 2" x 6" exterior walls
❖ This gorgeous country colonial offers a full front covered porch that has space for relaxing and taking in the great outdoors
❖ This beautiful design features all the amenities for comfortable family living and luxuries such as the first floor master bedroom and entire walls of windows
❖ 3 bedrooms, 3 baths, 3-car side entry garage
❖ Walk-out basement foundation

Special features

- ❖ 1,609 total square feet of living area
- ❖ The laundry area is adjacent to the kitchen for convenience
- ❖ Two storage areas; one can be accessed from the outdoors and the other from the garage
- ❖ Eating bar overlooks from kitchen into dining area
- ❖ 3 bedrooms, 2 baths, 2-car side entry garage
- ❖ Slab foundation

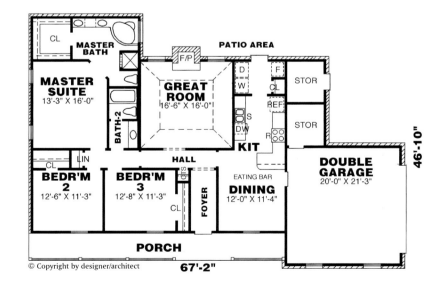

© Copyright by designer/architect

Painting over mildew doesn't mean it's gone - the sturdy spores are quite capable of growing right through paint film. Shady spots outdoors are particularly susceptible to this fungal pest. To kill mildew, wash it with a mixture of 1 part household bleach to 3 parts water. Then rinse the area thoroughly.

Second Floor
863 sq. ft.

© Copyright by designer/architect

Width: 68'-0"
Depth: 50'-0"

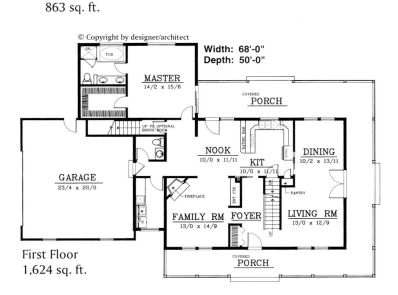

First Floor
1,624 sq. ft.

Special features

- ❖ 2,487 total square feet of living area
- ❖ Energy efficient home with 2" x 6" exterior walls
- ❖ Three second floor bedrooms and a convenient study loft share a hall bath
- ❖ Dining and living rooms feature French doors leading to a covered wrap-around porch
- ❖ First floor living spaces offer formal dining as well as a casual nook and kitchen with eating bar and pantry
- ❖ Second floor bonus room has an additional 338 square feet of living area
- ❖ 4 bedrooms, 2 1/2 baths, 2-car side entry garage
- ❖ Basement foundation

Special features

- 2,816 total square feet of living area
- A large wrap-around porch adds charming curb appeal to the front facade
- Bright and cheerful, the bayed breakfast room is a great way to start the day
- The master bath is large in size and features a whirlpool tub as the main focal point
- Insulated concrete formed exterior walls
- 3 bedrooms, 2 1/2 baths, 3-car garage
- Basement foundation

Pictures and ornaments give traditional bathrooms an inviting feel, but make sure any treasured items will tolerate a steamy atmosphere. You can protect paintings or photos by framing them behind glass or Lucite.

Second Floor
1,100 sq. ft.

BR. #2
11/6X11/4

M. BR.
15/10X17/2
COFFERED
CEILING

OPEN TO
ENTRY

BR. #3
10/5X10/7

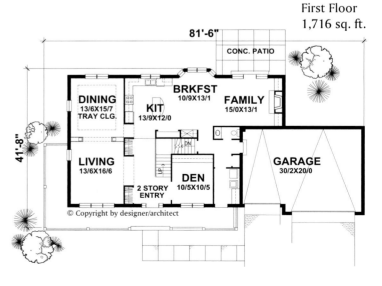

First Floor
1,716 sq. ft.

81'-6"

41'-8"

CONC. PATIO

DINING
13/6X15/7
TRAY CLG.

BRKFST
10/9X13/1

KIT
13/9X12/0

FAMILY
15/0X13/1

LIVING
13/6X16/6

DEN
10/5X10/5

GARAGE
30/2X20/0

2 STORY
ENTRY

© Copyright by designer/architect

Second Floor
574 sq. ft.

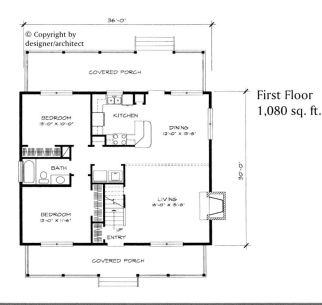

First Floor
1,080 sq. ft.

© Copyright by
designer/architect

Special features

- ❖ 1,654 total square feet of living area
- ❖ This country inspired home has plenty of quality space for family living
- ❖ A large extended counter in the kitchen creates instant dining space
- ❖ The second floor consists of a bedroom, full bath and a private loft
- ❖ 3 bedrooms, 2 baths
- ❖ Slab foundation

Plywood is a wonderful material, but the edges are unsightly. To hide them you can plan the project so the edges won't show in the finished item. Cover them with thin wood strips, or with veneer tape – thin strips of wood in flexible rolls.

Special features

- ❖ 2,002 total square feet of living area
- ❖ Energy efficient home with 2" x 6" exterior walls
- ❖ High ceilings throughout the house give it a feeling of spaciousness
- ❖ The gas fireplace warms the great room and is flanked by built-in cabinets
- ❖ The covered porch or patio is connected to the breakfast area, perfect for bringing meals outside
- ❖ 3 bedrooms, 2 baths, 2-car side entry garage
- ❖ Slab, crawl space or basement foundation, please specify when ordering

Duct tape is probably one of mankind's most useful inventions. Keep at least two rolls on hand, but don't skimp on quality. Inexpensive duct tape is not a good buy – the adhesive will be gummy and the tape may slip.

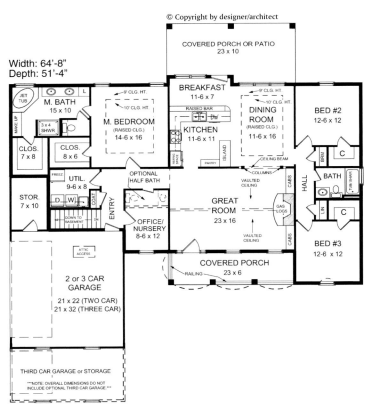

© Copyright by designer/architect

Width: 64'-8"
Depth: 51'-4"

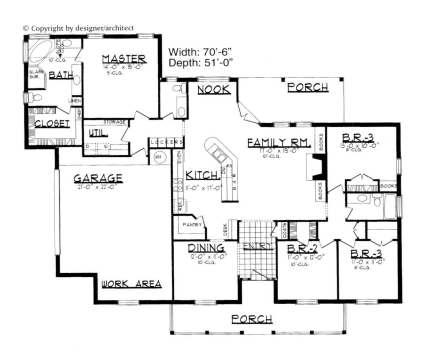

© Copyright by designer/architect

Width: 70'-6"
Depth: 51'-0"

Special features

- ❖ 2,164 total square feet of living area
- ❖ The charming front porch and dormers add a country touch to this classic home
- ❖ The stylish family room features a 10' ceiling and a fireplace flanked by built-in bookshelves
- ❖ A formal dining room is perfect for entertaining with the kitchen and entry nearby
- ❖ 4 bedrooms, 2 1/2 baths, 2-car side entry garage
- ❖ Slab foundation

An all brick home has many advantages. While easy to maintain, it offers beauty and a variety of colors perfect for creative design choices while building.

Special features

- ❖ 2,760 total square feet of living area
- ❖ Energy efficient home with 2" x 6" exterior walls
- ❖ Open formal living and dining areas combine creating a nice space for entertaining
- ❖ Cozy corner fireplace in the family room warms the area along with the adjacent breakfast nook
- ❖ Bonus room on the second floor is included in the square footage
- ❖ 4 bedrooms, 2 1/2 baths, 2-car side entry garage
- ❖ Crawl space foundation

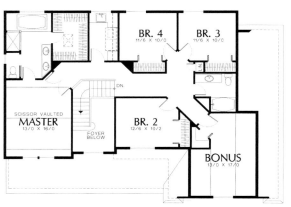

Second Floor
1,443 sq. ft.

© Copyright by designer/architect

First Floor
1,317 sq. ft.

Second Floor
952 sq. ft.

MBr
16-0x13-8

Br 3
12-4x10-0

Dn

open to below

Br 2
12-4x12-7

First Floor
1,228 sq. ft.

50'-0"

Family
16-2x17-0

vaulted

Dinette
9-0x12-2

Kit
10-0x12-2

Dining
11-3x15-0

L O

P R

W D

Living
12-0x15-6

40'-0"

Dn

Garage
21-9x21-8

Foyer

Up

Porch
25-0x5-0

© Copyright by designer/architect

Special features

- ❖ 2,180 total square feet of living area
- ❖ Energy efficient home with 2" x 6" exterior walls
- ❖ Informal dinette and formal dining area flank the kitchen
- ❖ The grand fireplace is the focal point in the vaulted family room
- ❖ Master bedroom includes a bath with a walk-in closet, a shower and corner garden tub
- ❖ 3 bedrooms, 2 1/2 baths, 2-car garage
- ❖ Basement foundation

Special features

- 2,129 total square feet of living area
- Energy efficient home with 2" x 6" exterior walls
- Home office has a double-door entry and is secluded from other living areas
- Corner fireplace in living area is a nice focal point
- Bonus room above the garage has an additional 407 square feet of living area
- 3 bedrooms, 2 1/2 baths, 2-car side entry garage
- Basement foundation

Heating and cooling account for 50% to 70% of the energy used in the home. Lighting, appliances, and everything else account for 10% to 30% of the energy used. Turning lights and appliances off when they are not in use, and reducing the amount of energy needed for heating and cooling will save even more.

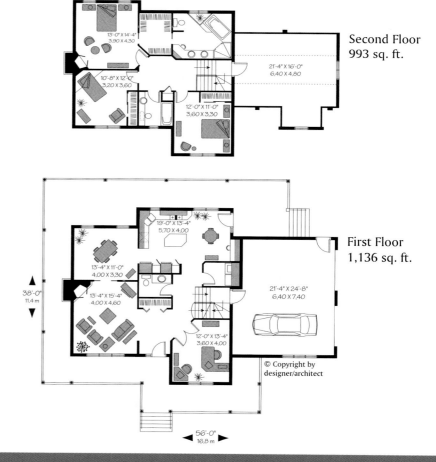

Second Floor
993 sq. ft.

First Floor
1,136 sq. ft.

© Copyright by designer/architect

Second Floor
925 sq. ft.

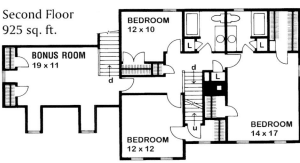

BEDROOM
12 x 10

BONUS ROOM
19 x 11

BEDROOM
12 x 12

BEDROOM
14 x 17

Special features

* 1,925 total square feet of living area
* Spacious foyer is flanked by the formal dining and living rooms
* The centrally located kitchen serves the dining room and breakfast nook with ease
* Expansive master bedroom enjoys a large walk-in closet and full private bath
* The bonus room above the garage has an additional 209 square feet of living area
* 3 bedrooms, 2 1/2 baths, 2-car garage
* Crawl space foundation

Heat loss through windows represents a significant amount of most heating bills. In home designs that feature multiple or large windows like this one, it is important to caulk cracks, install clear plastic film to the window trim inside the house or decorate windows for efficiency.

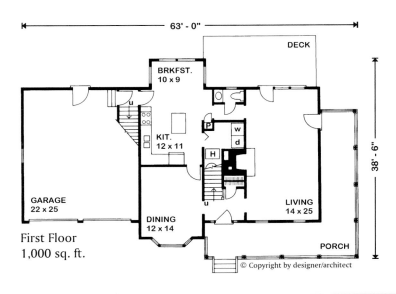

63' - 0"

DECK

BRKFST.
10 x 9

KIT.
12 x 11

38' - 6"

GARAGE
22 x 25

LIVING
14 x 25

DINING
12 x 14

First Floor
1,000 sq. ft.

PORCH

© Copyright by designer/architect

Special features

❖ 2,464 total square feet of living area

❖ Energy efficient home with 2" x 6" exterior walls

❖ The dining room is perfect for hosting elegant meals

❖ Master bedroom is oversized and offers a large shower and a separate dressing area

❖ The family room features a second fireplace and is open to the spacious country kitchen

❖ 4 bedrooms, 2 1/2 baths, 2-car garage

❖ Basement foundation

The key to a tidy kitchen is efficient storage. Make the most of cupboard space by fixing racks and shelves inside your units – most kitchen suppliers offer a range of clever interior fittings to help you get organized.

Second Floor
1,176 sq. ft.

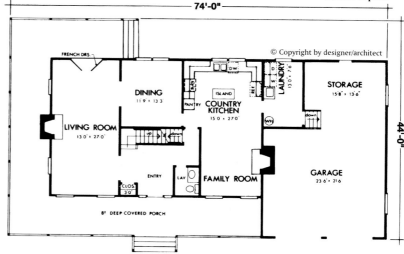

First Floor
1,288 sq. ft.

© Copyright by designer/architect

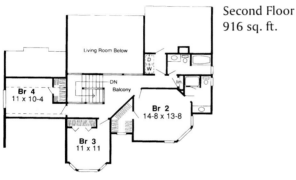

Second Floor
916 sq. ft.

Living Room Below

Br 4
11 x 10-4

DN
Balcony

lin.

Br 2
14-8 x 13-8

Br 3
11 x 11

Special features

❖ 2,541 total square feet of living area
❖ Energy efficient home with 2" x 6" exterior walls
❖ The living room is full of natural light shining down from the three skylights above
❖ The front porch opens to the foyer and wraps around to the breakfast room
❖ 4 bedrooms, 3 1/2 baths, 2-car side entry garage
❖ Basement foundation

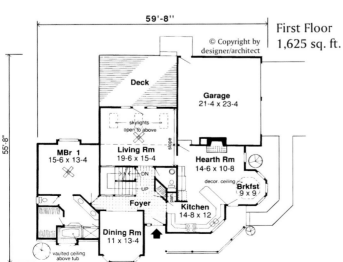

59'-8''

© Copyright by
designer/architect

First Floor
1,625 sq. ft.

Deck

Garage
21-4 x 23-4

55'-8"

skylights
open to above

slope

MBr 1
15-6 x 13-4

Living Rm
19-6 x 15-4

Hearth Rm
14-6 x 10-8

DN
UP

decor. ceiling

Brkfst
9 x 9

Foyer

Kitchen
14-8 x 12

Dining Rm
11 x 13-4

vaulted ceiling
above tub

Special features

- 1,409 total square feet of living area
- A trio of decorative dormers and a wide covered front porch give this charming one-story cottage a country flavor
- The spacious living room with its cozy fireplace leads into the dining room easily served by an efficient kitchen
- The deluxe master suite has a cathedral ceiling, sliding glass doors to a private terrace, a large walk-in closet and a private bath with whirlpool tub
- 3 bedrooms, 2 baths, optional 2-car garage
- Slab, crawl space or basement foundation, please specify when ordering

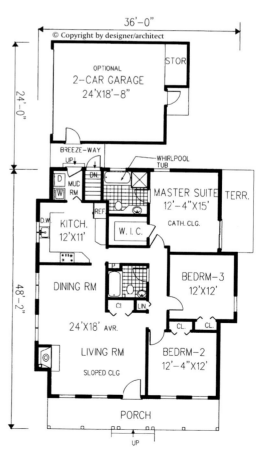

© Copyright by designer/architect

Second Floor
863 sq. ft.

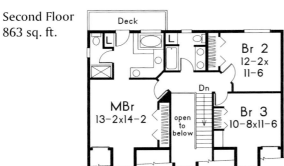

Special features

* 1,921 total square feet of living area
* Energy efficient home with 2" x 6" exterior walls
* Sunken family room includes a built-in entertainment center and coffered ceiling
* Sunken formal living room features a coffered ceiling
* Master bedroom dressing area has double sinks, spa tub, shower and French door to private deck
* Large front porch adds to home's appeal
* 3 bedrooms, 2 1/2 baths, 2-car garage
* Basement foundation

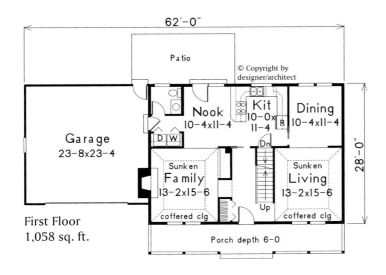

First Floor
1,058 sq. ft.

Special features

- ❖ 1,438 total square feet of living area
- ❖ A screened porch offers a perfect space for entertaining while enjoying the outdoors
- ❖ The open kitchen/dining area features an island with snack bar, pantry and bayed nook
- ❖ The spacious great room features a grand fireplace
- ❖ One of the secondary bedrooms could readily be converted to a home office
- ❖ 3 bedrooms, 1 bath
- ❖ Slab or crawl space foundation, please specify when ordering

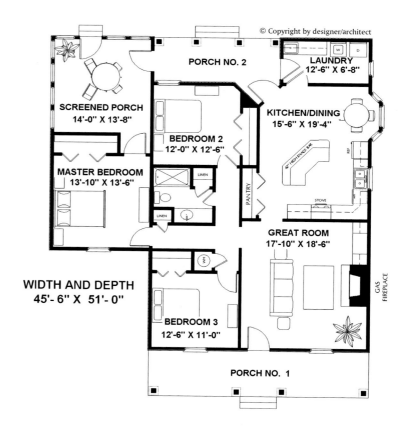

© Copyright by designer/architect

PORCH NO. 2

LAUNDRY
12'-6" X 6'-8"

SCREENED PORCH
14'-0" X 13'-8"

KITCHEN/DINING
15'-6" X 19'-4"

BEDROOM 2
12'-0" X 12'-6"

PANTRY

MASTER BEDROOM
13'-10" X 13'-6"

LINEN

LINEN

STOVE

GREAT ROOM
17'-10" X 18'-6"

**WIDTH AND DEPTH
45'- 6" X 51'- 0"**

GAS FIREPLACE

BEDROOM 3
12'-6" X 11'-0"

PORCH NO. 1

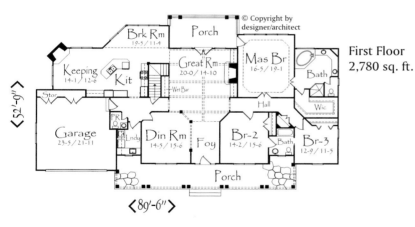

© Copyright by designer/architect

First Floor
2,780 sq. ft.

Brk Rm 19-5 / 11-4
Porch
Keeping 14-1 / 12-6
Kit
Great Rm 20-0 / 14-10
Mas Br 16-5 / 19-1
Bath
Wet Bar
Stor
Garage 23-5 / 21-11
Hall
Wic
Din Rm 14-5 / 15-6
Foy
Br-2 14-2 / 15-6
Bath
Br-3 12-9 / 11-5
Lndy
PR
Porch

< 52'-0" >
< 89'-6" >

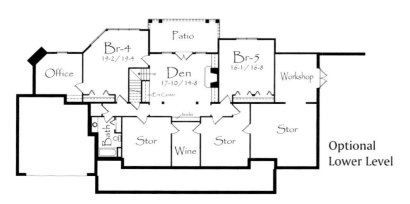

Patio
Br-4 19-2 / 19-4
Office
Den 17-10 / 14-8
Br-5 16-1 / 16-8
Workshop
Ent Center
books
Bath
Stor
Wine
Stor
Stor

Optional
Lower Level

Special features

❖ 2,780 total square feet of living area

❖ A beamed ceiling, grand fireplace, wet bar and porch access in the great room accent this rustic retreat

❖ The kitchen, breakfast and keeping rooms combine for a cozy gathering space

❖ The optional lower level offers an additional 1,347 square feet of living area and has space for two bedrooms, a full bath and an abundance of storage including a wine cellar

❖ 3 bedrooms, 2 1/2 baths, 2-car garage

❖ Walk-out basement foundation

When organizing the linen closets, cedar blocks help deter moths when placed on shelves where linens are stored. In addition, lavender sachets are a wise choice because they deter pests like moths from damaging fine linens.

Special features

- ❖ 2,147 total square feet of living area
- ❖ Living and dining rooms are adjacent to the entry foyer for easy access
- ❖ The kitchen is conveniently located next to the sunny breakfast nook
- ❖ Master bedroom includes a large walk-in closet and luxurious bath
- ❖ The breakfast area offers easy access to the deck
- ❖ 4 bedrooms, 2 1/2 baths, 2-car garage
- ❖ Basement foundation

Adding a second rod to a closet doubles space easily and inexpensively.

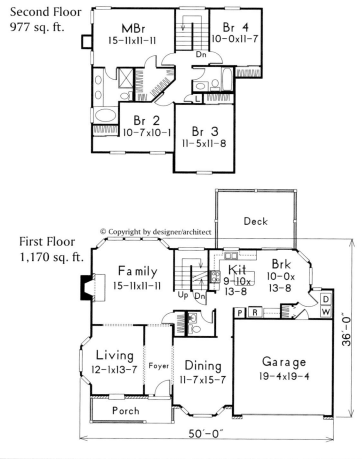

Second Floor
977 sq. ft.

MBr
15-11x11-11

Br 4
10-0x11-7

Dn

Br 2
10-7x10-1

Br 3
11-5x11-8

© Copyright by designer/architect

First Floor
1,170 sq. ft.

Deck

Family
15-11x11-11

Kit
9-10x
13-8

Brk
10-0x
13-8

Up Dn

P R

D
W

Living
12-1x13-7

Foyer

Dining
11-7x15-7

Garage
19-4x19-4

Porch

36'-0"

50'-0"

© Copyright by designer/architect

9'-0" X 10'-0"
2,70 X 3,00

9'-0" X 10'-0"
2,70 X 3,00

8'-4" X 10'-0"
2,50 X 3,00

9'-4" X 10'-4"
2,80 X 3,10

26'-4"
7,9 m

11'-0" X 12'-0"
3,30 X 3,60

12'-0" X 14'-4"
3,60 X 4,30

40'-0"
12,0 m

Special features

- ❖ 1,053 total square feet of living area
- ❖ Energy efficient home with 2" x 6" exterior walls
- ❖ Spacious kitchen and dining room
- ❖ Roomy bath includes an oversized tub
- ❖ Entry has a handy coat closet
- ❖ 3 bedrooms, 1 bath
- ❖ Basement foundation

Two laundry room necessities include an ironing board and folding table which can easily be hung on walls or doors and be folded down as needed. Don't forget these two features when designing your home.

Special features

* 2,598 total square feet of living area
* Energy efficient home with 2" x 6" exterior walls
* The large front porch opens to an elegant foyer flanked by formal living and dining rooms
* Bedrooms #3 and #4 each have their own sitting areas while sharing a common study area
* 4 bedrooms, 3 1/2 baths, 2-car side entry garage
* Crawl space foundation, drawings also include basement foundation

Vinyl decking costs more than wood decking. Synthetic decks or plastic decks are low maintenance and for the person who thinks sealing a deck is a hassle. But, in the long run, a wood deck might actually save you money.

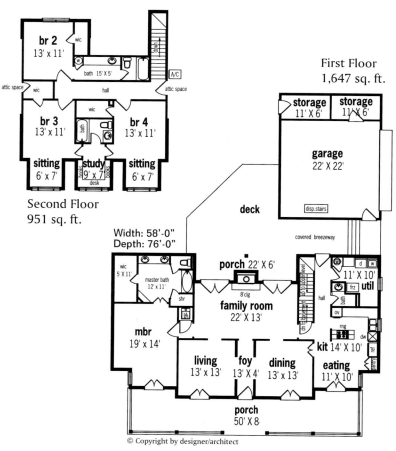

Second Floor
951 sq. ft.

First Floor
1,647 sq. ft.

Width: 58'-0"
Depth: 76'-0"

© Copyright by designer/architect

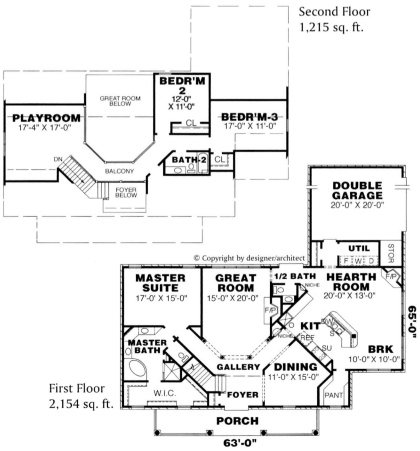

Second Floor
1,215 sq. ft.

GREAT ROOM BELOW

PLAYROOM
17'-4" X 17'-0"

BEDR'M 2
12'-0" X 11'-0"

CL

BEDR'M-3
17'-0" X 11'-0"

BATH-2 CL

DN

BALCONY

FOYER BELOW

© Copyright by designer/architect

DOUBLE GARAGE
20'-0" X 20'-0"

UTIL
F W D

STOR

MASTER SUITE
17'-0" X 15'-0"

GREAT ROOM
15'-0" X 20'-0"

1/2 BATH
NICHE

HEARTH ROOM
20'-0" X 13'-0"

F/P

MASTER BATH

F/P

KIT
REF

NICHE

D W S

SU

BRK
10'-0" X 10'-0"

65'-0"

GALLERY

DINING
11'-0" X 15'-0"

W.I.C.

FOYER

PANT

First Floor
2,154 sq. ft.

PORCH

63'-0"

Special features

- ❖ 3,369 total square feet of living area
- ❖ Large playroom overlooks to great room below and makes a great casual family area
- ❖ Extra storage is located in the garage
- ❖ Well-planned hearth room and kitchen are open and airy
- ❖ Foyer flows into unique diagonal gallery area creating a dramatic entrance into the great room
- ❖ 3 bedrooms, 2 1/2 baths, 2-car side entry garage
- ❖ Slab foundation

When using caulk to seal the joint between the wall tile and a bathtub, fill the tub with water first. The weight of the water will open the gap to the size it'll be when the tub is in use. Otherwise, the caulk's seal could break the first time you take a bath.

Special features

- 1,820 total square feet of living area
- Living room has a stunning cathedral ceiling
- Spacious laundry room with easy access to kitchen, garage and the outdoors
- Plenty of closet space throughout
- Covered front porch enhances outdoor living
- 3 bedrooms, 2 baths, 2-car garage
- Basement foundation

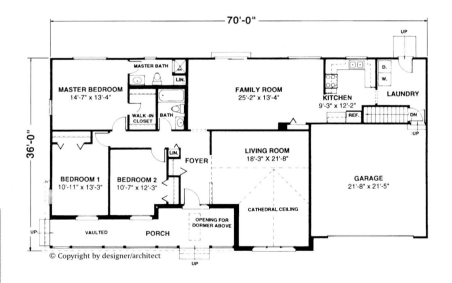

With so many perennials to choose from, it is easy to find one that suits your site, soil and style. Before buying always check the plant for signs of disease and poor growth. Things to look for: strong, healthy top growth; disease-free vigorous leaves; moist soil mix free of weeds; established thriving roots.

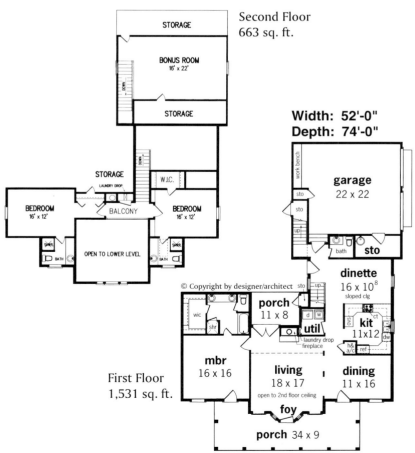

Second Floor
663 sq. ft.

STORAGE

BONUS ROOM
16' x 22'

STORAGE

STORAGE
LAUNDRY DROP

W.I.C.

BEDROOM
16' x 12'

BALCONY

BEDROOM
16' x 12'

OPEN TO LOWER LEVEL

BATH

BATH

Width: 52'-0"
Depth: 74'-0"

work bench

garage
22 x 22

sto

sto

up

bath

sto

dinette
16 x 10⁸
sloped clg

© Copyright by designer/architect

sto

up

porch
11 x 8

util
laundry drop
fireplace

d | w

kit
11x12

dw

ovs | ct

h&
a/c | ref

wic

shr

mbr
16 x 16

living
18 x 17
open to 2nd floor ceiling

dining
11 x 16

First Floor
1,531 sq. ft.

foy

porch 34 x 9

Special features

- ❖ 2,194 total square feet of living area
- ❖ Energy efficient home with 2" x 6" exterior walls
- ❖ A convenient laundry drop on the second floor leads to the centrally located utility room
- ❖ Both second floor bedrooms have large closets and their own bath
- ❖ Bonus room on the second floor has an additional 352 square feet of living space
- ❖ 3 bedrooms, 3 1/2 baths, 2-car side entry garage
- ❖ Crawl space foundation, drawings also include slab and basement foundations

Special features

- ❖ 1,553 total square feet of living area
- ❖ Two-story living area creates an open and airy feel to the interior especially with two dormers above
- ❖ First floor master bedroom is private and includes its own bath and walk-in closet
- ❖ Two secondary bedrooms share a full bath with double vanity
- ❖ 3 bedrooms, 2 1/2 baths, 2-car drive under garage
- ❖ Walk-out basement foundation

Topdressing means applying a layer of fertilizer, mulch or compost to enrich the soil.

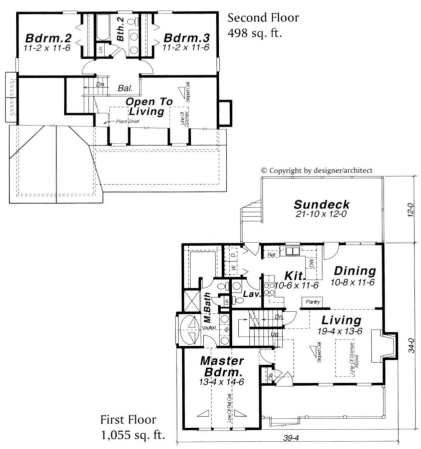

Second Floor
498 sq. ft.

Bdrm.2
11-2 x 11-6

Bth.2

Bdrm.3
11-2 x 11-6

Open To Living

© Copyright by designer/architect

Sundeck
21-10 x 12-0

12-0

Kit.
10-6 x 11-6

Dining
10-8 x 11-6

M.Bath

Lav.

Pantry

Living
19-4 x 13-6

Master Bdrm.
13-4 x 14-6

34-0

First Floor
1,055 sq. ft.

39-4

Special features

- 1,470 total square feet of living area
- Vaulted breakfast room is cheerful and sunny
- Private second floor master bedroom has a bath and walk-in closet
- Large utility room has access to the outdoors
- 3 bedrooms, 2 baths
- Basement, crawl space or slab foundation, please specify when ordering

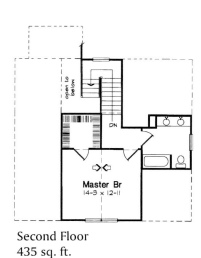

35'-0"

© Copyright by designer/architect

Deck

Brkfst
9-0 x 6-0

flat clg.

Kit.
11-6 x 9-8

Br #2
12-2 x 9-11

UP

42'-0"

Foyer
flat clg.

DN

Utility

Living Rm
18-11 x 12-11

Br #3
12-2 x 9-3

Porch

First Floor
1,035 sq. ft.

open to below

DN

Master Br
14-3 x 12-11

Second Floor
435 sq. ft.

Special features

- ❖ 1,200 total square feet of living area
- ❖ Enjoy lazy summer evenings on this magnificent porch
- ❖ Activity area has a fireplace and ascending stair to the cozy loft
- ❖ Kitchen features a built-in pantry
- ❖ Master bedroom enjoys a large bath, walk-in closet and cozy loft overlooking the activity room below
- ❖ 2 bedrooms, 2 baths
- ❖ Crawl space foundation

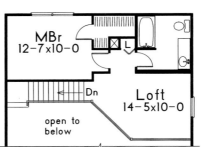

Second Floor
416 sq. ft.

MBr
12-7x10-0

Loft
14-5x10-0

open to
below

Dn

28'-0"

First Floor
784 sq. ft.

Bunk Rm
12-0x10-0

F

Kit
9-0x10-0

Stor

Up

Activity Rm
18-4x13-10

Nook
9-0x8-0

36'-0"

Covered Porch depth 8-0

© Copyright by designer/architect

Annual flowers germinate, grow and die within one year. Most produce a large number of flowers in one season, resulting in lots of seeds that help guarantee new plants the following year. Flowering quickly, they are ideal for impatient gardeners eager to experiment with color, texture and form.

Second Floor
1,147 sq. ft.

WALK-IN CLOSET

Bath

Bath

Bath

Bedroom
12' x 11'2"

WALK-IN CLOSET

Bonus
15'2" x 11'

Master Bedroom
15'4" x 15'7"

DOWN

Bedroom
12' x 10'2"

WALK-IN CLOSET

Special features

❖ 2,049 total square feet of living area
❖ The large covered porch creates an inviting entrance
❖ An angled counter defines the kitchen and provides additional seating
❖ The master bedroom enjoys a large walk-in closet and private bath with double-bowl vanity
❖ The parlor/library offers an elegant atmosphere
❖ The second floor bonus room is included in the total square footage
❖ 3 bedrooms, 2 1/2 baths, 2-car garage
❖ Basement foundation

First Floor
902 sq. ft.

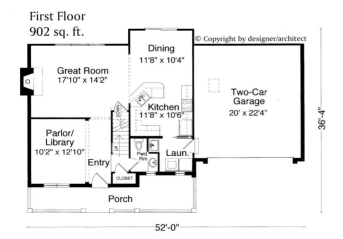

© Copyright by designer/architect

Dining
11'8" x 10'4"

Great Room
17'10" x 14'2"

Two-Car Garage
20' x 22'4"

Kitchen
11'8" x 10'6"

DOWN

Parlor/ Library
10'2" x 12'10"

Pwd Rm

Laun.

Entry

CLOSET

Porch

36'-4"

52'-0"

Protect against sparks by enclosing a fireplace's opening with glass doors or a sturdy screen. Never close the flue while a fire is still smoldering. Carbon monoxide can build up.

Special features

- ❖ 2,322 total square feet of living area
- ❖ Cedar shake siding, French style shutters and a multi-gabled roof line add warmth and character to the exterior
- ❖ The enormous great room offers a vaulted ceiling and fireplace flanked by patio doors
- ❖ A vaulted kitchen and breakfast room enjoy a large bay window and state-of-the-art design
- ❖ The vaulted master bedroom includes a large walk-in closet, luxury bath and five windows to embrace the sun
- ❖ 4 bedrooms, 3 baths, 3-car garage
- ❖ Basement foundation, drawings also include slab and crawl space foundations

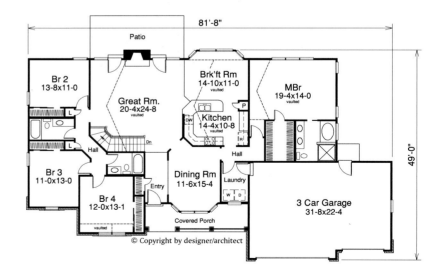

© Copyright by designer/architect

Second Floor
1,078 sq. ft.

Bedroom 4
10-4 x 10-10

DN

Bedroom 3
12-4 x 12-4

Bedroom 2
11-4 x 12-10

Master Suite
12-8 x 15-10
10' Tray Clg

First Floor
1,293 sq. ft.

73'-8"

34'-0"

D
W

DW

Kit/Dinette
20-0 x 13-4
9' Clg

Family
17-0 x 13-4
9'-6" Clg

Built-In

FP

Ref Desk

DN   DN

Built-In

P

Garage
30-0 x 22-0

Dining
12-4 x 14-4
9' Clg

UP

DN

Living
14-0 x 14-4
9' Clg

Covered Porch

© Copyright by designer/architect

Special features

❖ 2,301 total square feet of living area
❖ Formal living and dining rooms traditionally flank the foyer and offer excellent entertaining spaces
❖ The kitchen/dinette and family room combine creating a massive area for informal gatherings
❖ All bedrooms are located on the second floor for exceptional peace and quiet
❖ 4 bedrooms, 2 1/2 baths, 3-car garage
❖ Walk-out basement foundation

To reduce the likelihood of burglary do everything you can to make your home appear occupied when you are away: leave lights and a radio on timers, have the lawn mowed, and newspapers and mail collected.

Special features

- 1,823 total square feet of living area
- Vaulted living room is spacious and easily accesses the dining area
- The master bedroom boasts a tray ceiling, large walk-in closet and a private bath with a corner whirlpool tub
- Cheerful dining area is convenient to the U-shaped kitchen and also enjoys patio access
- Centrally located laundry room connects the garage to the living areas
- 3 bedrooms, 2 baths, 2-car garage
- Basement foundation

A single shelf or a collection of corner shelves are surprisingly appealing offering an opportunity to show off collectibles in an exciting new way. Plus, they also work well in more compact homes with smaller rooms.

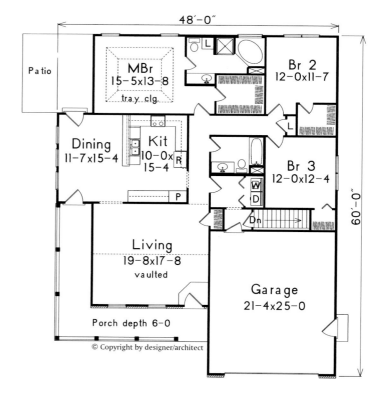

48'-0"

Patio

MBr
15-5x13-8
tray clg.

Br 2
12-0x11-7

Dining
11-7x15-4

Kit
10-0x
15-4

Br 3
12-0x12-4

Living
19-8x17-8
vaulted

Garage
21-4x25-0

60'-0"

Porch depth 6-0

© Copyright by designer/architect

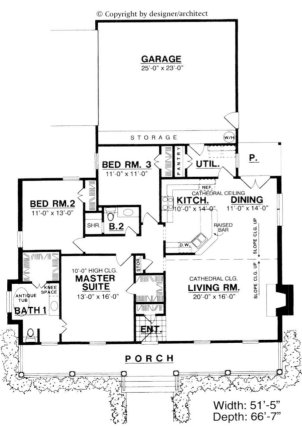

© Copyright by designer/architect

GARAGE
25'-0" x 23'-0"

STORAGE

W/H

BED RM. 3
11'-0" x 11'-0"

UTIL.

P.

PANTRY

REF.
CATHEDRAL CEILING

BED RM.2
11'-0" x 13'-0"

KITCH.
10'-0" x 14'-0"

DINING
11'-0" x 14'-0"

SHR.

B.2

RAISED BAR

D.W.

SLOPE CLG. UP

10'-0" HIGH CLG.
MASTER SUITE
13'-0" x 16'-0"

STOR.

CATHEDRAL CLG.
LIVING RM.
20'-0" x 16'-0"

SLOPE CLG. UP

ANTIQUE TUB
KNEE SPACE

BATH 1

ENT.

PORCH

Width: 51'-5"
Depth: 66'-7"

Special features

❖ 1,654 total square feet of living area
❖ Country touches including the full-length front porch and dormers invite people into this welcoming home
❖ A cathedral, sloped ceiling adorns the combined living room, kitchen and dining area
❖ A 10' ceiling, antique tub and two walk-in closets enhance the master suite
❖ 3 bedrooms, 2 baths, 2-car side entry garage
❖ Crawl space, slab or basement foundation, please specify when ordering

Mixing different fabrics on upholstered furniture adds a fun twist to a room. Be sure to use the "squint" test. When squinting if one pattern stands out a lot more than the others, it's probably best to choose another.

Special features

- ❖ 2,797 total square feet of living area
- ❖ Energy efficient home with 2" x 6" exterior walls
- ❖ 9' ceilings on the first floor
- ❖ A half wall divides the dining and living rooms maintaining an open feel
- ❖ A whirlpool tub with plant ledge above graces the private master bath
- ❖ An open kitchen overlooks the breakfast room
- ❖ 4 bedrooms, 3 baths, 2-car side entry garage
- ❖ Basement or crawl space foundation, please specify when ordering

A Palladian window is a window or a group of windows with an arched top of glass.

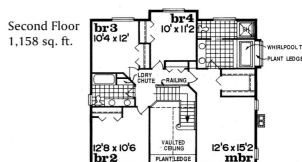

Second Floor
1,158 sq. ft.

First Floor
1,639 sq. ft.

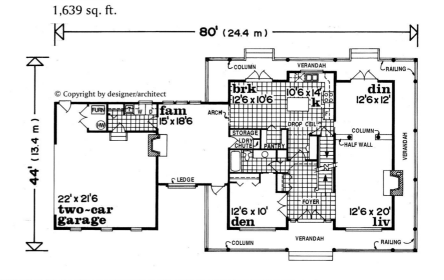

Special features

First Floor
1,009 sq. ft.

© Copyright by designer/architect

Second Floor
976 sq. ft.

- ❖ 1,985 total square feet of living area
- ❖ Cozy family room features a fireplace and double French doors opening onto the porch
- ❖ The open kitchen includes a convenient island
- ❖ The extraordinary master bedroom has a tray ceiling and a large walk-in closet
- ❖ Lovely bayed breakfast area has easy access to the deck
- ❖ 3 bedrooms, 2 1/2 baths
- ❖ Partial basement/crawl space foundation

Never use a wet mop on a wood floor. Squeeze out as much of the water as possible before beginning this chore.

Special features

- 2,200 total square feet of living area
- Master bedroom has a vaulted ceiling, spacious bath and an enormous walk-in closet
- Spacious kitchen has an efficient center island adding extra workspace
- Parlor/living room has a gorgeous bay window looking out to the covered front porch
- 9' ceiling on first floor
- 3 bedrooms, 2 1/2 baths, 2-car garage
- Crawl space or slab foundation, please specify when ordering

The best and most efficient way to clean mini-blinds is to use a lamb's wool duster. Close the blinds and gently sweep the entire surface starting at the top. If this is done regularly, there is no need to do anything more involved.

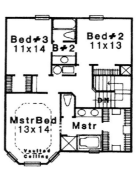

Second Floor
862 sq. ft.

Bed #3
11x14

Bed #2
11x13

MstrBed
13x14

Mstr

First Floor
1,338 sq. ft.

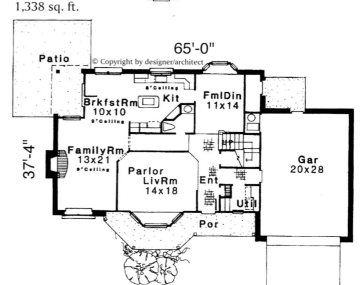

© Copyright by designer/architect

65'-0"

37'-4"

Patio

BrkfstRm
10x10

Kit

FmlDin
11x14

FamilyRm
13x21

Parlor
LivRm
14x18

Ent

Gar
20x28

Util

Por

Special features

- ❖ 1,944 total square feet of living area
- ❖ Spacious surrounding porch, covered patio and stone fireplace create an expansive ponderosa appearance
- ❖ The large entry leads to a grand-sized great room featuring a vaulted ceiling, fireplace, wet bar and access to the porch through three patio doors
- ❖ The U-shaped kitchen is open to the hearth room and enjoys a snack bar, fireplace and patio access
- ❖ A luxury bath, walk-in closet and doors to the porch are a few of the amenities of the master bedroom
- ❖ 3 bedrooms, 2 baths, 3-car detached garage
- ❖ Basement foundation

Special features

- ❖ 1,812 total square feet of living area
- ❖ A corner fireplace in the vaulted family room sets the stage for a cozy atmosphere
- ❖ The spacious kitchen includes a work island with seating for quick meals
- ❖ The master bedroom boasts a coffered ceiling and deluxe bath with whirlpool tub and walk-in closet
- ❖ Optional second floor has an additional 323 square feet of living area
- ❖ 3 bedrooms, 2 baths, 2-car side entry garage
- ❖ Slab foundation

Draperies are getting longer and longer. One of the best ways to add height to any room is to place window treatments just below the ceiling line. Use this designer trick in any room that could use a little lift.

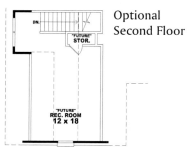

Optional Second Floor

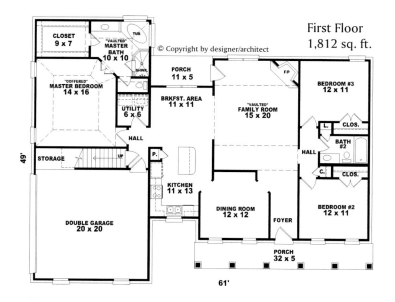

First Floor
1,812 sq. ft.

© Copyright by designer/architect

Second Floor
1,055 sq. ft.

First Floor
2,367 sq. ft.

62' - 0"

74' - 8"

© Copyright by designer/architect

Special features

- ❖ 3,422 total square feet of living area
- ❖ The oversized kitchen island includes space for the stove as well as a desk and bookshelves underneath
- ❖ Corner whirlpool tub is the focal point in the master bath
- ❖ A corner fireplace is enjoyed by both the hearth room and the breakfast room nearby
- ❖ Bonus room on the second floor has an additional 228 square feet of living area
- ❖ 4 bedrooms, 3 1/2 baths, 3-car side entry garage
- ❖ Basement foundation

Sealing a driveway is just as necessary in warmer climates as in cold ones. Asphalt sealers protect the pavement from oxidizing and becoming brittle in the harsh sun. This also provides prevention from water seeping through hairline cracks and reaching the base.

Special features

- 1,618 total square feet of living area
- Wrap-around porch offers a covered passageway to the garage
- Dramatic two-story entry, with balcony above and staircase provide an expansive feel with an added decorative oval window
- Dazzling kitchen features walk-in pantry, convenient laundry and covered rear porch
- 3 bedrooms, 2 1/2 baths, 1-car garage
- Basement foundation

Birdwatchers can attract their favorite species by growing plants birds love to eat. Plant sunflowers, black-eyed Susans, purple corn flowers and bee balm to bring the birds flocking to your garden.

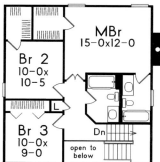

Second Floor
754 sq. ft.

MBr
15-0x12-0

Br 2
10-0x
10-5

Br 3
10-0x
9-0

Dn

open to below

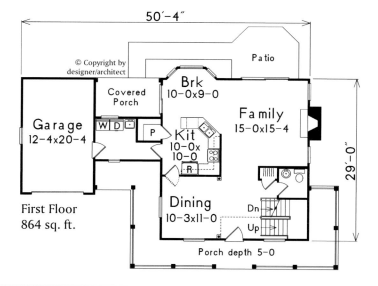

First Floor
864 sq. ft.

50'-4"

© Copyright by designer/architect

Patio

Covered Porch

Brk
10-0x9-0

Garage
12-4x20-4

W D

P

Kit
10-0x
10-0

Family
15-0x15-4

R

Dining
10-3x11-0

Dn

Up

29'-0"

Porch depth 5-0

Second Floor
796 sq. ft.

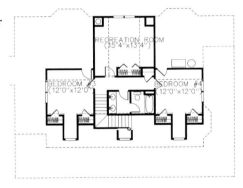

RECREATION ROOM
(15'4"x13'4")

BEDROOM #3
(12'0"x12'0")

BEDROOM #4
(12'0"x12'0")

First Floor
1,809 sq. ft.

Width: 58'-8"
Depth: 50'-10"

DECK
(16'0"x8'0")

MASTER
(12'0"x17'8")

BREAKFAST (7'8"x7'8")
(12'0"x7'8") UTILITY ROOM

GREAT ROOM
(15'4"x21'6")

KITCHEN
(12'0"x13'4")

DINING ROOM
(12'0"x12'8")

BEDROOM #2
(12'0"x11'0")

WRAP AROUND PORCH

© Copyright by designer/architect

Special features

- ❖ 2,605 total square feet of living area
- ❖ Bay windows add character and light to the master bedroom, breakfast area and formal dining room
- ❖ Bedroom #2 includes a walk-in closet and full bath nearby making it ideal as a guest suite
- ❖ The second floor bedrooms share a full bath and large recreation room
- ❖ 4 bedrooms, 3 baths
- ❖ Pier foundation

Special features

- 1,646 total square feet of living area
- Attractive cottage features two large porch areas
- The great room includes a corner fireplace and beautiful views provided by ten windows and doors
- A U-shaped kitchen with snack counter is open to the breakfast room and enjoys access to both the side and rear porch
- The master bedroom has a luxury bath with corner tub, double vanities with makeup counter and a huge walk-in closet
- 2 bedrooms, 2 baths, 2-car side entry garage
- Basement foundation, drawings also include slab and crawl space foundations

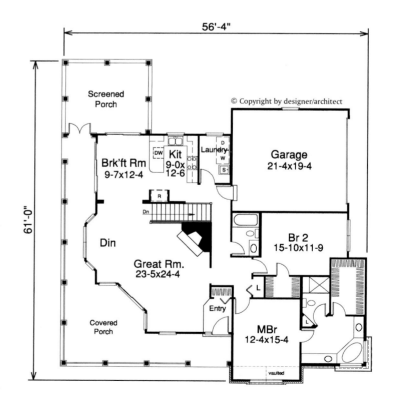

First Floor
1,845 sq. ft.

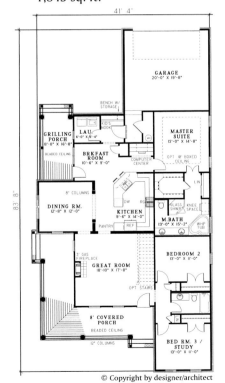

© Copyright by designer/architect

Optional
Bonus Room

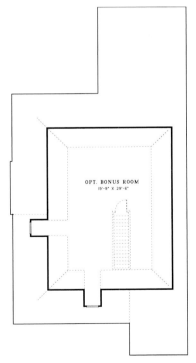

Special features

- ❖ 1,845 total square feet of living area
- ❖ Master suite has privacy from other bedrooms
- ❖ Dining room is convenient to kitchen and great room
- ❖ Breakfast room accesses outdoor grilling porch
- ❖ Optional bonus room has an additional 1,191 square feet of living area
- ❖ 3 bedrooms, 2 baths, 2-car rear entry garage
- ❖ Crawl space or slab foundation, please specify when ordering

Save your back when shoveling with proper technique. Bend at the knees, keeping your back straight, and tighten your stomach muscles as you lift with your legs. Don't overextend your arms though - the closer the load remains to your body, the lighter it feels. And don't twist your back when shoveling.

Special features

- ❖ 2,155 total square feet of living area
- ❖ Energy efficient home with 2" x 6" exterior walls
- ❖ The kitchen boasts a cooktop island and opens to the nook which features access to the screen porch
- ❖ The two-story great room includes an elegant window wall and fireplace
- ❖ The spacious master bedroom features a tray ceiling, walk-in closet and private bath with a relaxing whirlpool tub
- ❖ 4 bedrooms, 2 1/2 baths, 2-car side entry garage
- ❖ Basement foundation

As building materials go, drywall is the same: one manufacturer's product will be the same as another; there are no hidden defects. This material is either smooth and solid or it isn't. If you see it on sale, buy it.

Second Floor
592 sq. ft.

OPEN TO GREAT ROOM

BR.2
10'x12'

BR.3
10'6"x10'6"

BR.4
10'6"x14'6"

© Copyright by designer/architect

SCREEN PORCH
13'x12'

GRT.RM.
17'6"x18'6"

NK.
13'x11'6"

MBR.
TRAY CEILING
13'6"x16'

KIT.
15'x12'

DIN.
10'6"x10'6"

E.

2 CAR GAR.
22'-0"x 24'-0"

First Floor
1,563 sq. ft.

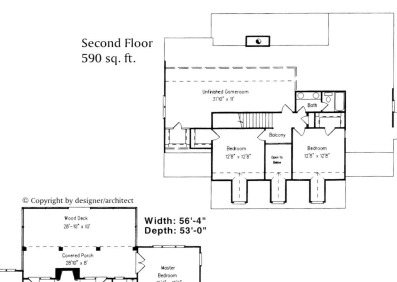

Second Floor
590 sq. ft.

© Copyright by designer/architect

Width: 56'-4"
Depth: 53'-0"

First Floor
1,910 sq. ft.

Special features

- 2,500 total square feet of living area
- Master bedroom has its own separate wing with front porch, double walk-in closets, private bath and access to back porch and patio
- Large unfinished gameroom on the second floor has an additional 359 square feet of living area
- Living area is oversized and has a fireplace
- 3 bedrooms, 3 baths
- Basement, slab or crawl space foundation, please specify when ordering

Ceramic tile made to look like real stone is a durable and affordable choice. It is easy to remove stains especially if you tint the grout to match the color of the stone.

Special features

- ❖ 920 total square feet of living area
- ❖ Energy efficient home with 2" x 6" exterior walls
- ❖ Bath has extra space for a washer and dryer
- ❖ Plenty of seating for dining at the kitchen counter
- ❖ 2 bedrooms, 1 bath
- ❖ Basement foundation

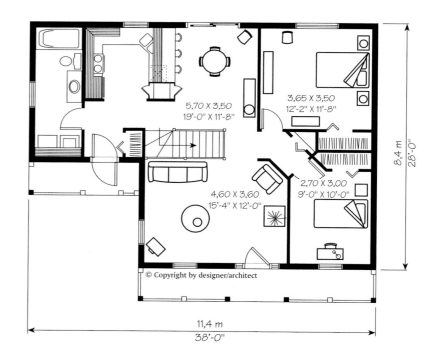

5,70 X 3,50
19'-0" X 11'-8"

3,65 X 3,50
12'-2" X 11'-8"

4,60 X 3,60
15'-4" X 12'-0"

2,70 X 3,00
9'-0" X 10'-0"

8,4 m
28'-0"

11,4 m
38'-0"

© Copyright by designer/architect

Double your storage capacity in even the smallest of closets by adding two tiers of hanging rods instead of one. It's a simple and inexpensive way to increase your closet space. However, don't forget to leave a small portion for longer items so you don't loose that length entirely for storage.

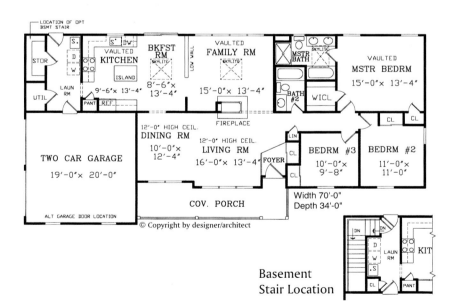

© Copyright by designer/architect

Width 70'-0"
Depth 34'-0"

Basement
Stair Location

Special features

- ❖ 1,667 total square feet of living area
- ❖ The centrally located fireplace lends warmth to the surrounding rooms
- ❖ Vaulted ceilings and skylights add elegance
- ❖ The foyer opens into the dining and living rooms with 12' ceilings and a wall of windows for a spacious feel
- ❖ The large laundry room offers an abundance of storage space
- ❖ 3 bedrooms, 2 baths, 2-car side entry garage
- ❖ Basement, crawl space or slab foundation, please specify when ordering

Special features

- ❖ 2,059 total square feet of living area
- ❖ Kitchen and nook share open view onto the covered porch
- ❖ Ample-sized secondary bedrooms
- ❖ Well-designed master bath
- ❖ Framing - only concrete block available
- ❖ 3 bedrooms, 2 baths, 2-car side entry garage
- ❖ Slab foundation

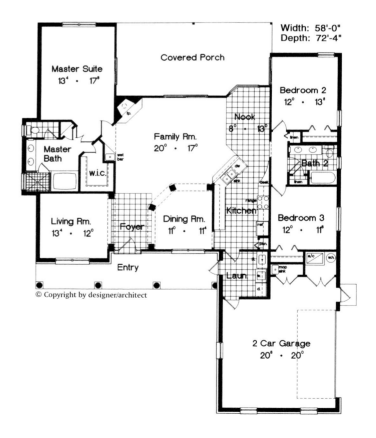

Width: 58'-0"
Depth: 72'-4"

Master Suite
13⁴ · 17⁸

Covered Porch

Bedroom 2
12⁰ · 13⁸

Nook
8⁰ · 13⁰

Family Rm.
20⁰ · 17⁰

Master Bath

w.i.c.

Kitchen

Bath 2

Living Rm.
13⁴ · 12⁰

Foyer

Dining Rm.
11⁰ · 11⁴

Bedroom 3
12⁰ · 11⁸

Entry

Laun.

2 Car Garage
20⁸ · 20⁰

© Copyright by designer/architect

Bricks are made from clay and other materials which are formed into shapes and then fired in a kiln to make them durable and strong. Red bricks contain large amounts of iron; yellow bricks contain little iron. Bricks can be sealed or unsealed. If they have been sealed they are easier to keep clean.

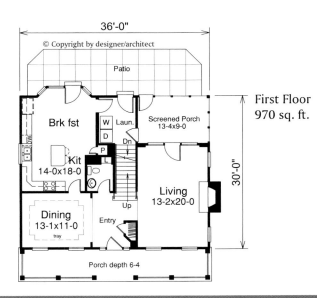

Second Floor
1,080 sq. ft.

Br 2
13-4x11-4

Dn

Br 3
14-0x13-5

MBr
13-4x16-6
vaulted

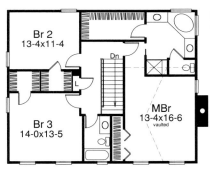

36'-0"

© Copyright by designer/architect

Patio

Brk fst

W | Laun.
D

Screened Porch
13-4x9-0

Dn

Kit
14-0x18-0

P
L

Dining
13-1x11-0
tray

Entry

Up

Living
13-2x20-0

First Floor
970 sq. ft.

30'-0"

Porch depth 6-4

Special features

- ❖ 2,050 total square feet of living area
- ❖ Large living room with fireplace enjoys a view to the front porch and access to the rear screened porch
- ❖ L-shaped kitchen has a built-in pantry, island snack bar and breakfast area with bay window
- ❖ Master bedroom is vaulted and has a luxury bath and abundant closet space
- ❖ The spacious secondary bedrooms each have a walk-in closet
- ❖ 3 bedrooms, 2 1/2 baths, 2-car detached garage
- ❖ Basement foundation, drawings also include slab and crawl space foundations

Special features

- 2,450 total square feet of living area
- Computer room is situated between bedrooms for easy access
- Two covered porches; one in front and one in rear of home
- Master bedroom includes bath with double walk-in closets and a luxurious step-up tub
- 4 bedrooms, 2 1/2 baths, 2-car side entry garage
- Slab foundation

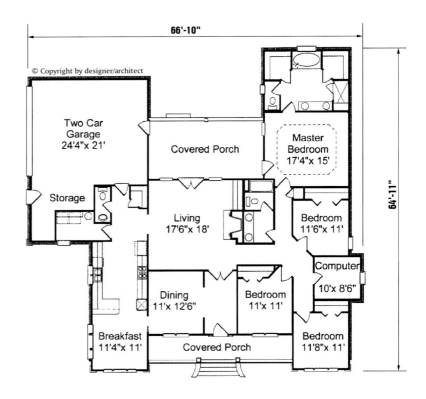

© Copyright by designer/architect

66'-10"

64'-11"

Two Car Garage 24'4"x 21'

Covered Porch

Master Bedroom 17'4"x 15'

Storage

Living 17'6"x 18'

Bedroom 11'6"x 11'

Computer 10'x 8'6"

Dining 11'x 12'6"

Bedroom 11'x 11'

Breakfast 11'4"x 11'

Covered Porch

Bedroom 11'8"x 11'

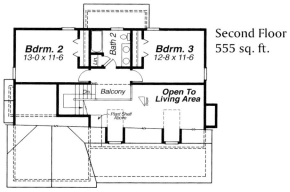

Second Floor
555 sq. ft.

Bdrm. 2
13-0 x 11-6

Bdrm. 3
12-8 x 11-6

Bath 2

Balcony

Open To Living Area

Plant Shelf Above

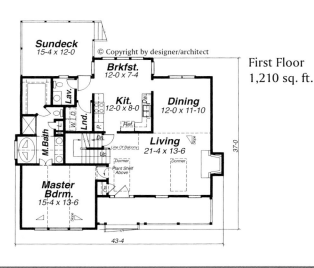

Sundeck
15-4 x 12-0

© Copyright by designer/architect

First Floor
1,210 sq. ft.

Brkfst.
12-0 x 7-4

Kit.
12-0 x 8-0

Dining
12-0 x 11-10

Lav.

Lnd.

Ref.

M.Bath

Living
21-4 x 13-6

Line Of Balcony Above

Plant Shelf Above

Dormer

Master Bdrm.
15-4 x 13-6

37-0

43-4

Special features

❖ 1,765 total square feet of living area
❖ A palladian window accenting the stone gable adds a new look to a popular cottage design
❖ Dormers above open the vaulted living room
❖ Kitchen extends to breakfast room with access to sundeck
❖ 3 bedrooms, 2 1/2 baths, 2-car drive under garage
❖ Basement foundation

As well as serving as decorative features and essential dressing aids, mirrors also play a less obvious role in a room scheme. They are invaluable for reflecting light, and can increase the illusion of space in a small room.

Special features

- 1,266 total square feet of living area
- Energy efficient home with 2" x 6" exterior walls
- Narrow frontage is perfect for small lots
- Prominent central hall provides a convenient connection for all main rooms
- Design incorporates full-size master bedroom complete with dressing room, bath and walk-in closet
- Angled kitchen includes handy laundry facilities and is adjacent to an oversized storage area
- 3 bedrooms, 2 baths, 2-car rear entry garage
- Crawl space foundation, drawings also include slab foundation

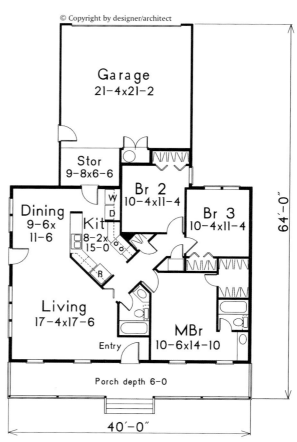

© Copyright by designer/architect

Garage
21-4x21-2

Stor
9-8x6-6

Br 2
10-4x11-4

Br 3
10-4x11-4

Dining
9-6x
11-6

Kit
8-2x
15-0

W
D

R

Living
17-4x17-6

MBr
10-6x14-10

Entry

Porch depth 6-0

64'-0"

40'-0"

Price Code E

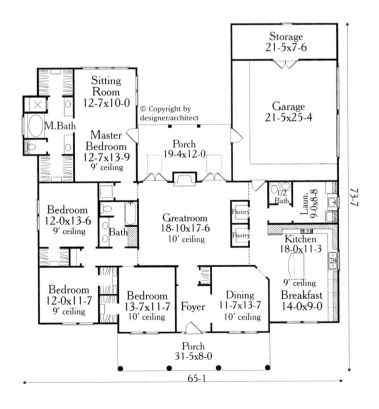

Special features

- 2,465 total square feet of living area
- Counterspace galore enhances the efficiency of the kitchen which features two walk-in pantries and a nearby dining room, laundry area and half bath
- French doors flank the fireplace in the great room
- The master bedroom is a luxurious retreat with a windowed sitting room and private bath with two walk-in closets and a deluxe tub
- 4 bedrooms, 2 1/2 baths, 2-car side entry garage
- Basement, crawl space or slab foundation, please specify when ordering

Special features

- 2,253 total square feet of living area
- Great room is joined by the rear covered porch
- Secluded parlor provides area for peace and quiet or a private office
- Sloped ceiling adds drama to the master bedroom
- Great room, kitchen and breakfast area combine for a large open living area
- 3 bedrooms, 2 1/2 baths, 2-car garage
- Basement foundation

Bay windows are combinations of three or more windows projecting outward from a room. These windows make a room appear more open and spacious, increase the flow of light into a home and can add counter area to any room.

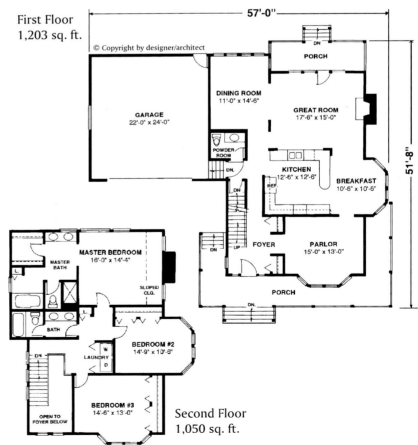

First Floor
1,203 sq. ft.

© Copyright by designer/architect

57'-0"

51'-8"

GARAGE
22'-0" x 24'-0"

DINING ROOM
11'-0" x 14'-6"

POWDER ROOM

PORCH

GREAT ROOM
17'-6" x 15'-0"

KITCHEN
12'-6" x 12'-6"

BREAKFAST
10'-6" x 10'-6"

REF.

FOYER

PARLOR
15'-0" x 13'-0"

UP

PORCH

MASTER BEDROOM
16'-0" x 14'-4"

MASTER BATH

SLOPED CLG.

BATH

LAUNDRY
W D

BEDROOM #2
14'-9" x 10'-6"

DN

BEDROOM #3
14'-6" x 13'-0"

OPEN TO FOYER BELOW

Second Floor
1,050 sq. ft.

Special features

- ❖ 1,778 total square feet of living area
- ❖ Angled walls in foyer add interest to this floor plan
- ❖ Secluded master suite maintains privacy
- ❖ Centralized kitchen is spacious in size with extras such as a nearby desk
- ❖ 3 bedrooms, 2 baths, 2-car side entry garage
- ❖ Slab foundation

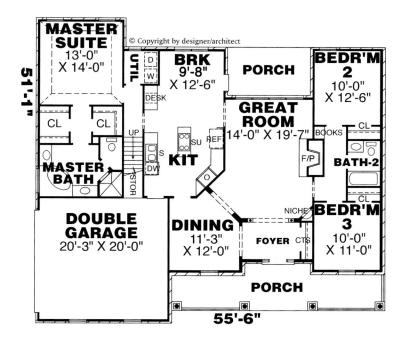

© Copyright by designer/architect

MASTER SUITE 13'-0" X 14'-0"

51'-1"

UTIL

D W DESK

BRK 9'-8" X 12'-6"

PORCH

BEDR'M 2 10'-0" X 12'-6"

CL

CL **CL**

UP

S SU REF

KIT

GREAT ROOM 14'-0" X 19'-7"

BOOKS

CL

MASTER BATH

S DW STOR

F/P

BATH-2

CL

DOUBLE GARAGE 20'-3" X 20'-0"

DINING 11'-3" X 12'-0"

NICHE

FOYER CTS

BEDR'M 3 10'-0" X 11'-0"

PORCH

55'-6"

To prevent a skin from forming on your paint while it's in storage, cut a circle of wax paper or aluminum foil and place it directly on the surface of the paint inside the can. This will protect the paint and keep it fresh.

Special features

- 1,852 total square feet of living area
- The stately great room features a vaulted ceiling and a corner gas fireplace
- The covered or screened-in porch is a great place to relax and enjoy the outdoors
- The future bonus room on the second floor has an additional 352 square feet of living space
- 3 bedrooms, 2 1/2 baths, 2-car garage
- Basement, crawl space or slab foundation, please specify when ordering

Optional Second Floor

FUTURE HALF BATH

SLOPED CEILING

FUTURE BONUS ROOM 14-8 x 24

SLOPED CEILING   CLOSET

First Floor
1,852 sq. ft.

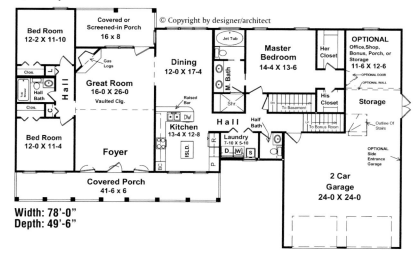

© Copyright by designer/architect

Bed Room
12-2 X 11-10

Covered or Screened-in Porch
16 x 8

Dining
12-0 X 17-4

Jet Tub

Master Bedroom
14-4 X 13-6

Her Closet

OPTIONAL
Office, Shop, Bonus, Porch, or Storage
11-6 X 12-6

Hall

Gas Logs

Great Room
16-0 X 26-0
Vaulted Clg.

M. Bath

OPTIONAL DOOR

OPTIONAL WALL

Hall Bath

Raised Bar

Shr.

His Closet

To Basement

Storage

Bed Room
12-0 X 11-4

Kitchen
13-4 X 12-8

ISLD.

Hall

To Bonus Room

Outline Of Stairs

Foyer

Half Bath

Laundry
7-10 X 5-10

D W S

OPTIONAL Side Entrance Garage

2 Car Garage
24-0 X 24-0

Covered Porch
41-6 x 6

Width: 78'-0"
Depth: 49'-6"

Second Floor
900 sq. ft.

81'-0"

© Copyright by
designer/architect

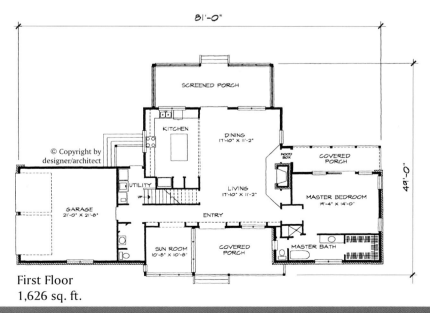

First Floor
1,626 sq. ft.

Special features

- ❖ 2,526 total square feet of living area
- ❖ An open playroom is enjoyed on the second floor by the children of the house
- ❖ A well designed sun room creates a natural extension of the front covered porch while offering year-round outdoor enjoyment
- ❖ The large center island in the kitchen provides plenty of extra workspace for many kitchen tasks
- ❖ 3 bedrooms, 2 1/2 baths, 2-car side entry garage
- ❖ Slab foundation

When a toilet begins to overflow, don't grab for the plunger and towels; reach for the shut-off valve. It's right at the base of the toilet and will close off the water supply so that you can deal with the clog.

Special features

❖ 1,434 total square feet of living area

❖ Private second floor master bedroom features a private bath and a roomy walk-in closet

❖ A country kitchen with peninsula counter adjoins the living room creating the feeling of a larger living area

❖ The living room has a warm fireplace and a tall ceiling

❖ 3 bedrooms, 2 baths, 2-car garage

❖ Basement, crawl space or slab foundation, please specify when ordering

Masking tape is one of the least expensive but most useful painting tools you'll find. But buy only the good stuff. Standard masking tape is often too sticky, and leaves behind a residue that can interfere with a painted finish.

Second Floor
416 sq. ft.

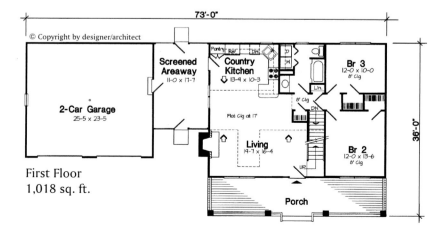

First Floor
1,018 sq. ft.

Second Floor
447 sq. ft.

BEDROOM #2
(10'0"x11'8")

ATTIC
STORAGE

BEDROOM #3
(10'0"x11'6"10

© Copyright by designer/architect

SIDE
PORCH

MASTER
BEDROOM
(12'4"x11'8")

DINING
AREA
(11'4"x10'0")

LIVING
ROOM
(16'4"x16'10")

KITCHEN
(9'0"x10'0")

ENTRY

Width: 36'-8"
Depth: 41'-0"

FRONT PORCH

First Floor
953 sq. ft.

Special features

- ❖ 1,400 total square feet of living area
- ❖ Energy efficient home with 2" x 6" exterior walls
- ❖ A wall of windows in the dining room is cheerful and brilliant
- ❖ Attic storage is a welcome addition to the second floor
- ❖ The master bedroom is enticing and elegant with a bay window, private bath and walk-in closet
- ❖ 3 bedrooms, 2 1/2 baths
- ❖ Crawl space foundation

If you choose to store pictures outside of albums, never stack them on top of each other, as the weight can damage them. And if the weather is humid, they could stick together. File them in boxes and store in a cool dry place.

Special features

- ❖ 1,148 total square feet of living area
- ❖ The large wrap-around porch is ideal for an early morning breakfast or for a late evening lounging
- ❖ A separate entry, full masonry fireplace and balcony/dining area that overlooks the two-story atrium with floor-to-ceiling window wall are some of the many amenities of the vaulted great room
- ❖ The spacious kitchen features an angled snack bar and enjoys easy access to the laundry and garage
- ❖ The atrium is open to 462 square feet of optional living area below
- ❖ 2 bedrooms, 1 bath, 1-car side entry garage
- ❖ Walk-out basement foundation

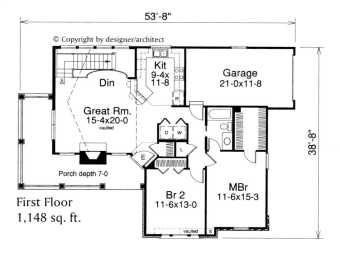

First Floor
1,148 sq. ft.

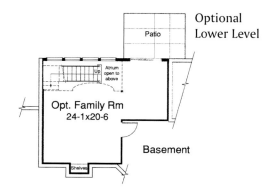

Optional Lower Level

Basement

WIDTH 65–0

DEPTH 58–8

SLOPE   SLOPE

MASTER BEDRM
12-8 X 14-6
10 FT CLG

FP

BRKFST RM
12-0 X 10-0
10 FT CLG

MASTER BATH
10 FT CLG

GREAT ROOM
18-6 X 15-6
10 FT CLG

UTIL
6-8 X 8-6

BATH 2

LIN

42" LEDGE

ARCH

PAN

ARCH   ARCH

KITCHEN
12-6 X 14-0
10 FT CLG

BEDRM 2
11-0 X 13-6

FOYER
10 FT CLG

DINING ROOM
12-2 X 14-0
10 FT CLG

BEDRM 3
12-6 X 13-4

PORCH

GARAGE

© Copyright by designer/architect

Special features

- ❖ 1,955 total square feet of living area
- ❖ Porch adds outdoor area to this design
- ❖ Dining and great rooms are visible from the foyer through a series of elegant archways
- ❖ The kitchen overlooks the great room and breakfast room
- ❖ 3 bedrooms, 2 baths, 2-car side entry garage
- ❖ Crawl space foundation, drawings also include slab foundation

A utility knife is one of the handiest tools to have around. Be sure to use sharp blades only; dull blades are inefficient and unsafe. Store with the blade retracted and hide it in your tool box to keep away from children.

Special features

* 3,072 total square feet of living area
* Charming window seats accent all the secondary bedrooms
* Master bedroom has a luxurious bath and an enormous walk-in closet
* French doors in both the study and the formal dining room lead to the covered front porch
* 4 bedrooms, 3 1/2 baths, 3-car side entry garage
* Slab foundation

One of the most confusing terms in the ornamental metals business is the phrase "wrought iron." However, the confusion is understandable since even dictionaries cannot agree on a single definition. The spelling can be just as confusing. Many consumers spell the metal "rod iron" or "rot iron."

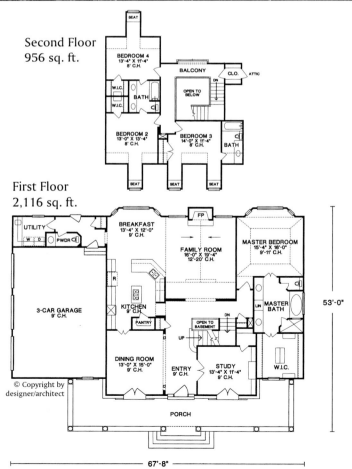

Second Floor
956 sq. ft.

First Floor
2,116 sq. ft.

© Copyright by designer/architect

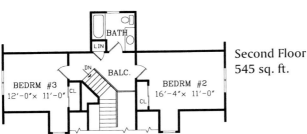

Second Floor
545 sq. ft.

BATH

LIN

BEDRM #3
12'-0" x 11'-0"

BALC.

DN

CL

BEDRM #2
16'-4" x 11'-0"

CL

Special features

❖ 1,679 total square feet of living area

❖ Wide, angled spaces in both the great room and the master bedroom create roomy appeal and year-round comfort

❖ Amenities in the luxurious master bedroom include a large walk-in closet, a whirlpool bath and double-vanity

❖ The nicely appointed kitchen offers nearby laundry facilities and porch access

❖ 3 bedrooms, 2 1/2 baths, 2-car drive under garage

❖ Basement, crawl space or slab foundation, please specify when ordering

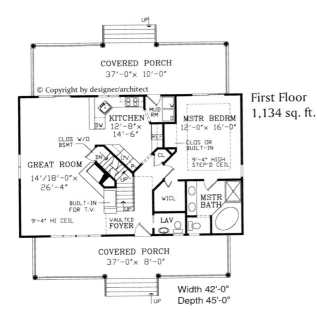

UP

COVERED PORCH
37'-0" x 10'-0"

© Copyright by designer/architect

First Floor
1,134 sq. ft.

KITCHEN
12'-8" x 14'-6"

MUD RM

DW

D

MSTR BEDRM
12'-0" x 16'-0"

CLOS W/D BSMT

REF

CLOS OR BUILT-IN
9'-4" HIGH STEP'D CEIL

GREAT ROOM
14'/18'-0" x 26'-4"

DN

TV

CL

UP

BUILT-IN FOR T.V.

9'-4" HI CEIL

WICL

MSTR BATH

UP

VAULTED FOYER

LAV

COVERED PORCH
37'-0" x 8'-0"

Width 42'-0"
Depth 45'-0"

UP

Special features

- 1,754 total square feet of living area
- Energy efficient home with 2" x 6" exterior walls
- Utilities are conveniently located in the first floor powder room
- U-shaped island in kitchen has a stovetop as well as additional dining space
- Bonus room on the second floor has an additional 421 square feet of living area
- 3 bedrooms, 2 1/2 baths, 2-car garage
- Basement foundation

Some say the noblest combination of forest trees in America is the Oak and Pine. This deciduous and evergreen combo will give your yard color and interest all year long. They are also good sources of food and shelter for birds and other wildlife.

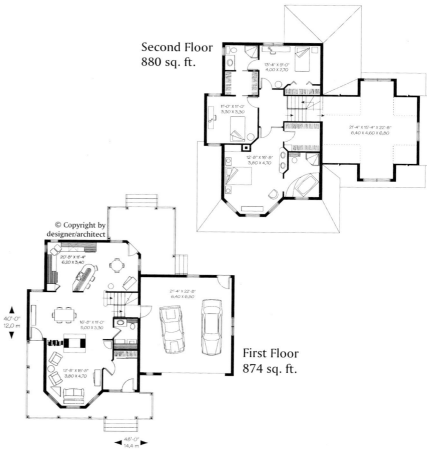

Second Floor
880 sq. ft.

First Floor
874 sq. ft.

© Copyright by designer/architect

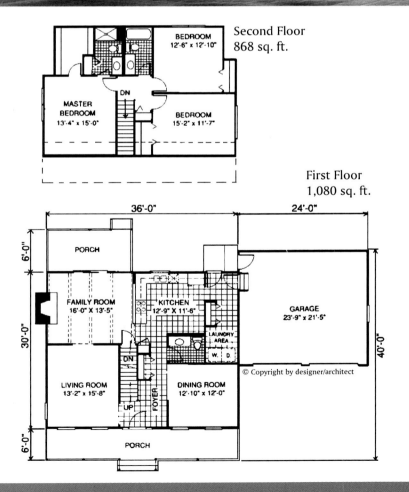

Second Floor
868 sq. ft.

BEDROOM
12'-6" x 12'-10"

MASTER
BEDROOM
13'-4" x 15'-0"

DN

BEDROOM
15'-2" x 11'-7"

First Floor
1,080 sq. ft.

36'-0"   24'-0"

6'-0"

PORCH

30'-0"

FAMILY ROOM
16'-0" X 13'-5"

KITCHEN
12'-9" X 11'-6"

GARAGE
23'-9" x 21'-5"

40'-0"

LAUNDRY
AREA

W.   D

DN

LIVING ROOM
13'-2" x 15'-8"

FOYER

DINING ROOM
12'-10" x 12'-0"

UP

© Copyright by designer/architect

6'-0"

PORCH

Special features

- ❖ 1,948 total square feet of living area
- ❖ Large elongated porch for moonlit evenings
- ❖ Stylish family room features a beamed ceiling
- ❖ Skillfully designed kitchen is convenient to an oversized laundry area
- ❖ Second floor bedrooms are all generously sized
- ❖ 3 bedrooms, 2 1/2 baths, 2-car garage
- ❖ Basement foundation, drawings also include crawl space foundation

Mildew is a nuisance in many parts of the country. To remove, mix a cup of household bleach into a gallon of water and apply the mix with a pump sprayer. Let the solution sit for about five minutes, taking caution to not let it dry out. Then pull out a hose and rinse the siding thoroughly from top to bottom.

Special features

- ❖ 1,299 total square feet of living area
- ❖ Large porch for enjoying relaxing evenings
- ❖ First floor master bedroom has a bay window, walk-in closet and roomy bath
- ❖ Two generous bedrooms with lots of closet space, a hall bath, linen closet and balcony overlook comprise the second floor
- ❖ 3 bedrooms, 2 1/2 baths
- ❖ Basement foundation

Place a storage bench in your entryway. Provide guests and household members a place to sit and take off shoes comfortably. And a bench with storage underneath keeps clutter at bay.

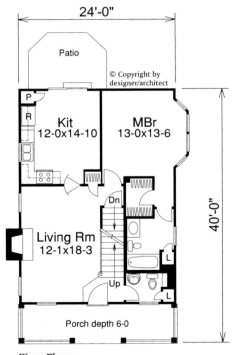

24'-0"

Patio

© Copyright by designer/architect

P
R
Kit
12-0x14-10

MBr
13-0x13-6

40'-0"

Dn

Living Rm
12-1x18-3

Up
L

Porch depth 6-0

First Floor
834 sq. ft.

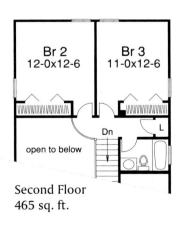

Br 2
12-0x12-6

Br 3
11-0x12-6

open to below

Dn
L

Second Floor
465 sq. ft.

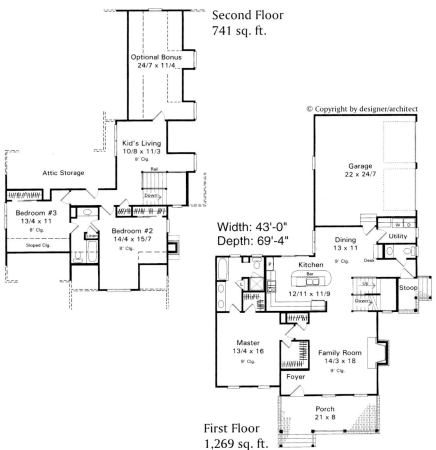

Second Floor
741 sq. ft.

Optional Bonus
24/7 x 11/4

Kid's Living
10/8 x 11/3
8' Clg.

Rail

Attic Storage

Down

Bedroom #3
13/4 x 11
8' Clg.

Sloped Clg.

Linen

Bedroom #2
14/4 x 15/7
8' Clg.

© Copyright by designer/architect

Garage
22 x 24/7

Width: 43'-0"
Depth: 69'-4"

W D

Dining
13 x 11
9' Clg.

Utility

Desk

P

Kitchen
12/11 x 11/9
Bar

L

Up

Down

Stoop

Master
13/4 x 16
9' Clg.

Family Room
14/3 x 18
9' Clg.

Foyer

Porch
21 x 8

First Floor
1,269 sq. ft.

Special features

❖ 2,010 total square feet of living area
❖ Oversized kitchen is a great gathering place with eat-in island bar, dining area nearby and built-in desk
❖ First floor master bedroom has privacy
❖ Unique second floor kid's living area for playroom
❖ Optional bonus room has an additional 313 square feet of living area
❖ 3 bedrooms, 2 1/2 baths, 2-car side entry garage
❖ Basement foundation

Prolonged exposure to the weather turns wood gray, and weathered wood makes a poor base for new paint. That's because the sunlight degrades the lining that holds wood cells together. Sand down to fresh wood, then prime the surface before painting.

Special features

- 1,643 total square feet of living area
- An attractive front entry porch gives this ranch a country accent
- Spacious family/dining room is the focal point of this design
- Kitchen and utility room are conveniently located near gathering areas
- Formal living room in the front of the home provides area for quiet and privacy
- Master bedroom has view to the rear of the home and a generous walk-in closet
- 3 bedrooms, 2 baths, 2-car garage
- Basement foundation, drawings also include crawl space and slab foundations

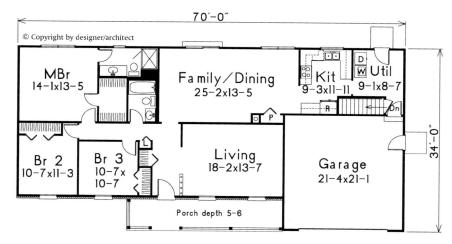

© Copyright by designer/architect

70'-0"

MBr 14-1x13-5

Family/Dining 25-2x13-5

Kit 9-3x11-11

Util 9-1x8-7

34'-0"

Br 2 10-7x11-3

Br 3 10-7x 10-7

Living 18-2x13-7

Garage 21-4x21-1

Porch depth 5-6

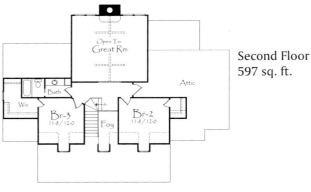

Second Floor
597 sq. ft.

© Copyright by
designer/architect

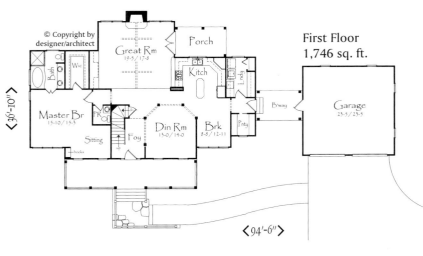

First Floor
1,746 sq. ft.

Special features

- ❖ 2,343 total square feet of living area
- ❖ Dormers and a large porch add country flair
- ❖ Elegant columns define the spacious dining room
- ❖ The secondary bedrooms enjoy cozy window seats and walk-in closets
- ❖ 3 bedrooms, 2 1/2 baths, 2-car detached garage
- ❖ Walk-out basement foundation

If you're stuck without electricity for a long time, here's what you should eat: first, perishable food from the refrigerator; second, foods from the freezer; third, crackers, cookies, snack foods; last, canned goods and non-perishables.

Special features

- ❖ 1,591 total square feet of living area
- ❖ Spacious porch and patio provide outdoor enjoyment
- ❖ Large entry foyer leads to a cheery kitchen and breakfast room which welcomes the sun through a wide array of windows
- ❖ The great room features a vaulted ceiling, corner fireplace, wet bar and access to the rear patio
- ❖ Double walk-in closets, private porch and a luxury bath are special highlights of the vaulted master bedroom suite
- ❖ 3 bedrooms, 2 baths, 2-car side entry garage
- ❖ Basement foundation

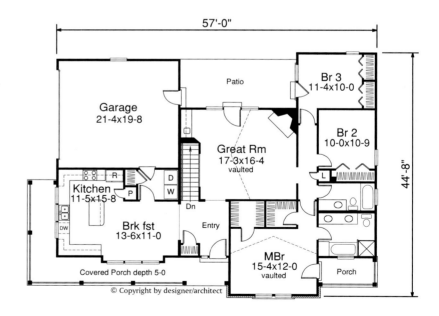

© Copyright by designer/architect

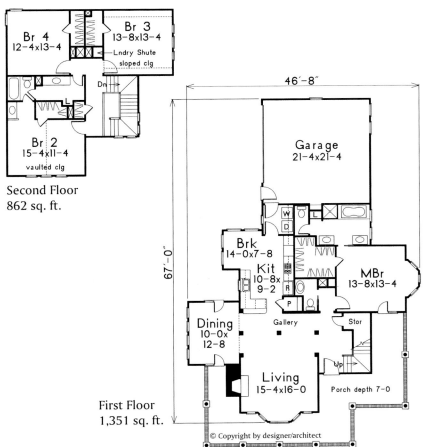

Second Floor
862 sq. ft.

Br 4
12-4x13-4

Br 3
13-8x13-4
Lndry Shute
sloped clg

Dn

Br 2
15-4x11-4
vaulted clg

46'-8"

Garage
21-4x21-4

67'-0"

W
D
L

Brk
14-0x7-8

Kit
10-8x
9-2

MBr
13-8x13-4

R
P

Dining
10-0x
12-8

Gallery

Stor

Up

Living
15-4x16-0

Porch depth 7-0

First Floor
1,351 sq. ft.

© Copyright by designer/architect

Special features

- ❖ 2,213 total square feet of living area
- ❖ Master bedroom features a full bath with separate vanities, large walk-in closet and access to the covered porch
- ❖ Living room is enhanced by a fireplace, bay window and columns framing the gallery
- ❖ 9' ceilings throughout the home add to the open feeling
- ❖ 4 bedrooms, 2 1/2 baths, 2-car side entry garage
- ❖ Slab foundation

Around 50% of heat loss in the average home is through loft space and walls. Proper insulation can be an investment initially, but could end up saving you hundreds of dollars over the life span of your home.

Special features

- ❖ 2,727 total square feet of living area
- ❖ Wrap-around porch and large foyer create an impressive entrance
- ❖ A state-of-the-art vaulted kitchen has a walk-in pantry and is open to the breakfast room and adjoining screen-in-porch
- ❖ A walk-in wet bar, fireplace, bay window and deck access are features of the family room
- ❖ Vaulted master bedroom enjoys a luxurious bath with skylight and an enormous 13' deep walk-in closet
- ❖ 4 bedrooms, 2 1/2 baths, 2-car side entry garage
- ❖ Walk-out basement foundation

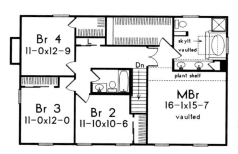

Second Floor
1,204 sq. ft.

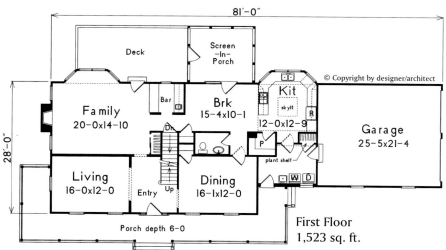

© Copyright by designer/architect

First Floor
1,523 sq. ft.

Special features

- ❖ 1,092 total square feet of living area
- ❖ Energy efficient home with 2" x 6" exterior walls
- ❖ Sunken family room adds interest
- ❖ Nice-sized bedrooms are convenient to the bath
- ❖ Handy work island in kitchen
- ❖ 3 bedrooms, 1 bath
- ❖ Basement foundation

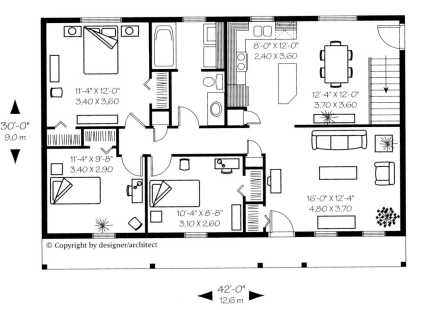

8'-0" X 12'-0"
2,40 X 3,60

12'-4" X 12'-0"
3,70 X 3,60

11'-4" X 12'-0"
3,40 X 3,60

30'-0"
9,0 m

11'-4" X 9'-8"
3,40 X 2,90

16'-0" X 12'-4"
4,80 X 3,70

10'-4" X 8'-8"
3,10 X 2,60

© Copyright by designer/architect

42'-0"
12,6 m

A long island has the ability to separate the kitchen from the living area while providing additional lower cabinet storage plus a great place to serve meals buffet-style.

Special features

❖ 4,217 total square feet of living area
❖ Energy efficient home with 2" x 6" exterior walls
❖ A sweeping staircase accentuates the great hall
❖ The gathering room invites family and friends to relax by the fireplace
❖ The master suite features a cozy sitting area with a bay window overlooking the backyard
❖ 4 bedrooms, 2 1/2 baths, 3-car side entry garage
❖ Walk-out basement foundation

Keep shoes stored up and away. Place shoes on shelves or racks or in clear or photo labeled boxes. Only put shoes on the floor if they are worn frequently otherwise they get too dusty.

Second Floor
2,109 sq. ft.

© Copyright by designer/architect

First Floor
2,108 sq. ft.

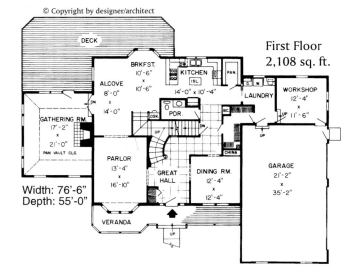

Width: 76'-6"
Depth: 55'-0"

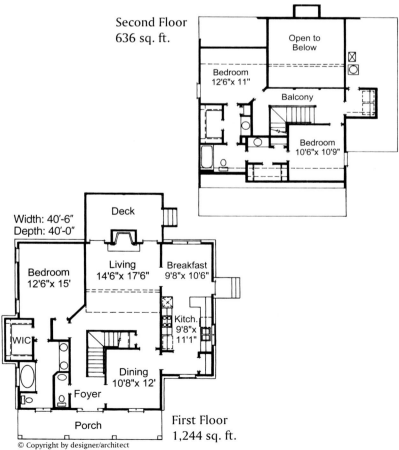

Second Floor
636 sq. ft.

Open to
Below

Bedroom
12'6"x 11"

Balcony

Bedroom
10'6"x 10'9"

Width: 40'-6"
Depth: 40'-0"

Deck

Bedroom
12'6"x 15'

Living
14'6"x 17'6"

Breakfast
9'8"x 10'6"

WIC

Kitch.
9'8"x
11'1"

Dining
10'8"x 12'

Foyer

Porch

First Floor
1,244 sq. ft.

© Copyright by designer/architect

Special features

* 1,880 total square feet of living area
* The large front porch is a perfect spot to sit back and relax
* The first floor bedroom includes a private bath with double-bowl vanity and a walk-in closet, creating an ideal master suite
* The secondary bedrooms enjoy walk-in closets and share a Jack and Jill bath
* 3 bedrooms, 2 1/2 baths
* Crawl space foundation

Special features

* 1,814 total square feet of living area
* This home enjoys a large country porch for a perfect leisure living area
* The vaulted great room, sunny breakfast room and kitchen with snack bar are all open to one another to create a very open sense of spaciousness
* A sensational lavish bath is the highlight of the master bedroom suite which features double vanities with a make-up counter, 5' x 5' shower with seat, separate toilet and a step-up whirlpool-in-a-sunroom
* 3 bedrooms, 2 baths, 3-car side entry garage
* Basement foundation

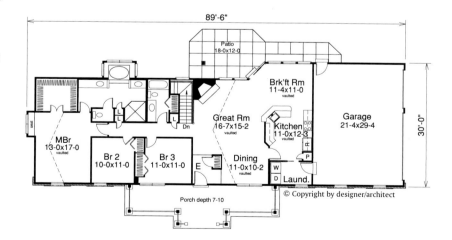

© Copyright by designer/architect

Special features

- ❖ 1,543 total square feet of living area
- ❖ Fireplace serves as the focal point of the large family room
- ❖ Efficient floor plan keeps hallways at a minimum
- ❖ Laundry room connects the kitchen to the garage
- ❖ Private first floor master bedroom has a walk-in closet and bath
- ❖ 3 bedrooms, 2 1/2 baths, 2-car detached side entry garage
- ❖ Slab foundation, drawings also include crawl space foundation

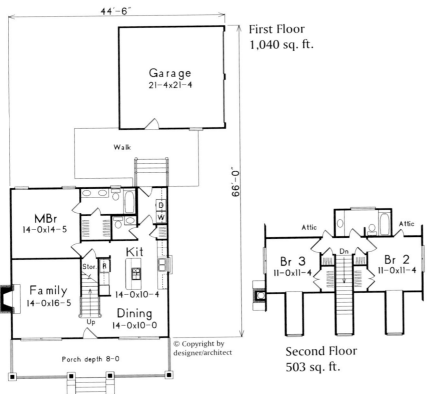

44'-6"

First Floor
1,040 sq. ft.

Garage
21-4x21-4

Walk

66'-0"

MBr
14-0x14-5

Kit
14-0x10-4

Stor. R

Family
14-0x16-5

Dining
14-0x10-0

Up

Porch depth 8-0

© Copyright by designer/architect

Attic   Attic

Br 3
11-0x11-4   Dn   Br 2
11-0x11-4

Second Floor
503 sq. ft.

Resist the temptation to mulch an area at the same time you plant seeds. Mulch can smother new seedlings and may keep the soil too cool to promote proper germination. One solution is to germinate seeds in six-pack trays.

Special features

- 2,828 total square feet of living area
- Multiple gables and wrap-around porch create a classic country exterior
- The spacious entry features a see-through stone fireplace and provides access to the study, guest bedroom and bath, dining room and staircase
- A well-designed kitchen has an island snack bar, built-in pantry and access to porch
- The two-story dining room includes a stone fireplace, master bedroom balcony overlook and 17' high window wall that accesses rear patio
- 4 bedrooms, 2 1/2 baths, 1-car and a 2-car rear entry garage
- Basement foundation

Second Floor
1,256 sq. ft.

Br 3
11-0x13-3

Dining Below
tray clg.

Br 2
13-9x10-9

MBr
21-0x14-0
tray clg.

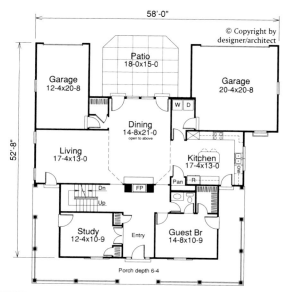

58'-0"

© Copyright by designer/architect

First Floor
1,572 sq. ft.

52'-8"

Garage
12-4x20-8

Patio
18-0x15-0

Garage
20-4x20-8

Dining
14-8x21-0
open to above

Living
17-4x13-0

Kitchen
17-4x13-0

Study
12-4x10-9

Entry

Guest Br
14-8x10-9

Porch depth 6-4

Special features

- 2,354 total square feet of living area
- 9' ceilings throughout this home
- Dramatic corner fireplace in the great room can be viewed from a lovely breakfast area
- Master bedroom is separated from other bedrooms for privacy and quiet
- 4 bedrooms, 2 1/2 baths
- Crawl space or slab foundation, please specify when ordering

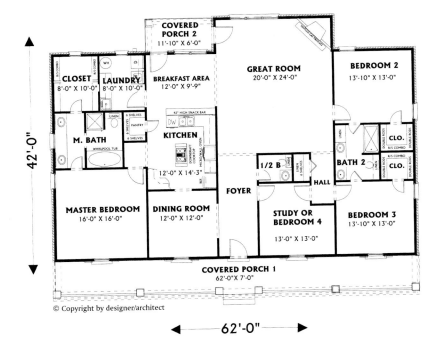

© Copyright by designer/architect

You can clear weeds out of large vegetable gardens with ease using a wheel hoe. There's no bending or stooping – just push the tool between the rows. Try one with double wheels for extra easy weeding. Just straddle the rows with the wheels.

Special features

❖ 2,043 total square feet of living area
❖ Energy efficient home with 2" x 6" exterior walls
❖ Two-story central foyer includes two coat closets
❖ Large combined space is provided by the kitchen, family and breakfast rooms
❖ Breakfast nook for informal dining looks out to the deck and screened porch
❖ 3 bedrooms, 2 1/2 baths, 2-car side entry garage
❖ Basement foundation, drawings also include slab foundation

Combine beauty and utility in your gardens by mixing edible flowers in with your veggies and planting a border of red-leaved lettuce or herbs around a flower bed.

Second Floor
534 sq. ft.

First Floor
1,509 sq. ft.

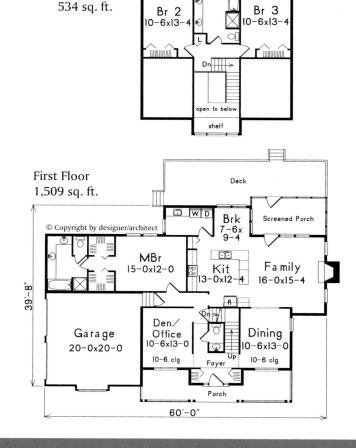

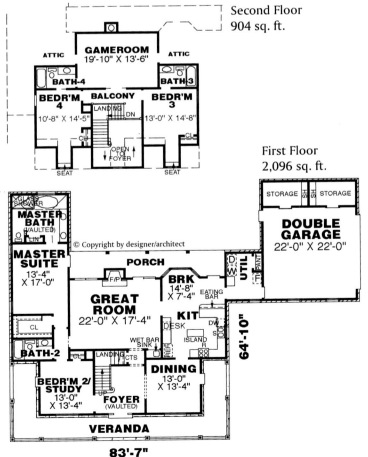

Second Floor
904 sq. ft.

ATTIC

GAMEROOM
19'-10" X 13'-6"

ATTIC

BATH-4

BEDR'M 4
10'-8" X 14'-5"

BALCONY
LANDING
DN

BATH-3

BEDR'M 3
13'-0" X 14'-8"

CL

OPEN TO FOYER

SEAT

SEAT

First Floor
2,096 sq. ft.

© Copyright by designer/architect

GLASS SHOWER

MASTER BATH (VAULTED)
LIN

STORAGE   STORAGE

MASTER SUITE
13'-4" X 17'-0"

PORCH

F/P

BRK
14'-8" X 7'-4"

EATING BAR

DW

UTIL

PANT

DOUBLE GARAGE
22'-0" X 22'-0"

GREAT ROOM
22'-0" X 17'-4"

KIT
DESK

DW

64'-10"

CL

WET BAR
SINK

ISLAND

REF

S

BATH-2
CL   LANDING

CTS

BEDR'M 2/ STUDY
13'-0" X 13'-4"

UP

FOYER (VAULTED)

DINING
13'-0" X 13'-4"

VERANDA

83'-7"

Special features

❖ 3,000 total square feet of living area

❖ Sliding pocket doors on the second floor lead to a spacious gameroom

❖ First floor master suite has direct access onto the porch, a vaulted private bath and walk-in closet

❖ Secondary bedrooms each have private baths and unique window seats

❖ 4 bedrooms, 4 baths, 2-car side entry garage

❖ Basement or slab foundation, please specify when ordering

When shoveling, place the shovel head perpendicular to the ground, keeping the handle well out in front and the blade close to your feet. Put the center of one foot on the step and push down. A concentrated push may be needed to sink the blade. Don't stomp too hard or jump on the head. If you have to jump on the shovel, you need a pick or a backhoe.

Special features

- 2,484 total square feet of living area
- Convenient first floor master bedroom features two walk-in closets and a dramatic bath with whirlpool tub and separate vanities
- Living room has 18' ceiling with a radius top window, decorative columns and a plant shelf
- Family room includes built-in bookcases and double French doors leading to an outdoor deck
- Bonus room has an additional 262 square feet of living area on the second floor
- 3 bedrooms, 2 1/2 baths, 2-car garage
- Crawl space foundation

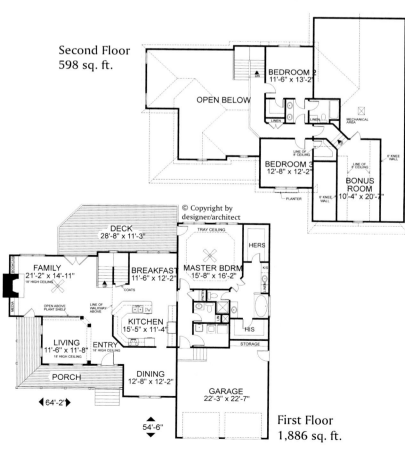

Second Floor
598 sq. ft.

First Floor
1,886 sq. ft.

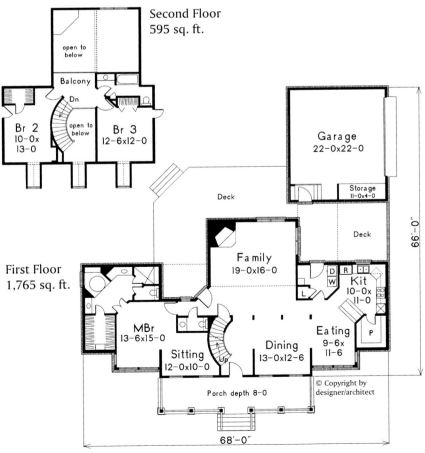

Second Floor 595 sq. ft.

open to below

Balcony

Dn

open to below

Br 2 10-0x 13-0

Br 3 12-6x12-0

First Floor 1,765 sq. ft.

Deck

Garage 22-0x22-0

Storage 11-0x4-0

Deck

66'-0"

Family 19-0x16-0

MBr 13-6x15-0

Kit 10-0x 11-0

Eating 9-6x 11-6

P

Sitting 12-0x10-0

Up

Dining 13-0x12-6

© Copyright by designer/architect

Porch depth 8-0

68'-0"

Special features

- ❖ 2,360 total square feet of living area
- ❖ Energy efficient home with 2" x 6" exterior walls
- ❖ Master bedroom includes a sitting area and large bath
- ❖ Sloped family room ceiling provides a view from the second floor balcony
- ❖ Kitchen features an island bar and walk-in butler's pantry
- ❖ 3 bedrooms, 2 1/2 baths, 2-car side entry garage
- ❖ Crawl space foundation, drawings also include slab and basement foundations

A fire safety tip, don't ever leave the dryer running when you are not at home. In 1998, there were 14,300 home fires related to dryers.

Special features

- ❖ 953 total square feet of living area
- ❖ Relax on porches fit for charming rocking chairs
- ❖ With two large bedrooms that feature oversized closets, a spacious kitchen and a family room with a fireplace, this home has everything you need to enjoy a vacation getaway
- ❖ The kitchen has a sunny corner double sink, roomy center island/snack bar and shares a vaulted ceiling with the family room
- ❖ 2 bedrooms, 1 1/2 baths
- ❖ Crawl space foundation

Keeping a phone list in the kitchen near the phone is not just convenient, but a safety feature as well. Jot down phone numbers for the police, fire department, doctors, family members or neighbors so if you have to act quickly you can.

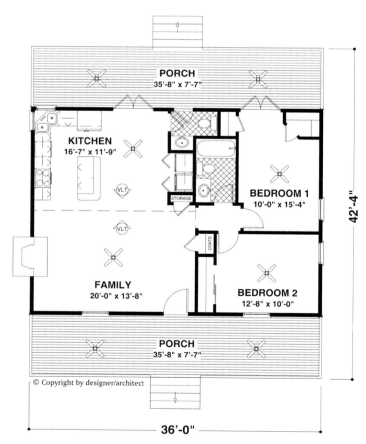

© Copyright by designer/architect

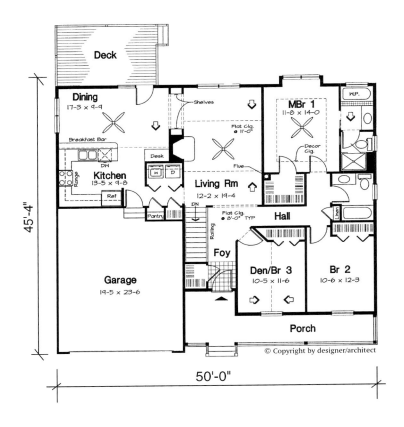

Special features

- ❖ 1,539 total square feet of living area
- ❖ Energy efficient home with 2" x 6" exterior walls
- ❖ A tray ceiling tops the master bedroom
- ❖ The peninsula counter in the kitchen doubles as a breakfast bar
- ❖ A walk-in closet in the foyer has space for additional storage
- ❖ 3 bedrooms, 2 baths, 2-car garage
- ❖ Basement, crawl space or slab foundation, please specify when ordering

Artwork that is hanging in a high traffic area often becomes crooked and misaligned. A way to alleviate such a problem is to use Velcro® circles (available at hardware stores) on the back of the picture. Stick one side of the Velcro® on the picture and the other side on the wall.

Special features

- 2,824 total square feet of living area
- 9' ceilings on the first floor
- Second floor bedrooms feature private dressing areas and share a bath
- Large great room includes a fireplace flanked by French doors leading to the rear patio
- Kitchen conveniently serves the formal dining room and breakfast area which features a large bay window
- 4 bedrooms, 3 baths, 2-car side entry garage
- Slab foundation, drawings also include crawl space foundation

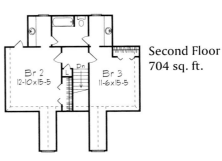

Second Floor
704 sq. ft.

Br 2
12-10x15-5

Br 3
11-6x15-5

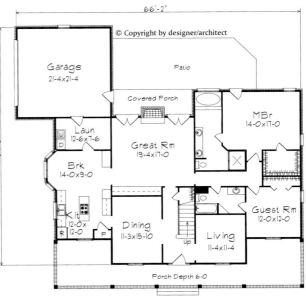

First Floor
2,120 sq. ft.

© Copyright by designer/architect

66'-2"

51'-9"

Garage
21-4x21-4

Patio

Covered Porch

Laun
12-6x7-6

Great Rm
19-4x17-0

MBr
14-0x17-0

Brk
14-0x9-0

Kit
12-0x12-0

Dining
11-3x15-10

Living
11-4x11-4

Guest Rm
12-0x12-0

Up

Porch Depth 6-0

Plan #597-017D-0006

Price Code E

Second Floor
1,138 sq. ft.

slope clg

MBr
17-8x13-0

slope clg

Br 2
12-6x10-9

Br 3
12-6x10-8

Br 4
12-6x11-0

open to below

Dn

Up

open

Third Floor
575 sq. ft.

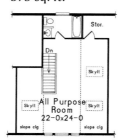

Stor.

Dn

Skylt

Skylt

All Purpose
Room
22-0x24-0

Skylt

slope clg

slope clg

Special features

- ❖ 3,006 total square feet of living area
- ❖ Energy efficient home with 2" x 6" exterior walls
- ❖ Large all-purpose room and bath on third floor
- ❖ Efficient U-shaped kitchen includes a pantry and adjacent planning desk
- ❖ 4 bedrooms, 3 1/2 baths, 2-car side entry garage
- ❖ Basement foundation, drawings also include slab foundation

63'-4"

© Copyright by designer/architect

Patio

Garage
20-0x20-0

Dinette
9-4x11-0

Kit
12-6x
15-8

D
W

R

46'-4"

Family
19-10x13-0

Dn

P

Living
12-6x16-8

Up

Dining
12-6x14-0

Foyer

Porch depth 7-0

First Floor
1,293 sq. ft.

Relaxing in a warm, bubbling spa or hot tub can relieve sore muscles, invigorate the skin, and contribute to a sense of calm. Once only available at great expense, many manufacturers now offer kits for home use that are affordable, easy to install, and can be adapted to just about any home.

Special features

- 2,351 total square feet of living area
- Coffered ceiling in dining room adds elegant appeal
- Wrap-around porch creates a pleasant escape
- Cozy study features a double-door entry and extra storage
- Double walk-in closets balance and organize the master bedroom
- 3 bedrooms, 2 1/2 baths, 2-car garage
- Basement foundation

A telescopic extension pole when painting high ceilings is an invaluable tool. Trying to balance yourself and a paint tray is a problem that gets eliminated when using this highly functional tool.

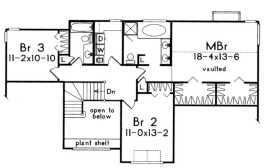

Second Floor
1,015 sq. ft.

Br 3
11-2x10-10

MBr
18-4x13-6
vaulted

Dn

open to
below

Br 2
11-0x13-2

plant shelf

© Copyright by designer/architect

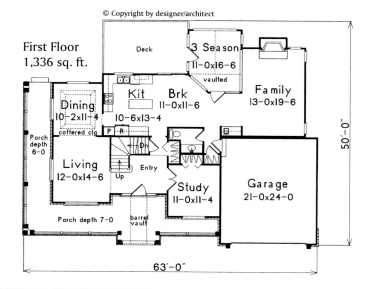

First Floor
1,336 sq. ft.

Deck

3 Season
11-0x16-6
vaulted

Dining
10-2x11-4
coffered clg

Kit

Brk
11-0x11-6
10-6x13-4

Family
13-0x19-6

Porch
depth
6-0

Living
12-0x14-6

P R

Dn

Entry

Up

Study
11-0x11-4

Garage
21-0x24-0

50'-0"

Porch depth 7-0

barrel
vault

63'-0"

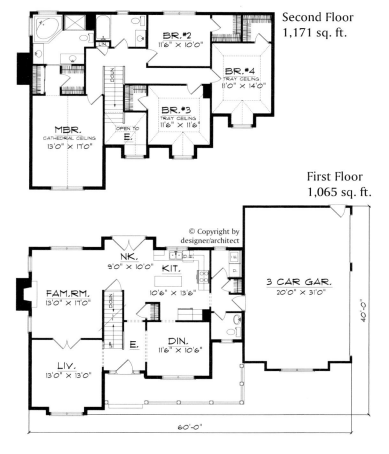

Second Floor
1,171 sq. ft.

BR.#2
11'6" × 10'0"

BR.#4
TRAY CEILING
11'0" × 14'0"

BR.#3
TRAY CEILING
11'6" × 11'6"

OPEN TO
E.

MBR.
CATHEDRAL CEILING
13'0" × 17'0"

First Floor
1,065 sq. ft.

© Copyright by
designer/architect

NK.
9'0" × 10'0"

KIT.
10'6" × 13'6"

3 CAR GAR.
20'0" × 31'0"

FAM. RM.
13'0" × 17'0"

DIN.
11'6" × 10'6"

E.

LIV.
13'0" × 13'0"

40'-0"

60'-0"

Special features

❖ 2,236 total square feet of living area
❖ Energy efficient home with 2" x 6" exterior walls
❖ The family room features double-door access into the formal living room and a grand fireplace flanked by windows
❖ All bedrooms are located on the second floor for privacy and enjoy walk-in closets
❖ The centrally located kitchen serves the charming nook and formal dining room with ease
❖ 4 bedrooms, 2 1/2 baths, 3-car side entry garage
❖ Basement foundation

Special features

- 2,694 total square feet of living area
- Inviting great room with fireplace and flanking windows is open to the kitchen and breakfast room
- The kitchen features a snack bar and adjacent breakfast room with bay window, large walk-in pantry and spacious laundry room
- The master bedroom includes a sumptuous bath, huge walk-in closet and nearby room ideal for a study or nursery
- A large two-story entry staircase leads to the second floor family and game room area, two bedrooms and a hall bath
- 4 bedrooms, 2 1/2 baths, 2-car side entry garage
- Basement foundation

Second Floor
782 sq. ft.

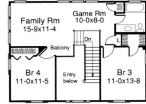

First Floor
1,912 sq. ft.

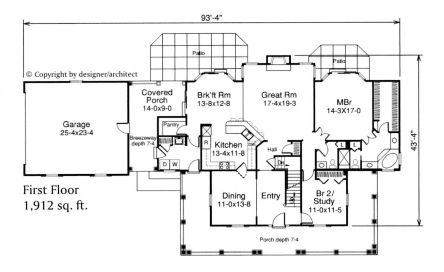

© Copyright by designer/architect

Special features

❖ 1,575 total square feet of living area
❖ The front and screened porches provide ample space for outdoor relaxation
❖ The master bedroom is a glorious retreat with a private bath, walk-in closet and double-door access onto the private deck
❖ Generously sized secondary bedrooms are located on the second floor and share a full bath
❖ 3 bedrooms, 2 1/2 baths
❖ Crawl space foundation

First Floor
1,050 sq. ft.

Width: 35'-0"
Depth: 57'-0"

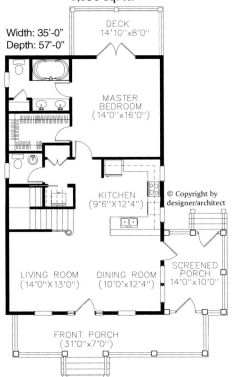

DECK
14'10"x8'0"

MASTER
BEDROOM
(14'0"x16'0")

KITCHEN
(9'6"X 12'4")

© Copyright by
designer/architect

LIVING ROOM
(14'0"x13'0")

DINING ROOM
(10'0"x12'4")

SCREENED
PORCH
14'0"x10'0"

FRONT PORCH
(31'0"x7'0")

Second Floor
525 sq. ft.

BEDROOM #2
(12'4"x15'8")

BEDROOM #3
(12'4"x13'0")

A variety of wrenches is a tool-box staple. The quality you pay for will be evident over the years: heavy, good-quality wrenches do not wear out. Cheap ones do, and can slip when in use, damaging the nut you are trying to loosen.

Special features

- 2,334 total square feet of living area
- Roomy front porch gives home a country flavor
- Vaulted great room boasts a fireplace, TV alcove, pass-through snack bar to kitchen and atrium featuring bayed window wall and an ascending stair to family room
- Oversized master bedroom features a vaulted ceiling, double-door entry and large walk-in closet
- 3 bedrooms, 2 baths, 2-car garage
- Walk-out basement foundation

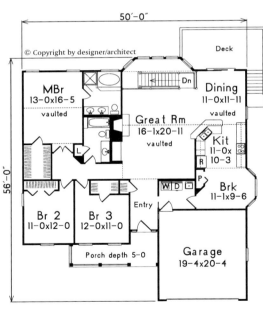

First Floor
1,777 sq. ft.

© Copyright by designer/architect

50'-0"

Deck

MBr
13-0x16-5
vaulted

Dining
11-0x11-11
vaulted

Dn

Great Rm
16-1x20-11
vaulted

Kit
11-0x
10-3

56'-0"

L

Brk
11-1x9-6

W D

Br 2
11-0x12-0

Br 3
12-0x11-0

Entry

Porch depth 5-0

Garage
19-4x20-4

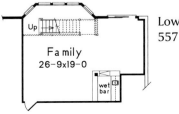

Up

Family
26-9x19-0

wet bar

Lower Level
557 sq. ft.

Special features

❖ 2,707 total square feet of living area
❖ A double-door entry leads into a handsome study
❖ Kitchen and breakfast room flow into the great room creating a terrific gathering place
❖ The second floor includes a game room/bonus room which is included in the total square footage
❖ 4 bedrooms, 3 baths, 2-car rear entry garage
❖ Crawl space or slab foundation, please specify when ordering

First Floor
1,713 sq. ft.

Second Floor
994 sq. ft.

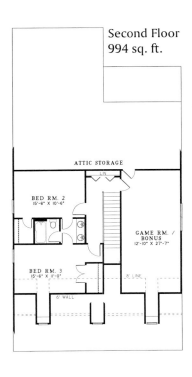

Any joints between building materials is a likely place to find heated air leaking out of the house. If two dissimilar materials meet, the chances of air leakage are even greater. When tightening up your house for the fall, scrutinize these areas with particular care.

Special features

- 2,384 total square feet of living area
- Bracketed box windows create an exterior with country charm
- Massive-sized great room features a majestic atrium, fireplace, box window wall, dining balcony and a vaulted ceiling
- An atrium balcony with large bay window off the deck is enjoyed by the spacious breakfast room
- 1,038 square feet of optional living area below with family room, wet bar, bedroom #4 and bath
- 3 bedrooms, 2 1/2 baths, 2-car side entry garage
- Walk-out basement foundation

First Floor
2,384 sq. ft.

© Copyright by
designer/architect

Optional
Lower Level

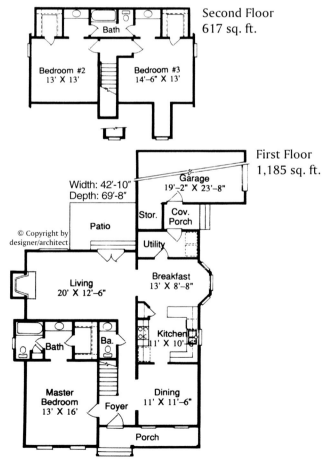

Second Floor
617 sq. ft.

Bath

Bedroom #2
13' X 13'

Bedroom #3
14'-6" X 13'

First Floor
1,185 sq. ft.

Width: 42'-10"
Depth: 69'-8"

Garage
19'-2" X 23'-8"

Stor.

Cov. Porch

© Copyright by designer/architect

Patio

Utility

Living
20' X 12'-6"

Breakfast
13' X 8'-8"

Bath

Ba.

Kitchen
11' X 10'-6"

Master Bedroom
13' X 16'

Foyer

Dining
11' X 11'-6"

Porch

Special features

- ❖ 1,802 total square feet of living area
- ❖ The secluded master bedroom includes a private master bath and large walk-in closet
- ❖ The efficient kitchen easily serves the dining room and bayed breakfast area
- ❖ The spacious secondary bedrooms enjoy walk-in closets and share the second floor bath
- ❖ 3 bedrooms, 2 1/2 baths, 2-car side entry garage
- ❖ Slab or crawl space foundation, please specify when ordering

Never use disinfectants to clean a refrigerator. The food inside will pick up the taste and odor of the cleaning solution. Warm soapy water works well and is a less harmful choice.

Special features

❖ 2,508 total square feet of living area
❖ Energy efficient home with 2" x 6" exterior walls
❖ Family room, bayed nook and kitchen combine for a spacious living area and is warmed by a grand fireplace
❖ The formal dining room provides an elegant entertaining space
❖ The master bedroom and family room feature double-door access onto the rear deck
❖ The bonus room above the garage has an additional 384 square feet of living area
❖ 3 bedrooms, 2 1/2 baths, 2-car side entry garage
❖ Basement or walk-out basement foundation, please specify when ordering

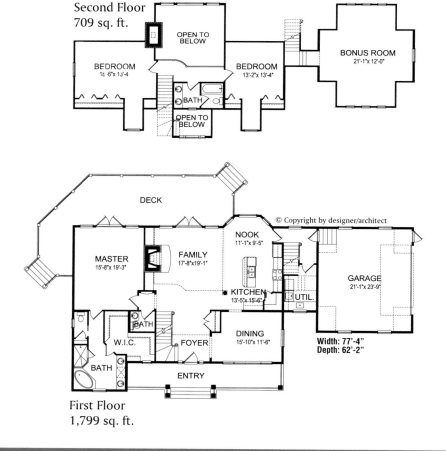

Second Floor
709 sq. ft.

First Floor
1,799 sq. ft.

Second Floor
525 sq. ft.

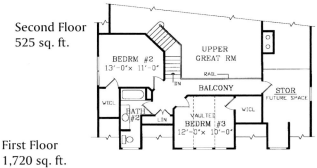

First Floor
1,720 sq. ft.

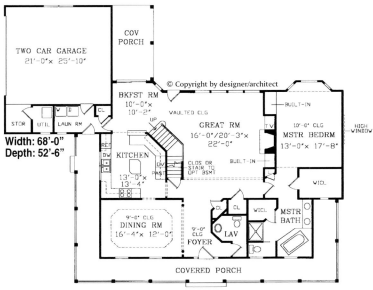

Width: 68'-0"
Depth: 52'-6"

© Copyright by designer/architect

Special features

- 2,245 total square feet of living area
- Covered wrap-around porch and arched windows create wonderful curb appeal
- Great room with an 18' vaulted ceiling has a fireplace set into a media wall
- Master bedroom has a 10' ceiling and bay window
- 3 bedrooms, 2 1/2 baths, 2-car side entry garage
- Basement, crawl space or slab foundation, please specify when ordering

One of the benefits of aluminum siding is that it generally requires less maintenance than wood siding. The material holds paint well so you don't have to worry about repainting it often. On the other hand, one of the drawbacks of is that it dents easily if a rock hits it or you drop your ladder against it.

Special features

- 2,270 total square feet of living area
- Great room and hearth room share a see-through fireplace
- Oversized rooms throughout
- First floor has a terrific floor plan for entertaining featuring a large kitchen, breakfast area and adjacent great room
- 4 bedrooms, 2 1/2 baths, 2-car garage
- Basement foundation

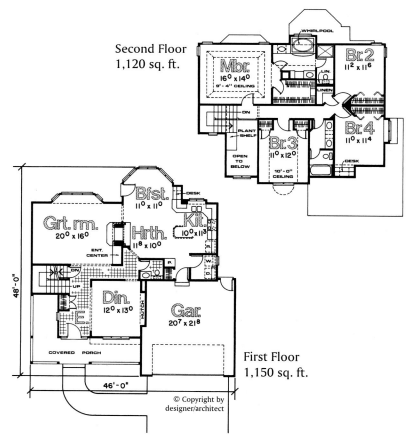

Second Floor
1,120 sq. ft.

First Floor
1,150 sq. ft.

© Copyright by designer/architect

When you're done painting for the day, and know you need to continue on the next day, scrape off the excess paint, stick your brush in a resealable plastic bag, press the air out and seal. This keeps the brush from drying out even if you don't get back to the job for a couple of days.

Second Floor
1,021 sq. ft.

Second Floor plan labels: Attic Space (Optional), WP. Tub, Skylt, Br #3 11-7 x 9-10, MBr #1 12-1 x 15-10 8' Clg, DN, Railing, Lin, Plant Shelf, Br #2 11-7 x 11-10, Open to Below, Flat Clg @ 10'

First Floor
1,260 sq. ft.

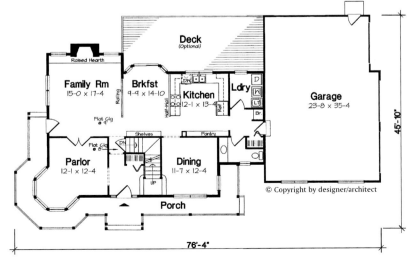

First Floor plan labels: Deck (Optional), Raised Hearth, Family Rm 15-0 x 17-4, Brkfst 9-9 x 14-10, Kitchen 12-1 x 13-4, Ldry, Garage 23-8 x 35-4, Flat Clg @ 9', Shelves, Pantry, Parlor 12-1 x 12-4, Flat Clg @ 8', DN, UP, Dining 11-7 x 12-4, Porch, 45'-10", 76'-4"

© Copyright by designer/architect

Special features

❖ 2,281 total square feet of living area
❖ Energy efficient home with 2" x 6" exterior walls
❖ Dramatic raised hearth in family room
❖ Kitchen is conveniently designed and features a large pantry closet
❖ Unique parlor offers privacy and quiet from the other more open living areas
❖ 3 bedrooms, 2 1/2 baths, 3-car side entry garage
❖ Basement, crawl space or slab foundation, please specify when ordering

A turret is a small tower that is attached to a part of a building. It is usually round or octagonal in shape. Turrets arose in the medieval period in castles and churches and usually contain stairs or were used as a watch tower.

Special features

- ❖ 2,100 total square feet of living area
- ❖ A large courtyard with stone walls, lantern columns and covered porch welcomes you into open spaces
- ❖ The great room features a stone fireplace, built-in shelves, vaulted ceiling and atrium with dramatic staircase and a two and a half story window wall
- ❖ Two walk-in closets, vaulted ceiling with plant shelf and a luxury bath adorn the master bedroom suite
- ❖ 1,391 square feet of optional living area on the lower level with family room, walk-in bar, sitting area, bedroom #3 and a bath
- ❖ 2 bedrooms, 2 baths, 3-car side entry garage
- ❖ Walk-out basement foundation

First Floor
2,100 sq. ft.

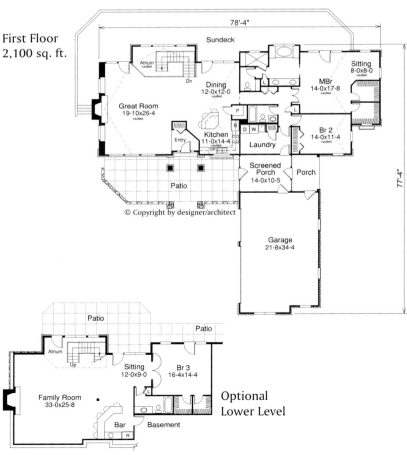

© Copyright by designer/architect

Optional
Lower Level

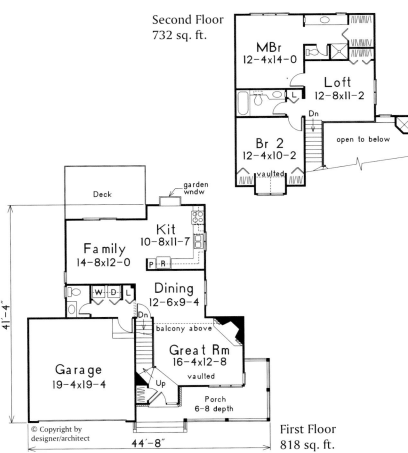

Second Floor
732 sq. ft.

MBr
12-4x14-0

Loft
12-8x11-2

Dn

Br 2
12-4x10-2

open to below

vaulted

Deck

garden
wndw

Kit
10-8x11-7

Family
14-8x12-0

P R

Dining
12-6x9-4

W D L

Dn

balcony above

Great Rm
16-4x12-8
vaulted

Up

Garage
19-4x19-4

Porch
6-8 depth

41'-4"

44'-8"

© Copyright by
designer/architect

First Floor
818 sq. ft.

Special features

- 1,550 total square feet of living area
- Impressive front entrance with a wrap-around covered porch and raised foyer
- Corner fireplace provides a focal point in the vaulted great room
- Loft is easily converted to a third bedroom or activity center
- Large kitchen/family room includes greenhouse windows and access to the deck and utility area
- The secondary bedroom has a large dormer and window seat
- 2 bedrooms, 2 1/2 baths, 2-car garage
- Basement foundation

The claw hammer is the most common, standard hammer. The 16-oz. size is best for most carpentry, but the 20-oz. size is highly recommended for construction work. Quality hammers have heads with slightly beveled edges to avoid chipping.

Special features

❖ 2,695 total square feet of living area

❖ A grand-scale great room features a fireplace with flanking shelves, handsome entry foyer with staircase and opens to a large kitchen and breakfast room

❖ Roomy master bedroom has a bay window, huge walk-in closet and bath

❖ Bedrooms #2 and #3 are generously oversized with walk-in closets and a Jack and Jill style bath

❖ 3 bedrooms, 2 1/2 baths, 2-car side entry garage

❖ Basement foundation

Put pots and cooking utensils near the range so they will be handy when cooking. While silverware, tableware, cleaning utensils and dishes for leftovers are best kept near the sink area.

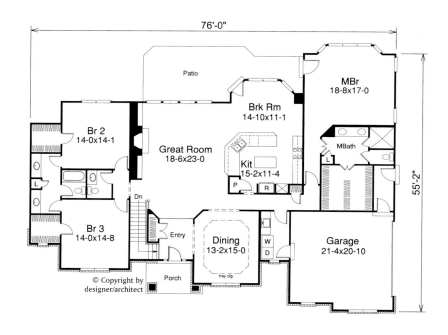

Second Floor
768 sq. ft.

First Floor
1,875 sq. ft.

Width: 72'-8"
Depth: 50'-10"

© Copyright by designer/architect

Special features

- 2,643 total square feet of living area
- Energy efficient home with 2" x 6" exterior walls
- Living and dining rooms combine to create a lovely area for entertaining
- Kitchen has a snack bar which overlooks an octagon-shaped dining area
- Family room is centrally located with entertainment center
- Private study at rear of home
- 4 bedrooms, 2 1/2 baths, 2-car side entry garage
- Basement foundation

55 million people work from home in North America; 1/3 of them (18 million people) run home-based businesses.

Special features

- ❖ 1,994 total square feet of living area
- ❖ Office/parlor/bedroom #4 has a double-door entry and is a very versatile space
- ❖ Sliding glass doors and many windows create a cheerful great room and breakfast room
- ❖ Double walk-in closets and vanity grace the master bath
- ❖ 3 bedrooms, 2 baths, optional 2-car side entry garage
- ❖ Basement, crawl space or slab foundation, please specify when ordering

Literally translated as "wind-water," feng shui is the art of placement. The three major concepts are the flow of energy; the balance of yin and yang; and the interaction of the five elements in the universe: fire, earth, metal, water and wood.

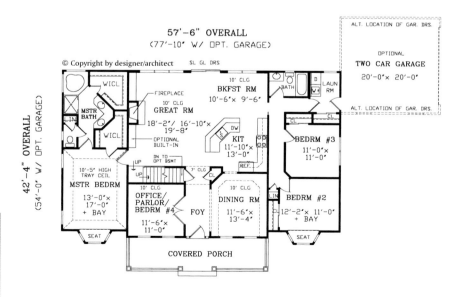

Special features

❖ 1,072 total square feet of living area
❖ Integrated open and screened front porches guarantee comfortable summer enjoyment
❖ Oversized garage includes area for shop and miscellaneous storage
❖ U-shaped kitchen and breakfast area is adjacent to the vaulted living room and has access to screened porch through sliding glass doors
❖ 345 square feet of optional living area on the lower level including a third bedroom and a bath
❖ 2 bedrooms, 2 baths, 2-car side entry garage
❖ Basement foundation

First Floor
1,072 sq. ft.

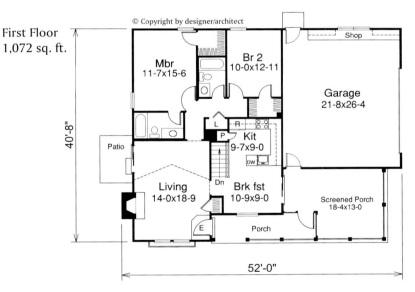

© Copyright by designer/architect

Mbr
11-7x15-6

Br 2
10-0x12-11

Shop

Garage
21-8x26-4

Patio

Kit
9-7x9-0

DW

Living
14-0x18-9

Dn

Brk fst
10-9x9-0

Screened Porch
18-4x13-0

E

Porch

40'-8"

52'-0"

Optional
Lower Level

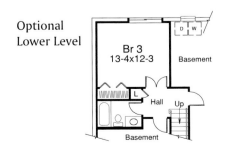

Br 3
13-4x12-3

Basement

D W

Hall

Up

Basement

Basement

Special features

- 2,646 total square feet of living area
- Energy efficient home with 2" x 6" exterior walls
- Casual living areas of the home are located in the rear, including a kitchen with eating bar overlooking an angled nook
- Private second floor master suite has a large walk-in closet, double sinks, spa tub and separate shower
- Two additional generous-sized bedrooms with dormered window seats and a large bonus room share a hall bath
- Bonus room on the second floor has 253 square feet of living area and is included in the total square footage
- 3 bedrooms, 2 1/2 baths, 3-car garage
- Basement foundation

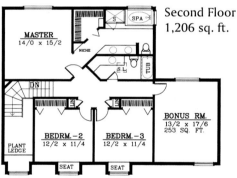

Second Floor
1,206 sq. ft.

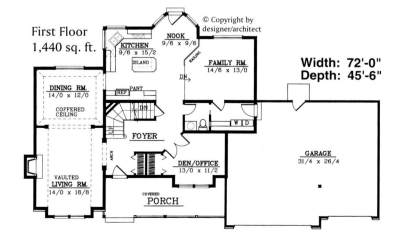

First Floor
1,440 sq. ft.

© Copyright by
designer/architect

Width: 72'-0"
Depth: 45'-6"

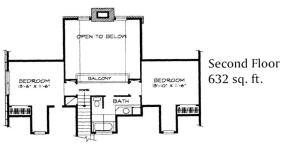

Second Floor
632 sq. ft.

BEDROOM
13'-6" X 11'-6"

BALCONY

OPEN TO BELOW

BEDROOM
13'-10" X 11'-6"

DOWN

BATH

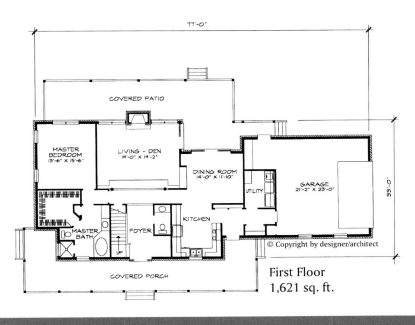

77'-0"

COVERED PATIO

MASTER BEDROOM
13'-6" X 15'-6"

LIVING – DEN
19'-0" X 19'-2"

DINING ROOM
14'-0" X 11'-10"

UTILITY

GARAGE
21'-2" X 23'-0"

33'-0"

MASTER BATH

FOYER

KITCHEN

UP

COVERED PORCH

© Copyright by designer/architect

First Floor
1,621 sq. ft.

Special features

- ❖ 2,253 total square feet of living area
- ❖ The spacious foyer includes a half bath on the way to the cozy living room/den
- ❖ The family will enjoy preparing meals in the U-shaped kitchen and eating in the quiet dining room or covered patio, accessed by sliding glass doors
- ❖ Secondary bedrooms enjoy added light and unique design created by the dormers
- ❖ 3 bedrooms, 2 1/2 baths, 2-car side entry garage
- ❖ Slab foundation

When landscaping your home, avoid overwhelming the home with landscape style. Do consider the size, shape and style of your home when planning the yard. Landscaping should harmonize with the house. Connect your yard and home with repeating design details, smooth transitions, and inside views.

Special features

- ❖ 1,621 total square feet of living area
- ❖ The front exterior includes an attractive gable-end arched window and extra-deep porch
- ❖ A grand-scale great room enjoys a coffered ceiling, fireplace, access to the wrap-around deck and is brightly lit with numerous French doors and windows
- ❖ The master bedroom suite has a sitting area, double walk-in closets and a luxury bath
- ❖ 223 square feet of optional finished space on the lower level
- ❖ 3 bedrooms, 2 baths, 2-car drive under side entry garage
- ❖ Basement foundation

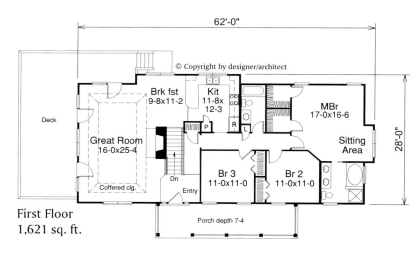

62'-0"

© Copyright by designer/architect

Deck

Brk fst
9-8x11-2

Kit
11-8x
12-3

MBr
17-0x16-6

Great Room
16-0x25-4

Sitting
Area

Coffered clg.

Dn

Br 3
11-0x11-0

Br 2
11-0x11-0

Entry

28'-0"

Porch depth 7-4

First Floor
1,621 sq. ft.

Lower Level With
Optional Laundry Area

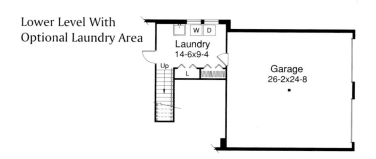

W D

Laundry
14-6x9-4

Garage
26-2x24-8

Up

L

Second Floor
1,052 sq. ft.

BR. #3
14/5X10/4

M. BR.
16/1X14/5
COFFERED CLG.

DN

BR. #2
12/5X12/2

First Floor
1,166 sq. ft.

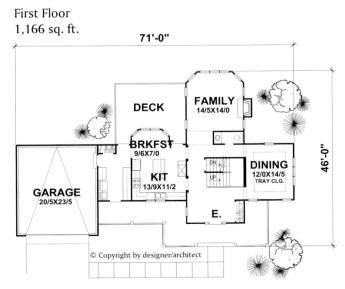

71'-0"

DECK

FAMILY
14/5X14/0

46'-0"

BRKFST
9/6X7/0

KIT
13/9X11/2

DN
UP

DINING
12/0X14/5
TRAY CLG.

GARAGE
20/5X23/5

E.

© Copyright by designer/architect

Special features

❖ 2,218 total square feet of living area
❖ Bay-shaped breakfast and family rooms maintain a cheerful atmosphere throughout the gathering areas
❖ An expansive walk-in closet in the master bedroom encourages organization
❖ Lots of counterspace in the laundry room is perfect for family chores
❖ 3 bedrooms, 2 1/2 baths, 2-car garage
❖ Basement foundation

A deck is usually built onto the back of a home creating an easy transition between the house and backyard. They are typically more private than porches.

Special features

- ❖ 1,768 total square feet of living area
- ❖ Upon entering you will get a feeling of spaciousness with the two-story living and dining rooms
- ❖ The bayed breakfast area is a refreshing place to start the day
- ❖ The covered porch off the breakfast area extends the dining to the outdoors
- ❖ 3 bedrooms, 2 1/2 baths
- ❖ Slab or crawl space foundation, please specify when ordering

First Floor
1,247 sq. ft.

Second Floor
521 sq. ft.

Width: 36'-6"
Depth: 57'-0"

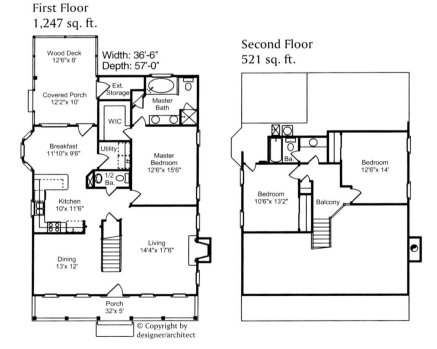

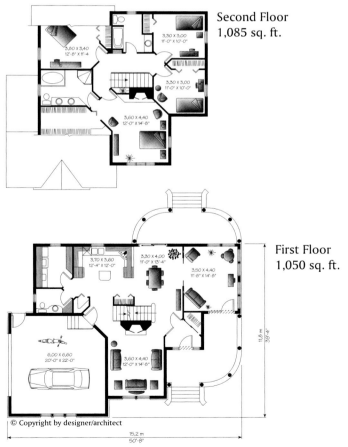

Second Floor
1,085 sq. ft.

3,80 X 3,40
12'-8" X 11'-4

3,30 X 3,00
11'-0" X 10'-0"

3,30 X 3,00
11'-0" X 10'-0"

3,60 X 4,40
12'-0" X 14'-8"

Special features

- ❖ 2,135 total square feet of living area
- ❖ Energy efficient home with 2" x 6" exterior walls
- ❖ All bedrooms on second floor for privacy
- ❖ 9' ceilings on the first floor
- ❖ 4 bedrooms, 2 1/2 baths, 2-car side entry garage
- ❖ Basement foundation

First Floor
1,050 sq. ft.

3,70 X 3,60
12'-4" X 12'-0"

3,30 X 4,00
11'-0" X 13'-4"

3,50 X 4,40
11'-8" X 14'-8"

11,8 m
39'-4"

6,00 X 6,60
20'-0" X 22'-0"

3,60 X 4,40
12'-0" X 14'-8"

© Copyright by designer/architect

15,2 m
50'-8"

Special features

- 1,873 total square feet of living area
- Energy efficient home with 2" x 6" exterior walls
- Sunny master bedroom has three large windows creating a cheerful feel
- U-shaped kitchen is open to a center island that looks beyond into the dining room
- Cozy den in the front of the home includes a large closet for storage
- 3 bedrooms, 2 baths, 3-car garage
- Crawl space foundation

Over time mulch can lose color making it somewhat less desirable in decorative planting areas. Aged pine bark mulch holds a great, uniform brown color for an entire season. Straight compost, which is black, will do the same. Light-colored mulch, such as cedar and hemlock, loses its color quickly.

© Copyright by designer/architect

Width: 63'-0"
Depth: 74'-11"

Special features

❖ 2,597 total square feet of living area
❖ Dormer windows and stone accent complete the unique look of this home
❖ The formal dining room features a barreled ceiling and is perfect for entertaining with an adjacent butler's pantry that leads to a huge gourmet kitchen
❖ A spacious family room boasts a media center and bookcases flanking the cozy fireplace
❖ A large, secluded master bedroom boasts a lavish bath with a huge walk-in closet and whirlpool tub
❖ 4 bedrooms, 2 baths, 2-car side entry garage
❖ Slab or crawl space foundation, please specify when ordering

Special features

- 2,188 total square feet of living area
- Master bedroom includes a private covered porch, sitting area and two large walk-in closets
- Spacious kitchen features a center island, snack bar and laundry access
- Great room has a 10' ceiling and a dramatic corner fireplace
- 3 bedrooms, 2 baths, 3-car side entry garage
- Basement foundation

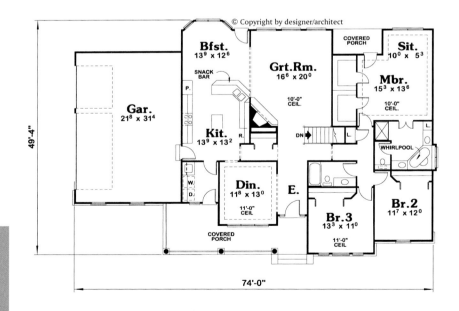

© Copyright by designer/architect

Floral furnishings and decorations create a look, but fresh flowers and plants can really bring a room to life. Display potted orchids to enhance an oriental theme, colorful spring blooms for country style or lush green foliage for a colonial room.

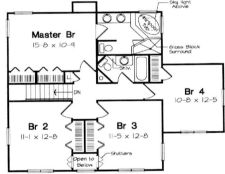

Second Floor
983 sq. ft.

Master Br
15-8 x 10-9

Sky light Above

Glass Block Surround

Shlv.

DN

Br 4
10-8 x 12-5

Br 2
11-1 x 12-8

Br 3
11-5 x 12-8

Open to Below — Shutters

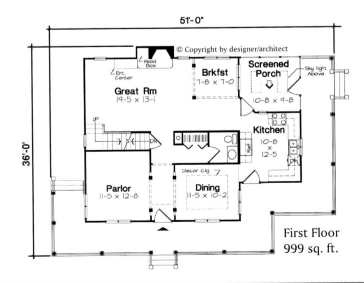

51'-0"

36'-0"

© Copyright by designer/architect

Wood Box

Ent. Center

Brkfst
7-8 x 7-0

Screened Porch
10-8 x 9-8

Sky light Above

Great Rm
19-5 x 13-1

UP

DN

Kitchen
10-8 x 12-5

Ref

Decor Clg

Parlor
11-5 x 12-8

Dining
11-5 x 10-2

First Floor
999 sq. ft.

Special features

❖ 1,982 total square feet of living area
❖ Spacious master bedroom has a bath with corner whirlpool tub and sunny skylight above
❖ Breakfast area overlooks into the great room
❖ Screened porch with skylight above extends the home outdoors and allows for another entertainment area
❖ 4 bedrooms, 2 1/2 baths
❖ Basement foundation

To prevent scalding, make sure your water heater temperature is set no higher than 120 degrees Fahrenheit.

Special features

- ❖ 1,993 total square feet of living area
- ❖ Charming front and rear porches
- ❖ 12' ceiling in living room
- ❖ Exquisite master bath with large walk-in closet
- ❖ 3 bedrooms, 2 baths, 2-car side entry garage
- ❖ Crawl space foundation, drawings also include slab foundation

If you have a small room don't paint it white to make it seem bigger. Instead, go with the architecture of the space and paint it a rich, warm color to make it more intimate and cozy. Let your big rooms expand with light, while your small rooms should wrap around you with the use of warm paint tones.

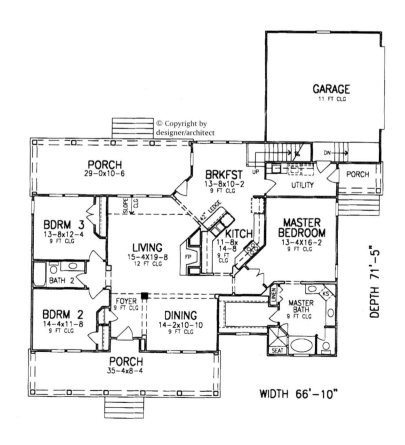

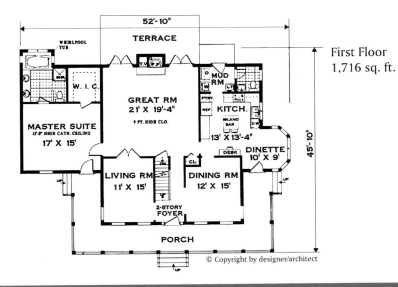

Second Floor
942 sq. ft.

BEDRM-2
12' X 14'

BEDRM-3
12' X 16'

CL.   HALL   CL.   CL.

BEDRM-5
11' X 12'

DN.

LIN

BEDRM-4
12' X 12'

CL.   CL.   CL.

First Floor
1,716 sq. ft.

52'-10"

WHIRLPOOL TUB

TERRACE

W. I. C.

GREAT RM
21' X 19'-4"
9 FT. HIGH CLG.

MUD RM

KITCH.

PTRY.

REF.

MASTER SUITE
17'-4" HIGH CATH. CEILING
17' X 15'

ISLAND BAR
13' X 13'-4"

DESK

DINETTE
10' X 9'

45'-10"

LIVING RM
11' X 15'

CL.

DINING RM
12' X 15'

2-STORY FOYER

UP

PORCH

UP

© Copyright by designer/architect

Special features

❖ 2,658 total square feet of living area

❖ A wrap-around porch, round-top windows and a trio of dormers enhance this Traditional design

❖ Formal areas flank the foyer, which leads to an expansive great room featuring a fireplace and a built-in media center

❖ Varied ceiling heights add character to the entire home

❖ 5 bedrooms, 2 1/2 baths

❖ Slab, crawl space or basement foundation, please specify when ordering

Elegant arched windows can be challenging to dress. A rounded track or rod can be installed to follow the line of an arch. Alternatively, a rod may be fixed across the window below the semicircular part. Leave the arched portion bare, or fill it with a fixed, shaped shade or fan-shaped curtain.

Special features

❖ 1,792 total square feet of living area
❖ Great curb appeal makes this a popular design
❖ First floor master bedroom maintains privacy
❖ Dining area has sliding glass doors leading to the outdoors
❖ Formal dining and living rooms combine for added gathering space
❖ 3 bedrooms, 2 1/2 baths, 2-car garage
❖ Basement foundation

Learn the "rule of threes" and apply to your home decorating projects. Overall, odd numbers of objects when decorating are more eye-catching and interesting than even numbers.

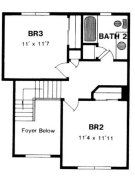

Second Floor
511 sq. ft.

BR3
11' x 11'7

BATH 2

Foyer Below

BR2
11'4 x 11'11

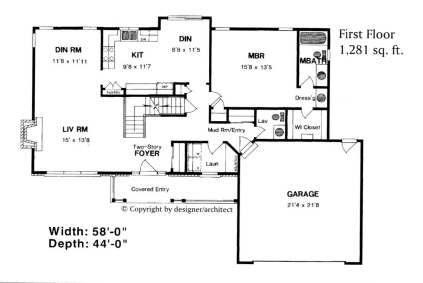

First Floor
1,281 sq. ft.

DIN RM
11'8 x 11'11

KIT
9'8 x 11'7

DIN
8'8 x 11'5

MBR
15'8 x 13'5

MBATH

PANTRY

REF

Dress'g

LIV RM
15' x 13'8

Lav

WI Closet

Two-Story
FOYER

Mud Rm/Entry

Laun

Covered Entry

GARAGE
21'4 x 21'8

© Copyright by designer/architect

Width: 58'-0"
Depth: 44'-0"

Special features

- ❖ 1,288 total square feet of living area
- ❖ Energy efficient home with 2" x 6" exterior walls
- ❖ Convenient snack bar in kitchen
- ❖ The first floor half bath has laundry facilities
- ❖ Both second floor bedrooms easily access a full bath
- ❖ 2 bedrooms, 1 1/2 baths, 1-car rear entry garage
- ❖ Basement foundation

First Floor
691 sq. ft.

Second Floor
597 sq. ft.

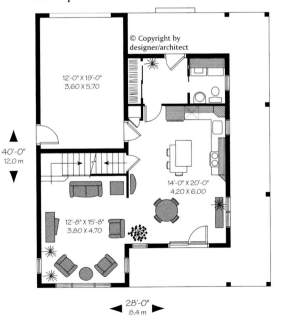

© Copyright by designer/architect

12'-0" X 19'-0"
3,60 X 5,70

14'-0" X 20'-0"
4,20 X 6,00

12'-8" X 15'-8"
3,80 X 4,70

40'-0"
12,0 m

28'-0"
8,4 m

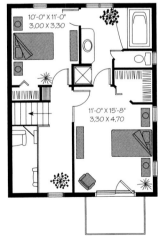

10'-0" X 11'-0"
3,00 X 3,30

11'-0" X 15'-8"
3,30 X 4,70

Flexible lighting is essential for a living room. Aim to include three different types of light source: ambient, for general illumination; task lamps to focus on activities such as reading or sewing; and decorative lighting, which gives you the chance to introduce unusual and attractive fittings or interesting effects.

Special features

- ❖ 1,533 total square feet of living area
- ❖ Multiple gables and stonework deliver a warm and inviting exterior
- ❖ The vaulted great room has a fireplace and spectacular views accomplished with a two-story atrium window wall
- ❖ A covered rear porch is easily accessed from the breakfast room or garage
- ❖ The atrium provides an ideal approach to an optional finished walk-out basement
- ❖ 3 bedrooms, 2 baths, 2-car garage
- ❖ Walk-out basement foundation

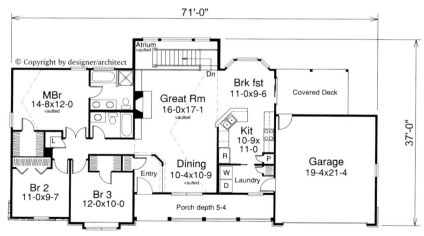

First Floor
1,288 sq. ft.

Second Floor
359 sq. ft.

Special features

- ❖ 1,647 total square feet of living area
- ❖ Enormous great room boasts a vaulted ceiling
- ❖ Located in the great room is an open kitchen with an island and breakfast bar
- ❖ Stunning loft overlooks the great room
- ❖ 2 bedrooms, 1 bath
- ❖ Slab or basement foundation, please specify when ordering

Brown, beige and tan colors represent spring, youth, prosperity, family, harmony, nutrition, strength, growth and vitality.

Special features

- 1,957 total square feet of living area
- The grand family room with a 10' ceiling and fireplace flanked by transom windows creates a relaxing escape
- The combined kitchen and bayed breakfast area has access to the outdoors
- The second floor includes a massive unfinished storage area
- 4 bedrooms, 2 1/2 baths, 2-car garage
- Basement foundation

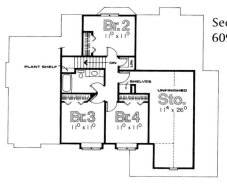

Second Floor
609 sq. ft.

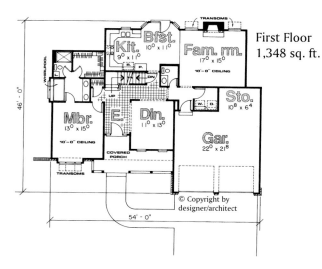

First Floor
1,348 sq. ft.

Heavy objects that could shatter dangerously should be securely attached to walls with screws and metal straps. This is particularly important in areas prone to earthquakes.

Second Floor
728 sq. ft.

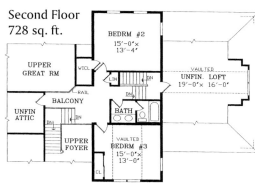

BEDRM #2
15'-0" x
13'-4"

UPPER GREAT RM

WICL

LIN

VAULTED
UNFIN. LOFT
19'-0" x 16'-0"

DN

DN

UNFIN ATTIC

BALCONY

RAIL

BATH

DN DN

UPPER FOYER

VAULTED
BEDRM #3
15'-0" x
13'-0"

CL

Special features

- ❖ 2,874 total square feet of living area
- ❖ Energy efficient home with 2" x 6" exterior walls
- ❖ Openness characterizes the casual areas
- ❖ The kitchen is separated from the bayed breakfast nook by an island workspace
- ❖ Stunning great room has a dramatic vaulted ceiling and a corner fireplace
- ❖ Unfinished loft on the second floor has an additional 300 square feet of living area
- ❖ 4 bedrooms, 3 baths, 3-car side entry garage
- ❖ Basement, crawl space or slab foundation, please specify when ordering

© Copyright by designer/architect

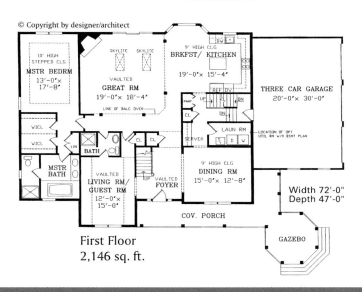

10' HIGH STEPPED CLG
MSTR BEDRM
13'-0" x
17'-8"

SKYLITE SKYLITE

9' HIGH CLG
BRKFST/ KITCHEN
19'-0" x 15'-4"

VAULTED
GREAT RM
19'-0" x 18'-4"

THREE CAR GARAGE
20'-0" x 30'-0"

LINE OF BALC. OVER

WICL

WICL

BATH

LIN

CL CL

REF DW

UP

PANT

DN

CL

LAUN RM

SERVER

S D W

LOCATION OF OPT
UTIL RM W/O BSMT PLAN

MSTR BATH

VAULTED
LIVING RM/
GUEST RM
12'-0" x
15'-0"

UP

VAULTED
FOYER

9' HIGH CLG
DINING RM
15'-0" x 12'-8"

Width 72'-0"
Depth 47'-0"

COV. PORCH

GAZEBO

First Floor
2,146 sq. ft.

Special features

❖ 2,535 total square feet of living area

❖ Energy efficient home with 2" x 6" exterior walls

❖ The foyer is flanked by formal living and dining spaces, which open to the family room and is great for entertaining

❖ The master bedroom features a sitting area and lavish bath with double-bowl vanity, makeup counter and giant walk-in closet

❖ The family room enjoys a grand fireplace and twin French doors to the rear porch and deck

❖ 4 bedrooms, 3 1/2 baths, 2-car side entry garage

❖ Crawl space foundation, drawings also include basement foundation

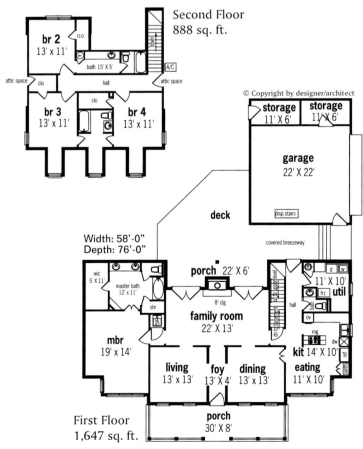

Second Floor
888 sq. ft.

br 2
13' x 11'

bath 15' X 5'

attic space

clo

hall

clo

br 3
13' x 11'

br 4
13' x 11'

© Copyright by designer/architect

storage
11' X 6'

storage
11' X 6'

garage
22' X 22'

deck

disp. stairs

covered breezeway

Width: 58'-0"
Depth: 76'-0"

wic
5' x 11'

master bath
12' x 11'

shr

porch
22' X 6'

8' clg

11' X 10'

util

mbr
19' x 14'

family room
22' X 13'

hall

kit
14' X 10'

eating
11' X 10'

living
13' x 13'

foy
13' x 4'

dining
13' x 13'

First Floor
1,647 sq. ft.

porch
30' X 8'

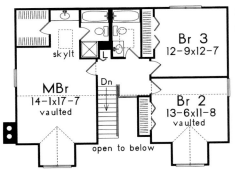

Second Floor
896 sq. ft.

Br 3
12-9x12-7

skylt

MBr
14-1x17-7
vaulted

Dn

Br 2
13-6x11-8
vaulted

open to below

38'-0"

First Floor
1,216 sq. ft.

Nook
7-6x9-6

Kit
9-6x
12-0

D

W

Family
14-1x15-10

Dn

P

R

L

32'-2"

Living
14-1x15-5

Up

Foyer

Dining
13-6x12-3

Porch depth 8-0

© Copyright by designer/architect

Special features

- ❖ 2,112 total square feet of living area
- ❖ Kitchen efficiently connects to the formal dining area
- ❖ Nook located between the family room and kitchen creates an ideal breakfast area
- ❖ Both baths on the second floor feature skylights
- ❖ 3 bedrooms, 3 baths
- ❖ Basement foundation, drawings also include crawl space foundation

Talcum powder works really well in quieting a squeaky floor. Sprinkle a generous amount wherever the floor makes noise and then work the powder into the joints and around exposed nail heads.

Special features

- 1,958 total square feet of living area
- Spacious kitchen and breakfast area is open to the rear deck
- A charming rail separates the family room and breakfast area keeping an open feel
- Dormers add interest and spaciousness in bedroom #2
- Bonus room on the second floor is included in the square footage
- 3 bedrooms, 2 1/2 baths, 2-car side entry garage
- Basement foundation, drawings also include slab and crawl space foundations

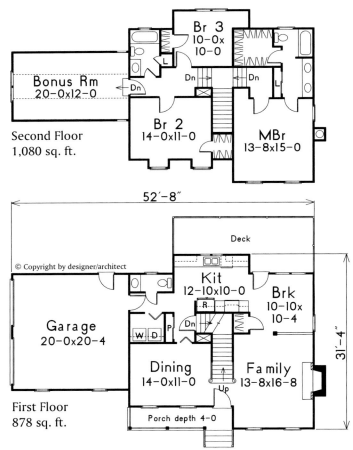

Br 3
10-0x
10-0

Bonus Rm
20-0x12-0

Dn

Dn

Dn

Second Floor
1,080 sq. ft.

Br 2
14-0x11-0

MBr
13-8x15-0

52'-8"

Deck

© Copyright by designer/architect

Kit
12-10x10-0

Brk
10-10x
10-4

R

Garage
20-0x20-4

W D

P

Dn

31'-4"

Dining
14-0x11-0

Family
13-8x16-8

Up

First Floor
878 sq. ft.

Porch depth 4-0

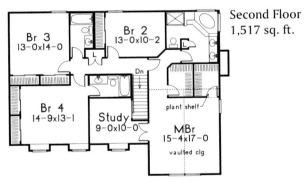

Second Floor 1,517 sq. ft.

Br 3
13-0x14-0

Br 2
13-0x10-2

Br 4
14-9x13-1

Study
9-0x10-0

plant shelf

Dn

MBr
15-4x17-0
vaulted clg

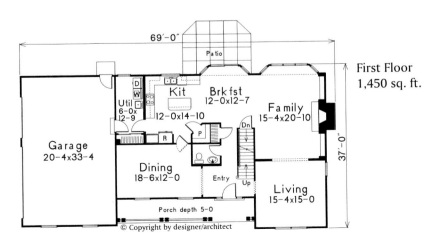

First Floor 1,450 sq. ft.

69'-0"

Patio

Kit
12-0x14-10

Brkfst
12-0x12-7

Family
15-4x20-10

Util
6-0x 12-9

D W

R

P

Dn

37'-0"

Garage
20-4x33-4

Dining
18-6x12-0

Entry

Up

Living
15-4x15-0

Porch depth 5-0

© Copyright by designer/architect

Special features

- ❖ 2,967 total square feet of living area
- ❖ The charming exterior is graced with a country porch and multiple arched projected box windows
- ❖ Dining area is oversized and adjoins a fully equipped kitchen with walk-in pantry
- ❖ Two bay windows light up the enormous informal living area to the rear
- ❖ 4 bedrooms, 3 1/2 baths, 3-car side entry garage
- ❖ Basement foundation

For easy storage, use an old silverware organizer in the bathroom or bedroom to organize brushes, combs, bobby pins, razor blades, and all sorts of other things that clutter your space.

Special features

- 2,420 total square feet of living area
- The huge great room has a fireplace with flanking shelves, a wide bay window and dining area surrounded with windows
- Many excellent features adorn the kitchen including a corner window sink, island snack bar, walk-in pantry and breakfast area with adjoining covered patio
- The apartment with its own exterior entrance and entry with coat closet accesses the dining and great rooms of the primary residence
- 1,014 square feet of optional living area on the lower level includes a large family room with fireplace and home theater room with walk-in bar and half bath
- 4 bedrooms, 3 1/2 baths, 2-car side entry garage
- Basement foundation

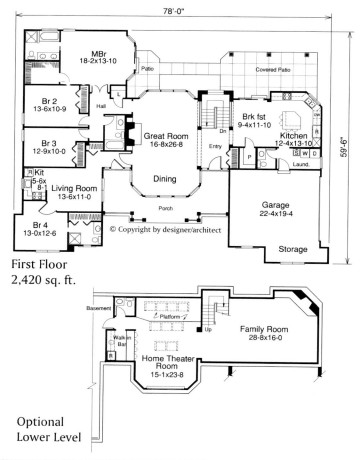

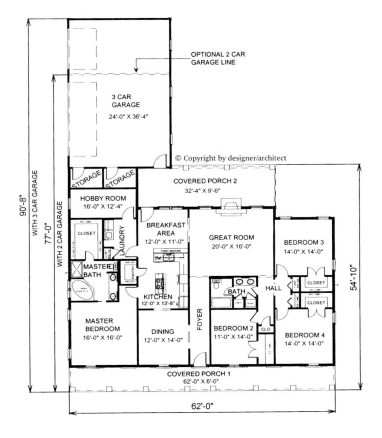

OPTIONAL 2 CAR
GARAGE LINE

3 CAR
GARAGE
24'-0" X 36'-4"

© Copyright by designer/architect

90'-8"
WITH 3 CAR GARAGE

77'-0"
WITH 2 CAR GARAGE

STORAGE   STORAGE

COVERED PORCH 2
32'-4" X 9'-6"

HOBBY ROOM
16'-0" X 12'-4"

CLOSET

LAUNDRY

MASTER
BATH

BREAKFAST
AREA
12'-0" X 11'-0"

GREAT ROOM
20'-0" X 16'-0"

BEDROOM 3
14'-0" X 14'-0"

KITCHEN
12'-0" X 13'-8"

BATH

HALL

CLOSET

CLOSET

MASTER
BEDROOM
16'-0" X 16'-0"

DINING
12'-0" X 14'-0"

FOYER

BEDROOM 2
11'-0" X 14'-0"

CLO.

BEDROOM 4
14'-0" X 14'-0"

54'-10"

COVERED PORCH 1
62'-0" X 6'-0"

62'-0"

Special features

- ❖ 2,423 total square feet of living area
- ❖ All bedrooms have large walk-in closets
- ❖ Unique hobby room located off the laundry area is a nice workshop
- ❖ Kitchen boasts a walk-in pantry and snack bar open to the breakfast area
- ❖ 4 bedrooms, 2 baths, 3-car side entry garage
- ❖ Crawl space or slab foundation, please specify when ordering

Clean the inside of the dishwasher once a month. Use some lemonade mix to fill the soap cup and then run it through a cycle. The citric acid in the lemonade will clean the racks, the jets and the interior walls.

Special features

- 2,414 total square feet of living area
- 9' ceilings throughout this home
- Versatile screened porch connects to master suite, outdoor porch and breakfast room for convenience
- Quiet parlor in the front of the home makes an ideal place for reading or a cozy home office
- Future playroom on the second floor has an additional 305 square feet of living area
- 3 bedrooms, 2 1/2 baths, 2-car side entry garage
- Slab foundation

Garden furniture can be found in a variety of materials. Wicker has a traditional look but needs protection from weather. Metal is highly durable, but it usually needs cushions. Resin is an inexpensive and light material and is easily cleaned with soap and water. Weather-resistant hardwood can be left natural and is low maintenance.

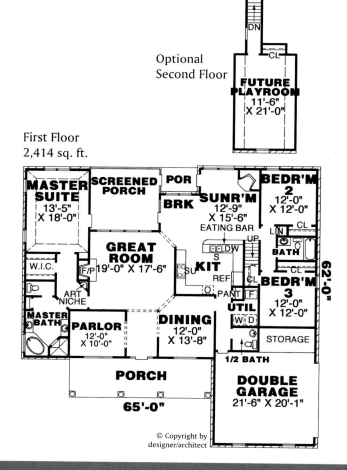

Optional Second Floor

First Floor 2,414 sq. ft.

© Copyright by designer/architect

Plan #597-001D-0061

Price Code C

Special features

- ❖ 1,875 total square feet of living area
- ❖ Country-style exterior with wrap-around porch and dormers
- ❖ Large second floor bedrooms share a dressing area and bath
- ❖ Master bedroom includes a bay window, walk-in closet, dressing area and bath
- ❖ 2" x 6" exterior walls available, please order plan #597-001D-0114
- ❖ 3 bedrooms, 2 baths, 2-car side entry garage
- ❖ Crawl space foundation, drawings also include basement and slab foundations

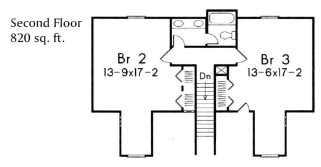

Second Floor
820 sq. ft.

Br 2
13-9x17-2

Br 3
13-6x17-2

Dn

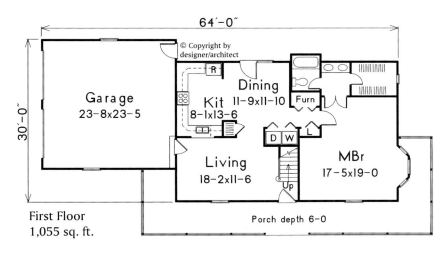

64´-0˝

30´-0˝

© Copyright by designer/architect

R

Garage
23-8x23-5

Dining
11-9x11-10

Kit
8-1x13-6

Furn

D W L

Living
18-2x11-6

Up

MBr
17-5x19-0

First Floor
1,055 sq. ft.

Porch depth 6-0

Special features

- 647 total square feet of living area
- Large vaulted room for living/sleeping has plant shelves on each end, stone fireplace and wide glass doors for views
- Roomy kitchen is vaulted and has a bayed dining area and fireplace
- Step down into a sunken and vaulted bath featuring a 6'-0" whirlpool tub-in-a-bay with shelves at each end for storage
- A large palladian window adorns each end of the cottage giving a cheery atmosphere throughout
- 1 living/sleeping room, 1 bath
- Crawl space foundation

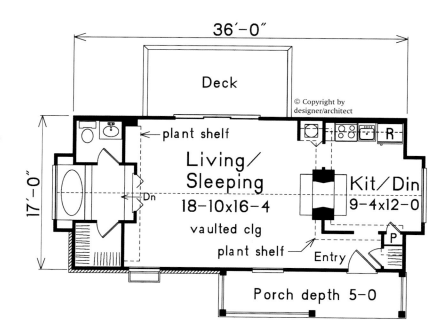

36'-0"

Deck

© Copyright by designer/architect

17'-0"

plant shelf

Living/ Sleeping
18-10x16-4

vaulted clg

plant shelf

Dn

Kit/Din
9-4x12-0

Entry

P

Porch depth 5-0

Second Floor
585 sq. ft.

BED RM.2
12'-0" x 13'-0"

STUDY AREA

BED RM.3
12'-0" x 13'-0"

BENCH WITH STORAGE

BOOKS

BOOKS

STOR.

W.I. CLOS.

B.3

1/2 WALL

LINEN

STAIR DOWN

ATTIC ACCESS

STAINED GLASS

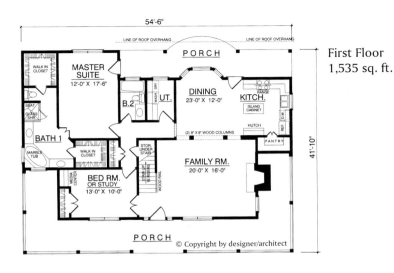

54'-6"

LINE OF ROOF OVERHANG

LINE OF ROOF OVERHANG

PORCH

First Floor
1,535 sq. ft.

41'-10"

WALK IN CLOSET

MASTER SUITE
12'-0" X 17'-6"

B.2

UT.

WASH DRY

DINING
23'-0" X 12'-0"

KITCH.

RANGE

ISLAND CABINET

REF. D.W.

SEAT GLASS SHR.

HUTCH

PANTRY

BATH 1

MARBLE TUB

WALK IN CLOSET

(2) 8" X 8" WOOD COLUMNS

STOR. UNDER STAIR

MEDIA CENTER

BED RM. OR STUDY
13'-0" X 10'-0"

STAIR UP W/ INSERTS

WOOD RAIL

FAMILY RM.
20'-0" X 16'-0"

PORCH

© Copyright by designer/architect

Special features

❖ 2,143 total square feet of living area

❖ Enter the home into the expansive family room and view the bayed dining area defined by wood columns

❖ The kitchen includes an island, hutch, extra-large pantry and access to the rear porch

❖ A study area in a box-bay on the second floor includes built-in bookshelves and a bench with storage

❖ 4 bedrooms, 3 baths

❖ Basement, slab or crawl space foundation, please specify when ordering

Don't darken your hallway with an excess of art and family pictures. Keep a balance of empty spaces and hanging objects.

Special features

- ❖ 3,035 total square feet of living area
- ❖ Front facade showcases a large porch
- ❖ Private master bedroom with windowed sitting area, walk-in closet, sloped ceiling and skylight
- ❖ Formal living and dining rooms adjoin the family room through attractive French doors
- ❖ Energy efficient home with 2" x 6" exterior walls
- ❖ 4 bedrooms, 3 1/2 baths, 2-car detached side entry garage
- ❖ Crawl space foundation, drawings also include slab and basement foundations

Whatever makes your family room stand out should be the main focal point. So, if you have a beautiful painting or a stunning fireplace, accent it with lighting or furniture arrangements that draw the eye to this feature.

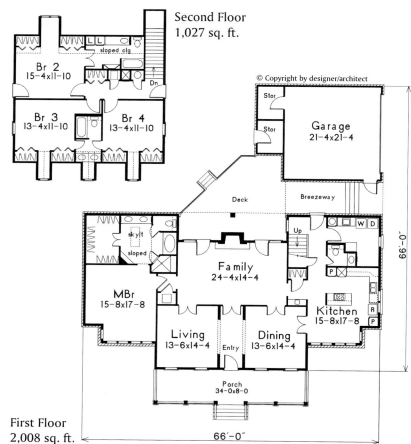

Second Floor
1,027 sq. ft.

Br 2
15-4x11-10

Br 3
13-4x11-10

Br 4
13-4x11-10

© Copyright by designer/architect

First Floor
2,008 sq. ft.

Stor

Stor

Garage
21-4x21-4

Deck

Breezeway

66'-0"

Family
24-4x14-4

Kitchen
15-8x17-8

MBr
15-8x17-8

Living
13-6x14-4

Entry

Dining
13-6x14-4

Porch
34-0x8-0

66'-0"

Second Floor
1,091 sq. ft.

Second Floor plan labels:
- Window Seat
- Shelves
- Bedroom 13'6" x 13'9"
- Computer Loft 8'5" x 19'
- Great Room Below
- Bath
- Balcony
- Hall Below
- Bedroom 13'6" x 14'3"
- Bath
- Bedroom 13'2" x 13'6" Irreg
- Foyer Below
- Stairs Down
- Arched Opening

Special features

- ❖ 3,816 total square feet of living area
- ❖ Beautifully designed master bedroom enjoys a lavish dressing area as well as access to the library
- ❖ Second floor computer loft is centrally located and includes plenty of counterspace
- ❖ The two-story great room has an arched opening and a beautiful beamed ceiling
- ❖ The outdoor covered deck has a popular fireplace
- ❖ 4 bedrooms, 3 1/2 baths, 3-car side entry garage
- ❖ Basement foundation

First Floor plan labels:
- Stairs Down
- DECK
- Hearth Room 23'4" x 15'4"
- Breakfast
- Dressing
- Three Car Garage 22'10" x 38' Irreg.
- Laun.
- Kitchen 15'9" x 16'6"
- Great Room 17'9" x 17'
- Bath
- Master Bedroom 15' x 19'10"
- Gallery
- Wood Stair Rail
- Stairs Up
- Mud Room
- Walk-in Closet
- Butler Pantry
- Dining Room 13'2" x 13'6"
- Foyer
- Library 14'8" x 11'2"
- Window Seat
- Dropped Soffit
- Porch
- © Copyright by designer/architect

First Floor
2,725 sq. ft.

69'10"

90'

Special features

- ❖ 2,098 total square feet of living area
- ❖ Covered porch wraps around the entire house, leading to the deck and screened porch in the back
- ❖ Spacious kitchen has plenty of cabinet space as well as counterspace
- ❖ Convenient laundry chute is located near the second floor bathroom
- ❖ 3 bedrooms, 2 1/2 baths, 3-car side entry detached garage
- ❖ Crawl space or basement foundation, please specify when ordering

Violet is the color of luxury, from pale lilac to saturated purple. This color scheme can be exotic, regal and magical. Use strategically placed candles and lamps to illuminate the jewel tones and create an atmosphere of richness.

Second Floor
586 sq. ft.

First Floor
1,512 sq. ft.

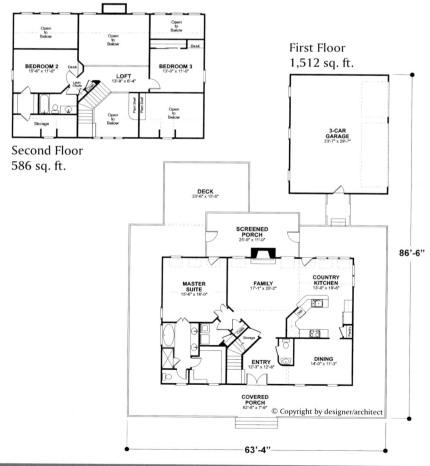

Second Floor
1,171 sq. ft.

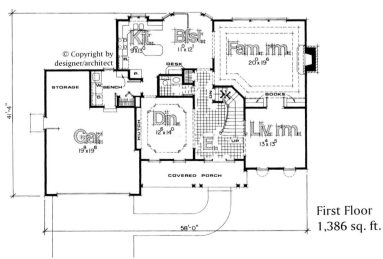

First Floor
1,386 sq. ft.

© Copyright by
designer/architect

Special features

❖ 2,557 total square feet of living area
❖ All bedrooms are located on the second floor for privacy
❖ The spacious family room provides a relaxing atmosphere with a cozy fireplace
❖ The built-in desk off the combined kitchen and breakfast room offers a convenient space for home office work
❖ 9' ceilings on the first floor
❖ 4 bedrooms, 2 1/2 baths, 3-car garage
❖ Basement foundation

A dining room table's style and shape affects the look of a room. As a general rule, many designers suggest buying a table that mimics the shape of your room for clean lines that are appealing to the eye.

Special features

- ❖ 1,979 total square feet of living area
- ❖ Striking corner fireplace is a stylish addition to the great room
- ❖ Open dining room allows the area to flow into the great room for added spaciousness
- ❖ Large pantry in the kitchen
- ❖ 3 bedrooms, 2 baths, 2-car side entry garage
- ❖ Slab foundation

When hanging artwork, be aware of whether sunlight will be directly hitting it or if it will be underneath another direct light source. Try to avoid hot spotlights when displaying art because they can cause quicker fading and overall deterioration to a special or cherished piece.

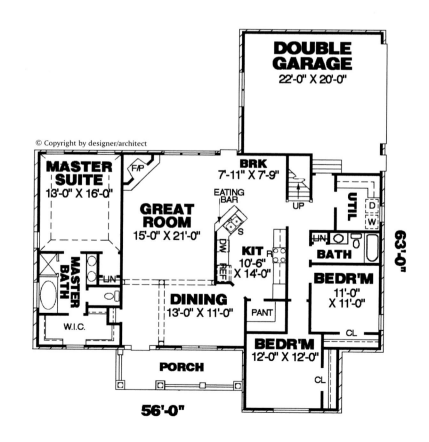

© Copyright by designer/architect

© Copyright by designer/architect

Special features

- ❖ 1,798 total square feet of living area
- ❖ French doors lead into the home with a view of the vaulted great room
- ❖ A coffered ceiling tops the formal dining room providing an elegant atmosphere
- ❖ The cozy breakfast area has access to the rear patio easily extending dining opportunities to the outdoors
- ❖ 3 bedrooms, 2 baths, 2-car side entry garage
- ❖ Slab foundation

A colored ceiling can make a room much more interesting. If the walls have been painted, but the ceiling is still white, the eye is drawn to the white ceiling because of the contrast. Why not make the contrast an unexpected color to complement the space creating an element of surprise?

Special features

❖ 1,559 total square feet of living area

❖ A cozy country appeal is provided by a spacious porch, masonry fireplace, roof dormers and a perfect balance of stonework and siding

❖ Large living room enjoys a fireplace, bayed dining area and separate entry

❖ A U-shaped kitchen is adjoined by a breakfast room with bay window and large pantry

❖ 3 bedrooms, 2 1/2 baths, 2-car drive under side entry garage

❖ Basement foundation

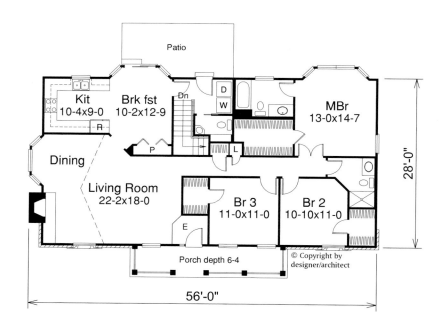

Never run an empty microwave. It can cause overheating and serious damage.

Special features

- 2,139 total square feet of living area
- The foyer leads into the spacious living and dining rooms
- The living and breakfast rooms open onto the relaxing rear porch
- Two walk-in closets and a corner whirlpool tub enhance the master bedroom bath
- The bonus room above the garage has an additional 532 square feet of living area
- 3 bedrooms, 2 baths, detached 2-car side entry garage
- Crawl space foundation

First Floor
2,139 sq. ft.

MASTER BEDROOM (19'0"x15'4")

STUDY/ BEDROOM #3 (13'4"x12'0")

BEDROOM #2 (13'4"x11'0")

FOYER

LIVING ROOM (16'10"x16'8")

REAR PORCH (26'8"x10'0")

DINING ROOM (12'0"x14'0")

BREAKFAST (12'0"x14'6")

KITCHEN (12'0"x10'4")

FRONT PORCH (40'0"x7'8")

FRONT OF HOME

SERVICE YARD (7'8"x8'0")

LAUNDRY (6'0"x9'4")

Width: 67'-8"
Depth: 98'-11"

Optional
Second Floor

BONUS ROOM (13'0"x24'2")

© Copyright by designer/architect

2-CAR GARAGE (23'4"x24'6")

A few precautions can go a long way toward protecting your home from termites. Fixing all leaks, cleaning overflowing gutters and diverting water from the foundation will keep your house dry and uninviting for pests. Trimming shrubbery and keeping wood mulch away from your house will also keep termites at bay.

Special features

- ❖ 2,044 total square feet of living area
- ❖ Elegant French doors lead from the kitchen to the formal dining room
- ❖ Two-car garage features a workshop area for projects or extra storage
- ❖ Second floor includes loft space ideal for an office area and a handy computer center
- ❖ Colossal master bedroom boasts double walk-in closets, a private bath and bay window seat
- ❖ 3 bedrooms, 2 1/2 baths, 2-car side entry garage
- ❖ Basement, crawl space or slab foundation, please specify when ordering

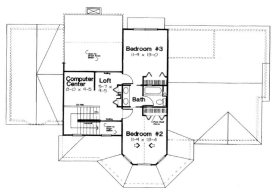

Second Floor
641 sq. ft.

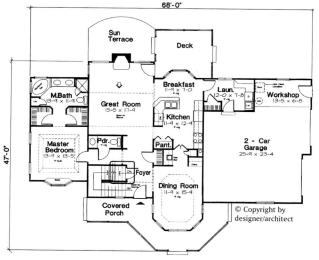

First Floor
1,403 sq. ft.

© Copyright by designer/architect

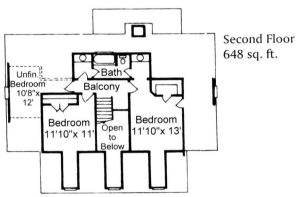

Second Floor
648 sq. ft.

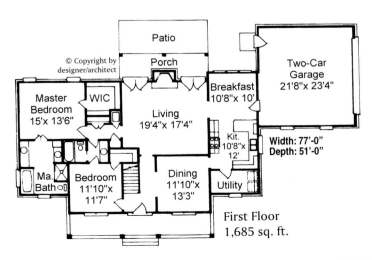

© Copyright by
designer/architect

Width: 77'-0"
Depth: 51'-0"

First Floor
1,685 sq. ft.

Special features

- ❖ 2,333 total square feet of living area
- ❖ Two sets of French doors flank the fireplace in the delightful living room
- ❖ The private master bedroom enjoys a walk-in closet and the pampering private bath
- ❖ Two additional bedrooms located on the second floor share a convenient Jack and Jill bath
- ❖ 4 bedrooms, 3 baths, 2-car side entry garage
- ❖ Slab, crawl space or basement foundation, please specify when ordering

Paint is flammable. Store in a climate-controlled area away from heat sources. Cans exposed to heat can expand, causing leakage.

Special features

- 1,941 total square feet of living area
- Interesting roof lines and a spacious front porch with flanking stonework help to fashion this beautiful country home
- The vaulted great room has a separate entry and bayed dining area suitable for a large family and friends
- The master bedroom enjoys a big walk-in closet and a gracious bath
- Four additional bedrooms complete the home, one of which is ideal for a study off the great room
- 5 bedrooms, 3 baths, 2-car side entry drive under garage
- Walk-out basement foundation

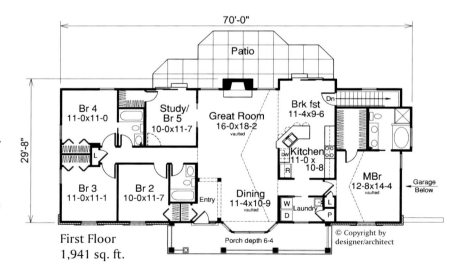

First Floor
1,941 sq. ft.

© Copyright by designer/architect

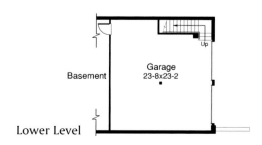

Lower Level

Plan #597-015D-0039

Price Code B

Second Floor
677 sq. ft.

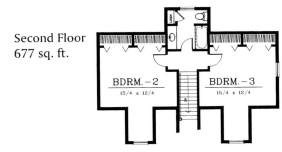

BDRM. – 2
15/4 x 12/4

BDRM. – 3
15/4 x 12/4

Width: 60'-0"
Depth: 36'-0"

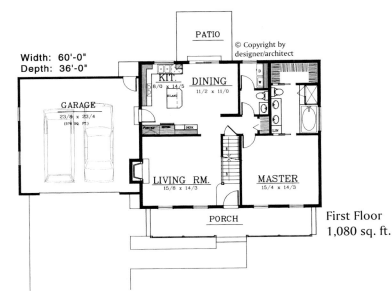

PATIO

© Copyright by
designer/architect

KIT.
8/0 x 14/5

DINING
11/2 x 11/0

GARAGE
23/8 x 23/4
(576 SQ. FT.)

LIVING RM.
15/8 x 14/3

MASTER
15/4 x 14/3

PORCH

First Floor
1,080 sq. ft.

Special features

- ❖ 1,757 total square feet of living area
- ❖ Energy efficient home with 2" x 6" exterior walls
- ❖ First floor master bedroom has privacy as well as its own bath and walk-in closet
- ❖ Cozy living room includes fireplace for warmth
- ❖ 3 bedrooms, 2 1/2 baths, 2-car garage
- ❖ Crawl space, basement or slab foundation, please specify when ordering

Change the batteries in your smoke and carbon monoxide detectors with the beginning and ending of Daylight Savings Time. They're lifesavers and should always be treated that way.

Special features

- ❖ 2,503 total square feet of living area
- ❖ 10' ceilings throughout the first floor
- ❖ A secondary entrance into the kitchen is convenient and casual
- ❖ First floor master bedroom has its own bath and walk-in closet
- ❖ The living room features a fireplace flanked by doors leading to the rear porch
- ❖ 4 bedrooms, 3 1/2 baths, 2-car drive under garage
- ❖ Walk-out basement foundation

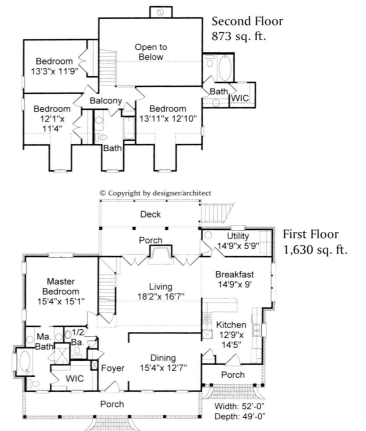

Second Floor
873 sq. ft.

Bedroom 13'3"x 11'9"

Open to Below

Bath WIC

Bedroom 12'1"x 11'4"

Balcony

Bedroom 13'11"x 12'10"

Bath

Bath

© Copyright by designer/architect

First Floor
1,630 sq. ft.

Deck

Porch

Utility 14'9"x 5'9"

Breakfast 14'9"x 9'

Master Bedroom 15'4"x 15'1"

Living 18'2"x 16'7"

Kitchen 12'9"x 14'5"

Ma. Bath

1/2 Ba.

Foyer

Dining 15'4"x 12'7"

Porch

WIC

Porch

Width: 52'-0"
Depth: 49'-0"

Second Floor
826 sq. ft.

slope
plant shelf

Guest Br 4
11-4 x 11-8

Br 3
12-2 x 13-4

open to below   DN

Balcony

slope   open to below

plant shelf

Br 2
13 x 11-2

linen

© Copyright by
designer/architect

First Floor
1,737 sq. ft.

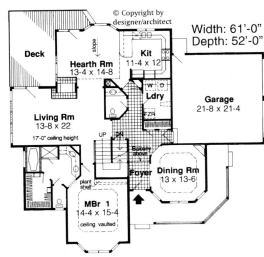

Deck

slope

Hearth Rm
13-4 x 14-8

Kit
11-4 x 12

W D

Ldry

FZR

Garage
21-8 x 21-4

Living Rm
13-8 x 22

17'-0" ceiling height

UP DN

Balcony above

Foyer

Dining Rm
13 x 13-6

plant shelf

MBr 1
14-4 x 15-4

ceiling vaulted

Width: 61'-0"
Depth: 52'-0"

Special features

❖ 2,563 total square feet of living area
❖ Energy efficient home with 2" x 6" exterior walls
❖ A distinctive see-through fireplace connects and warms the hearth and living rooms
❖ The living room boasts an impressive 17' ceiling and beautiful high windows
❖ The front porch wraps around the outside of the dining room
❖ 4 bedrooms, 3 1/2 baths, 2-car side entry garage
❖ Basement foundation

Special features

- 1,806 total square feet of living area
- Covered porch in the rear of the home adds an outdoor living area
- Private and formal living room
- Kitchen has snack counter that extends into family room
- 3 bedrooms, 2 baths, 2-car garage
- Slab foundation

Never water plants with tap water direct from the faucet; it contains chemicals that could harm your plants. Let tap water sit overnight before using it to water plants.

© Copyright by designer/architect

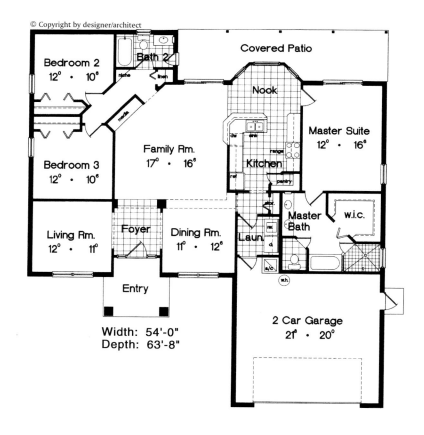

Bedroom 2
12⁰ · 10⁶

Bath 2

Covered Patio

Nook

Master Suite
12⁰ · 16⁶

Family Rm.
17⁰ · 16⁶

Kitchen

Bedroom 3
12⁰ · 10⁶

Master Bath

w.i.c.

Living Rm.
12⁰ · 11⁰

Foyer

Dining Rm.
11⁰ · 12⁶

Laun

Entry

2 Car Garage
21⁰ · 20⁰

Width: 54'-0"
Depth: 63'-8"

Special features

- 1,735 total square feet of living area
- Living and dining rooms offer 9' stepped ceilings
- Family room has an 11' ceiling, fireplace and French doors to the porch
- Master bedroom features a tray ceiling and includes a relaxing sitting bay
- 3 bedrooms, 2 baths, 2-car side entry garage
- Basement, crawl space, slab or walk-out basement foundation, please specify when ordering

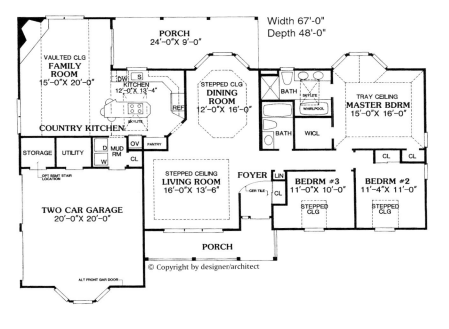

Width 67'-0"
Depth 48'-0"

© Copyright by designer/architect

Many house plants thrive in the steamy and humid atmosphere of a kitchen, so use their lush foliage to enhance a country scheme or liven up a windowsill.

Special features

- ❖ 2,594 total square feet of living area
- ❖ Snack bar in kitchen creates an extra place for dining
- ❖ Master bath has an interesting bayed whirlpool tub
- ❖ A wonderful sun room extends off the breakfast room creating a beautiful area for gathering
- ❖ 4 bedrooms, 2 1/2 baths, 2-car side entry garage
- ❖ Basement foundation

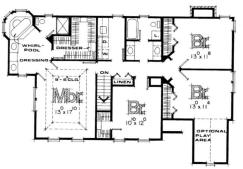

Second Floor
1,272 sq. ft.

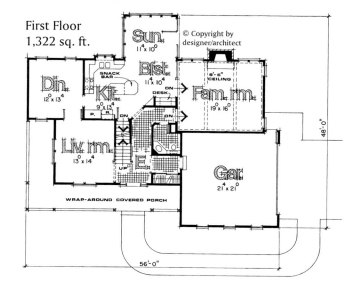

First Floor
1,322 sq. ft.

© Copyright by designer/architect

No fruit is more fickle about its habitat than the strawberry. Each region has favorite varieties; the same sort may give radically different results on neighboring lots. Consult your local extension agent or plant nurseries for recommendations.

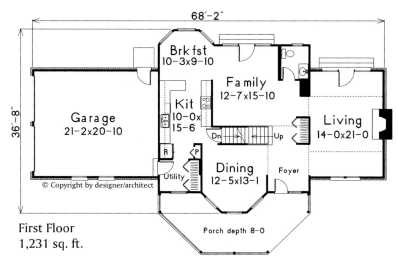

Second Floor
1,049 sq. ft.

MBr
16-9x15-4

Br 3
10-0x
10-8

Br 4
10-0x
10-0

Br 2
12-4x13-4

Dn

L

plant
shelf

open to
below

68'-2"

36'-8"

Garage
21-2x20-10

Brkfst
10-3x9-10

Family
12-7x15-10

Kit
10-0x
15-6

Living
14-0x21-0

Dn   Up

R

P

Dining
12-5x13-1

Utility

Foyer

© Copyright by designer/architect

First Floor
1,231 sq. ft.

Porch depth 8-0

Special features

- ❖ 2,280 total square feet of living area
- ❖ Laundry area is conveniently located on the second floor
- ❖ Compact, yet efficient kitchen
- ❖ Unique shaped dining room overlooks the front porch
- ❖ Cozy living room is enhanced with a sloped ceiling and fireplace
- ❖ 4 bedrooms, 2 1/2 baths, 2-car side entry garage
- ❖ Basement foundation

When you light the fire in your fireplace, keep the flue fully open, for maximum airflow to feed the flames. Once it's roaring, close the flue to the point where the chimney starts smoking, then open it just a tad for optimal heat. To keep airflow constant, open the window closest to the fire by a half-inch.

Special features

- 1,365 total square feet of living area
- Home is easily adaptable for physical accessibility featuring no stairs and extra-wide hall baths, laundry and garage
- Living room has separate entry and opens to a spacious dining room with view of rear patio
- L-shaped kitchen is well equipped and includes a built-in pantry
- All bedrooms are spaciously sized and offer generous closet storage
- 3 bedrooms, 2 baths, 1-car garage
- Slab foundation

If you don't have a green thumb or you need greenery in a hard-to-reach place, it is best to go with dried or artificial arrangements rather than not using them at all. Greenery adds natural sereneness to a space.

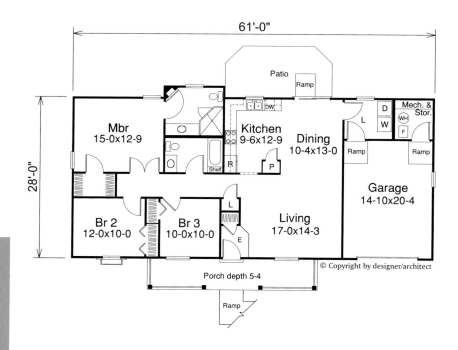

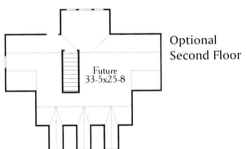

Optional
Second Floor

Future
33-5x25-8

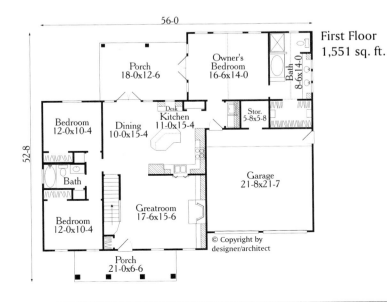

56-0

52-8

First Floor
1,551 sq. ft.

Porch
18-0x12-6

Owner's
Bedroom
16-6x14-0

Bath
8-6x14-0

Bedroom
12-0x10-4

Dining
10-0x15-4

Desk

Kitchen
11-0x15-4

Stor.
5-8x5-8

Bath

Bedroom
12-0x10-4

Greatroom
17-6x15-6

Garage
21-8x21-7

© Copyright by
designer/architect

Porch
21-0x6-6

Special features

- ❖ 1,551 total square feet of living area
- ❖ Enter the home and view the spacious great room with grand fireplace flanked by built-ins
- ❖ The kitchen boasts a large island with seating and a built-in desk
- ❖ The private owner's bedroom enjoys a deluxe bath, porch access and nearby laundry closet
- ❖ The optional second floor has an additional 684 square feet of living area
- ❖ 3 bedrooms, 2 baths, 2-car garage
- ❖ Basement, crawl space or slab foundation, please specify when ordering

Special features

- 2,054 total square feet of living area
- A sweeping porch leads to the large foyer with staircase, powder room and handy coat closet
- Spacious living room has a fireplace, triple door to patio and an adjacent computer room
- Kitchen features a snack bar, island counter, pantry and breakfast area with bay window
- Large master bedroom has two spacious closets and accesses a luxury bath with separate toilet and corner tub
- 3 bedrooms, 2 1/2 baths, 2-car detached garage
- Basement foundation

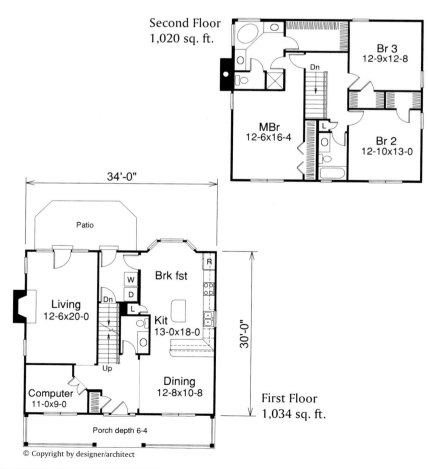

Second Floor 1,020 sq. ft.

First Floor 1,034 sq. ft.

© Copyright by designer/architect

Special features

- ❖ 1,364 total square feet of living area
- ❖ Master bedroom features a spacious walk-in closet and private bath
- ❖ Living room is highlighted with several windows
- ❖ Kitchen with snack bar is adjacent to the dining area
- ❖ Plenty of storage space throughout
- ❖ 3 bedrooms, 2 baths, optional 2-car garage
- ❖ Basement foundation, drawings also include crawl space foundation

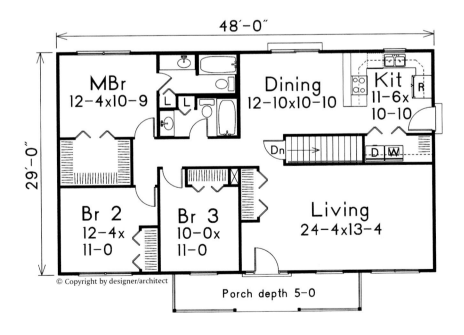

48'-0"

29'-0"

MBr
12-4x10-9

Dining
12-10x10-10

Kit
11-6x
10-10

Dn

D W

Br 2
12-4x
11-0

Br 3
10-0x
11-0

Living
24-4x13-4

© Copyright by designer/architect

Porch depth 5-0

Trees are a huge influence on a landscape so take time to locate them properly. Don't plant a tree beneath power lines if it will grow to be 25 feet tall or more. Don't plant above underground utility lines. For help locating electric, cable, phone and water lines on your property, contact each of your utility companies directly.

Special features

- ❖ 2,008 total square feet of living area
- ❖ A unique flex space could be used for extra storage or a small office area
- ❖ An enormous master bath is inviting with a center whirlpool tub and double walk-in closets
- ❖ The dining area is substantial in size and is ideal for entertaining
- ❖ Bonus room on the second floor has an additional 354 square feet of living area
- ❖ 3 bedrooms, 2 1/2 baths, 2-car side entry garage
- ❖ Crawl space or slab foundation, please specify when ordering

Sage is a peculiar herb. It is known as a happiness barometer and thought to follow the fortunes of the house. Its growth will dwindle when evil days befall and miraculously revive when things are bright again.

Optional Second Floor

First Floor
2,008 sq. ft.

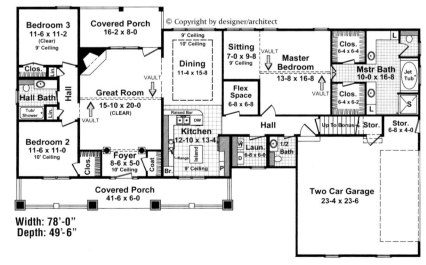

Width: 78'-0"
Depth: 49'-6"

© Copyright by designer/architect

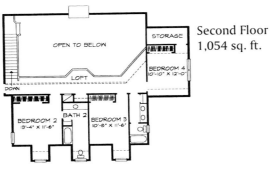

Second Floor
1,054 sq. ft.

Within floor plan labels:
- OPEN TO BELOW
- STORAGE
- LOFT
- BEDROOM 4 10'-10" X 12'-0"
- DOWN
- BEDROOM 2 13'-4" X 11'-6"
- BATH 2
- BEDROOM 3 10'-8" X 11'-6"

Special features

- ❖ 3,519 total square feet of living area
- ❖ Wide porch and triple dormers add country flair to this spacious home
- ❖ The entry has views of the quiet study and dining room while leading into the massive living room
- ❖ There is plenty of room for a large family with a grand master bedroom on the first floor and three bedrooms and two baths on the second floor
- ❖ 4 bedrooms, 3 1/2 baths, 2-car carport
- ❖ Slab foundation

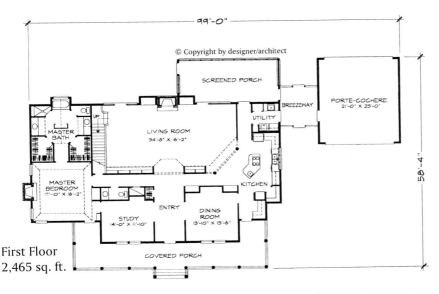

© Copyright by designer/architect

Within first floor plan labels:
- 99'-0"
- SCREENED PORCH
- BREEZEWAY
- PORTE-COCHERE 21'-0" X 23'-0"
- UTILITY
- MASTER BATH
- LIVING ROOM 34'-8" X 16'-2"
- UP
- 58'-4"
- KITCHEN
- MASTER BEDROOM 17'-10" X 16'-2"
- ENTRY
- STUDY 14'-0" X 11'-10"
- DINING ROOM 13'-10" X 13'-6"
- COVERED PORCH

First Floor
2,465 sq. ft.

When you're heading out to the garden, grab your child's sled. Load the tools and plants on board and slide them easily around the yard. This is also a great way to gather weeds.

Special features

- ❖ 1,735 total square feet of living area
- ❖ Angled kitchen wall expands space into the dining room
- ❖ Second floor has a cozy sitting area with cheerful window
- ❖ Two spacious bedrooms on the second floor share a bath
- ❖ 3 bedrooms, 2 1/2 baths, 2-car drive under garage
- ❖ Basement foundation

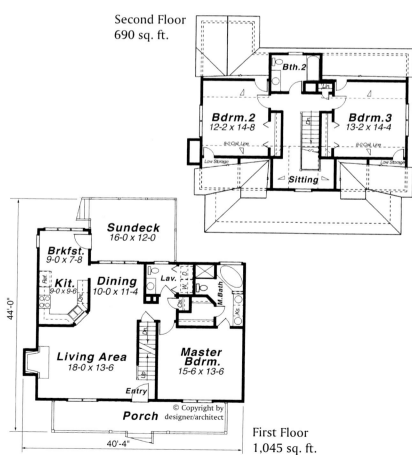

Second Floor
690 sq. ft.

Bth.2

Bdrm.2
12-2 x 14-8

Bdrm.3
13-2 x 14-4

Low Storage   Low Storage

Sitting

Sundeck
16-0 x 12-0

Brkfst.
9-0 x 7-8

Kit.
9-0 x 9-6

Dining
10-0 x 11-4

Lav.   W. D.

M.Bath

Living Area
18-0 x 13-6

Master Bdrm.
15-6 x 13-6

Entry

Porch

© Copyright by
designer/architect

44'-0"

40'-4"

First Floor
1,045 sq. ft.

Second Floor
927 sq. ft.

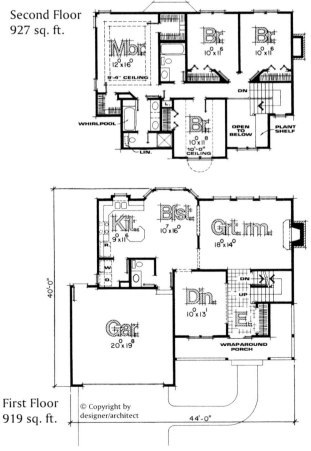

First Floor
919 sq. ft.

© Copyright by designer/architect

Special features

- ❖ 1,846 total square feet of living area
- ❖ All bedrooms are on the second floor for privacy
- ❖ Large breakfast room extends off the kitchen
- ❖ Great room has a beautiful wall of windows and a cozy fireplace
- ❖ 4 bedrooms, 2 1/2 baths, 2-car garage
- ❖ Basement foundation

Freestanding metal fireplaces or pottery chimneys are fun and enjoyable for small outdoor fires. Just make sure not to put them on wooden decks or other flammable surfaces.

Special features

- 1,832 total square feet of living area
- Energy efficient home with 2" x 6" exterior walls
- Distinctive master bedroom enhanced by skylights, garden tub, separate shower and walk-in closet
- U-shaped kitchen features convenient pantry, laundry area and full view to breakfast room
- Foyer opens into spacious living room
- Large front porch creates enjoyable outdoor living
- 3 bedrooms, 2 baths
- Crawl space foundation, drawings also include basement and slab foundations

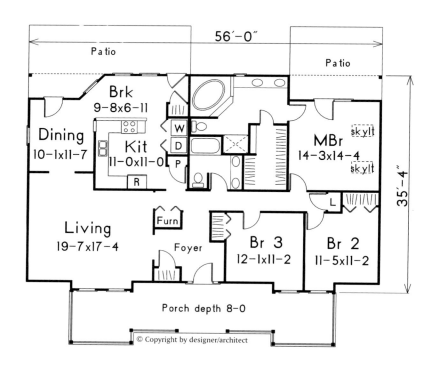

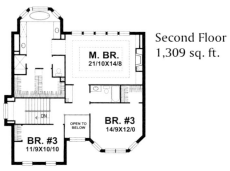

Second Floor
1,309 sq. ft.

M. BR.
21/10X14/8

BR. #3
14/9X12/0

OPEN TO
BELOW

DN

BR. #3
11/9X10/10

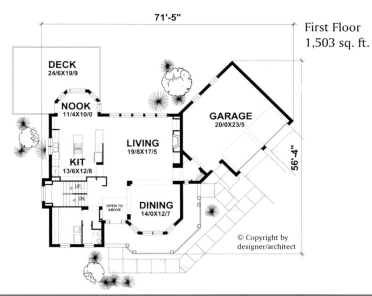

71'-5"

First Floor
1,503 sq. ft.

DECK
24/6X19/9

NOOK
11/4X10/0

KIT
13/6X12/8

GARAGE
20/0X23/5

LIVING
19/8X17/5

56'-4"

UP

DN

OPEN TO
ABOVE

DINING
14/0X12/7

© Copyright by
designer/architect

Special features

- ❖ 2,812 total square feet of living area
- ❖ The bayed dining nook takes in lovely views of an outdoor deck
- ❖ Decorative columns help define the formal dining room
- ❖ A gorgeous master bedroom features a beautiful fireplace and includes an enormous bath with a whirlpool tub-in-a-bay and a large walk-in closet
- ❖ Insulated concrete formed exterior walls
- ❖ 3 bedrooms, 2 1/2 baths, 2-car side entry garage
- ❖ Basement foundation

Don't crowd out a small spare room with a double bed, especially if you have to place one of its sides against a wall. A single bed and futon combination frees up floor space and also provides more flexibility for sleeping arrangements.

Special features

- ❖ 2,801 total square feet of living area
- ❖ 9' ceilings on the first floor
- ❖ Full view dining bay with elegant circle-top windows
- ❖ Wrap-around porches provide outdoor exposure in all directions
- ❖ Secluded master bedroom with double vanities and walk-in closets
- ❖ Convenient game room
- ❖ 5 bedrooms, 3 baths, 2-car side entry garage
- ❖ Slab foundation

First Floor
1,651 sq. ft.

Second Floor
1,150 sq. ft.

© Copyright by designer/architect

Special features

- ❖ 1,550 total square feet of living area
- ❖ Convenient mud room between the garage and kitchen
- ❖ Oversized dining area allows plenty of space for entertaining
- ❖ Master bedroom has a private bath and ample closet space
- ❖ Large patio off the family room brings the outdoors in
- ❖ 3 bedrooms, 2 baths, 2-car side entry garage
- ❖ Basement foundation, drawings also include crawl space or slab foundations

According to feng shui principles, choose bedding and linens in solid colors. If they have patterns, avoid geometric, angular designs that emanate negative energy and disturb your rest.

PATIO   76'-0"

FAMILY ROOM
13'-3" x 20'-10"

BATH

MASTER BEDROOM
14'-6" x 13'-5"

KITCHEN
12'-7" x 11'-6"

BATH

40'-0"

GARAGE
20'-4" x 21'-4"

MUD ROOM

dn

china

STOR

LIVING ROOM
23'-4" x 12'

ENTRY

BEDROOM
10'-5" x 10'

BEDROOM
10' x 13'-6"

alternate garage door location

PORCH

© Copyright by designer/architect

Special features

- ❖ 1,310 total square feet of living area
- ❖ The combination of brick quoins, roof dormers and an elegant porch creates a classic look
- ❖ Open-space floor plan has vaulted kitchen, living and dining rooms
- ❖ The master bedroom is vaulted and enjoys privacy from other bedrooms
- ❖ A spacious laundry room is convenient to the kitchen and master bedroom with access to an oversized garage
- ❖ 3 bedrooms, 2 baths, 2-car garage
- ❖ Basement foundation, drawings also include crawl space and slab foundations

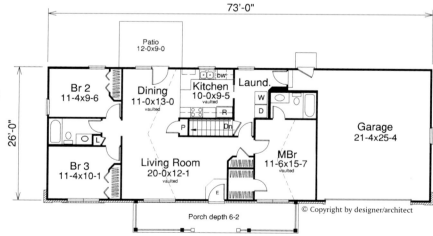

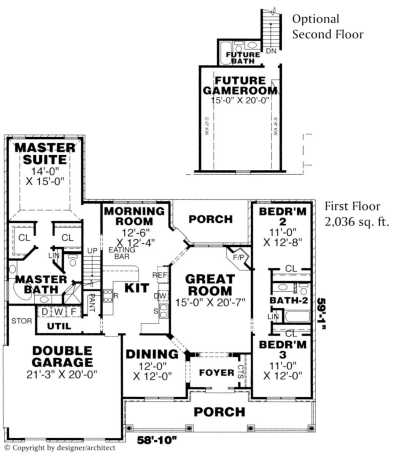

Optional
Second Floor

FUTURE BATH

FUTURE GAMEROOM
15'-0" X 20'-0"

MASTER SUITE
14'-0" X 15'-0"

CL   CL

LIN

MORNING ROOM
12'-6" X 12'-4"

EATING BAR

UP

PORCH

BEDR'M 2
11'-0" X 12'-8"

First Floor
2,036 sq. ft.

MASTER BATH

KIT

REF

PANT

GREAT ROOM
15'-0" X 20'-7"

F/P

CL

DW

BATH-2

LIN

CL

DWF

STOR

UTIL

DOUBLE GARAGE
21'-3" X 20'-0"

DINING
12'-0" X 12'-0"

FOYER

BEDR'M 3
11'-0" X 12'-0"

59'-1"

PORCH

58'-10"

© Copyright by designer/architect

Special features

- ❖ 2,036 total square feet of living area
- ❖ Corner fireplace in great room adds warmth and style
- ❖ A bright and cheerful morning room is a lovely place to start the day
- ❖ Secluded master suite has an impressive bath with a whirlpool tub perfect for an escape
- ❖ Future gameroom on the second floor has an additional 370 square feet of living area
- ❖ 3 bedrooms, 2 baths, 2-car side entry garage
- ❖ Slab foundation

A chalkboard is great for jotting down notes and for kids to draw. An easy and inexpensive way to make your own is with chalkboard paint. It looks like spray paint, but dries to a chalkboard finish you can write on and wipe off.

Special features

❖ 1,966 total square feet of living area

❖ Private dining room remains the focal point when entering the home

❖ Kitchen and breakfast room join to create a functional area

❖ Lots of closet space in the second floor bedrooms

❖ 3 bedrooms, 2 1/2 baths, 2-car side entry garage

❖ Basement foundation

Inexpensive canvas Roman shades or bamboo blinds may be all you need for window treatments in a room that features a natural palette. Alternatively, consider leaving windows bare, as natural interiors embrace light.

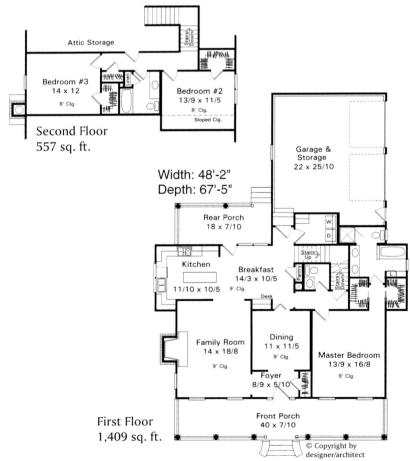

Width: 48'-2"
Depth: 67'-5"

Second Floor
557 sq. ft.

First Floor
1,409 sq. ft.

© Copyright by
designer/architect

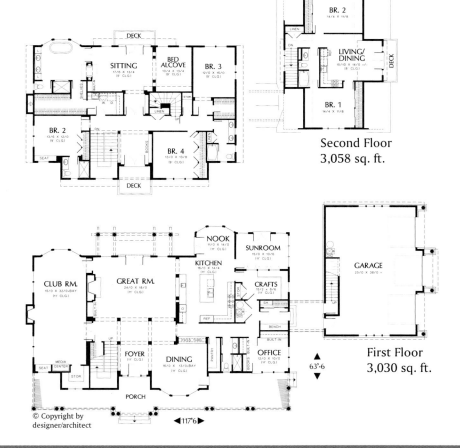

Second Floor
3,058 sq. ft.

First Floor
3,030 sq. ft.

© Copyright by
designer/architect

◀117'6▶

Special features

❖ 6,088 total square feet of living area

❖ Energy efficient home with 2" x 6" exterior walls

❖ Master suite is a unique style with separate bed alcove and a large central sitting area with a view onto the deck

❖ The first floor features amenities including a club room for entertaining, an office with direct deck access and a craft room for hobbies

❖ The guest quarters above the garage is included in the total square footage and features two bedrooms, a full kitchen and bath

❖ 6 bedrooms, 5 baths, 3-car side entry detached garage

❖ Crawl space foundation

Special features

- 2,533 total square feet of living area
- The sizeable living room includes a fireplace flanked by large windows overlooking the backyard
- The secluded master bedroom accesses the rear porch and features a large walk-in closet and private bath
- The kitchen includes a cooktop island and opens to a sunny bayed breakfast area
- 3 bedrooms, 3 1/2 baths, 2-car side entry garage
- Slab or crawl space foundation, please specify when ordering

Some paint manufacturers offer kitchen and bathroom collections specially formulated for steamy rooms. Designed to resist moisture and inhibit mildew growth, they also give a wipe-clean finish.

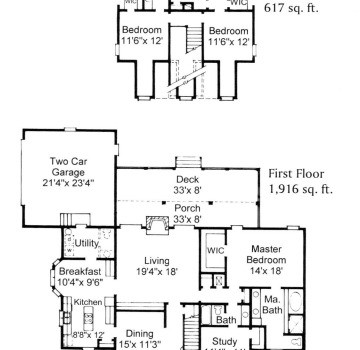

Second Floor 617 sq. ft.

First Floor 1,916 sq. ft.

Width: 66'-0"
Depth: 64'-0"

© Copyright by designer/architect

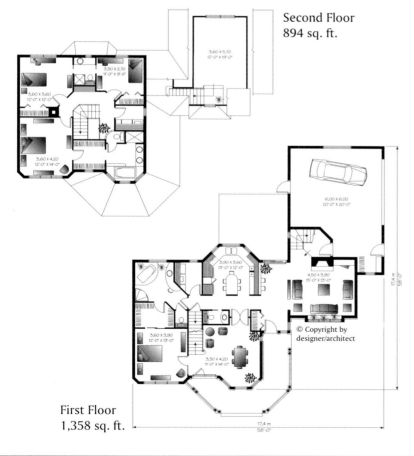

Second Floor
894 sq. ft.

3.30 x 2.70
11'-0" x 9'-0"

3.60 x 3.60
12'-0" x 12'-0"

3.60 x 5.70
12'-0" x 19'-0"

3.60 x 4.20
12'-0" x 14'-0"

6.00 x 6.00
20'-0" x 20'-0"

3.90 x 3.60
13'-0" x 12'-0"

4.50 x 3.90
15'-0" x 13'-0"

3.60 x 3.90
12'-0" x 13'-0"

3.30 x 4.20
11'-0" x 14'-0"

© Copyright by
designer/architect

17.4 m
58'-0"

17.4 m
58'-0"

First Floor
1,358 sq. ft.

Special features

- ❖ 2,252 total square feet of living area
- ❖ Energy efficient home with 2" x 6" exterior walls
- ❖ Cathedral ceiling in the family room adds spaciousness
- ❖ 9' ceilings on the first floor
- ❖ 4 bedrooms, 3 1/2 baths, 2-car side entry garage
- ❖ Basement foundation

Special features

- ❖ 2,333 total square feet of living area
- ❖ 9' ceilings on the first floor
- ❖ Master bedroom features a large walk-in closet and an inviting double-door entry into a spacious bath
- ❖ Convenient laundry room is located near the kitchen
- ❖ 4 bedrooms, 3 baths, 2-car side entry garage
- ❖ Slab foundation, drawings also include crawl space and partial crawl space/basement foundations

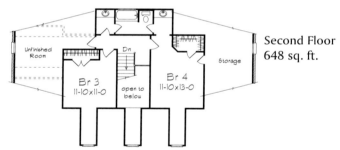

Second Floor
648 sq. ft.

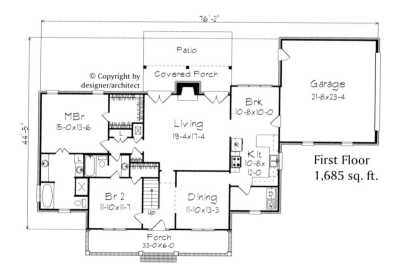

First Floor
1,685 sq. ft.

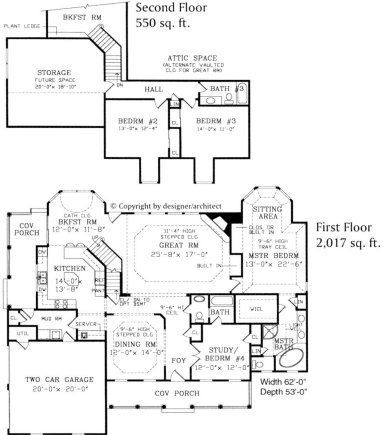

Second Floor
550 sq. ft.

PLANT LEDGE

BKFST RM

STORAGE
FUTURE SPACE
20'-0"x 18'-10"

ATTIC SPACE
(ALTERNATE VAULTED
CLG FOR GREAT RM)

HALL   BATH #3
DN

BEDRM #2   BEDRM #3
13'-0"x 12'-4"   14'-0"x 11'-0"

© Copyright by designer/architect

COV
PORCH

CATH CLG
BKFST RM
12'-0"x 11'-8"

UP

SITTING
AREA

CLOS. OR
BUILT IN

11'-4" HIGH
STEPPED CLG
GREAT RM
25'-8"x 17'-0"

9'-6" HIGH
TRAY CEIL
MSTR BEDRM
13'-0"x 22'-6"

BUILT IN

KITCHEN
14'-0"x
13'-8"

REF
PANT

DV
DW

EL DN TO
OPT BSMT

9'-6" HT
CEIL

BATH   WICL

CL   MUD RM
CL   SERVER

UTIL

9'-6" HIGH
STEPPED CLG
DINING RM
12'-0"x 14'-0"

FOY

LIGHT
WELL

STUDY/
BEDRM #4
12'-0"x 12'-0"

MSTR
BATH

TWO CAR GARAGE
20'-0"x 20'-0"

COV PORCH

First Floor
2,017 sq. ft.

Width 62'-0"
Depth 53'-0"

Special features

❖ 2,567 total square feet of living area
❖ Breakfast room has a 12' cathedral ceiling and a bayed area full of windows
❖ Great room has a stepped ceiling, built-in media center and a corner fireplace
❖ Bonus room on the second floor has an additional 300 square feet of living area
❖ 4 bedrooms, 3 baths, 2-car side entry garage
❖ Basement, crawl space or slab foundation, please specify when ordering

Special features

- 1,560 total square feet of living area
- Two-story master bedroom has sunny dormer above, large walk-in closet and private bath
- Great room has unique two-story ceiling with dormers
- Spacious kitchen has large center island creating an ideal workspace
- 3 bedrooms, 2 1/2 baths
- Basement, crawl space or slab foundation, please specify when ordering

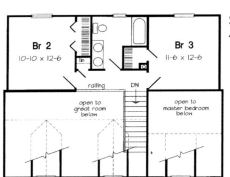

Second Floor
499 sq. ft.

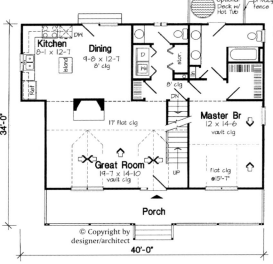

First Floor
1,061 sq. ft.

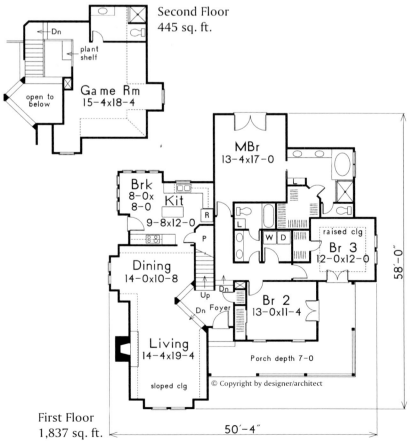

Second Floor
445 sq. ft.

Dn

plant shelf

open to below

Game Rm
15-4x18-4

First Floor
1,837 sq. ft.

MBr
13-4x17-0

Brk
8-0x8-0

Kit
9-8x12-0

raised clg

Br 3
12-0x12-0

Dining
14-0x10-8

Up

Dn

Dn Foyer

Br 2
13-0x11-4

Living
14-4x19-4

Porch depth 7-0

sloped clg

© Copyright by designer/architect

58'-0"

50'-4"

Special features

- ❖ 2,282 total square feet of living area
- ❖ Living and dining rooms combine to create a large, convenient entertaining area that includes a fireplace
- ❖ Comfortable covered porch allows access from secondary bedrooms
- ❖ Second floor game room overlooks the foyer and includes a full bath
- ❖ Kitchen and breakfast areas are surrounded by mullioned windows
- ❖ 3 bedrooms, 3 baths, 2-car detached garage
- ❖ Slab foundation, drawings also include crawl space foundation

Special features

❖ 1,892 total square feet of living area

❖ Victorian home includes folk charm

❖ This split bedroom plan places a lovely master bedroom on the opposite end of the other two bedrooms for privacy

❖ Central living and dining areas combine creating a great place for entertaining

❖ Bonus room on the second floor has an additional 285 square feet of living area

❖ 3 bedrooms, 2 1/2 baths, 2-car side entry garage

❖ Basement, crawl space or slab foundation, please specify when ordering

Use light tints when painting expansive interiors that feature multiple windows. For example, paint the walls of a great room a very light ice blue to create a spacious environment for daily life.

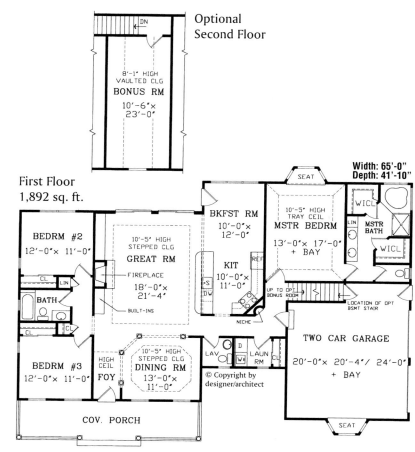

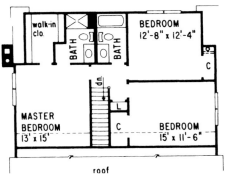

Second Floor
868 sq. ft.

walk-in clo.

BATH

BATH

BEDROOM
12'-8" x 12'-4"

MASTER BEDROOM
13' x 15'

BEDROOM
15' x 11'-6"

dn.

roof

Special features

❖ 1,948 total square feet of living area

❖ Family room offers warmth with an oversized fireplace and rustic beamed ceiling

❖ Fully-appointed kitchen extends into the family room

❖ Practical mud room is adjacent to the kitchen

❖ 3 bedrooms, 3 baths

❖ Basement foundation, drawings also include crawl space foundation

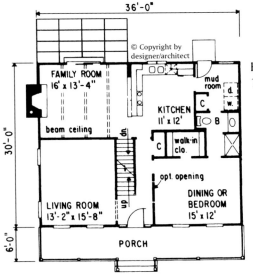

36'-0"

© Copyright by designer/architect

FAMILY ROOM
16' x 13'-4"

beam ceiling

mud room

KITCHEN
11' x 12'

walk-in clo.

30'-0"

LIVING ROOM
13'-2" x 15'-8"

opt. opening

DINING OR BEDROOM
15' x 12'

6'-0"

PORCH

First Floor
1,080 sq. ft.

Wattle fences have been used for hundreds of years in Europe and Africa. "Wattle and daub" houses, made of interwoven twigs covered with mud, are waterproof and were used as long ago as the Stone Age.

Special features

- 1,348 total square feet of living area
- Ideal retirement home or lakeside retreat with a country flavor
- The living room has a stone corner fireplace and carefully planned shelving for a flat panel TV and components
- A luxury bath, huge walk-in closet and covered deck adjoin the master bedroom
- The lower level is comprised of a guest bedroom, hall bath and garage with space for two cars and a boat
- 2 bedrooms, 2 1/2 baths, 3-car rear entry garage
- Walk-out basement foundation

First Floor
1,008 sq. ft.

© Copyright by designer/architect

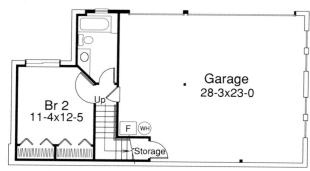

Lower Level
340 sq. ft.

Special features

- 1,595 total square feet of living area
- Dining room has a convenient built-in desk and provides access to the outdoors
- L-shaped kitchen features an island cooktop
- Family room has a high ceiling and fireplace
- Private master bedroom includes a large walk-in closet and bath with separate tub and shower units
- 3 bedrooms, 2 baths, 2-car side entry garage
- Slab foundation, drawings also include crawl space foundation

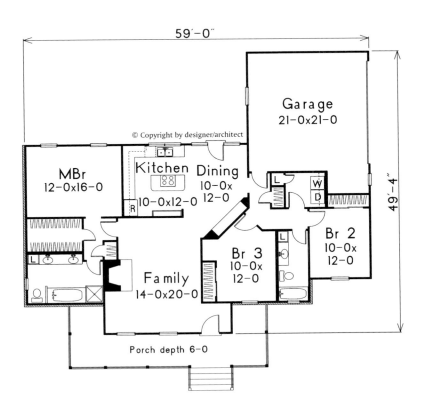

59'-0"

49'-4"

Garage
21-0x21-0

© Copyright by designer/architect

MBr
12-0x16-0

Kitchen
10-0x12-0

Dining
10-0x
12-0

Br 2
10-0x
12-0

Br 3
10-0x
12-0

Family
14-0x20-0

Porch depth 6-0

Special features

- 2,214 total square feet of living area
- Great room has built-in cabinets for an entertainment system, a fireplace and French doors leading to a private rear covered porch
- Dining room has an arched opening from foyer
- Breakfast room has lots of windows for a sunny open feel
- 3 bedrooms, 2 baths, 2-car side entry garage
- Crawl space or slab foundation, please specify when ordering

Outdoor faucets mounted on the side of a house can freeze in cold weather, causing pipes to burst. Be sure to drain them before the first freeze. To do this, shut off the water supply leading to the faucet, then open the faucet to drain off any remaining water trapped between the faucet and the shut-off valve.

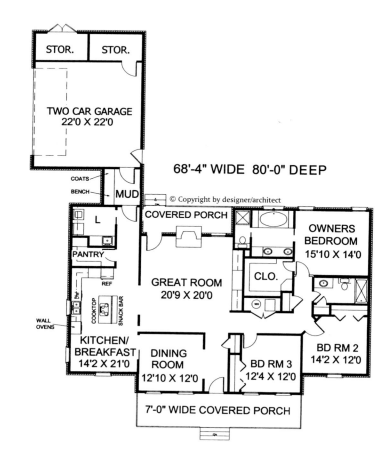

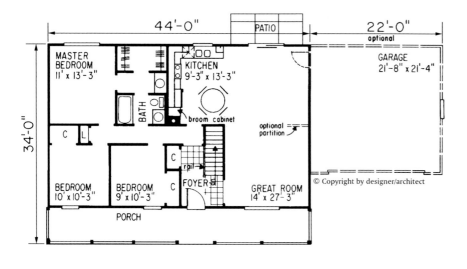

Special features

- ❖ 1,232 total square feet of living area
- ❖ Ideal porch for quiet quality evenings
- ❖ Great room opens to dining room for those large dinner gatherings
- ❖ Functional L-shaped kitchen includes broom cabinet
- ❖ Master bedroom contains a large walk-in closet and compartmented bath
- ❖ 3 bedrooms, 1 bath, optional 2-car garage
- ❖ Basement foundation, drawings also include crawl space and slab foundations

© Copyright by designer/architect

Organic gardeners like to quote an old Chinese proverb: "The best fertilizer in the garden may be the gardener's own shadow." It is their belief that the daily attendance of a living presence, as opposed to a chemical or artificial one, may be the best tonic growing plants can have.

Special features

- 2,126 total square feet of living area
- Hearth room has corner fireplace for warmth
- Great room features entertainment center and a dramatic wall of windows
- Covered front porch is charming
- 1,058 square feet of optional living area available on the second floor
- 3 bedrooms, 2 baths, 2-car side entry garage
- Slab foundation

A garden hose makes a handy tool for choosing a shape for a new flower bed. Arrange and rearrange the hose until you find an outline you like. Push your mower alongside the hose to see how maintenance-friendly the border is.

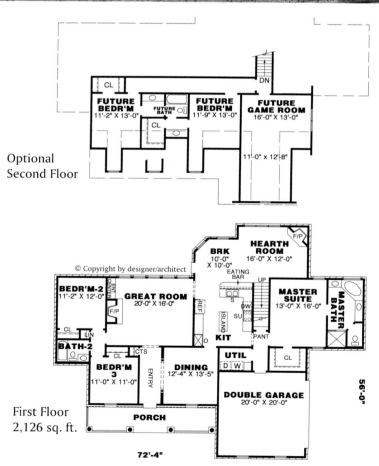

Optional Second Floor

First Floor
2,126 sq. ft.

© Copyright by designer/architect

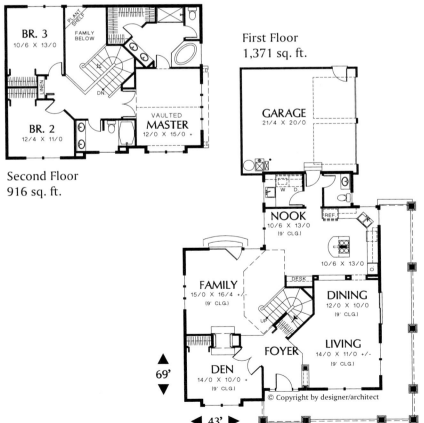

BR. 3
10/6 X 13/0

PLANT SHELF

FAMILY BELOW

BR. 2
12/4 X 11/0

LINEN

DN.

VAULTED
MASTER
12/0 X 15/0 +

Second Floor
916 sq. ft.

First Floor
1,371 sq. ft.

GARAGE
21/4 X 20/0

NOOK
10/6 X 13/0
(9' CLG.)

REF

10/6 X 13/0

W   D

DESK

FAMILY
15/0 X 16/4 +
(9' CLG.)

DINING
12/0 X 10/0
(9' CLG.)

UP

FOYER

LIVING
14/0 X 11/0 +/-
(9' CLG.)

DEN
14/0 X 10/0 +
(9' CLG.)

69'

43'

© Copyright by designer/architect

Special features

- ❖ 2,287 total square feet of living area
- ❖ Energy efficient home with 2" x 6" exterior walls
- ❖ Wrap-around porch creates an inviting feeling
- ❖ First floor windows have transom windows above
- ❖ Den has a see-through fireplace into the family area
- ❖ 3 bedrooms, 2 1/2 baths, 2-car side entry garage
- ❖ Crawl space foundation

A small raised garden can be planted earlier in the spring, with more plants close together, and watered only when the weather is dry. They are easy to grow plants in and you can have something growing nearly all the time.

Special features

- ❖ 2,695 total square feet of living area
- ❖ Formal living room includes built-in bookshelves making this a perfect private retreat or study
- ❖ Master bedroom has a dramatic cathedral ceiling, double closets and a luxurious bath with corner whirlpool tub
- ❖ Octagon-shaped breakfast room has a cheerful atmosphere
- ❖ 4 bedrooms, 3 1/2 baths, 3-car side entry garage
- ❖ Basement foundation

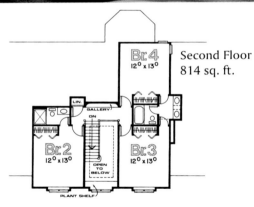

Second Floor
814 sq. ft.

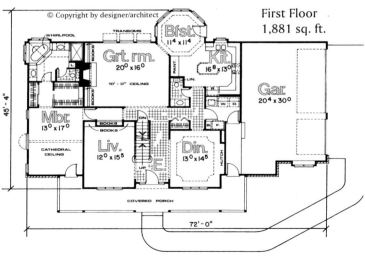

First Floor
1,881 sq. ft.

Arrange to have the chimney or flue cleaned. Blocked residue or even a bird's nest can disrupt ventilation and endanger your health or family.

Second Floor
810 sq. ft.

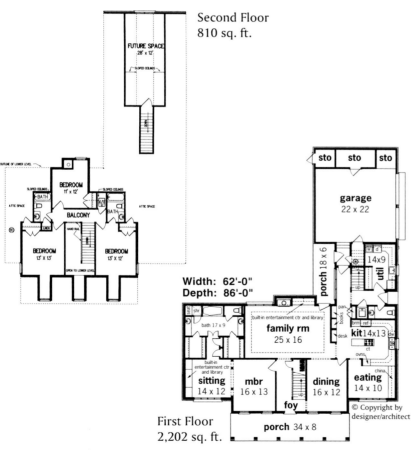

FUTURE SPACE
28' x 12'
SLOPED CEILINGS

OUTLINE OF LOWER LEVEL

BEDROOM
11' x 12'

ATTIC SPACE

BATH

SLOPED CEILINGS

BALCONY
HAND RAIL

BATH

ATTIC SPACE

BEDROOM
13' x 13'

BEDROOM
13' x 12'

OPEN TO LOWER LEVEL

Width: 62'-0"
Depth: 86'-0"

sto   sto   sto

garage
22 x 22

porch 18 x 6

14x9
util

built-in entertainment ctr and library

family rm
25 x 16

bath 17 x 9

pan.
books

brm ref.
desk

kit 14x13
ct

built-in entertainment ctr and library

sitting
14 x 12

mbr
16 x 13

dining
16 x 12

ovns

china

eating
14 x 10

foy

© Copyright by designer/architect

First Floor
2,202 sq. ft.

porch 34 x 8

Special features

- ❖ 3,012 total square feet of living area
- ❖ Energy efficient home with 2" x 6" exterior walls
- ❖ Master bedroom has a sitting area with an entertainment center/library
- ❖ Utility room has a sink and includes lots of storage and counterspace
- ❖ Future space above garage has an additional 336 square feet of living area
- ❖ 4 bedrooms, 3 1/2 baths, 2-car side entry garage
- ❖ Crawl space foundation, drawings also include slab and basement foundations

Special features

- ❖ 2,764 total square feet of living area
- ❖ A balcony leads to a small study area while offering a dramatic view to the family room and fireplace
- ❖ Master bedroom provides convenience and comfort with its whirlpool tub, double-bowl vanity, shower and large walk-in closet
- ❖ Delightful library is a nice quiet place to relax
- ❖ 4 bedrooms, 2 1/2 baths, 2-car side entry garage
- ❖ Basement foundation

Tranquil interiors are mood enhancing and nurturing. A cool palette will blend comfortably with a wide assortment of furnishings and often feature a variety of greens, one of nature's most abundant, peaceful colors.

Second Floor
821 sq. ft.

First Floor
1,943 sq. ft.

© Copyright by designer/architect

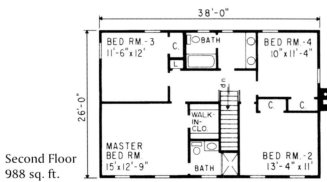

Second Floor
988 sq. ft.

38'-0"

BED RM.-3
11'-6"x12'

BATH

BED RM.-4
10"x11'-4"

26'-0"

WALK-IN-CLO.

MASTER BED RM.
15'x12'-9"

BATH

BED RM.-2
13'-4" x 11'

Special features

❖ 2,137 total square feet of living area
❖ Spacious porch for plants, chairs and family gatherings
❖ Huge living room includes front and rear views
❖ U-shaped kitchen features abundant storage
❖ Laundry room with large closet has its own porch
❖ 4 bedrooms, 2 1/2 baths, 2-car garage
❖ Partial basement/crawl space foundation

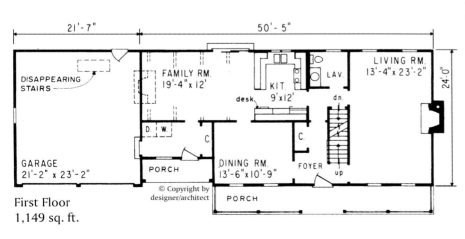

21'-7"

50'-5"

DISAPPEARING STAIRS

FAMILY RM.
19'-4"x 12'

KIT.
9'x12'

LAV.

LIVING RM.
13'-4"x 23'-2"

24'-0"

desk

D. W.

C.

C.

dn.

GARAGE
21'-2" x 23'-2"

PORCH

DINING RM.
13'-6"x10'-9"

FOYER

up

© Copyright by designer/architect

PORCH

First Floor
1,149 sq. ft.

Special features

- 2,024 total square feet of living area
- Energy efficient home with 2" x 6" exterior walls
- King-size master bedroom includes a sitting area
- Living room features a corner fireplace, access to the covered rear porch, 18' ceiling and a balcony
- Closet for handling recyclables
- Future bonus room has an additional 475 square feet of living area
- 3 bedrooms, 2 1/2 baths, 2-car side entry garage
- Crawl space foundation, drawings also include slab and basement foundations

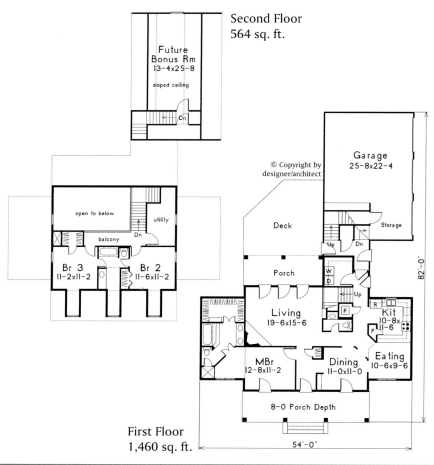

Second Floor
564 sq. ft.

Future Bonus Rm
13-4x25-8
sloped ceiling

Dn

open to below

utility

balcony

Dn

Br 3
11-2x11-2

Br 2
11-6x11-2

© Copyright by designer/architect

Garage
25-8x22-4

Deck

Storage

Porch

Up   Dn

W   D

Living
19-6x15-6

F

Up

Kit
10-8x11-6

R

P

MBr
12-8x11-2

Dining
11-0x11-0

Eating
10-6x9-6

8-0 Porch Depth

82-0"

54'-0"

First Floor
1,460 sq. ft.

Special features

- 1,196 total square feet of living area
- Home includes an extra-deep porch for evening relaxation
- The large living room enjoys a corner fireplace, dining area featuring a wide bay window with sliding doors to the rear patio, and a snack bar open to the kitchen
- The master bedroom has a nice walk-in closet, its own linen closet and a roomy bath with a double-bowl vanity and garden tub
- 3 bedrooms, 2 baths, 1-car side entry garage
- Crawl space foundation, drawings also include slab foundation

40'-0"

42'-0"

© Copyright by designer/architect

Patio

MBr
12-3x12-0

Dining
8-4x10-2

Living Rm
13-0x20-8

Kit
8-0x
12-6

DW

R

P

W/D

Br 2
11-0x8-6

Entry

Garage
20-4x12-0

Br 3
11-0x9-6

Porch depth 6-8

Special features

- 1,792 total square feet of living area
- A massive family room with fireplace and access onto the porch is the perfect place to relax or entertain
- The spacious kitchen and dining area includes a cooktop island and walk-in pantry
- All the bedrooms are located on the second floor for extra peace and quiet
- 3 bedrooms, 2 1/2 baths
- Slab foundation

Second Floor
932 sq. ft.

MASTER BEDROOM
16 x 14

MASTER BATH
12 x 10

BATH #3

PLANTS

LIN. LIN.

DOWN

HALL

CLOSET
6 x 8

BEDROOM #2
12 x 13

BEDROOM #3
11 x 13

CLOSET
6 x 5

CLOS.
4 x 5

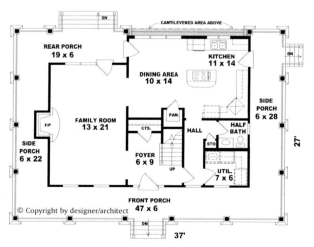

First Floor
860 sq. ft.

CANTILEVERED AREA ABOVE

REAR PORCH
19 x 6

KITCHEN
11 x 14

DN

DINING AREA
10 x 14

SIDE PORCH
6 x 28

FAMILY ROOM
13 x 21

F/P

PAN.

SIDE PORCH
6 x 22

CTS.

HALL

HALF BATH

FOYER
6 x 9

STO.

UP

UTIL.
7 x 6

FRONT PORCH
47 x 6

© Copyright by designer/architect

27'

37'

DN

Coastal colors, from watery pale aquamarine to dark blue-green, refresh and invigorate. Seek the colors of this palette for their renewing properties. A variety of marine hues are rejuvenating, crisp, clean and ever-popular for the bath and bedrooms.

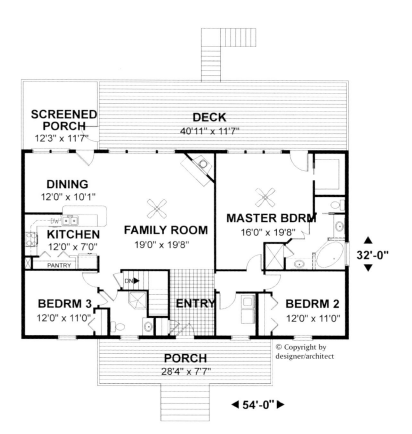

© Copyright by designer/architect

SCREENED PORCH 12'3" x 11'7"

DECK 40'11" x 11'7"

DINING 12'0" x 10'1"

FAMILY ROOM 19'0" x 19'8"

MASTER BDRM 16'0" x 19'8"

KITCHEN 12'0" x 7'0"

PANTRY

DN

BEDRM 3 12'0" x 11'0"

ENTRY

BEDRM 2 12'0" x 11'0"

PORCH 28'4" x 7'7"

32'-0"

◄ 54'-0" ►

Special features

- ❖ 1,728 total square feet of living area
- ❖ Large entry leads to the family room featuring a corner fireplace and a window wall overlooking an enormous deck
- ❖ Master bedroom is adorned with a dramatic bath featuring an angled entry and a corner tub
- ❖ Design also includes a detached garage option
- ❖ 3 bedrooms, 2 baths, 3-car drive under garage
- ❖ Basement or crawl space foundation, please specify when ordering

Listening to music, watching a movie or even having a conversation can be very unpleasant in a room with too many parallel hard surfaces. Adding texture and soft surfaces like carpet and cozy seating can create a fuller sound to acoustics and make movie watching or listening to music much more enjoyable.

Special features

❖ 2,073 total square feet of living area
❖ Energy efficient home with 2" x 6" exterior walls
❖ U-shaped kitchen connects with cozy nook and formal dining room
❖ Expansive great room creates a wonderful entertaining space and features a fireplace
❖ All bedrooms are located on the second floor for privacy
❖ 4 bedrooms, 2 1/2 baths, 2-car garage
❖ Basement foundation

When planning a computer desk, you need a desk surface that is at least 24 inches deep unless you are using a laptop. But, keep in mind even more surface space will be welcomed for files and papers.

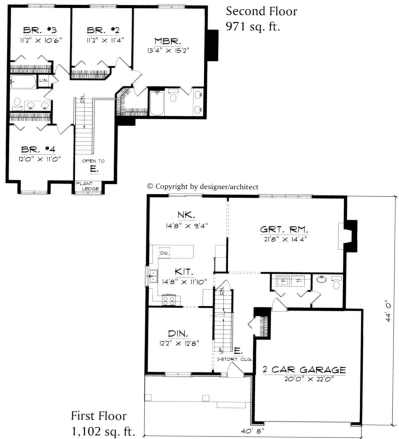

Second Floor
971 sq. ft.

BR. #3
11'2" x 10'6"

BR. #2
11'2" x 11'4"

MBR.
13'4" x 15'2"

LIN.

BR. #4
12'0" x 11'0"

OPEN TO E.

PLANT LEDGE

© Copyright by designer/architect

NK.
14'8" x 9'4"

GRT. RM.
21'8" x 14'4"

DW.

KIT.
14'8" x 11'10"

DIN.
12'2" x 12'8"

E.

2-STORY CLG.

2 CAR GARAGE
20'0" x 22'0"

44' 0"

40' 8"

First Floor
1,102 sq. ft.

Price Code   C

Special features

❖ 1,536 total square feet of living area
❖ Energy efficient home with 2" x 6" exterior walls
❖ Sliding glass doors in the master bedroom lead to a terrific screened porch offering a quiet place to retreat
❖ Galley-style kitchen is compact yet convenient
❖ A sunny dining area extends off the kitchen
❖ 3 bedrooms, 2 1/2 baths
❖ Pier foundation

Second Floor
498 sq. ft.

© Copyright by designer/architect

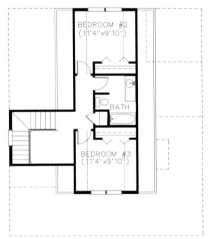

First Floor
1,038 sq. ft.

Width: 36'-0"
Depth: 43'-8"

Special features

- 2,185 total square feet of living area
- Formal dining room has direct access into kitchen
- Symmetrical master bath has double walk-in closets, a step-up tub, double vanity and a separate shower
- Double storage spaces in garage make organizing lawn equipment or tools easy
- Optional second floor has an additional 719 square feet of living area
- 3 bedrooms, 2 baths, 2-car side entry garage
- Slab foundation

According to the Center for Disease Control, 40% of homes have some lead-based paint in them especially if the home was built before 1980.

Optional Second Floor

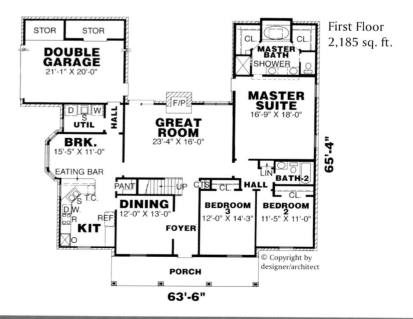

First Floor 2,185 sq. ft.

© Copyright by designer/architect

Second Floor
1,233 sq. ft.

3-CAR GARAGE
24'-0" X 36'-4"
GARAGE LOCATION TO BE DETERMINED

Special features

❖ 3,706 total square feet of living area
❖ Master bedroom has walk-in closets, a private bath and an exercise/hobby room that accesses a sun room/ screened porch
❖ Breakfast room with counter seating joins kitchen and dining area
❖ The optional media room on the second floor has an additional 155 square feet of living space
❖ 3 bedrooms, 2 1/2 baths, 3-car detached garage
❖ Crawl space foundation

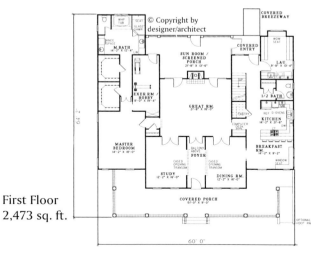

© Copyright by
designer/architect

First Floor
2,473 sq. ft.

Piles of comfy pillows on a bed look inviting, but often pose a problem for guests. Stick to a pair of pillows neatly arranged and stack extra quilts, pillows and blankets in the guest room closet.

Special features

❖ 2,718 total square feet of living area
❖ The two-story foyer opens into the kitchen which enjoys an island work area
❖ The vaulted master bedroom offers two walk-in closets and a private bath with garden tub
❖ An optional loft easily converts into a fourth bedroom and has an additional 223 square feet of living area
❖ 4 bedrooms, 2 1/2 baths, 2-car side entry garage
❖ Basement, crawl space or slab foundation, please specify when ordering

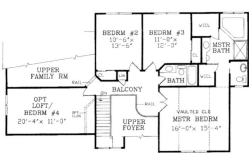

Second Floor
1,203 sq. ft.

First Floor
1,515 sq. ft.

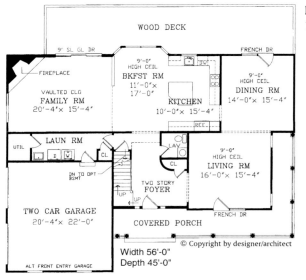

Width 56'-0"
Depth 45'-0"

© Copyright by designer/architect

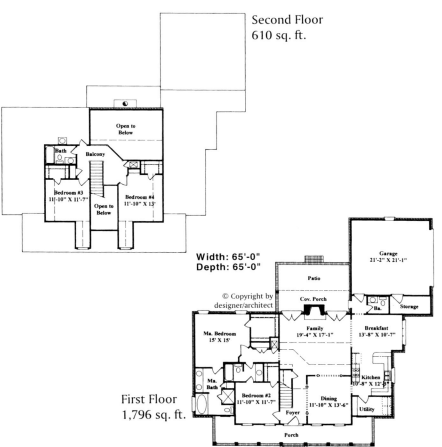

Second Floor
610 sq. ft.

Open to Below

Bath

Balcony

Bedroom #3
11'-10" X 11'-7"

Open to Below

Bedroom #4
11'-10" X 13'

Width: 65'-0"
Depth: 65'-0"

Garage
21'-2" X 21'-1"

© Copyright by
designer/architect

Patio

Cov. Porch

Ba.

Storage

Ma. Bedroom
15' X 15'

Family
19'-4" X 17'-1"

Breakfast
13'-8" X 10'-7"

Ma. Bath

Bedroom #2
11'-10" X 11'-7"

Kitchen
10'-8" X 12'-9"

Dining
11'-10" X 13'-6"

Foyer

Utility

First Floor
1,796 sq. ft.

Porch

Special features

- 2,406 total square feet of living area
- Beautiful family area with fireplace surrounded by double French doors
- Covered rear porch and patio
- Sunny breakfast room located off kitchen and adjacent to family area
- Plenty of closet space for a growing family
- 4 bedrooms, 3 1/2 baths, 2-car side entry garage
- Crawl space or slab foundation, please specify when ordering

Have you ever wondered how long perishable food items will keep in the refrigerator or freezer if you lose electricity? Items in a full freezer will stay frozen for about two days with the door kept closed. Refrigerated foods can keep up to four hours. Discard any perishable refrigerated foods that have been above 40 degrees for more than two hours.

Special features

- ❖ 2,326 total square feet of living area
- ❖ Energy efficient home with 2" x 6" exterior walls
- ❖ A glorious sun room with skylights brightens the home and creates a relaxing atmosphere
- ❖ The centrally located kitchen serves the formal and informal dining areas with ease
- ❖ The secondary bedrooms share a private bath with double-bowl vanity
- ❖ The bonus room above the garage has an additional 358 square feet of living area
- ❖ 3 bedrooms, 2 1/2 baths, 2-car side entry garage
- ❖ Basement, walk-out basement or slab foundation, please specify when ordering

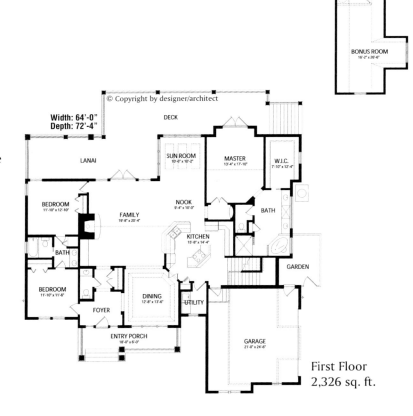

Optional Second Floor

First Floor
2,326 sq. ft.

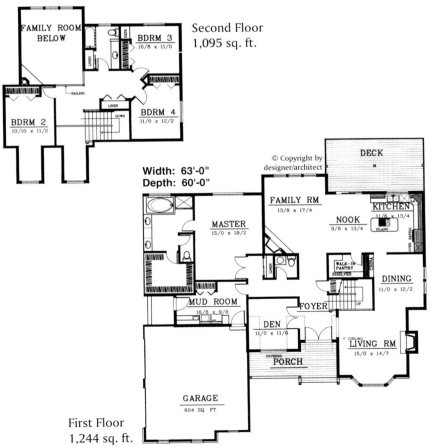

FAMILY ROOM BELOW

BDRM 3
10/8 x 11/0

Second Floor
1,095 sq. ft.

BDRM 2
10/10 x 11/2

LINEN

BDRM 4
11/0 x 12/2

RAILING

DOWN

Width: 63'-0"
Depth: 60'-0"

© Copyright by
designer/architect

DECK

FAMILY RM
13/8 x 17/4

KITCHEN

NOOK
9/8 x 13/4

ISLAND

MASTER
15/0 x 19/2

WALK-IN
PANTRY
SHELVES

DINING
11/0 x 12/2

LINEN

MUD ROOM
16/8 x 9/8

FOYER

UP

DEN
11/0 x 11/6

LIVING RM
15/0 x 14/7

COVERED
PORCH

GARAGE
604 SQ FT

First Floor
1,244 sq. ft.

Special features

❖ 2,339 total square feet of living area
❖ Large island kitchen is complete with a generous walk-in pantry
❖ Dining room has a built-in china cabinet
❖ First floor master bedroom offers an alternate handicap accessible version
❖ 4 bedrooms, 2 1/2 baths, 2-car side entry garage
❖ Crawl space or slab foundation, please specify when ordering

The slotted and Phillips screwdrivers are the two predominately used types. Slotted ones have a flat tip and Phillips have a pointed, criss-cross end. Cheap, low-quality screwdrivers are worthless. Get screwdrivers with the bigger, softer handles.

Special features

- ❖ 1,712 total square feet of living area
- ❖ Laundry closet is conveniently located near the bedrooms
- ❖ Formal living room connects to the dining room and kitchen
- ❖ Den/study makes a cozy retreat with built-in bookcases
- ❖ 3 bedrooms, 2 1/2 baths, 2-car garage
- ❖ Basement, crawl space or slab foundation, please specify when ordering

To remove musty smells from a cabinet or piece of furniture, fill plastic containers with white vinegar and punch holes in the top. Putting one container in each drawer overnight absorbs odors.

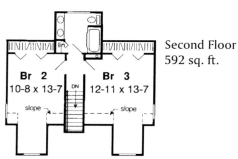

Second Floor
592 sq. ft.

Br 2
10-8 x 13-7

Br 3
12-11 x 13-7

slope   slope

DN

First Floor
1,120 sq. ft.

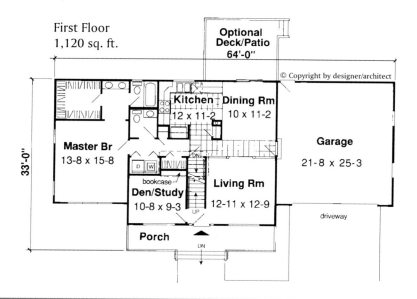

Optional Deck/Patio
64'-0"

© Copyright by designer/architect

Kitchen
12 x 11-2

Dining Rm
10 x 11-2

Master Br
13-8 x 15-8

Garage
21-8 x 25-3

bookcase

Den/Study
10-8 x 9-3

Living Rm
12-11 x 12-9

33'-0"

DN

UP

driveway

Porch

DN

Optional
Second Floor

OPT.
BATH
DORMER

BALCONY

CL

BEDRM #3
14'-0"× 12'-0"

DN

BEDRM #4
12'-8"× 12'-0"

WICL

© Copyright by designer/architect

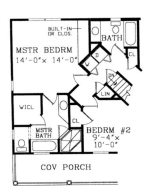

BUILT-IN
OR CLOS.

BATH

CL

MSTR BEDRM
14'-0"× 14'-0"

D

DN

LIN

WICL

CL

MSTR
BATH

BEDRM #2
9'-4"×
10'-0"

COV PORCH

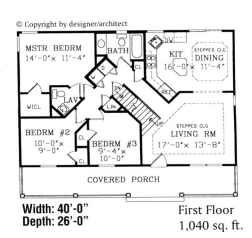

MSTR BEDRM
14'-0"× 11'-4"

BATH

DW

KIT
16'-0"

STEPPED CLG

DINING
11'-4"

CL

D

REF.

WICL

LAV.

DN

LIN

BEDRM #2
10'-0"×
9'-0"

BEDRM #3
9'-4"×
10'-0"

CL

UP

STEPPED CLG

LIVING RM
17'-0"× 13'-8"

COVERED PORCH

Width: 40'-0"
Depth: 26'-0"

First Floor
1,040 sq. ft.

Special features

- 1,040 total square feet of living area
- An island in the kitchen greatly simplifies your food preparation efforts
- A wide archway joins the formal living room to the dramatic angled kitchen and dining room
- Optional second floor has an additional 597 square feet of living area
- Optional first floor design has two bedrooms including a large master bedroom that enjoys a private luxury bath
- 3 bedrooms, 1 1/2 baths
- Basement, crawl space or slab foundation, please specify when ordering

Special features

- 2,156 total square feet of living area
- Secluded master bedroom has a spa-style bath with a corner whirlpool tub, large shower, double sinks and a walk-in closet
- Kitchen overlooks rear patio
- Plenty of windows add an open, airy feel to the great room
- 4 bedrooms, 3 baths, 2-car side entry garage
- Basement, crawl space or slab foundation, please specify when ordering

Combing is a paint technique that transforms a piece of furniture into a treasure. Apply a base coat, then apply a glaze in a complementary or contrasting color. While wet, drag the teeth of a comb over the glaze to reveal the base coat.

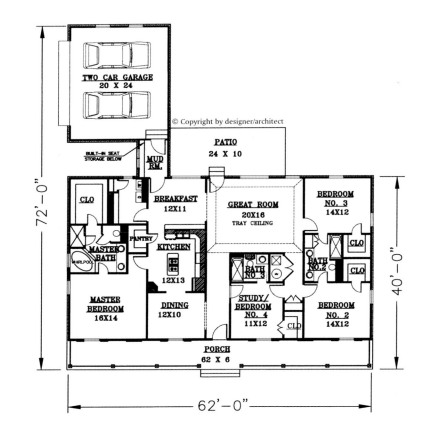

© Copyright by designer/architect

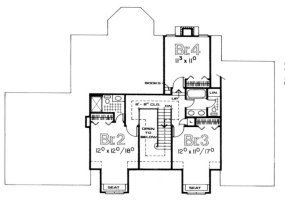

Second Floor
815 sq. ft.

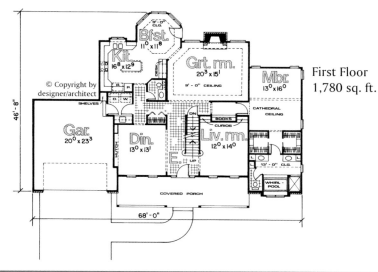

© Copyright by
designer/architect

First Floor
1,780 sq. ft.

Special features

- ❖ 2,595 total square feet of living area
- ❖ Cathedral ceiling in master bedroom adds spaciousness
- ❖ Windows seats add interest in bedrooms #2 and #3
- ❖ Formal living and dining rooms accent the front of this home
- ❖ 4 bedrooms, 3 1/2 baths, 2-car garage
- ❖ Basement foundation

Ebony is an extremely hard, close-grained wood used as an early inlay and for turned woods. Today, although expensive, it is used to make handsome staircases and furniture.

Special features

- 1,865 total square feet of living area
- Family and friends will easily enjoy the spacious living room with 9' ceiling, fireplace, access to the rear porch and openness to the kitchen
- All bedrooms enjoy walk-in closets for easy organization
- The optional second floor has an additional 1,245 square feet of living area
- 3 bedrooms, 2 1/2 baths, 2-car side entry garage
- Basement, crawl space or slab foundation, please specify when ordering

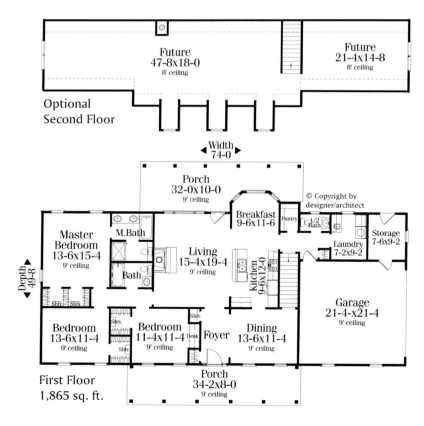

Second Floor
926 sq. ft.

Width: 52'-2"
Depth: 40'-0"

First Floor
961 sq. ft.

© Copyright by designer/architect

Special features

- ❖ 1,887 total square feet of living area
- ❖ Energy efficient home with 2" x 6" exterior walls
- ❖ Enormous great room is the heart of this home with an overlooking kitchen and dining room
- ❖ Formal dining room has a lovely bay window
- ❖ Master bedroom has spacious bath with corner step-up tub, double vanity and walk-in closet
- ❖ 3 bedrooms, 2 1/2 baths, 2-car garage
- ❖ Basement foundation

Your home should be a place of safe refuge, but every year 21 million injuries and 20,000 deaths occur unintentionally in our homes. Falls cause the most injuries by a wide margin. Make sure stairwells are well-lit, and for the elderly remove throw rugs or affix them with double-sided tape.

Special features

❖ 1,760 total square feet of living area

❖ Second floor master bedroom is large enough for a sitting area and features a luxury bath

❖ 9' ceilings on the first floor

❖ Energy efficient home with 2" x 6" exterior walls

❖ Bonus room on the second floor has an additional 256 square feet of living area

❖ 3 bedrooms, 2 1/2 baths, 1-car garage

❖ Basement foundation

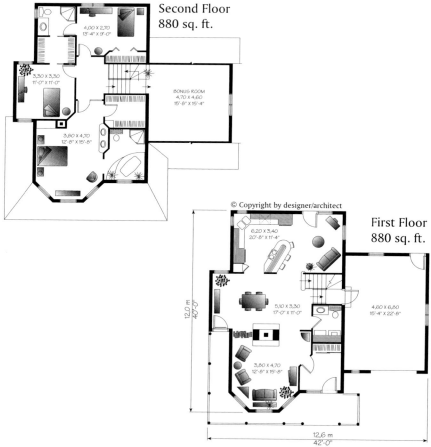

Second Floor
880 sq. ft.

First Floor
880 sq. ft.

© Copyright by designer/architect

Decorating with a dynamic mix, hunt for colorful accessories that recall the mid-twentieth century (think big dots, psychedelics and arrows). Well-placed dashes of vibrant color add energy and vigor to a dynamic decor.

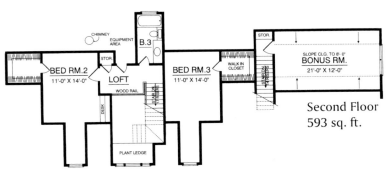

Second Floor
593 sq. ft.

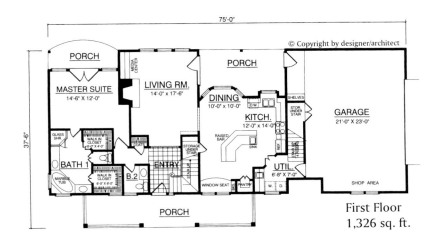

First Floor
1,326 sq. ft.

© Copyright by designer/architect

Special features

- ❖ 1,919 total square feet of living area
- ❖ The spacious kitchen and bayed dining area feature a raised bar island with sink, window seat and large pantry
- ❖ The relaxing master suite boasts double-door access to a private porch and a lavish bath including two walk-in closets and a whirlpool tub
- ❖ Both secondary bedrooms include a walk-in closet and charming dormer
- ❖ Second floor bonus room has an additional 306 square feet of living area
- ❖ 3 bedrooms, 2 1/2 baths, 2-car side entry garage
- ❖ Slab or crawl space foundation, please specify when ordering

Special features

- 3,176 total square feet of living area
- Energy efficient home with 2" x 6" exterior walls
- Varied ceiling heights throughout
- Beautifully designed foyer has a prominent center staircase and a lovely adjacent gallery space
- A casual sitting room connects the secondary bedrooms
- 3 bedrooms, 3 1/2 baths, 2-car side entry garage
- Basement, crawl space or slab foundation, please specify when ordering

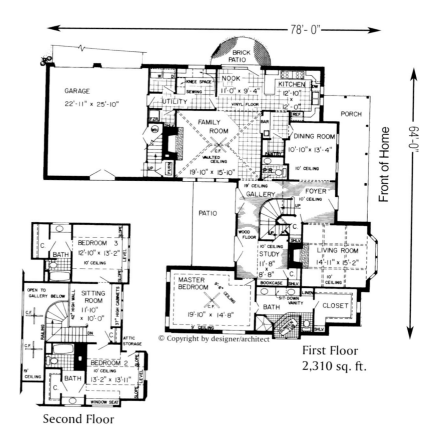

© Copyright by designer/architect

First Floor
2,310 sq. ft.

Second Floor
866 sq. ft.

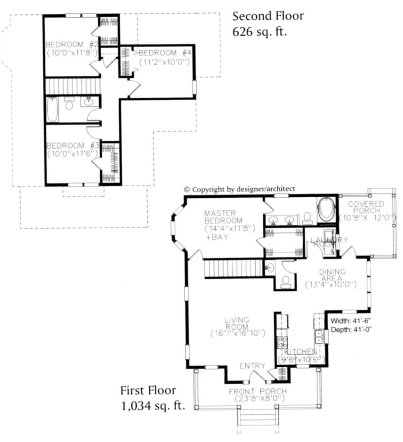

Second Floor
626 sq. ft.

BEDROOM #2
(10'0"x11'8")

BEDROOM #4
(11'2"x10'0")

BEDROOM #3
(10'0"x11'6")

© Copyright by designer/architect

MASTER BEDROOM
(14'4"x11'8")
+BAY

COVERED PORCH
(10'8"X 12'0")

LAUNDRY ROOM

DINING AREA
(13'4"x10'0")

Width: 41'-6"
Depth: 41'-0"

LIVING ROOM
(16'1"x16'10")

KITCHEN
(9'0"x10'0")

ENTRY

FRONT PORCH
(23'8"X8'0")

First Floor
1,034 sq. ft.

Special features

- ❖ 1,660 total square feet of living area
- ❖ The charming dining room accesses the covered porch to expand the entertaining opportunities
- ❖ The roomy living room is perfect for relaxing or fun family activities
- ❖ Three bedrooms on the second floor create an ideal family home
- ❖ 4 bedrooms, 2 1/2 baths
- ❖ Crawl space foundation

Special features

- ❖ 2,100 total square feet of living area
- ❖ Lovely covered porches front and rear provide an abundance of outdoor living space
- ❖ The efficient kitchen easily serves the formal dining room and bright breakfast area/sunroom with a raised bar for quick meals
- ❖ The elegant master bedroom includes his and her baths and large closets
- ❖ Bonus room above the garage has an additional 405 square feet of living area
- ❖ 3 bedrooms, 3 baths, 2-car garage
- ❖ Basement, crawl space or slab foundation, please specify when ordering

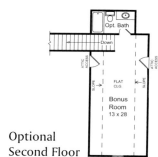

Optional
Second Floor

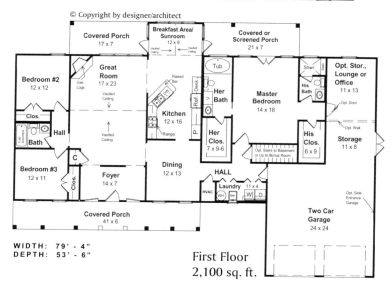

© Copyright by designer/architect

WIDTH: 79' - 4"
DEPTH: 53' - 6"

First Floor
2,100 sq. ft.

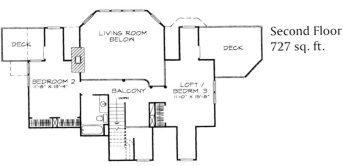

Second Floor
727 sq. ft.

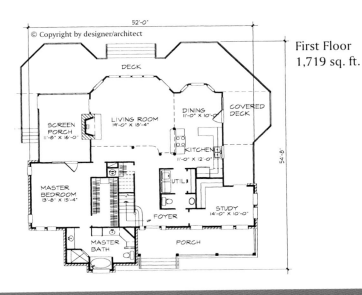

First Floor
1,719 sq. ft.

Special features

- ❖ 2,446 total square feet of living area
- ❖ A cheerful and private study would make a perfect home office
- ❖ A nice-sized kitchen offers a pass-through into the living room for easy entertaining
- ❖ A lovely screen porch is accessible from the living room as well as the master bedroom
- ❖ 3 bedrooms, 2 1/2 baths
- ❖ Slab foundation

According to the techniques of feng shui, it is a good idea to keep a bowl or arrangement of fruit on your dining room table. This represents continuous sustenance for your family. Add a mirror on the west or northwest wall of the dining room to double the food on your table.

Special features

❖ 3,114 total square feet of living area

❖ Unique ceiling treatments such as a tray ceiling in the master bedroom and a two-story ceiling in the living room add character throughout the home

❖ An appealing swing suite on the first floor is the perfect place for guests or in-laws

❖ A tantalizing bath in the master bedroom will no doubt be enjoyed by the homeowners

❖ 5 bedrooms, 4 baths, 3-car garage

❖ Basement foundation

Along with providing an abundance of fun and excitement, finishing a billiards room will increase the value of your property. Well designed game rooms are becoming more and more popular with today's need for homeowners to have their own space to relax and enjoy themselves.

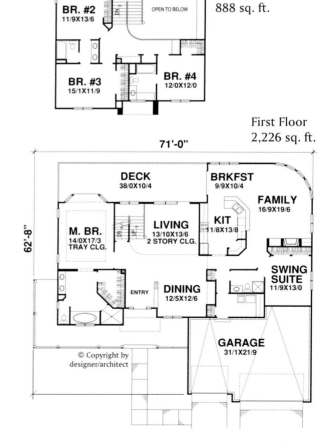

Second Floor
888 sq. ft.

First Floor
2,226 sq. ft.

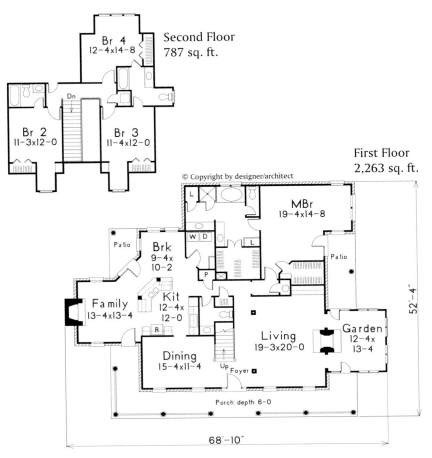

Br 4
12-4x14-8

Second Floor
787 sq. ft.

Dn

Br 2
11-3x12-0

Br 3
11-4x12-0

First Floor
2,263 sq. ft.

© Copyright by designer/architect

MBr
19-4x14-8

Patio

W D

Brk
9-4x
10-2

Patio

L

P

Family
13-4x13-4

Kit
12-4x
12-0

R

Living
19-3x20-0

Garden
12-4x
13-4

Dining
15-4x11-4

Up
Foyer

Porch depth 6-0

52'-4"

68'-10"

Special features

- ❖ 3,050 total square feet of living area
- ❖ Sunny garden room and two-way fireplace create a bright, airy living room
- ❖ Front porch is enhanced by arched transom windows and bold columns
- ❖ Sitting alcove, French door access to side patio, walk-in closets and abundant storage enhance the master bedroom
- ❖ 4 bedrooms, 3 1/2 baths, 2-car detached garage
- ❖ Slab foundation, drawings also include crawl space foundation

Romanesque columns were first used by American architect Henry Robson Richardson in the mid-1800's to support the massive Roman arches in Romanesque Revival homes. Simple pier columns, similar to the ones used above, often have wider bottoms than tops and are common in Mission and Craftsman homes.

Special features

❖ 1,714 total square feet of living area
❖ Master bedroom has a luxurious bath and private rear porch
❖ Angled kitchen counter allows for views into the family room and breakfast area
❖ Spacious secondary bedrooms enjoy walk-in closets
❖ 3 bedrooms, 2 baths, 2-car detached side entry garage
❖ Slab or crawl space foundation, please specify when ordering

For odors coming from the garbage disposal, drop a bunch of ice cubes and a cup of vinegar in it. Run for a minute or so. The ice will scour the blades to get rid of stuck-on stuff, and the vinegar will kill germs.

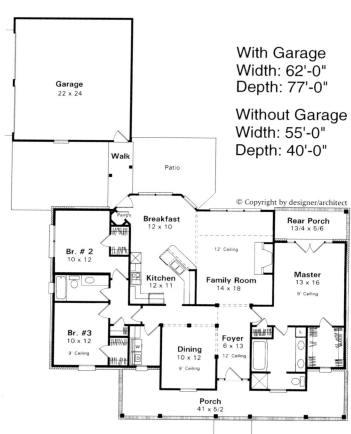

With Garage
Width: 62'-0"
Depth: 77'-0"

Without Garage
Width: 55'-0"
Depth: 40'-0"

© Copyright by designer/architect

Our Blueprint Packages Offer...

Quality plans for building your future, with extras that provide unsurpassed value, ensure good construction and long-term enjoyment.

A quality home - one that looks good, functions well, and provides years of enjoyment - is a product of many things - design, materials, craftsmanship.

But it's also the result of outstanding blueprints - the actual plans and specifications that tell the builder exactly how to build your home.

And with our BLUEPRINT PACKAGES you get the absolute best. A complete set of blueprints is available for every design in this book. These "working drawings" are highly detailed, resulting in two key benefits:

- Better understanding by the contractor of how to build your home and...
- More accurate construction estimates.

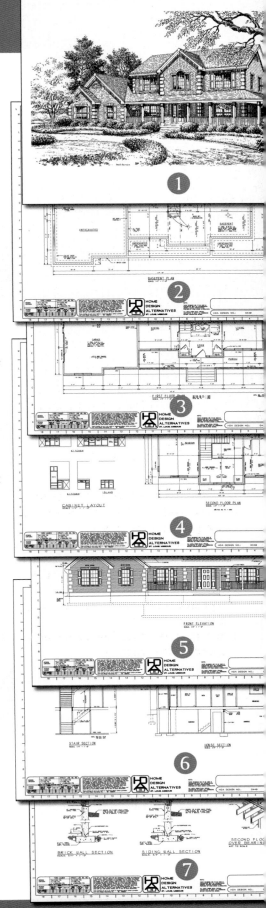

1. **Cover Sheet** is the artist's rendering of the exterior of the home and is included with many of the plans. It will give you an idea of how your home will look when completed and landscaped.

2. **Foundation** plan shows the layout of the basement, crawl space, slab or pier foundation. All necessary notations and dimensions are included. See the plan page for the foundation types included. If the home plan you choose does not have your desired foundation type, our Customer Service Representatives can advise you on how to customize your foundation to suit your specific needs or site conditions.

3. **Floor Plans** show the placement of walls, doors, closets, plumbing fixtures, electrical outlets, columns, and beams for each level of the home.

4. **Interior Elevations** provide views of special interior elements such as fireplaces, kitchen cabinets, built-in units and other features of the home.

5. **Exterior Elevations** illustrate the front, rear and both sides of the house, with all details of exterior materials and the required dimensions.

6. **Sections** show detail views of the home or portions of the home as if it were sliced from the roof to the foundation. This sheet shows important areas such as load-bearing walls, stairs, joists, trusses and other structural elements, which are critical for proper construction.

7. **Details** show how to construct certain components of your home, such as the roof system, stairs, deck, etc.

Home Plan Index

Plan Number	Square Feet	Price Code	Page	Material List	Right Read. Reverse	Can. Shipping
597-038D-0085	2,541	F	247		•	
597-038D-0089	1,960	C	196	•		
597-038D-0091	2,525	F	136			
597-039D-0001	1,253	A	38			
597-039D-0002	1,333	A	109			
597-039D-0004	1,406	A	85			
597-039D-0007	1,550	B	93			
597-039D-0010	1,714	B	444			
597-039D-0012	1,815	C	99			
597-039D-0017	1,966	C	398			
597-039D-0020	2,010	C	299			
597-039D-0022	2,158	C	199			
597-040D-0001	1,833	D	70	•		
597-040D-0002	1,958	D	358	•		
597-040D-0003	1,475	B	16	•		
597-040D-0014	1,595	B	409	•		
597-040D-0015	1,655	B	108	•		
597-040D-0016	3,013	E	162	•		
597-040D-0027	1,597	C	50	•		
597-040D-0030	1,543	B	309	•		
597-040D-0033	1,829	C	207	•		
597-045D-0006	2,351	D	320	•		
597-045D-0007	2,685	E	218	•		
597-045D-0017	954	AA	119	•		
597-046D-0016	2,812	E	393			
597-046D-0027	3,114	E	442			
597-046D-0034	2,218	D	341			
597-046D-0036	2,150	C	138			
597-046D-0063	2,816	E	238			
597-047D-0005	1,885	C	156			
597-047D-0025	1,806	C	380			
597-047D-0050	2,293	D	129			
597-047D-0069	2,059	C	280			
597-047D-0076	2,326	D	180			
597-047D-0077	2,326	D	428			
597-047D-0079	2,508	D	328			
597-047D-0080	2,508	D	228			
597-049D-0005	1,389	A	110	•		
597-049D-0006	1,771	B	63	•		
597-049D-0008	1,937	C	39	•		
597-049D-0009	1,673	B	71	•		
597-049D-0010	1,669	B	59			
597-049D-0012	1,295	A	116	•		
597-051D-0011	2,155	C	276			
597-051D-0020	2,491	D	177			
597-051D-0025	2,367	D	127			
597-051D-0089	2,073	D	422			
597-051D-0124	2,236	E	321			
597-051D-0155	3,172	F	221			
597-052D-0011	1,325	A	78	•		
597-052D-0020	1,553	B	258			
597-052D-0026	1,675	B	137			
597-052D-0031	1,735	B	390	•		
597-052D-0032	1,765	B	283			
597-052D-0052	1,936	C	178			
597-052D-0055	1,993	C	65	•		
597-053D-0001	1,582	B	123	•		
597-053D-0007	1,922	C	223	•		
597-055D-0016	2,698	E	76	•	•	
597-055D-0022	2,107	C	126	•	•	
597-055D-0035	3,059	E	174	•	•	
597-055D-0045	2,707	E	325	•	•	
597-055D-0049	1,845	C	275	•	•	
597-055D-0088	2,261	D	120	•	•	
597-055D-0098	3,060	E	225	•	•	
597-055S-0001	3,706	S1	425	•	•	
597-058D-0006	1,339	A	20	•	•	
597-058D-0020	1,428	A	44	•	•	
597-062D-0015	2,797	E	266			•
597-062D-0041	1,541	B	66	•	•	•
597-062D-0042	2,582	D	166	•	•	•
597-062D-0050	1,408	A	36	•	•	•
597-065D-0027	1,595	B	210	•		
597-065D-0028	1,611	B	24	•	•	
597-065D-0031	2,764	E	416	•		
597-065D-0043	3,816	F	367	•	•	
597-065D-0046	2,049	C	261	•	•	
597-065D-0164	1,860	C	161			
597-065D-0166	1,698	B	53	•		
597-067D-0004	1,698	B	91		•	
597-067D-0008	2,327	D	82		•	
597-067D-0009	2,198	C	92		•	
597-067D-0014	2,599	D	60		•	
597-068D-0002	2,266	D	95	•		
597-069D-0012	1,594	B	81	•		
597-069D-0018	2,069	C	54	•		
597-070D-0006	1,841	C	128			
597-072D-0005	2,729	E	41			
597-072D-0009	2,464	D	246			
597-076D-0035	2,368	D	153			
597-076D-0103	2,844	E	213			
597-077D-0045	1,799	C	140	•	•	
597-077D-0053	1,852	D	288	•	•	
597-077D-0058	2,002	D	240	•	•	
597-077D-0063	2,100	D	440	•	•	
597-077D-0082	2,008	D	388	•	•	
597-077D-0101	2,250	E	188	•	•	
597-077D-0128	3,379	C	30	•	•	
597-078D-0002	1,925	D	245	•		
597-078D-0007	2,600	D	145	•		
597-078D-0049	1,480	D	164	•		
597-080D-0007	2,414	B	143	•		•
597-081D-0010	1,400	C	291		•	
597-081D-0021	1,536	C	423		•	
597-081D-0027	1,575	C	323		•	
597-081D-0028	1,578	C	222		•	
597-081D-0034	1,660	C	439		•	
597-081D-0041	2,038	D	121		•	
597-081D-0043	2,139	D	373		•	
597-081D-0052	2,605	D	273		•	
597-081D-0053	2,157	D	171		•	
597-082D-0004	1,529	G	10		•	
597-082D-0015	2,343	H	301		•	
597-082D-0019	2,780	H	251		•	
597-082D-0021	2,896	G	151		•	
597-084D-0018	1,865	D	434	•		
597-084D-0026	1,551	D	385	•		
597-084D-0033	2,465	E	285	•		
597-084D-0037	1,688	D	182	•		
597-084D-0038	1,894	D	232	•		
597-087D-0145	1,792	G	420			
597-087D-0147	1,798	G	371			
597-087D-0262	1,812	H	270			
597-087D-0298	2,200	H	158			
597-087D-0569	2,759	I	211			
597-089D-0013	2,658	F	349	•		
597-089D-0052	1,409	C	248	•		
597-089D-0064	1,522	D	186	•		
597-091D-0002	2,301	D	263			
597-091D-0017	2,982	E	163			
597-095D-0002	3,519	G	389			
597-095D-0008	2,526	D	289			
597-095D-0009	2,928	E	134			
597-095D-0016	1,479	A	190			
597-095D-0017	2,446	D	441			
597-095D-0026	2,253	D	339			
597-095D-0034	1,654	B	239			
597-095D-0035	1,790	AA	139			
597-099D-0013	2,375	D	117			
597-099D-0017	2,556	E	216			

What Kind of Plan Package Do You Need?

Once you find the home plan you've been looking for, here are some suggestions on how to make your Dream Home a reality.
To get started, order the type of plans that fit your particular situation.

Your Choices:

The 1-Set Package - We offer a 1-set plan package so you can study your home in detail. This one set is considered a study set and is marked "not for construction." It is a copyright violation to reproduce blueprints.

The Minimum 5-Set Package - If you're ready to start the construction process, this 5-set package is the minimum number of blueprint sets you will need. It will require keeping close track of each set so they can be used by multiple subcontractors and tradespeople.

The Standard 8-Set Package - For best results in terms of cost, schedule and quality of construction, we recommend you order eight (or more) sets of blueprints. Besides one set for yourself, additional sets of blueprints will be required by your mortgage lender, local building department, general contractor and all subcontractors working on foundation, electrical, plumbing, heating/air conditioning, carpentry work, etc.

Reproducible Masters - If you wish to make some minor design changes, you'll want to order reproducible masters. These drawings contain the same information as the blueprints but are printed on reproducible paper that is easy to alter and clearly indicates your right to copy or reproduce. This will allow your builder or a local design professional to make the necessary drawing changes without the major expense of redrawing the plans. This package also allows you to print copies of the modified plans as needed. The right of building only one structure from these plans is licensed exclusively to the buyer. You may not use this design to build a second or multiple dwellings without purchasing another blueprint. Each violation of the Copyright Law is punishable in a fine.

Mirror Reverse Sets - Plans can be printed in mirror reverse. These plans are useful when the house would fit your site better if all the rooms were on the opposite side than shown. They are simply a mirror image of the original drawings causing the lettering and dimensions to read backwards. Therefore, when ordering mirror reverse drawings, you must purchase at least one set of right-reading plans. Some of our plans are offered mirror reverse right-reading. This means the plan, lettering and dimensions are flipped but read correctly. See the Home Plan Index on pages 446-448 for availability.

Other Great Products...

The Legal Kit - Avoid many legal pitfalls and build your home with confidence using the forms and contracts featured in this kit. Included are request for proposal documents, various fixed price and cost plus contracts, instructions on how and when to use each form, warranty statements and more. Save time and money before you break ground on your new home or start a remodeling project. All forms are reproducible. The kit is ideal for homebuilders and contractors. **Cost: $35.00**

Detail Plan Packages - Electrical, Plumbing and Framing Packages - Three separate packages offer homebuilders details for constructing various foundations; numerous floor, wall and roof framing techniques; simple to complex residential wiring; sump and water softener hookups; plumbing connection methods; installation of septic systems, and more. Each package includes three dimensional illustrations and a glossary of terms. Purchase one or all three. Note: These drawings do not pertain to a specific home plan. **Cost: $20.00 each or all three for $40.00**

More Helpful Building Aids

Your Blueprint Package contains the necessary construction information to build your home. We also offer the following products and services to save you time and money in the building process.

Express Delivery - Most orders are processed within 24 hours of receipt. Please allow 7-10 business days for delivery. If you need to place a rush order, please call us by 11:00 a.m. Monday-Friday CST and ask for express service (allow 1-2 business days).

Technical Assistance - If you have questions, please call our technical support line at 1-314-770-2228 between 8:00 a.m. and 5:00 p.m. Monday-Friday CST. Whether it involves design modifications or field assistance, our designers are extremely familiar with all of our designs and will be happy to help you.

Material List - Material lists are available for many of the plans in this publication. Each list gives you the quantity, dimensions and description of the building materials necessary to construct your home. You'll get faster and more accurate bids from your contractor while saving money by paying for only the materials you need. See the Home Plan Index on pages 446-448 for availability.
Note: Material lists are not refundable. **Cost: $125.00**

Making Changes to Your Plan

We understand that it is difficult to find blueprints for a home that will meet all your needs. That is why HDA, Inc. (Home Design Alternatives) is pleased to offer home plan modification services.

Typical home plan modifications include:

- Changing foundation type
- Adding square footage to a plan
- Changing the entry into a garage
- Changing a two-car garage to a three-car garage or making a garage larger
- Redesigning kitchen, baths, and bedrooms
- Changing exterior elevations
- Or most other home plan modifications you may desire!

Some home plan modifications we cannot make include:

- Reversing the plans
- Adapting/engineering plans to meet your local building codes
- Combining parts of two different plans (due to copyright laws)

Our plan modification service is easy to use. Simply:

1. Decide on the modifications you want. For the most accurate quote, be as detailed as possible and refer to rooms in the same manner as the floor plan (i.e. if the floor plan refers to a "den," use "den" in your description). Including a sketch of the modified floor plan is always helpful.

2. Complete and e-mail the modification request form that can be found online at www.houseplansandmore.com.

3. Within two business days, you will receive your quote. Quotes do not include the cost of the reproducible masters required for our designer to legally make changes.

4. Call to accept the quote and purchase the reproducible masters. For example, if your quote is $850 and the reproducible masters for your plan are $800, your order total will be $1650 plus two shipping and handling charges (one to ship the reproducible masters to our designer and one to ship the modified plans to you).

5. Our designer will send you up to three drafts to verify your initial changes. Extra costs apply after the third draft. If additional changes are made that alter the original request, extra charges may be incurred.

6. Once you approve a draft with the final changes, we then make the changes to the reproducible masters by adding additional sheets. The original reproducible masters (with no changes) plus your new changed sheets will be shipped to you.

Other Important Information:

- Plans cannot be redrawn in reverse format. All modifications will be made to match the reproducible master's original layout. Once you receive the plans, you can make reverse copies at your local blueprint shop.

- Our staff designer will provide the first draft for your review within 4 weeks (plus shipping time) of receiving your order.

- You will receive up to three drafts to review before your original changes are modified. The first draft will totally encompass all modifications based on your original request. Additional changes not included in your original request will be charged separately at an hourly rate of $75 or a flat quoted rate.

- Modifications will be drawn on a separate sheet with the changes shown and a note to see the main sheet for details. For example, a floor plan sheet from the original set (i.e. Sheet 3) would be followed by a new floor plan sheet with changes (i.e. Sheet A-3).

- Plans are drawn to meet national building codes. Modifications will not be drawn to any particular state or county codes, thus we cannot guarantee that the revisions will meet your local building codes. You may be required to have a local architect or designer review the plans in order to have them comply with your state or county building codes.

- Time and cost estimates are good for 90 calendar days.

- All modification requests need to be submitted in writing. Verbal requests will not be accepted.

2 Easy Steps for FAST service

1. Visit www.houseplansandmore.com to download the modification request form.

2. E-mail the completed form to customize@hdainc.com or fax to 913-856-7751.

   If you are not able to access the internet, please call 1-800-373-2646 (Monday-Friday, 8am-5pm CST).

Before You Order

Exchange Policies

Since blueprints are printed in response to your order, we cannot honor requests for refunds. However, if for some reason you find that the plan you have purchased does not meet your requirements, you may exchange that plan for another plan in our collection within 90 days of purchase. At the time of the exchange, you will be charged a processing fee of 25% of your original plan package price, plus the difference in price between the plan packages (if applicable) and the cost to ship the new plans to you. Please note: Reproducible drawings can only be exchanged if the package is unopened.

Building Codes & Requirements

At the time the construction drawings were prepared, every effort was made to ensure that these plans and specifications meet nationally recognized codes. Our plans conform to most national building codes. Because building codes vary from area to area, some drawing modifications and/or the assistance of a professional designer or architect may be necessary to comply with your local codes or to accommodate specific building site conditions. We advise you to consult with your local building official for information regarding codes governing your area.

Additional Sets✦

Additional sets of the plan ordered are available for an additional cost of $45.00 each. Five-set, eight-set, and reproducible packages offer considerable savings.

Mirror Reverse Plans✦

Available for an additional $15.00 per set, these plans are simply a mirror image of the original drawings causing the dimensions and lettering to read backwards. Therefore, when ordering mirror reverse plans, you must purchase at least one set of right-reading plans. Some of our plans are offered mirror reverse right-reading. This means the plan, lettering and dimensions are flipped but read correctly. To purchase a mirror reverse right-reading set, the cost is an additional $150.00. See the Home Plan Index on pages 446-448 for availability.

One-Set Study Package

We offer a one-set plan package so you can study your home in detail. This one set is considered a study set and is marked "not for construction." It is a copyright violation to reproduce blueprints.

✦Available only within 90 days after purchase of plan package or reproducible masters of same plan.

Blueprint Price Schedule

BEST VALUE

Price Code	1-Set	5-Sets (Save $110)	8-Sets (Save $200)	Reproducible Masters
AAA	$310	$380	$425	$525
AA	$410	$480	$525	$625
A	$470	$540	$585	$685
B	$530	$600	$645	$745
C	$585	$655	$700	$800
D	$635	$705	$750	$850
E	$695	$765	$810	$910
F	$750	$820	$865	$965
G	$850	$920	$965	$1065
H	$945	$1015	$1060	$1160
I	$995	$1065	$1110	$1210
S1	N/A	N/A	N/A	$2500

Plan prices are subject to change without notice.
Please note that plans and material lists are not refundable.

Shipping & Handling Charges

U.S. Shipping - (AK and HI express only)	1-4 Sets	5-7 Sets	8 Sets or Reproducibles
Regular (allow 7-10 business days)	$15.00	$17.50	$25.00
Priority (allow 3-5 business days)	$25.00	$30.00	$35.00
Express* (allow 1-2 business days)	$35.00	$40.00	$45.00

Canada Shipping (to/from)** - Plans with suffix 032D, 062D and 080D - see index

	1-4 Sets	5-7 Sets	8 Sets or Reproducibles
Standard (allow 8-12 business days)	$35.00	$40.00	$45.00
Express* (allow 3-5 business days)	$60.00	$70.00	$80.00

Overseas Shipping/International -
Call, fax, or e-mail (plans@hdainc.com) for shipping costs.

* For express delivery please call us by 11:00 a.m. Monday-Friday CST
** Orders may be subject to custom's fee and/or duties/taxes.

Questions? Call Our Customer Service Number
1-800-373-2646

Many of our plans are available in CAD. For availability, please call our Customer Service Number above.

How to Order

1.) **Call** toll-free 1-800-373-2646 for credit card orders.
Mastercard, Visa, Discover and American Express are accepted.

2.) **Fax** your order to 1-314-770-2226.

3.) **Mail** the Order Form to: **HDA, Inc.**
944 Anglum Road
St. Louis, MO 63042
ATTN: Customer Service Dept.

4.) **Online** visit www.houseplansandmore.com

For fastest service, Call Toll-Free
1-800-DREAM HOME (1-800-373-2646) day or night

Order Form

Please send me -

PLAN NUMBER 597-_____

PRICE CODE _____   (see pages 446-448)

Specify Foundation Type (see plan page for availability)

☐ Slab   ☐ Crawl space   ☐ Pier

☐ Basement   ☐ Walk-out basement

☐ Reproducible Masters $_____

☐ Eight-Set Plan Package $_____

☐ Five-Set Plan Package $_____

☐ One-Set Study Package (no mirror reverse) $_____

Additional Plan Sets❖ (see page 451)

☐ ____ (Qty.) at $45.00 each $_____

Mirror Reverse❖ (see page 451)

☐ Right-reading $150 one-time charge
(see index on pages 446-448 for availability) $_____

☐ Print in Mirror Reverse
(where right-reading is not available)

____ (Qty.) at $15.00 each $_____

☐ Material List❖ $125 (see pages 446-448 for availability)
(see page 449 for more information)
                                                $_____

☐ Legal Kit (002D-9991, see page 449) $_____

Detail Plan Packages: (see page 449)

☐ Framing   ☐ Electrical   ☐ Plumbing
(002D-9992)   (002D-9993)   (002D-9994)
                                                $_____

SUBTOTAL $_____

Sales Tax (MO residents add 6%) $_____

☐ Shipping/Handling (see page 451) $_____

TOTAL (US funds only - sorry no CODs) $_____

I hereby authorize HDA, Inc. to charge this purchase to my credit card account (check one):

☐ MasterCard   ☐ VISA   ☐ DISCOVER   ☐ AMERICAN EXPRESS Cards

Plan prices are subject to change without notice. Please note that plans and material lists are not refundable.

Credit Card number _____

Expiration date _____

Signature_____

Name_____
(Please print or type)

Street Address_____
(Please do not use a P.O. Box)

_____

City _____

State _____

Zip _____

Daytime phone number   (_____) -_____

E-mail address_____

I am a   ☐ Builder/Contractor
         ☐ Homeowner
         ☐ Renter

I ☐ have ☐ have not selected my general contractor.

Thank you for your order!

❖Available only within 90 days after purchase of plan package or reproducible masters of same plan.

Casual Country
❖ Project Plans ❖

Casual country project plans include a variety of functional and easy-to-build projects. The following pages include 60 indoor and outdoor project plans perfect for your needs while adding a charming complement to your surroundings. Everything from birdhouses to storage cabinets, these do-it-yourself projects are sure to spice up your country home.

Plan #597-066D-0012

Small Wishing Well
- ❖ Size - 27" diameter x 40" high
- ❖ Perfect addition to any garden
- ❖ Complete list of materials
- ❖ Step-by-step instructions
- ❖ Full-size traceable patterns

Price Code P3

Plan #597-097D-0001

Wishing Well
- ❖ Size - 29" x 29" x 64" high
- ❖ Flower planters add character to this lovely yard decoration
- ❖ Simple design is pleasing
- ❖ Complete list of materials
- ❖ Step-by-step instructions

Price Code P3

Plan #597-066D-0002

Wishing Well
- ❖ Size - 4' diameter x 7' high
- ❖ Includes patterns for authentic bucket and operating windlass and crank handle
- ❖ Complete list of materials
- ❖ Step-by-step instructions
- ❖ Full-size traceable patterns

Price Code P3

Plan #597-066D-0013

Wheelbarrow Planter
- ❖ Size - 40" x 10" x 15" high
- ❖ Wheel turns to move planter easily
- ❖ Complete list of materials
- ❖ Step-by-step instructions
- ❖ Full-size traceable patterns

Price Code P3

Plan #597-097D-0008

Covered Wagon Planter
- ❖ Size - 27" x 14" x 30" high
- ❖ A decorative touch for your plants
- ❖ Will add character to your yard, patio or deck
- ❖ Complete list of materials
- ❖ Step-by-step instructions

Price Code P3

Plan #597-097D-0009

Water Pump Planter
- ❖ Size - 23" x 23" x 53" high
- ❖ Add style and character to your planting scheme
- ❖ Easy to build and sturdy construction
- ❖ Complete list of materials
- ❖ Step-by-step instructions

Price Code P3

Plan #597-066D-0009

Birdhouses
- ❖ Country birdhouse size -
  7" x 9" x 10" high
- ❖ Victorian birdhouse size -
  8 1/2" x 7" x 18" high
- ❖ Complete list of materials
- ❖ Step-by-step instructions
- ❖ Full-size traceable patterns

Price Code P3

Plan #597-066D-0017

Birdhouse Assortment
- ❖ Seven plans: four houses and three feeders
- ❖ Projects require only standard hand tools and inexpensive materials
- ❖ Traceable pieces
- ❖ Complete list of materials
- ❖ Step-by-step instructions

Price Code P3

Plan #597-066D-1506

Deer Planter Trio
- ❖ Sizes -
  16" high
  24" high
  32" high
- ❖ Simple design for indoor/outdoor use
- ❖ Complete list of materials
- ❖ Step-by-step instructions
- ❖ Full-size traceable patterns

Price Code P3

Plan #597-097D-0014

Hexagon Picnic Table
- ❖ Size - 27" x 23" x 12" high
- ❖ Enhance your backyard or deck
- ❖ Complements any setting
- ❖ Complete list of materials
- ❖ Step-by-step instructions

Price Code P3

Plan #597-097D-0011

Flower Bed Planter
- ❖ Size 24" x 12" x 17" high
- ❖ Create a wonderful flower and plant display with this charming planter
- ❖ Simple construction for easy assembly
- ❖ Complete list of materials
- ❖ Step-by-step instructions

Price Code P3

Plan #597-097D-0015

Hanging Planter Box
- ❖ Size - 37" x 37" x 74" high
- ❖ Ideal for any yard
- ❖ Attractive and sturdy design
- ❖ Complete list of materials
- ❖ Step-by-step instructions

Price Code P3

Plan #597-066D-0006

Canopy Glider Swing
- ❖ Size - 8'-0" x 6'-5" x 8'-0" high
- ❖ Seats four adults
- ❖ Includes small table with cut-outs for drinks
- ❖ Complete list of materials
- ❖ Step-by-step instructions
- ❖ Full-size traceable patterns

Price Code P3

Plan #597-066D-0001

Tree Seat
- ❖ Easily adjusts to fit most trees
- ❖ Complete list of materials
- ❖ Step-by-step instructions
- ❖ Full-size traceable patterns

Price Code P3

Plan #597-066D-0016

Water Wheel
- ❖ Size - 4' x 3' x 4' high
- ❖ Submersible pump keeps water circulating and wheel turning
- ❖ Complete list of materials
- ❖ Step-by-step instructions
- ❖ Full-size traceable patterns

Price Code P3

Plan #597-097D-0013

Ground Level Planter
- ❖ Size - 33" x 13" x 28" high
- ❖ Enhance your garden, patio or deck
- ❖ Complements any outdoor setting
- ❖ Complete list of materials
- ❖ Step-by-step instructions

Price Code P3

Plan #597-066D-0014

Water Pump
- ❖ Size - 14" square x 44" high
- ❖ Designed for use with submersible pump
- ❖ Complete list of materials
- ❖ Step-by-step instructions
- ❖ Full-size traceable patterns

Price Code P3

Plan #597-066D-0023

Adirondack Quartet
- ❖ Four easy-to-build Adirondack projects
- ❖ Complete list of materials
- ❖ Step-by-step instructions

Price Code P3

Plan #597-066D-1521

Corner Cabinet

❖ Size - 72" tall x 27" across the front x 23 1/2" deep on the two sides
❖ Display space above with large cabinet below
❖ Complete list of materials
❖ Step-by-step instructions
Price Code P3

Plan #597-097D-1508

Tall Country Hutch

❖ Size - 34 1/2" x 10 1/4" x 64" high
❖ Provides essential storage in a stylish design
❖ Easy to build and sturdy construction
❖ Complete list of materials
❖ Step-by-step instructions
Price Code P3

Plan #597-066D-1519

Craftsman Bookcase

❖ Size - 60" tall x 36" wide x 12" deep
❖ Features tempered glass doors and three shelves
❖ Complete list of materials
❖ Step-by-step instructions
Price Code P3

Plan #597-097D-1514

Window & Bath Shelves

❖ Sizes -
   Window - 48" x 7" x 15" high
   Bath - 22" x 7 1/2" x 32" high
❖ Attractive and sturdy design
❖ Complete list of materials
❖ Step-by-step instructions
Price Code P3

Plan #597-097D-1512

Three Shelves

❖ Sizes -
   Sofia - 22" x 10" x 10.5" high
   Phone - 22" x 10" x 10.5" high
   Wall - 37.5" x 8" x 41" high
❖ Complements any room of the house
❖ Complete list of materials
❖ Step-by-step instructions
Price Code P3

Plan #597-097D-1513

Collectible Shelves

❖ Sizes -
   23" x 5" x 28" high
   15" x 6 1/2" x 32" high
❖ A stylish way to display your collectibles
❖ Complete list of materials
❖ Step-by-step instructions
Price Code P3

Plan #597-097D-1504

Quilt Rack
- ❖ Size - 24" x 11" x 30" high
- ❖ Store and display your fine-crafted quilts
- ❖ Complete list of materials
- ❖ Step-by-step instructions

Price Code P3

Plan #597-066D-1529

Jewelry & Lingerie Chest
- ❖ Size - 39" tall x 19" wide x 15" deep
- ❖ Mahogany, with porcelain knobs and felt-lined drawers
- ❖ Mostly straight cuts make this an easy project
- ❖ Complete list of materials
- ❖ Step-by-step instructions

Price Code P3

Plan #597-066D-1522

Roll-Top Desk
- ❖ Size - 43" tall x 50" long x 28" deep
- ❖ Timeless pigeon-hole design
- ❖ Nine drawers, two draw boards, 16 nooks, pull-down cover
- ❖ Complete list of materials
- ❖ Step-by-step instructions

Price Code P3

Plan #597-066D-1503

Heritage Cradle
- ❖ Size - 33" x 27" x 27" high
- ❖ Beautiful, sturdy construction with limited rocking motion
- ❖ Complete list of materials
- ❖ Step-by-step instructions
- ❖ Full-size traceable patterns

Price Code P3

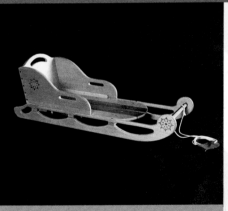

Plan #597-066D-0005

Sled
- ❖ Size - 40" x 15"
- ❖ Plans are designed with a removable seat
- ❖ Complete list of materials
- ❖ Step-by-step instructions
- ❖ Full-size traceable patterns

Price Code P3

Plan #597-066D-1508

Storage Bins
- ❖ Size - 19" x 12" x 40" high
- ❖ Wire mesh allows air to circulate
- ❖ Two pull-out bins and a shelf
- ❖ Complete list of materials
- ❖ Step-by-step instructions

Price Code P3

Plan #597-066D-1507

Blanket Chest and Seat
- Size - 48" x 19" x 36" high
- Simple country styling with a hinged bench seat
- Complete list of materials
- Step-by-step instructions

Price Code P3

Plan #597-097D-1501

Personalized Toy Chest
- Size - 40" x 19" x 24" high
- Great for children and grandchildren to have their own space for toys
- Complete list of materials
- Step-by-step instructions

Price Code P3

Plan #597-066D-1518

Entertainment Armoire
- Size - 70" tall x 39" wide x 23" deep
- Pine armoire holds 27-inch TV, VCR, stereo equipment and more
- Complete list of materials
- Step-by-step instructions

Price Code P3

Plan #597-097D-1507

Sunflower Plant Stand
- Size - 12" x 12" x 14" high
- Stylish details will enhance any room
- Complete list of materials
- Step-by-step instructions

Price Code P3

Plan #597-097D-1511

Cow Table
- Size - 34" x 18" x 30" high
- Fun design will brighten any room
- Complete list of materials
- Step-by-step instructions

Price Code P3

Plan #597-097D-1506

Paper Towel Holders
- Choose from three country designs or make all
- Perfect to use for yourself or to make as a gift
- Complete list of materials
- Step-by-step instructions

Price Code P3

Plan #597-097D-1523

Design #597-097D-1520

Plan #597-097D-1522

Doll Bunk Beds

❖ Size - 23 1/2" x 11" x 24" high
❖ Comes complete with a step ladder
❖ Complete list of materials
❖ Step-by-step instructions
  Price Code P3

Doll's Seat & Storage Bin

❖ Size - 17" x 10" x 16" high
❖ The bench seat lifts up for a small storage area, perfect for doll clothes
❖ Complete list of materials
❖ Step-by-step instructions
  Price Code P3

Doll's Cradle

❖ Size - 20 3/4" x 10 1/4" x 11 1/4" high
❖ Charming design for the doll-lover in the family
❖ Complete list of materials
❖ Step-by-step instructions
  Price Code P3

Plan #597-066D-1505

Plan #597-066D-1526

Plan #597-002D-1520

Pony Rocker

❖ Size - 44" x 12" x 25" high
❖ A classic design with the mane and tail made from yarn and scrap leather for the ears
❖ Complete list of materials
❖ Step-by-step instructions
❖ Full-size traceable patterns
  Price Code P3

Child's Rocker

❖ Size - 25" tall x 21" long
❖ Extra safe and sturdy, with no sharp points or edges
❖ Oak and oak dowels
❖ Traceable pieces
❖ Complete list of materials
❖ Step-by-step instructions
  Price Code P3

Rocking Horse

❖ Size - 30" x 11" x 23 3/4"
❖ A child's dream come true
❖ Complete list of materials
❖ Step-by-step instructions
  Price Code P3

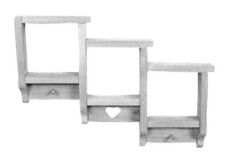

Plan #597-002D-1545

Heart Shadow Box
- Size - 22 1/2" x 2 3/4" x 17 1/2"
- Creative stair-stepped design
- Complete list of materials
- Step-by-step instructions

Price Code P3

Plan #597-002D-1541

Star Shelf with Pegs
- Size - 12" x 3 3/4" x 19 1/2"
- Shelf for displaying, pegs for hanging
- Complete list of materials
- Step-by-step instructions

Price Code P3

Plan #597-002D-1514

Towel Bar with Shelf
- Size - 25 1/2" x 7" x 12"
- Perfect for any bathroom with classic heart-shaped design
- Complete list of materials
- Step-by-step instructions

Price Code P3

Plan #597-002D-1517

2 Shelf Plant Stand
- Size - 31 1/2" x 9 1/4" x 33"
- Plenty of room for all your plants
- Complete list of materials
- Step-by-step instructions

Price Code P3

Plan #597-002D-1551

Key Rack with Doors
- Size - 9" x 3" x 13 1/2"
- Key slots for many sets
- Complete list of materials
- Step-by-step instructions

Price Code P3

Plan #597-002D-1528

Heart Magazine Rack
- Size - 16 1/2" x 7" x 15"
- Magazine rack features heart accents
- Complete list of materials
- Step-by-step instructions

Price Code P3

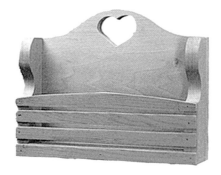

Plan #597-002D-1538

Key/Mail Holder
- ❖ Size - 11" x 3" x 9"
- ❖ Easy way to keep track of your keys and important mail
- ❖ Complete list of materials
- ❖ Step-by-step instructions
- Price Code P3

Plan #597-002D-1533

Corner Heart Shelf
- ❖ Size - 7 1/2" x 7 1/2" x 11"
- ❖ Display your special collectibles
- ❖ Complete list of materials
- ❖ Step-by-step instructions
- Price Code P3

Plan #597-002D-1535

Heart Shaped Stool
- ❖ Size - 13 3/4" x 10 1/4" x 6 1/4"
- ❖ Sturdy design for those hard-to-reach places
- ❖ Complete list of materials
- ❖ Step-by-step instructions
- Price Code P3

Plan #597-002D-1526

Cup Holder
- ❖ Size - 8 1/4" x 8 1/4" x 19 1/4"
- ❖ Coffee cups within easy reach
- ❖ Complete list of materials
- ❖ Step-by-step instructions
- Price Code P3

Plan #597-002D-1506

Curio
- ❖ Size - 15" x 4 1/2" x 30"
- ❖ Unique curio with pegs for hanging decorative items
- ❖ Complete list of materials
- ❖ Step-by-step instructions
- Price Code P3

Plan #597-002D-1522

Phone Stand
- ❖ Size - 14" x 9" x 32"
- ❖ Stand with lower shelf for phone directories
- ❖ Complete list of materials
- ❖ Step-by-step instructions
- Price Code P3

Plan #597-002D-1508

34" Heart Shelf
❖ Size - 34" x 5 1/2" x 6 1/4"
❖ Large shelf unit with pegs for handing items
❖ Complete list of materials
❖ Step-by-step instructions
  Price Code P3

Plan #597-002D-1509

18" Heart Shelf
❖ Size - 18" x 4 1/2" x 6 1/2"
❖ Perfect size and styling for any room
❖ Complete list of materials
❖ Step-by-step instructions
  Price Code P3

Plan #597-002D-1507

24" Heart Shelf
❖ Size - 24" x 5 1/2" x 6 1/4"
❖ Attractive styling for any room
❖ Complete list of materials
❖ Step-by-step instructions
  Price Code P3

Plan #597-002D-1516

Quilt Rack
❖ Size - 25 1/2" x 9 1/4" x 32"
❖ Classic quilt rack fits any decor
❖ Complete list of materials
❖ Step-by-step instructions
  Price Code P3

Plan #597-002D-1515

Heart Quilt Rack
❖ Size - 25 1/2" x 9 1/4" x 32"
❖ Display your favorite quilts on the heart-accented rack
❖ Complete list of materials
❖ Step-by-step instructions
  Price Code P3

Plan #597-002D-1554

Blanket/Quilt Rack
❖ Size - 26 1/2" x 14 1/4" x 30"
❖ Simple design accents any room
❖ Complete list of materials
❖ Step-by-step instructions
  Price Code P3

For fastest service, Call Toll-Free
1-800-373-2646 day or night

FOUR Easy Ways To Order

1. CALL toll free 1-800-373-2646 for credit card orders. MasterCard, Visa, Discover and American Express are accepted.

2. FAX your order to 1-314-770-2226.

3. MAIL the Order Form to:

   HDA, Inc.
   944 Anglum Road
   St. Louis, MO 63042

   Attn: Customer Service Department

4. ONLINE visit **www.projectplans.com**

QUESTIONS?
Call Our Customer Service Number
1-800-373-2646

order form

Please send me -

PLAN NUMBER 597-_____

           PRICE CODE_____ *(see Plan Page)*

Reproducible Masters *(see chart at right)* $ _____
Initial Set of Plans $ _____
Additional Plan Sets *(see chart at right)*
_____ (Qty) at $ _____ each $ _____

                              SUBTOTAL $ _____
SALES TAX (MO residents add 7%) $ _____
☐ Shipping/Handling *(see chart at right)* $ _____
   (each additional set add $2.00 to shipping charges)

   TOTAL ENCLOSED (US funds only) $ _____

☐ Enclosed is my check or money order payable
   to HDA, Inc. (Sorry, no COD's)

I hereby authorize HDA, Inc. to charge this purchase to my credit card account (check one):

☐   ☐   ☐   ☐ ☐

Credit Card number _____

Expiration date _____

Signature_____

Name_____
                  (Please print or type)
Street Address_____
                  (Please do not use PO Box)
City _____

State _____ Zip _____

Daytime phone number (_____) -_____

E-mail address_____

Important Information To Know Before You Order

◆ **Exchange Policies** - Since blueprints are printed in response to your order, we cannot honor requests for refunds. However, if for some reason you find that the plan you have purchased does not meet your requirements, you may exchange that plan for another plan in our collection. At the time of the exchange, you will be charged a processing fee of 25% of your original plan package price, plus the difference in price between the plan packages (if applicable) and the cost to ship the new plans to you.

Please note: Reproducible drawings can only be exchanged if the package is unopened, and exchanges are allowed only within 90 days of purchase.

◆ **Building Codes & Requirements** - At the time the construction drawings were prepared, every effort was made to ensure that these plans and specifications meet nationally recognized codes. Our plans conform to most national building codes. Because building codes vary from area to area, some drawing modifications and/or the assistance of a professional designer or architect may be necessary to comply with your local codes or to accommodate specific building site conditions. We advise you to consult with your local building official for information regarding codes governing your area.

blueprint price schedule

Price Code	1-Set	Additional Sets	Reproducible Masters
P3	$15.00	$10.00	$65.00

**Plan prices are subject to change without notice.
Please note that plans are not refundable.**

Shipping & Handling Charges
EACH ADDITIONAL SET ADD $2.00 TO SHIPPING CHARGES

U.S. SHIPPING - Alaska & Hawaii express only

Regular *(allow 7-10 business days)* $5.95
Priority *(allow 3-5 business days)* $15.00
Express* *(allow 1-2 business days)* $25.00

CANADA SHIPPING**

Standard *(allow 8-12 business days)* $15.00
Express* *(allow 3-5 business days)* $40.00

OVERSEAS SHIPPING/INTERNATIONAL
Call, fax, or e-mail (plans@hdainc.com) for shipping costs.

* For express delivery please call us by 11:00 a.m. CST
** Orders may be subject to custom's fees and/or duties/taxes.

Thank you for your order!